90 02???11 0

KW-380-083

SLIPPERY CUSTOMERS:
ESTATE AGENTS, THE PUBLIC AND REGULATION

FROM
UNIVERSITY OF PLYMOUTH
LIBRARY SERVICES

SLIPPERY CUSTOMERS: ESTATE AGENTS, THE PUBLIC AND REGULATION

Dr Michael Clarke
Senior Lecturer, Department of Sociology,
University of Liverpool

Dr David Smith
Senior Research Fellow, Centre for Policy Studies in Education,
University of Leeds

and

Professor Mike McConville
Director, Legal Research Institute, University of Warwick

UNIVERSITY OF ...
LIBRARY ...

Item
No.

233911

Class
No.

No.

BLACKSTONE
PRESS LIMITED

First published in Great Britain 1994 by Blackstone Press Limited,
9-15 Aldine Street, London W12 8AW. Telephone: 081-740 1173

© M. Clarke, D. Smith and M. McConville

ISBN: 1 85431 377 0

British Library Cataloguing in Publication Data
A CIP catalogue record for this book is available from the British Library.

−1. MAY 1995   ②

UNIVERSITY OF PLYMOUTH
LIBRARY SERVICES

Item No.	900 223911-0
Class No.	333.3322 CLA
Contl. No.	1 85431 3770

Typeset by Montage Studios Limited, Tonbridge, Kent
Printed by Livesey Limited, Shrewsbury, Shropshire

All rights reserved. No part of this book may be reproduced or transmitted
in any form or by any means, electronic or mechanical, including
photocopying, recording, or any information storage or retrieval system
without prior permission from the publisher.

Contents

Preface

The research on which this book is based was directed towards understanding what it is that estate agents do and the constraints, pressures, outlook and aspirations which characterise their work in order to understand the regulatory situation. Rather than attempting to identify and quantify abuses, our aim was to understand the working world of estate agents, the way in which existing regulation operates and the structured constraints and conflicts of interest to which they are subject and which may give rise to abuse.

To that end we began in September 1990 with an initial phase in which we brought ourselves up-to-date with the current situation in estate agency, including the initiation of a round of meetings with leading figures in the professional and regulatory bodies and the corporates. All of the key people and bodies offered their help.

This was followed by a division of labour. With the support of the research directors, David Smith negotiated access to a series of estate agencies and their branches, both corporate and independent. Most of David Smith's time was thereafter taken up with observation at various sites, interviews with estate agents, managers, members of professional bodies and others and the collation of information on estate agency work, and the preparation of extensive reports on each observation site based on field notes. Regular meetings were held by all three of us to monitor progress and to keep ourselves up-to-date with regulatory and other developments.

One of the research directors, Michael Clarke, was able to undertake supplementary research on the history of professionalisation and attempts at registration and on the organisation of estate agency in other countries, notably Scotland, to which he undertook a brief research trip to interview leading figures. All three of us collaborated on the preparation and organisation of a sample of consumers of estate agents services, and mailing of the interview survey which was sent out in early Spring 1992. By this time fieldwork was coming to an end and a further round of meetings, telephone contacts and letters was initiated with a wide variety of professional bodies, regulators and others, including all the corporate estate agents, so as to ensure that all relevant and available information was collected and up-to-date, and the contribution of no significant participant ignored. The initial drafting of the manuscript was undertaken by Michael Clarke and reviewed and revised by all the project team.

Dr Michael Clarke
Dr David Smith
Professor Michael McConville
May 1994

Acknowledgements

This book arises out of a research project generously funded by the Leverhulme Trust whose staff have been supportive throughout the period of the research and writing up. The funding provided by the Leverhulme Trust allowed David Smith to undertake field work on a full-time basis from September 1990 to September 1992, Michael Clarke a term's writing up time free of teaching responsibilities and for all ancillary support.

The project could not have taken place without the strong support of all relevant regulatory and professional bodies. In this regard we are indebted to the National Association of Estate Agents, the Royal Institute of Chartered Surveyors, the Incorporated Society of Valuers and Auctioneers, the Office of Fair Trading, the Consumers' Association, the Law Society, and local Trading Standards Officers, all of whom have assisted us with help and advice. Others who provided particular help include Francis Bennion, George Clark, Tony Clark, Neil Dalton, Dr Coull, David Perkins and Frank Rutherford.

The research would not have been possible without the co-operation of estate agents themselves, who allowed us to spend time observing them at work and gave us every assistance possible. The guarantees of confidentiality and anonymity we gave prevent us from expressing our thanks in anything other than general terms, but this does not detract from our genuine gratitude to all those who helped.

We have been helped throughout the research by Aileen Stockham who in her capacity as project secretary helped co-ordinate the field work and typed and re-typed fieldnotes and the manuscript with professionalism and good humour. At Liverpool University, Lorraine Campbell provided additional secretarial support for which we are grateful.

Finally, we thank our partners and our families for keeping us going throughout the project.

Acknowledgments

List of Tables

ONE

Introduction

In the public mind, the world of estate agency enjoys a status similar to that of second-hand car sellers: rogue characters employing artful techniques to market services of a dubious character. Everyone has a perspective on and a story about estate agents, sometimes based in their own experiences but more usually founded in received wisdom and common knowledge. The allegations will be familiar to any reader, even those who have not used the services of an estate agent: active misdescription of properties, touting, pressured selling tactics, misleading prospective purchasers as to the intentions or even existence of other interested bidders, extracting fees at unjustified levels, talking up the market, and exploiting vulnerable sellers by purchasing properties themselves at below market rates by using sleeping partners. Between sellers and buyers, it would seem, estate agency inhabits a murky world.

We were of course aware, before we went into the field, of the negative stereotypes to which the estate agent is subject, a matter on which we continually attempted to reserve judgment, but which we took to be in substantial part an outcome of the history and current practice of estate agency in England. One of the features evident on even limited inquiry into estate agency in other countries is that hostility to estate agents is widespread and very similar. A combination of smarminess and arrogance, an unctuous solicitude masking a ruthless manipulativeness in the drive to complete the deal and earn commission — and, perhaps even worse, exploit the vendor by underpricing or the purchaser by overpricing — is by no means unique to Britain as a stereotype of estate agents. It was not with great surprise then that one of the first images we came across was the 'white socks and earring' salesman, the definitely uncouth youth whose arrogance was only surpassed by his ignorance, and who had his heyday as the gatekeeper to properties with ever-rising values during the boom of the latter 1980s. These staff, taken on to cope with escalating demand and largely inexperienced and untrained greatly discredited estate agency, it was generally agreed by older and sager agents by the time our research started. However, nearly all of them had now left for greener pastures with the slump in the market.

What surprised us more was that alongside this contemporary image of fecklessness and exploitation and the established negative stereotype of estate agents went an equally hostile stereotype of the public: rude, ignorant, unscrupulous and at times downright dishonest. A stream of anecdotes and invective supported this throughout our research. One of the first stories we were told, and repeatedly encountered throughout the research, was of the time-wasting 'purchaser' whose idea of a Sunday afternoon's entertainment is to turn up, by prior arrangement or otherwise, to view a number of properties in which they have not the slightest interest, nor often the capacity to buy. Such people we were assured, are bored, nosey, like to see the inside of other people's homes, and confidently anticipate the anxious vendor's provision of tea and biscuits in the process. A blunter stereotype later related in one agency we observed at length is that 'buyers are liars', that is, they can be expected to misrepresent their financial capacity and to claim that they have sold their property when they have not. Gazumping was universally and readily identified as the seller's responsibility with the unfortunate agent caught in the middle between a greedy vendor* snapping at an extra £500 or £1,000 and an angry purchaser frustrated after having had a survey and instructed solicitors. 'And in the end it does clients no good', the agent would say, 'because the sale is delayed and the price of the property they want to purchase goes up too.' Further tales in which estate agents were subjected to wholly unscrupulous and dishonest propositions were also related, which served to confirm estate agents' experience. Whilst there are honest and indeed naïve members of the public in the housing market, a good many are characterised rather by greed and dishonesty.

Whilst, therefore, estate agents are easy targets for public disapprobation and abuse, the world of estate agents is characterised by mutual stigmatisation between agents and the public. The epithet in the title of our book is, therefore, not intended to apply to one party in the property market but to all three of them: agents, vendors and purchasers and it is this complex world that we sought to understand and enlighten.

REGULATORY CONTEXT

Our interest in estate agency was first aroused by a conjunction of events affecting it in the late 1980s. Not only did the property boom which reached a crescendo in August 1988, as the Chancellor's deadline for the elimination of double tax relief on mortgages approached, stimulate a predictable wave of complaints about abuses and unscrupulousness among estate agents, but estate agents were involved with others in other abuses, notably mortgage

---

*Throughout the text, 'vendor' and 'seller' are used interchangeably and potential purchasers are sometimes referred to as 'applicants'.

fraud.[1] This drew our attention to the housing market. A cursory inspection revealed that, in comparison to other actors in the property transfer process, estate agents are astonishingly little regulated. Further inquiry revealed the efforts of estate agents over half a century to promote self-regulation through their professional bodies, with the sanction of Parliament for the statutory registration and regulation of estate agents, alas, to no avail. The ultimate outcome of this protracted effort was the Estate Agents Act 1979, a statute, we soon discovered, that is widely condemned as weak, poorly drafted, and in any case at the time largely unimplemented.

Around 1989 there were other reasons for anticipating that the apparent regulatory anomaly of estate agents would soon be addressed. The financial institutions (banks, building societies and insurance companies notably) were at that time in the middle of a spectacular spending spree, in the course of which they expected to transform British estate agency. They hoped to create national chains under their own august supervision which, it almost went without saying, would confer on estate agency for the first time the stamp of those financial institutions' reliability, concern for uniform good service and absolute propriety when dealing with the public. The image and nature of estate agency was, it seemed, in the process of being transformed from a local service of varying quality into a limited number of national services of absolutely reliable quality.

At the same time there were exciting new prospects for the public. The new corporate estate agents were already offering their financial services — mortgages, insurance etc. — to their customers and there were also prospects for the reform of conveyancing which would usher in the era of 'one-stop property shopping' with all services to the transaction carried out by one omnicompetent institution, with great benefits of convenience and cost to the customer. Although eagerly anticipated in some quarters,[2] the transformation of the legal side of property transfer did not progress as far or rapidly as it might have. The new Lord Chancellor, Lord Mackay of Clashfern, under pressure from the Law Society, was reluctant to allow in-house conveyancing by the financial institutions who now ran estate agency chains, though the threat of this reform had quite an impact upon the competitive practices and pricing of solicitors' services in respect of conveyancing.

In addition, however, there were anxieties about these developments. Mortgage lenders were competing vigorously for market share reflecting not only the property boom but the aggressive involvement of the banks and centralised lenders alongside the building societies, themselves recently deregulated and diversifying into banking territory. The ground was being cultivated for the over-borrowing which led in the 1990s to an unprecedented wave of repossessions.[3] Further, the financial institutions were

---

[1] M. J. Clarke, *Mortgage Fraud* (Chapman and Hall, 1991).
[2] See, e.g., *Towards Easier Buying and Selling: Taking the Trauma out of Moving House*, Report by the interprofessional working party on the transfer of property (RICS, 1989); *Let the Buyer be Well Informed*, Recommendations of the Conveyancing Standing Committee of the Law Commission (1989); *Estate Agency: Moving Forward* (Access Parliamentary Public Affairs, 1988).
[3] See S. Jenkinson, *Repossessed* (CHAS, 1992).

peddling their products to house purchasers with unparalleled ferocity, amounting in some cases to making their take-up a condition of purchasing a property on their estate agency's books. This practice — 'tied sales' — gave rise to considerable public resentment and media coverage and to the intervention of the main regulatory body, the Office of Fair Trading (OFT), to attempt to outlaw it. With the collapse of the market after 1988 and the introduction in 1988 of the regulatory regime under the Financial Services Act 1986, these excesses were mitigated, but the arrival of the corporate estate agents plainly contributed a major new regulatory challenge.

As a result of anxieties generated by these developments, as well as long-term pressures from professional bodies unhappy with the Estate Agents Act 1979, in 1989 the OFT responded by issuing a consultative document in 1989[4] followed by a report the following year.[5] This established the basis for government policy on estate agency: intervene as little as possible. Comprehensive regulation was to be avoided, still less government-backed registration. Rather, specific abuses were to be targeted, regulations introduced under the 1979 Act to control them, and consideration given to the extension of the Trade Descriptions Act 1968 to estate agency. On the whole the problem was identified as one of unethical behaviour by estate agents which would not be eliminated by extensive regulation — notably, it was said, by the introduction of compulsory registration and tests of competence as favoured by most of the professional bodies. Could this narrow anti-interventionism, supported, with one exception, by ultra-dry Ministers for Consumer Affairs and, to the consternation of many in the field of estate agency, by the OFT, be sustained as an adequate response to the very limited regulation of estate agents and the increasingly complex institutional nature of estate agency?

OBJECTIVES OF THE RESEARCH

Our purpose in undertaking the research was to attempt to identify the key regulatory issues in estate agency, an industry in the housing market that stands out as under-regulated in relation to other professions involved, notably lawyers. Given the importance of house sale and purchase to the average citizen, for the majority of whom it is now the way in which they make their home and much the largest financial commitment into which they ever enter, we found it odd that estate agency is so little regulated in Britain that anyone can set up with an office and begin to solicit custom without either qualifications or experience. Was it this simple lack of regulation, we wondered, that had given rise to abuses, of which there was widespread anecdotal evidence during the property boom of the 1980s, much of it only echoing laments voiced by the public in earlier periods? We realised that no previous research had been undertaken on what estate agents actually do and what their practical expectations and capacities are in their work. We

---

[4] *Estate Agency: a Consultation Document* (OFT, 1989).
[5] *Estate Agency: a Report* (OFT, 1990).

therefore wanted to avoid a simple portrait of the incidence of misconduct, though we did want to ensure that the public would be able to give vent to their views and experiences. Accordingly our research effort concentrated on looking at how a limited number of estate agencies work, backing this up with interviews and the collection of documentation from regulatory and professional bodies. We also conducted a survey of those who had recently used the services of estate agents as well as observing estate agents in action with clients.

These points will be elaborated in many ways throughout this book. An appreciation of them forms the foundation of our approach to the research. We did not enter the field in the anticipation of catching estate agents engaging in deception or dishonesty. Not only was it unlikely that they would let us observe this if they did engage in it, but we were not interested in such point scoring. Rather we sought to identify the working environment and life of the estate agent so as to become aware of the pressures, opportunities, fears, aspirations and rewards to which they are subject. It was for this reason that field observation and semi-structured interviews were at the heart of our research. Our approach to regulation derived from this. We have not tried to identify a list of abuses or to calculate relative incidence rates, though where we have come across abuses we have recorded them. We have, however, also attempted to understand their sources, and to investigate and discuss those sources with a view to controlling or mitigating undesirable conduct by that route. More fundamentally our concern has been with the conflicts of interest which are inherent in the work of estate agents and the ways and extent to which these can be eliminated or, if not, publicly recognised and managed.

The review of regulation with which this book concludes, like the discussion of practising estate agents which forms its bulk, should be understood in this light. Our objective has been to understand estate agency, not to itemise its malpractices. The intention is to use that understanding to appraise past attempts at regulation, the existing regulatory machinery and the potential for regulatory reform which might make both estate agents and their customers less slippery.

RESEARCH METHODS AND LIMITATIONS

In the light of the above considerations our judgment was that the most fruitful way to conduct the research was through a series of case studies of estate agencies in which the fieldworker could observe agents at work, and conduct informal and more formal interviews. The disadvantage of such an approach is obviously that the number of agencies that can be observed is limited in comparison to the opposite approach which involves the application of structured questionnaires to a large national sample. Our problem was that in the absence of existing authoritative research it was quite unclear what was to go into any such questionnaire. To have constructed and applied one in the absence of such knowledge would have been to risk merely perpetuating stereotypes and prejudices.

Although we were able to vary our use of observation to achieve a grasp on practice and occupational outlooks in the agencies that we studied (so that, for example, it might at times be useful to supplement a more extended study of one branch of an agency with a limited visit to another branch), for the best results it was essential that the fieldworker maintained fairly extended contact with a limited number of agencies. This led to the preparation of long and detailed field reports on each agency — based on field notes taken during the observation period. This was supplemented with semi-structured interviews with individuals in each agency which were subsequently transcribed and in which issues covering the work of estate agents were discussed in particular focus.

Overall this meant that we were unable to study more than a limited number of agencies but in an attempt to be representative we spread them widely. We divided fieldwork time between the corporates and the independents, observing five independents in the North, the South and the Midlands, one of them an up-market agency whose offices in both London and the country we investigated. We also looked at branches of three of the corporates, two with national chains and one with a regional chain. In one case we looked at branches of the same corporate in both the North and the South. Whilst access to observing the independents was not a matter of breezing in and explaining our interest, we experienced little resistance, probably because the upheavals in the market as a result of the arrival of the corporates and the sudden slump after 1989 had made many independents eager to present their own view of estate agency.

In the case of the corporates access was less easy, reflecting the difficulties they had experienced in realising the ambitious projects they had set themselves when they entered estate agency. At the point at which our interest was first aroused the corporates were firmly established but suffering losses, and were concerned at the lack of financial services sales through estate agency, and at the very variable quality of the staff they had acquired. The corporates were also highly sensitive to each other as competitors. This and the sense that they had not yet got estate agency right made them more resistant to observation. We made wide-ranging contacts with senior staff in many of the corporates which enabled us to identify those who were willing to talk further and those who were not interested. In the event once access was granted in the three cases we needed, there were no further difficulties at the observational level. The only constraint that we suffered was that the corporates especially were unwilling to release financial information in anything like systematic detail, perhaps not surprisingly in view of their sustained losses over the years. As will be seen, we were able to obtain financial information from staff about such matters as payment and bonus systems, and to obtain from other sources broad estimates of the financial success (or otherwise) of the corporates.

STRUCTURAL CONTRADICTIONS OF ESTATE AGENCY

Whilst government has tended to target specific abuses and identify these as problems deriving from unethical behaviour of estate agents, it is our view that the world of estate agency is subject to two fundamental contradictions which give estate agency its slippery character, and the subjection to which in turn elicits clients' and customers' slippery conduct.

The first source of ambivalence lies in the nature of estate agency as simultaneously a selling operation and a professional service. This has frustrated attempts at professionalisation and sustained the faith of a government which idolises the market and suspects, like Shaw, that all professions are no more than a conspiracy against the laity. Such beliefs tend to reinforce the view that estate agency should be left largely alone. Thus no-one needs qualifications to be an estate agent, because what an agent does is sell property on commission, and selling is an art capable of being developed by those with the appropriate innate capacity. All the rest is professional flim flam. One wonders whether this does not amount to an endorsement of the graffito: 'Gary Whitesocks rules OK'.

There is more, as we show at length, to estate agency than selling, particularly selling in a crude, 'shifting the product' sense: estate agency is a highly sensitive and specialised form of selling that needs to be hedged about with all manner of circumspection and delicacy if it is be conducted ethically and to the satisfaction of all parties. The point, however, for present purposes is that it is a mixture of selling and professional services, and as such requires the assertive, outgoing, eager to please, confident individuals whose stock in trade (and one of whose prime sources of satisfaction) is relating to the customer. From the customer's point of view, however, this constitutes a recipe for the transmission of mixed messages: are agents selling you something (i.e., trying to get you to buy something you do not want), or are they offering professional services, that is dispassionate expert advice based on your individual circumstances and aspirations?

The second source of ambiguity lies in the interests or obligations of the agent. The agent is retained, in England, by the vendors, to sell the property on commission. In order to achieve the sale the purchaser has to be attracted to come forward, vetted for their capacity and desire to purchase the property in question, and persuaded to go ahead at a price acceptable to the vendor. The vendor, meanwhile, has to accept that the price offered is the best practically available, that the purchaser will complete the deal, and that any prejudices the vendor may have against the purchaser are beside the point. In this process the agent acts not just as the representative of the vendor, as contracted, but as an intermediary broking the deal between vendor and purchaser. Whose side is the agent on? Especially in a weak market with few purchasers around, a great deal of effort may be spent cultivating the purchaser, and in a falling market offers may be put to vendors in forcible terms as the best obtainable, even though well below what they hoped for and anticipated. Furthermore, both parties at certain points in the negotiations may realise that the agent's own interest does not coincide with either of theirs: the agent's interest is to conclude the deal and earn commission, not to ensure that vendor and purchaser are entirely happy. As estate agents have it, vendors are greedy, and purchasers are always looking for ideal properties, which do not exist (still less at a price they can afford).

Many vendors and purchasers are only dimly or intermittently aware of these features of estate agency and experience them in projected form as deviousness on the part of the agents. At the same time they are also vague, in many cases, about the kind of property they want to buy and indeed whether they intend to move at all, since most moves are voluntary. This, along with the high level of emotion generated by moving house, can produce contradictory and indeed contrary behaviour: aggressiveness and rudeness; confusion and changes of mind, which arouses the estate agent's contempt and his belief that people never buy what they say they want, and cannot afford it anyway, so sell them what you have on your list; and deviousness deriving from confusion about what is wanted, together with the perception that the agent is attempting to manipulate them and hence that protective tactics to outmanoeuvre this are in order.

The ambiguities in the nature of estate agency will constitute persistent themes in the detailed account which follows in later chapters. It is these ambiguities that make the effective regulation of estate agency and the achievement of consistent standards of conduct by practitioners so difficult to achieve.

CONTENTS

This outline of the work of the project gives an indication of the contents of this book. Chapters 2 and 3 are concerned with the history of attempts at the professional regulation of estate agency and at statutory recognition through registration, leading up to the Estate Agents Act 1979. Chapter 4 explores the organisation and structure of independent estate agents whose work and focal concerns are considered in chapters 5 and 6. Chapter 7 reviews the entry of the corporates into estate agency and considers the issues this raises. The way in which the corporates are seeking to confront these issues is explored in three case studies detailed in chapter 8. Chapter 9 presents the results of a consumer survey of the public experience and views of estate agents based on their recent experience. Chapter 10 looks briefly at estate agency in a number of other countries: at Scotland at some length, and then at the USA, France and Australia. Finally chapter 11 reviews the existing fragmented machinery for regulating estate agency. It then takes up themes and issues identified in the preceding chapters which bear on regulation, and examines the possibilities for regulatory reforms and for improvement in the standards and standing of estate agency, and is able to make some concrete recommendations.

TWO

Professionalisation of Estate Agency

INTRODUCTION

The contemporary customer of an estate agent is no doubt vaguely aware that some agents at any rate are members of the Royal Institution of Chartered Surveyors (RICS), the largest and most senior of the professional bodies. Awareness of other leading professional bodies such as the Incorporated Society of Valuers and Auctioneers (ISVA) and the National Association of Estate Agents (NAEA) is probably lower, and the significance of membership of any of these bodies for the quality of service a customer may expect to receive, and the rights of redress offered through professional bodies in case of complaint are not, we believe, well known. Nor is this surprising, as the evidence of the coming chapters will demonstrate.

The professional position of estate agents, even before the arrival of the corporates, offering their size and reputation as a guarantee of service, backed by the Ombudsman for Corporate Estate Agents, has been weak and confused. The contrast with solicitors, regulated by a single professional body, the Law Society, which has legal recognition as the regulatory body, could not be starker. Nevertheless, the history of the regulation of estate agency, until at least the 1970s, could more or less be identified with attempts at professional self-regulation, and at obtaining the registration of their occupation through Parliamentary legislation and the conferring on the professional bodies of regulatory responsibility, including, crucially, the right to control entry to the profession. The reasons for the failure of these attempts, despite repeated efforts and despite the successes of other service occupations during the same period such as accountants and loss adjusters,[1]

---

[1] See H. Wilmott, 'Organising the profession: a theoretical and historical examination of the development of the major accounting bodies in the UK', *Accounting Organizations and Society*, vol. 11, No. 6 (1986); E.F. Cato-Carter, *Order out of Chaos: a History of the Loss Adjusting Profession*, vol. 1 (London, Chartered Institute of Loss Adjusters, 1989); M.J. Clarke, 'Insurance fraud', *British Journal of Criminology* (1989).

are instructive not only in themselves, but in laying bare the character of estate agency. For this reason, this and the next chapter are resolutely historical and, although concerned mainly with developments in the 1960s and subsequently, make no apology for beginning where the wave of professionalisation began,[2] in the 19th century.

There is plain evidence from the latter 19th century onwards of a desire for professionalisation, but only as the 'professions of the land' differentiated themselves over time did it become clear how intractable estate agency itself is to professionalisation.

The market in owner-occupied housing in Britain has grown steadily, though more rapidly in some periods than in others, since the mid 19th century. Each surge in the market has given rise to a new batch of aspirant estate agents eager to take advantage of the opportunities and with no obstacles in the way to practice: regulation by the State has until recently been negligible and the capital costs of setting up as an estate agent are limited. As we shall see, however, estate agency proved extremely difficult to professionalise. Other services related to property, such as surveying and valuation, came to achieve more or less professional status and organisation, but estate agency, as it became more explicitly identified as a separate practice as a result of these successes elsewhere, remained ambiguous. It did so because of its fundamentally ambivalent character, incorporating both client services (but without achieving clarity as to whether vendor or purchaser is the client, no matter that the vendor pays the commission) and acting as an unabashed salesman. In time this division between the professionally oriented and the market oriented aspects of estate agency produced separate organisations and powerfully informed government policy on regulation. Professionalisation then came to be seen as the means to overcoming the ambiguities of estate agency, dealing with complaints of abuses and achieving respectability. It had, in other words, a regulatory project, to be achieved by a degree of professional market closure: professionalisation would establish an ethical code, training and disciplinary procedures, and so eliminate 'the cowboys'. The problem with this project is that it generated constant antagonism by just those who might be thus stigmatised as outsiders and it proved ultimately impossible for the established professional bodies in the latter 20th century to reach a professional accommodation with the constantly arriving new generations of incoming estate agents.

There is then an identity between the project of professionalisation and the increasingly recognised necessity for regulation, but with the latter coming to the fore increasingly as time went on, and professionalisation still had not been achieved. Matters came to a head in the 1960s with the creation of the Estate Agents Registration Council (EARC), at which point professional self-regulation was seen starkly as the alternative to State regulation. With the failure of the EARC and the advent of the corporates complicating the regulatory environment further, State regulation became increasingly the

---

[2]See H. Perkin, *The Rise of Professional Society* (Routledge, 1989).

accepted option. In order to make this long historical development more accessible to the reader we have divided it into two chapters. The present one deals with the professionalisation project itself, whilst the next concentrates on the regulatory issues. Because these became more pressing in recent years, and because professionalisation reached a critical point from a regulatory point of view with the EARC, we have broken the story at 1966 with chapter 3 taking it up to date, with an emphasis on the regulatory issues which came to the fore during this more recent period.

1868–1934: PROFESSIONALISATION VIA REGISTRATION

The importance of this first period lies in the ascendancy which was achieved by the three senior bodies among the professions of the land: the Royal Institution of Chartered Surveyors (RICS), the Chartered Land Agents Society and the Chartered Auctioneers and Estate Agents Institute. These ultimately merged under the name of the RICS in 1970, but they all established themselves firmly during this early period. The RICS was founded in 1868 and received its royal charter in 1881. The Land Agents Society was founded in 1902 and chartered in 1929. The Institute of Estate and House Agents was founded in 1872 and renamed the Estate Agents Institute in 1902. It merged with the Auctioneers Institute in 1912, the latter having been founded in 1886 as the Institute of Auctioneers and Surveyors and changed its name in 1889. The new body was named the Auctioneers and Estate Agents Institute. Although it did not receive its charter until 1947, it clearly achieved ascendancy over its rivals, and was explicitly associated on a number of occasions with the RICS and Chartered Land Agents Society (CLAS) before their eventual merger. Its success may have contributed to the formation of the Incorporated Society of Auctioneers and Landed Property Agents (ISALPA) in 1923/4, which survived as a significant body until 1968, when it merged with the Incorporated Society of Valuers and Auctioneers. The Valuers Institution was founded in 1928, absorbing the National Association of Auctioneers (founded in 1924) in 1949, and the Valuers Association (founded in 1936) in 1953. The history of these institutions is shown in Figure 2.1.

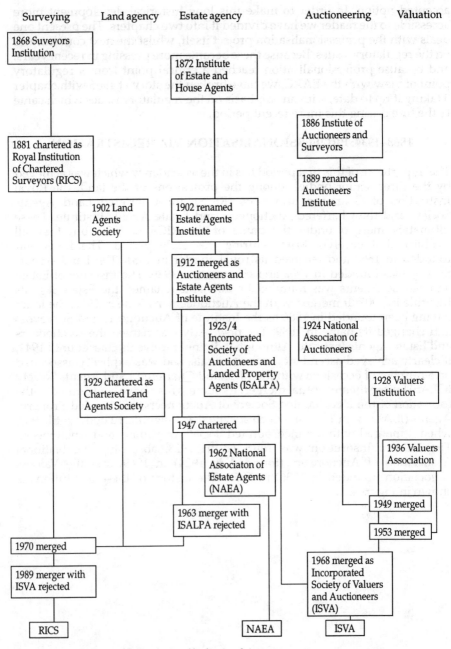

Figure 2.1 Development of the professional bodies involving estate agency
Sources: F.A.R. Bennion, 'History of estate agents registration', *Estates Gazette*, 25 May 1968; D.B.C. Symonds, *Some Notable Dates in the Estate Agency Profession* (NAEA, 1990).

Crudely it might therefore be said that the four principal professions of the land developed in a sequence, beginning with surveyors, then land agents, and followed by auctioneers and valuers. Practitioners of all these professions and members of the professional bodies might at all times also practice as estate agents, but no professional body to represent the specific skills and duties of estate agents, as property sellers, emerged.

Estate agency has always had two overlapping meanings: the specific business of selling property on commission and the wider sense that comprehends all that takes place under the sign of 'Smith and Jones Estate Agents'. This may include commercial as well as residential estate agency and, in the former especially, advice on town planning and development, valuation for rating, insurance, mortgage and other purposes, and property management. Most, though not all, estate agents have long had mixed practices with a staff including members with qualifications from the professional bodies. Although the marketing of residential property — house agency as it has been called — may be the work that is most familiar to the public, it is not therefore necessarily that which predominates in an estate agency business. This has been essential to the stability of estate agency businesses because of the fluctuations in the housing market. In periods of boom agents may concentrate on house agency, and survive the slumps on fee-based professional work. This has meant conversely that not all estate agents have ever felt it appropriate to be members of any one professional body and that not all members of most of the professional bodies have engaged in estate agency proper: in 1990, for example, of the 62,000 members of the RICS, only about 13,000 were estimated to derive some or all of their income from estate agency.[3]

The differentiation of the professions of the land reflected the changes in land use and especially tenure that took place with gathering speed from the latter 18th century onwards. Carr-Saunders and Wilson[4] describe graphically the circumstances giving rise to the surveyors and land agents' professions:

The enclosure of the commons and wastes, the commutation of ecclesiastical tithes, the enfranchisement of copyholds, and the compulsory acquisition of land for purposes of railway construction, called for a new type of expert, competent to prepare plans of land about to be enclosed, or, it might be, to assess the respective interests of lord and tenant in copyholds about to be enfranchised. At the same time the supersession of traditional farming methods by commercial agriculture and the growth of large urban areas greatly enhanced the value of property in land, so that the landed proprietor found it advantageous to employ the services of an expert manager. For such employment the qualifications required were essentially those of the surveyor. (p. 195.)

The effect of the enclosure movement, and of the revolution in the agricultural economy which accompanied it, was to present the landowner

---

[3] According to estimates given to us by the RICS.
[4] A.M. Carr-Saunders and P.A. Wilson, *The Professions* (Oxford University Press, 1933).

with an extremely profitable investment, though one which required expert management if it was to yield the full return of which it was capable. But the supersession of the farmer-bailiff and the estate-solicitor by the trained surveyor or land agent was a slow process which was not completed until after the agricultural depression which began in the late 'seventies of the last century. The country firms of surveyors, though they secured some, did not secure the bulk of this work. Owing to the very large units in which property was then held in this country it became the practice to appoint one or more whole-time resident agents to be responsible for the management of each estate; and the typical agent, residing on the estate he managed, was bound to his employer by a close personal tie. Only very gradually did he come to think of himself as possessing interests which he shared with the managers of other estates. Moreover the realization, even when it came, was not one of community of interest with the general body of members of the Surveyors' Institution, with most of the energies of which it was felt were devoted to urban and suburban properties; while its country organization was admittedly extremely defective. In these circumstances the Land Agents' Society came into being in 1902. (pp. 199–200.)

Auctioneers similarly differentiated themselves in the 19th century from solicitors. Initially they were called in only to take charge of the actual auction, but came in time to take responsibility for the preparation of particulars and the advertising of the sale, leaving the solicitor with purely legal matters, so creating a natural combination of estate agency and auctioneering both of real property and chattels which persists to the present, especially in rural areas.

A number of residues of this process of differentiation are worthy of note. First, the place of lawyers — solicitors in particular — in relation to estate agency and other matters connected with real property remains ambivalent. In Scotland, especially in the eastern half, solicitors continue to act as estate agents and dominate the market.[5] In England they still retain an active interest in estate agency in a minority of practices, and the profession as a whole is on guard to see that they are not excluded from its practice.[6]

Secondly, relations between the various professional bodies became, from quite early on, touchy on certain matters. In some respects this appears as little more than snobbery, yet in others it is rooted in a proper appreciation of the dangers to a profession of conflict of interest. Carr-Saunders and Wilson for example, quote the by-laws of the Chartered Land Agents Society (CLAS) effective in the 1930s by which 'the expression "genuine manager of a landed estate" is not to include a practising solicitor, house agent, auctioneer, accountant or others who undertake the management of estates as part of their business, nor a land agent who holds an auctioneers licence'.[7] In part

---

[5] A fuller account is available in chapter 9.
[6] They obtained exemption from the Estate Agents Act 1979 — see chapter 3.
[7] Op. cit. (note 4), pp. 200–1.

such professional anxieties reflected the tension between the practical side of the work, which relied on experience, and the difficulty in successfully codifying this in objective written terms which could form the basis for professional examination. Thus the CLAS also insisted at the time that a member must have had experience of managing estates of at least 2,000 acres for at least five years and that if he ceased to practice, his membership automatically ceased.[8] Other sensitive areas include dealing in property, canvassing, advertising and secondary activities such as furniture retailing, on which we will comment further later. Suffice it to say for the present that the issues of what distinguishes one of the professions of the land from another, the necessarily practical and experience-based nature of much of the work and the difficulty in translating it successfully into examination syllabuses and codified professional training, and the regular concern with conflicts of interests and their capacity to compromise the professional standing of the practitioner, have been sustained features of the professions of the land.

The net effect has been a historic tendency for the more established bodies to look down on the aspirant ones and to resist amalgamation. Thus the two senior bodies, the RICS and the CLAS finally amalgamated, but their tendency to look askance at auctioneers and estate agents did not disappear. This has been reinforced both by the more overt ambiguity of residential estate agency as between its selling and professional service aspects, and by the fact that estate agency was the last of the professions of the land to emerge, reflecting as they did changes in the economic position and tenure of real property.

Growth of the housing market and of owner-occupation

More specifically estate agency, particularly in its residential form, could not develop until owner-occupation became substantial and involved significant population migration. Practically this took place in waves, the first in the latter part of the 19th century with the development of Victorian suburbs, the second in the inter-war period, the third in the reconstruction boom of the 1950s developing into the affluence of the 1960s, and the fourth in the expansion in home ownership deliberately stimulated by the Thatcher administration.

Each wave of expansion of home ownership affected both members of the existing professional bodies and new and unqualified practitioners, some of whom did very well, some of whom failed and some of whom were unscrupulous or downright criminal. Two examples from the 19th century are appropriate in the overall context. Treen[9] describes the growth of estate agency in Leeds:

... throughout the nineteenth century there continued to be a considerable overlap between some of the activities of those calling themselves architects, surveyors, land and estate agents. The estate agents' role of

---

[8] Ibid.
[9] C. Treen, 'The process of suburban development in north Leeds, 1870–1914' in *The Rise of Suburbia*, ed. F.M.L. Thompson (Leicester University Press, 1982), p. 185.

bringing together buyers and sellers of property grew rapidly in importance in Leeds during the second half of the nineteenth century. Headingley
property was first advertised by estate agents in the local press in 1855; the
first were Hobson and Hindle who had offices in Park Row, Leeds. By 1857
W.B. Hindle handled cottage property for sale in Lower Burley and houses
to let in Headingley. Not until 1864, however, did the compilers of
Leeds directories recognise estate agency as a separate occupational
category.

Throughout the nineteenth century estate agency included men without
training who were agents for the sale of their own building land.
B.H. Richardson, an insurance agent in 1871, had become an estate agent
by 1874 and was developing land on the former Headingley Glebe estate.
Richardson and his partner, T.H. Watson, announced in May 1874 that they
were forming 'a Club for the Erection of Terrace Houses, with eight rooms
each and large gardens ... to be called Oakfield Terrace'. The scheme was
to enlist 16, later 18, members in a building club for the erection of £500
houses. Richardson and Watson were members of the club and its
secretaries. Having purchased 2.5 acres at 1s. 11½d. per square yard, the
pair promptly resold it to the building club at 3s. 5d. per square yard, a
gross profit of £900.

Jackson[10] describes the rise of a London estate agent, Ernest Owers:

> Owers (1860–1938), now almost a legendary figure in the world of estate
> agents, started business life as a solicitor's clerk. After some experience in
> the Stock Exchange and his father's small estate agency at Shepherd's
> Bush, he set up an agency, with virtually no capital, in 1879, living frugally
> above his office adjoining West Hampstead Metropolitan station. His
> vitality and financial acumen brought sufficient success to enable him to
> secure a strong position in the Golders Green bonanza in which he made
> his name and fortune. A small hut opened at the station site in 1905 was
> replaced by an office in 'The Hawthorns' and later by more palatial
> accommodation in the new shopping parade, directly opposite the station,
> on a fine corner site. In 1920 Owers formed a limited company with his
> partner Charles Death and with Charles Handman, and this firm par-
> ticipated in the rather less dramatic Edgware development after 1924.
> Retiring from daily business in 1931, Owers sold his interests three years
> later to Handman and to W. Charles Williams. Hospitals benefited from
> generous bequests out of his estate of £400,790.

The significance of the 1930s and the persistence of the new estate agents'
body, ISALPA, in seeking registration is clarified by the significant changes in
the housing market and the growth of suburbanisation, backed by unprece-
dentedly easy financial terms. As Carr puts it in his account of London:[11]

---

[10] A.A. Jackson, *Semi-Detached London* (London: Allen and Unwin, 1973), p. 74.
[11] M.C. Carr, 'The development and character of a metropolitan suburb: Bexley, Kent' in F.M.L.
Thompson (ed.) op. cit. (note 9), p. 244.

For the house purchaser the two outstanding benefits of the 1930s were a fall in house prices compared to those of the 1920s, and easier facilities for raising the money to buy a house. Until 1936 the cheapest houses in the district sold for £350 to £395 compared to £525 to £550 in the late 1920s. The intermediate range lay between about £570 and £700, and the highest price range from £975 upwards.

The most important fall in house prices was that for the cheapest houses. As wages also rose and employment opportunities expanded after 1932, the effective fall in house prices was even more than the difference between the advertised prices indicates. Families with an income of £3 to £4 a week generally bought this cheaper type of house. The somewhat better houses, as for example those on the Davis Estate near Bexleyheath Station, went to families with an income of £4 to £8; sometimes the wife and family of a factory foreman or supervisor, but more commonly of a lower grade civil servant or local small businessman.

In contrast to the 1920s, the local authority played little part in financing house purchase. Most of this was done through the local offices of building societies, working in conjunction with an estate agent or directly with the builder. Building society advances were normally limited to 75 per cent of the purchase price, leaving a deposit of 25 per cent to be found by the purchaser, an amount usually beyond the resources of the lower middle class family. This raised a serious problem, which was solved by the cooperative efforts of the building society and the builder. The deposit required from the purchaser was reduced to a nominal amount because the building society advanced almost all the 25 per cent by arrangement with the builder against cash and/or other collateral deposited by him. The house purchaser then repaid the total advance by instalments in the usual way, including interest, so that in the course of time the builder's collateral was automatically redeemed. As a result of this system, keys to the cheapest houses could be had for a deposit of £5. If the purchaser had not the £5 readily available it was common practice for him to be lent it by the estate agent or builder. Repayments on the mortgage advance could be made at 11s. weekly over 20 or 21 years, a weekly outlay which compared very favourably with 10s. 3d. rent on a council house or 8s. rent on an old terrace house lacking in any modern conveniences and in particular a bathroom and hot water supply.

This easy and revolutionary means of house purchase was a major factor in the spread of cheaper housing in this and other similar outer suburbs. Never before or since has house purchase been made so easy. It was also a method used to finance the purchase of better quality housing. For example, Ideal Homestead offered houses on the Falconwood Estate at Welling, costing £675, for an initial deposit of only £10, and a further £25 on possession. Weekly mortgage repayments were a modest 22s. and rates 4s. 5d.

Attempts at self-registration

In this early period the emphasis was upon attempting to achieve recognition of estate agency skills as a means to achieving the professional goal of legal registration. This, it was repeatedly argued, was the only sure means to protect the public against abuses which were regularly identified — overcharging, bankruptcy, underhand contracts and at times grosser frauds. The model was the legal profession, which had succeeded in achieving registration both of function and of appellation, that is, of a compulsory register of all those engaging in legal work as principals and of all those wishing to call themselves barrister or solicitor. Accordingly a series of attempts were made through private members' Bills to obtain registration, beginning with Duncan in 1888, then Boyton in 1914, and Clarke in 1923.[12] None of these made great progress even when, as in the latter case, the three senior societies (RICS, CLAS, AEAI) were behind it, partly because private members' Bills are notoriously hard to take through Parliament, but more immediately because those in estate agency likely to be affected, but not members of the sponsoring professional bodies, naturally raised objections.

Although estate agents who were not members of the professional bodies sponsoring the 1923 Clarke bill were one important group which blocked its passage, there were, as Carr-Saunders and Wilson pointed out, others probably more powerful and certainly better organised:[13]

> To guard against opposition and to protect the members of other professions, a saving clause was added exempting from the provisions of the bill all solicitors and any architect or civil engineer belonging to one of the well recognized professional associations in those fields. The architects and civil engineers seem to have been satisfied with this; but the Law Society opposed the bill strenuously from the first. Opposition also came from the house and estate agents in the employment of commercial firms, from the National Farmers' Union whose members do a certain amount of auctioneering, and from the National Federation of Building Trades Employers. During the following year the joint committee were still hopeful of overcoming the opposition by suitable amendment; and it was antici- pated that the bill would again be introduced. This, however, proved not to be the case; in 1926 the joint committee had to recommend that 'in view of the uncompromising attitude of the Law Society . . . no steps should be taken in the direction of re-introducing a Registration Bill at the present time'.

The obstacle was hence early identified of failure to mobilise the overwhelm- ing majority of estate agents or, to put it the other way round, of needlessly granting a monopoly to the best established bodies. In a move that was in many respects similar to a more decisive one in 1962, the estate agents opposed to the Clarke Bill in 1923 formed ISALPA in 1924, not as a basis to oppose registration, which they supported, but to resist their exclusion, and the apparently snobbish requirement of the Bill that would make it possible

---

[12]This account draws on F.A.R. Bennion, 'A history of estate agents registration', *Estates Gazette*, 25 May 1968, and also on D.B.C. Symonds, *Some Notable Dates in the Estate Agents Profession* (NAEA, 1990); and R. Card, *The Estate Agents Act 1979*, (London: Butterworths, 1979), ch. 1.
[13]Op. cit. (note 4), pp. 207–8.

for the proposed governing board to exclude from membership any estate agents who 'have entered into any profession, business or occupation which in the opinion of the Board, cannot properly be carried on in conjunction with the performance of the specified duties'.[14] This was directed particularly at the habit of combining estate agency with furniture retailing, a reminder both of the differences of estate agency practice during this period and of the very much smaller percentage of the population (perhaps 20 per cent) who were owner-occupiers.

The opposition of the established professional bodies to secondary commercial activities was not, however, purely based on snobbery, but on anxieties about the use of estate agency services to coerce sales of other services. Thus the concern was that an estate agent might use the sale of a house as a basis to sell his furniture to the purchaser, so creating a conflict of interest with the vendor, whose commission he takes and whose agent he is. Similar dangers were perceived to arise from the sale of central heating, which was then just beginning to feature in new houses.[15]

ISALPA made the same mistake as the three senior bodies in promoting the Harvey Bill in 1928, which failed for lack of a broad basis of support. It did not give up, but prepared another Bill in the early 1930s, and opposed the registration of architects and accountants in 1929. The fate of these other groups is instructive by comparison. Architects achieved registration in 1931, but only on the basis that they were permitted to establish a register, not of compulsory registration. Accountants had a number of advantages which the professions of the land lacked: they were increasingly important in the regulation of company affairs, and in the State's strategy for the legitimation of business and profit, they were of critical importance in achieving a managed economy in time of war, and they performed a clear and increasingly technical set of services both for business and for individuals. Nonetheless, accountants failed to achieve registration and were bedevilled by failure, which persists to the present, to consolidate into a few representative bodies based on function. Every time the leading bodies looked likely to make a successful attempt at registration the newer marginal practitioners formed associations to protest, and the point was made that the proponents of registration did not command the widest support, and that in any case, accounting, like the professions of the land, may include exact techniques and an exacting experience, but is not an exact science and can reasonably include a diversity of levels of skill.[16]

1934–62: STALEMATE

In 1934 the three senior societies (RICS, CLAS, AEAI) abandoned the pursuit of registration, citing as reasons for doing so failure to achieve it after 20 years

[14]Cited by Bennion, op. cit. (note 12), p. 14.
[15]See Carr-Saunders and Wilson, op. cit. (note 4), p. 205.
[16]See Wilmott, op. cit. (note 1).

of deliberate effort, the permissive nature of the registration achieved by architects in 1931, and the importance of professional qualifications (of the type that they would by this date claim to administer) in protecting the public. A slightly different interpretation would add that the three societies had achieved considerable recognition and stability and a sense of ascendancy over the other would-be professional bodies, whose coming and goings on the political scene had nonetheless proved to be a serious obstacle to the three societies achieving registration on anything like their own terms.

ISALPA put the matter rather more assertively, saying that the decision was illogical, and if registration had been essential for the protection of the public in the past why was it not so in the present; exclusive, in that it failed to comprehend the interests of other professional bodies and the public in registration; and that it left Britain noticeably out of line with other industrialised countries, including the British Dominions. ISALPA soldiered on in the pursuit of registration and turned its attention to the excise licences which were the only form of State regulation of estate agents then required, and which were available on demand and the payment of a fee. ISALPA castigated the government for exercising no supervision over the fitness of those it licensed to practise and as being more interested in the income from the sale of licences than the protection of the public. The government was sufficiently stung to establish a committee under Lord Mersey to consider the matter, which recommended that a magistrate oversee the issuing of licences, that references be required of applicants, and that cases involving evidence of dishonesty should be turned down.

The intervention of war in 1939 put a stop to further professional skirmishing, and at its conclusion in 1945 the political landscape looked rather different. The RICS and AEAI again rejected registration, pointing out that registration of appellation was inadequate for estate agency, because of the number of firms that would need to be included, and that registration of function would be almost impossible to achieve. On the other hand the postwar regulation of housing and land was a potential route to a general increase in the specification of standards by the State, in which the estate agency professions should participate. The AEAI remained in favour of registration as the only real basis for the protection of the public, but recognised that it was unlikely to be attainable in current political and legislative circumstances.

By 1952 alliances had shifted somewhat and, whereas the RICS and CLAS repeated their opposition to registration, ISALPA and the CAEAI objected and pointed to a rash of fraudulent abuses. Some of these were addressed the following year in the Hutchinson Bill, which became the Accommodation Agencies Act 1953 and which banned a number of abuses in respect of rented accommodation agencies which, it was claimed, had defrauded the public of £100,000. Rented accommodation was not part of most estate agents' work and was often undertaken by independent accommodation agencies.

In 1959, however, Denis Howell MP identified alleged abuses by estate agents over deposits and commissions involving 2,000 people and £200,000 in Birmingham. This was followed by a London County Council report in 1960 alleging substantial abuses of commissions, contracts and deposits in the capital. In 1961 an anonymous writer in the *Estates Gazette* alleged substantial abuses by business transfer agents.[17]

Britain had by this point entered the Macmillan era of rapid housing construction, both private and public, rising incomes, and the 'never had it so good' ebullience of the prime minister. Wartime restraints upon property sales and development were long gone and commercial and domestic property business was, despite fluctuations, doing very well. Many new faces had come into estate agency in the postwar years, taking advantage of the strong market and expanding home ownership. Evidence of abuses thus threatened to upset the apple cart, but as ever there was a need to draw in all interested bodies if registration was to be achieved. Failure yet again to do this provoked a crisis, the consequences of which have affected the regulatory picture down to the present. In 1959 the three senior bodies and ISALPA reached agreement on registration but, ominously, issued a warning on the need for professional bodies which might be recognised in legislation to be of 'rigorous and well governed organisation'.

1962–6: SO NEAR AND YET SO FAR: RENEWED ATTEMPTS AT REGISTRATION

In 1962 a further attempt was made at registration with the Legge-Bourke Bill. This envisaged registration of function and regulation by an Estate Agents Council dominated by eight representatives of each of the three senior bodies, leaving only six to represent the other bodies. After three years the three senior bodies' representation would remain at 24 and the representation of other bodies and independents would rise, by various provisions, to 18. Professional competence was stressed as necessary to public protection and registration as essential to outlaw abuses. It was quite plainly a bid for effective domination of estate agency by the established bodies, claiming that only they could really be trusted to protect the public.

In taking this stance the senior bodies had underestimated the changes in the postwar scene. The Bill's sponsors claimed overwhelming support and that their membership dominated estate agency. The independents were galvanised by the Bill to form themselves into an association, the National Association of Estate Agents (NAEA), which lobbied vigorously, not against registration, but against a Bill which they believed would lead to professional monopoly. The NAEA campaign was decisive in defeating the Bill. Research was commissioned which showed that of about 11,000 identifiable estate agency firms, at least a third were operated by independents. This was enough to persuade the current, like previous governments, to withhold support for the Bill, because it did not represent a sufficient majority of estate agents.

More significant in the longer term, however, was the view of estate agency professed by the NAEA. It distinguished estate agency as selling property as an agent on commission from the professional skills ancillary to

---

[17]See Bennion, op. cit. (note 12).

the property market, and claimed that estate agency should be marked out by the quality of service given to clients and by agents' skills in obtaining the best price for clients' properties. Estate agents were thus identified not as the providers of professional services for a fee, but as market intermediaries. In order to act as estate agents they needed the skills, experience and ability to sell houses which were not conferred by professional qualifications, useful adjuncts though these might be. Competition between agents to make their names in the market was seen as part of the bedrock of estate agency, and there was great antagonism to the notion that rights of access to the market should be exclusive to members of the existing professional bodies. It was vital that new unqualified people should be able to come into the market to keep it working at its most efficient. The NAEA hence took a strong line against proposed restrictions on advertising.

A critical point then became what view the NAEA took of tests of competence. If selling houses was no different from selling cars or furniture, was there any need for such tests? The solution that experience as a practising estate agent should be accepted in lieu of professional qualifications was the same as had been advanced by junior bodies in the past, and not only in respect of estate agency but also other professions, notably accountancy, but the basis of the argument for it was different. For estate agency it was not that experience generates enough of the professional skills to justify public reliance on the practitioner, it was that experience in selling houses is more important for that purpose — getting the best price for the client and getting the sale through — than professional qualifications.

Parliamentary interest in estate agency regulation did not evaporate with the demise of the Legge-Bourke Bill, and indeed with the advent of Labour administrations the issue gradually moved on to the government's agenda.

In contrast to the Conservative government which had been content to confine itself to benevolent neutrality during the professions' attempts to obtain registration, the incoming Labour government in 1964 demonstrated a more consumerist view of the public interest, to the point of effectively questioning the place of established estate agents in the market. Not only was its attitude to registration more critical, as we shall see, but it took steps, albeit not very well thought out, to promote the establishment of property registers run by local authorities at minimum costs.[18] Eight cities embarked on schemes but, with very little support or guidance from the Ministry of Housing, they varied in their precise pattern. All, however, limited themselves to what estate agents would call multi-listing, that is, circulating the particulars of properties without further marketing or ancillary services, though local authorities were enabled to embark upon mortgage lending by the Labour government. The multi-listing initiative was replied to in various guises by the private sector — a cooperative scheme by Manchester agents, a half-scale fee operation in Hayes, for example. As with the similar efforts of the 1980s, such initiatives were not shown to be fruitless but did not result in

---

[18]See J. Goudie, *House Agents*, Young Fabian Pamphlet, No. 13 (Fabian Society, 1966).

the wholesale takeover of the estate agency market as clients flocked to a simple cheap listing service. For all the scepticism as to the benefit to the public of estate agents and the questioning of what they do to earn their commissions, which reinforced their dubious image, the public seemed disinclined to abandon them when offered an alternative. There were a series of more detailed reasons for estate agents to retain their negative image, which fuelled the continuing campaign for registration as a route to controlling them. The question which arose now, however, was whether this was to be achieved by the effective cooperation of the professional bodies and self-regulation or be imposed by government regulation.

In the early 1960s there were complaints of the problems posed by the bankruptcy of estate agents, a problem that had arisen several times in the past and for which the solution was known to be compulsory bonding (as indeed was done for travel agents following the Court Line disaster in the 1960s). There were also complaints about the wilful misdescription of properties and abuse of deposits. According to Goudie, a contemporary commentator:

> ... at the end of 1964, in twelve cases known to a London Citizens Advice Bureau, twelve people, all West Indians, lost deposits ranging from £200 to £600 through the breakdown of mortgage negotiations, consequent upon an agent's falsification of mortgage applications to a building society. These deposits have never been recovered and are not like to be.
>
> A deposit is not the only money a purchaser stands to lose. To push a sale through, the agent may well help the purchaser to raise mortgage finance. The agent may introduce a mortgage broker, who will charge a fee for his services, which he may divide with the agent or the agent may act as his own broker and charge a procuration fee himself. Agents and brokers often obtain the procuration fee in advance. This is sometimes partly to evade the Moneylenders Act, which makes brokerage fees irrecoverable from the borrower when the lender is in law a 'money-lender'. Where the fee is paid in advance it is not always readily refunded if the loan is not granted, whether because the lender withdraws after approving the loan in principle or because the borrower declines to take up the loan after discovering the true rate of interest. There can be a very wide variation in the rate of interest depending on whether it is expressed as flat (on the full amount of the loan throughout the period of repayment) or reducing (on the balance from time to time remaining owing) and whether it is expressed as gross or net (after deduction of tax).

Commissions were also subject to abuse:

> The type of agent, who wishes to stipulate that his commission is payable at some stage in the process being reached short of completion and payment of the purchase price, usually has an expertly drafted and very one-sided form of contract to which he endeavours to obtain the signature of the vendor. The vendor is bound by what he signs unless he can prove

that he was misled by something the agent said and as a result had no idea that the document which he was signing had anything to do with the agent's entitlement to commission.

Those who sign these documents do not mean to pay commission unless the sale goes through, or to put themselves at the risk of becoming liable to two agents, both of whom do what they stipulated they had to do to earn commission. They simply do not bother to consider the small print and are scarcely likely to be encouraged to do so by the agent. There are cases in the Law Reports of agents collecting a commission in respect of a person introduced by them who completed the purchase and then suing for a second commission in respect of an earlier applicant for the same house who did not go on to complete.[19]

In 1965 the attitude of some Labour MPs to the issues raised by estate agency was indicated in the Winterbottom Bill, which aimed to limit the fees which estate agents could charge, and to encourage local authorities to go into estate agency. The professional bodies widened access to their Parliamentary committee and made concessions, and ultimately, following additional concessions, admitted the NAEA. When Winterbottom's Bill failed 10 societies became involved in the preparation of a Bill to achieve registration: RICS, CLAS, CAEAI, ISALPA, NAEA, Incorporated Association of Architects and Surveyors, Rating and Valuation Association, Valuers Institution, Institution of Business Agents, and the Faculty of Architects and Surveyors. It is worth noting the conditions exacted by the NAEA for joining the group:

1.   That the test of competence for future admission to the register should be related to the specific functions to be controlled without creating artificially high barriers.

2.   That in determining representation in the Estate Agents Council a registered agent who was a member of more than one representative body should be counted only once.

3.   It was recognised that estate agency was not a purely professional function and such restrictions as were imposed should not be designed to favour one type of business as against another and should prohibit only those practices which were prejudicial to the public. In particular care must be taken that rules should not inhibit new techniques and the provision of an efficient and up-to-date service to the public.'[20]

These points reflected not only the NAEA's market orientation, but the diversity of practices involved in estate agency in the broad sense and represented in the societies which had come together to promote registration. For example, some practices, particularly rural ones, included auctioneering, but that did not imply that any restrictions necessary to secure the public

---

[19]Goudie, op. cit. (note 18), pp. 3, 4, 5.
[20]Quoted in Bennion, op. cit. (note 12).

interest at auctions need be applied to practices whose sole concern was the sale of domestic and commercial property.

The Ten Societies Committee promoted a new Bill, the Jones Bill in 1965/6 which took the concept of an Estate Agents Council forward on the basis of membership being allocated at one per 1,000 members of the recognised professional bodies. Parliamentary concern had been evident in the preceding years and the lesson of past attempts and the need to mobilise all interested parties had finally been learned; the Bill hence commanded wide Parliamentary support. Abuses such as oppressive contracts, extortionate commissions and outright fraud were cited in the debate on the Bill, and there was also an attempt to include a ban on property dealing by estate agents, though this was resisted on the basis that a compulsory declaration of interest would be sufficient. More significantly, questions were raised as to whether the proposed council should not have some lay members to represent the public interest. The presumption was that the proposed regulatory body (the Council, or in previous initiatives a Board) would contain members of the main professional bodies who would discipline their members, suspending or expelling them for misconduct and so debarring them from legitimate practice. Specific abuses would be identified and outlawed when and insofar as they became a problem. On the positive side, codes of conduct and good practice, coupled with tests of competence applied by the professional bodies would increasingly secure adequate levels of performance both as regards probity and competence. Whilst the Jones Bill, like its predecessors, contained some measures to protect the public interest, for example, compulsory bonding and audit of client accounts, the burden of detailed regulation was left to the council. The public, however, would be further protected by the fact that the code of conduct, scale of charges, and particulars of registration would all be subject to the approval and amendment of the Board of Trade. Solicitors were, as in previous bills, excepted from the requirement to register.

One matter seemed in retrospect ominously prophetic of the outcome of efforts on registration. The practice of estate agents also dealing in property is long established, as was evident in the 19th-century examples quoted above, but created a clear conflict of interest which has regularly given rise to allegations of abuse. The Code of Conduct of the Chartered Auctioneers and Estate Agents Institute (CAEAI) provided that '... agency and dealing are two incompatible occupations and any attempt to combine them in one person or firm must inevitably be fatal to any pretension to a professional reputation'. Several of the other professional bodies have similar provisions in their codes of conduct.[21] The response of Arthur Jones to the issue when it was put to him as sponsor of the 1966 Bill is therefore interesting: 'I do not accept that they are incompatible'. Jones was a fellow of the Valuers Institution (VI) which amalgamated with ISALPA in 1968. The CAEAI had held discussions with ISALPA earlier in the decade with a view to merger but these failed. Many regarded this as an important lost opportunity to form

---

[21]Goudie, op. cit. (note 18), p. 2; Carr-Saunders and Wilson, op. cit. (note 4), p. 205.

a body which could primarily represent estate agents, so finally delineating that profession of the land. After the rebuff and the ISALPA/VI merger to form ISVA the CAEAI merged with the RICS in 1970.

THREE

Professional Crisis and Regulatory Dilemma

In the late 1960s the various professional bodies attempted to coordinate themselves for the 'final big push' to achieve registration and legislative recognition, it now being realised that the cooperation of all the bodies representing estate agents was essential to achieving this end. The formation of the Ten Societies Committee was a significant achievement and the proposed Estate Agents Council (EAC) looked as if it might succeed.

1966–9: ESTATE AGENTS REGISTRATION COUNCIL

Arthur Jones's private member's Bill incorporating these aspirations stood a good chance of passing and had government support, but the 1966 general election intervened and it was lost. The Ten Societies Committee then agreed to sustain the Estate Agents Council themselves, but in the clear expectation of legislation:

We regard the setting up of the Council as a step towards statutory control and not as a substitute for it. As soon as the Council becomes operative, it will prepare a licensing Bill and press for its early passage through Parliament. We are already assured of government support for this[1]

The composition of the Council was as envisaged in the Bill. The chairman, nominated by the Board of Trade was Sir Ronald German, who had recently retired as Director General of the General Post Office. The Council's ambitions were considerable:

---

[1] A statement by the Ten Societies Committee on Estate Agency addressed to members of the societies, p. 3, emphasis in original.

It will be the purpose of the Council to secure adequate standards of competence and conduct amongst estate agents; to improve the techniques used in estate agency; to increase public knowledge of the services provided by estate agents; to establish and maintain a register of all persons entitled to use the term 'Recognised by the Estate Agents Council'; and to make regulations as to the requirements which must be fulfilled before any person can be entered on the Register.

The Council will have the right to lay down the form of qualification for entry on the register. It will be able to discipline those registered for unethical acts and require that the activities of each registered estate agent shall be covered by an 'honesty bond'.

Additionally it is the purpose of the Council to prevent the exploitation of the public by unscrupulous men. This has indeed been the aim of the efforts in the past and has arisen largely because there has been the opportunity for exploitation. Provided the public treats only with those entitled to the description 'recognised by the Estate Agents Council', the risks will be appreciably reduced.

The other principal advantage, and this must be related to the preceding paragraph, will be the drawing together of estate agents' interests and the promotion of those interests by one body. Dispersal of effort has in the past resulted in inadequate public relations but in future, for the 'recognised estate agent', promotion will come from one source with obvious advantage.

Estate agency has long been recognised as essentially one function of the professions of the land and it is vitally important that at long last this function should be properly controlled for the public protection.[2]

In practice it was registration which was crucial to the council, reflecting the central objective of successive Bills. It was hence vital that it succeeded in attracting as many estate agents as possible to register. This was promoted by funding the council directly from the 10 societies for the first two years after its establishment on 7 October 1967 and only thereafter requiring fees of the societies' members, though non-members of the societies were charged a fee from the start. Though the question of qualification by examination was present as a practical aspiration, and the drawing up of an appropriate syllabus was soon looked into by the Admissions Committee, which sought to come to an agreement as regards teaching with the College of Estate Management at Reading University, in practice membership of one of the 10 societies conferred access to registration with the Council. For non-members evidence of good character, together with practice full time as an estate agent in two out of the preceding 10 years was initially deemed acceptable as a basis for registration. Even in the future, the expectation was that qualification as a registered estate agent should be at a lower level than qualification for the professional accreditation of the 10 societies, and four O levels including maths and English were agreed as the entry requirement to the Council's proposed diploma. The Council further asserted that it:

---

[2] Ibid., p. 4.

will not attempt to exclude anyone who satisfies reasonable tests of competence and character. The constitution explicitly recognises that estate agency has both professional and commercial attributes and that it is desirable to encourage estate agents to make proper use of new techniques and to provide in other ways an efficient service to the public.

Further,

> ... it is not envisaged that the rules of conduct will prohibit a person recognised by the Estate Agents Council from canvassing or restrict his advertising except in any case where the public is prejudiced, but members of the societies will remain bound by the rules of conduct of their respective societies.[3]

The Council was therefore from the start a holding operation riding on the goodwill of the constituent member societies sponsoring the Jones Bill and was vulnerable to any dissent among them until legislation was enacted creating a statutory framework to which all were required to adhere. Problems soon arose at all levels. By early 1968, for example, the registration working group was struggling with the practical problem of how to verify the bona fides and good character of individuals on the register when they applied to become registered as principals. The Council agreed to accredit status, but the organisation recommended for verifying this, Tracing Services Ltd, proved to have come in for some adverse publicity and the group decided to rely on the conventional resources of bankers, solicitors and accountants.[4]

From this point — early 1968 — onwards the tension between the EAC (its title amended to the Estate Agents Registration Council at the end of March) and the governing societies (reduced to nine by amalgamation) was evident. Even the cordial welcome given to a letter from the Nine Societies EAC Committee had to be reiterated to avoid misunderstanding. The fundamental sources of this tension were, on the Council's side, its dependence upon the support of the societies to urge their members to register so that as nearly comprehensive a register as possible could be produced. Difficulties in its production delayed the deadline for applications from 31 May to 30 September, with the result that the first register could not be published until January 1969. Arrangements for bonding went ahead, with a minimum level of £10,000 per individual principal or £20,000 per firm.

By the turn of the year, however, the seeds of the crisis that was to overwhelm the Council in 1969 were already sown. A letter drafted for circulation to members, of whom about 12,000 were said to be registered, identified legislation as the most important task of the Council, and expressed every hope that a Bill could be introduced in the coming few

---

[3] Ibid., p. 7.
[4] Registration Working Group Minutes, 22 February 1968, EAC/55/68. Here and below papers of the Council are cited by their internal reference numbers.

months which would be acceptable to the Council, the societies and the government. This, everyone seemed to be agreed, was the Holy Grail which would finally secure statutory recognition of estate agency, bind all practitioners to common standards, outlaw excesses, reassure the public, and provide a foundation for a statutorily recognised Council to build better standards in the future. If legislation were not obtained, however, disagreement among the societies threatened to reemerge, alongside fears that the Council would assert its independence from its sponsors. Certainly no major short-term gains in credibility were to be anticipated apart from bonding — it was evident that teaching on the new qualifications could not start until September 1970.

When the Council published its conduct and bonding rules in January 1969 they proved modest indeed. All members were to be bonded, as indicated above, against dishonesty and default. The conduct rules specifically excluded professional activities not carried on as part of an agency transaction, such as valuations, surveys and planning applications, so narrowing the scope of the Council's remit and leaving ample room for the societies' professional regulatory role to continue. Estate agents were enjoined as a paramount duty to protect and promote the legitimate interests of their clients and a series of offences was specified amounting to disgraceful conduct contrary to the public interest — a significant combination of professional and consumerist terms. The first five are the most significant and notable for their lack of complexity — some might even say naïvety:

1   Acting for a client whose interests conflict directly or indirectly with the estate agent's or with those of another of his clients without having made full disclosure of all relevant facts to the first-mentioned client and without having pointed out to him the desirability of taking independent advice.

Examples of conflicts of interests:

(a)   Where the estate agent is instructed to sell property and introduces as a prospective purchaser a company in which the estate agent is a substantial shareholder or a director.

(b)   Where the estate agent is retained by a client to find property and offers to the client a property owned by the estate agent's wife.

2   Receiving from another person in connection with the affairs of a client any commission, discount, rebate or other profit without prior disclosure to the client.

3   Seeking instructions in a manner which is oppressive or unconscionable.

4   Publishing particulars of any property without having taken reasonable steps to ensure that they are accurate and not misleading.

5 (a)   Accepting instructions without ensuring that the terms and conditions of his engagement (including terms and conditions as to remuneration) are clearly known to his client.

(b)   Making a charge which is unreasonably high.

It was item three of this code that was to prove the undoing of the EARC. In November 1968 John Fraser MP had agreed to introduce a registration Bill in Parliament but withdrew when approached by members of ISVA. It soon became apparent that these members represented deep-seated anxieties about giving immediate statutory backing to the EARC. ISVA's practical objection was that of timing — that it was inopportune, particularly given the recent reference of estate agency to the Monopolies Commission, whose report was expected in early 1969. This was likely to attack the scale fees then charged by estate agents, but might also be expected to comment on other restrictive and anti-competitive practices, which might include professional codes of conduct and restrictions on entry. In brief the Commission might very well come down firmly on the commercial side of estate agency to the detriment of the professional societies who were sponsoring the Council and legislation. These fears were articulated at the first annual dinner of the newly formed society (the amalgamation of the Valuers Institution and ISALPA) in February 1969, by the ISVA president:

The form and content of a Bill and the timing of its introduction into Parliament must be agreed by all parties who are concerned with it. There must be a code of conduct no less stringent, particularly on the question of personal canvassing, than that which has been adhered to by the major bodies for over 30 years and which was imposed voluntarily by ourselves on ourselves, especially to protect the public from the door-to-door canvasser. And there must be a proper test of competence imposed on all those who, without adequate practice qualifications, seek admission to an estate agents' register.

The formula for success of any operation, whether in peace or in war, is dependent on correct timing and it seemed to us that it would be extremely unwise to have a Bill in the House when the report of the Monopolies Commission was published and before it had even been considered by the profession. Not so much through fear of what the government might do, but rather because the government might find itself unable to resist amendments introduced by those who do not consider estate agents as their best friends. The many might well find themselves suffering for the misdemeanours of the few.

On the question of a code of conduct, it surely cannot be right to accept a standard lower than the best. Well over 80 per cent of the practising estate agents in the country are agreed on this and I can see no reason whatsoever why the remaining few should reap the benefit of our persistence and hard work over many years without also accepting the limitations and obligations which are inherent in the receipt of any privilege. And on the third point — an adequate standard of competence — this is too obvious. It is a *sine qua non* and needs no further amplification from me. Given agreement on those points, my society will support legislation to the hilt.[5]

---

[5] As reported in *Estates Gazette*, 15 February 1969.

This *démarche* provoked critics in the EARC, which at its meeting on 18 December 1968 debated a motion to 'give serious consideration to liquidation unless the prospect of early legislation can be assured'.[6] Although the majority of members were reluctant to contemplate the demise of the EARC, given both their own efforts over the preceding months and the achievement of a common Council after so many years of struggle, the severity of the crisis was widely acknowledged. Two immediate steps towards a solution were taken, one by the EARC and one by the NAEA.

The most significant was a meeting between the EARC, the Nine Societies EARC Committee, ISVA and the Board of Trade (Parliamentary and Permanent Secretaries). The substance of this meeting was to clarify the extent of ISVA's objections and the willingness of the government to legislate. The Nine Societies Committee had in the interim recommended that the EARC should continue in being, whether or not legislation was imminent. ISVA remained implacable in its insistence on dealing with the Monopolies Commission report before legislation was initiated and in requiring that the matters of the code of conduct, especially as regards canvassing and entry qualifications to the profession, be resolved by the council before legislation. Legislation was clearly seen by ISVA as a potential problem, not as a solution, and a threat to what ISVA believed was hard-won professional progress. It seemed to believe that in default of legislation, further progress would have to be achieved by the efforts of the professional bodies, jointly or severally, and the Council's aspiration to establish minimum standards for all estate agents, whether members of one of the professional bodies or not, was something worth leaving to the public and its support of a voluntary EARC. As an ISVA representative had put it at the 19 December EARC meeting:

> He did not consider that liquidation was inevitable in the absence of a registration Bill. There were already about 12,000 registered practitioners, and if the public were persuaded to deal only with registered persons, then undoubtedly all those persons would remain registered and even more would seek registration. If, on the other hand, the public did not support them, then this would itself indicate that the public did not want legislation and did not support the need for a Council. Given sufficient registrations he did not foresee financial difficulty for the Council. Nevertheless he felt that the Council did have a duty towards all registered persons to seek legislation at the first opportunity when the time was appropriate.[7]

Mrs Dunwoody, the minister, was clearly upset at this situation and expressed herself 'desperately unhappy' if the work of the Council were to stop. She warmly commended the work of the Council in outlining voluntary registration but said that government legislation on estate agency was virtually impossible in the current session. In response to pressure she

[6]EAC/301/68 item 4.
[7]EAC/301/68 item 22.

undertook to seek help from the government in introducing legislation, though she was made aware that the Nine Societies Committee did not see this as quite the priority that the EARC did.[8]

The initiative by the NAEA, though, as it turned out, little more than a gesture, went more to the heart of ISVA concerns. It asked Sir Edward Boyle, the leading liberal Tory, to extend his private member's Industrial Information Bill to include the practice of estate agents impersonating potential property buyers in order to obtain details of properties from rivals and then going on to canvass them intensively. Such a legal prohibition would give more practical force to the EARC's point three on 'seeking instructions in a manner which is oppressive or unconscionable'. Whether it could have satisfied ISVA is another matter, but in any event the initiative came to nothing. More significant in practice were the comments on this topic by the Under-Secretary to the Board of Trade at the 21 January meeting. He was minuted as saying that:

> A code of this sort must be a matter of compromise, both for the Council and the Board of Trade whose approval was required. The Board of Trade were interested rather in consumer protection than in seeking to prevent reasonable competition between estate agents. In the opinion of the Board of Trade, the code published by the Council appeared to be a fully acceptable compromise.[9]

The tone of these remarks clearly foreshadowed the government's likely response to the Monopolies Commission report, which would tend to construe extended codes of conduct concerned with interprofessional relations and canvassing as likely to involve restrictive practices and the frustration of the consumer's interest. The questions then became, first how tough the Commission's report would be and secondly, whether ISVA's insistence on retaining the fruits of professional progress even at the cost of registration found support among the other professional bodies. ISVA's view on the importance of professional standards in respect of canvassing was shortly expressed more articulately:

> It is my belief that canvassing and touting for business is against the public interest. It is only the fact that four-fifths or more of those engaged in estate agency accept and adhere to the rules of the professional societies which prevents unrestricted touting from becoming the intolerable public nuisance that it was before the war. Canvassing and touting for business is not particularly noticed by the public as contrary to their interest while only a few indulge in it. If we returned to a free-for-all there would soon be a public outcry, and we should be in danger of putting the estate agents' profession into the same position as it was before the First World War.
>
> Now there is no immediate prospect of legislation the time is right to re-examine, or perhaps examine properly for the first time, the conse-

---

[8] EAC/10/69 minutes of meeting.
[9] EAC/10/69 item 7.

quences and the problems arising from having one voluntary code for the majority and trying to introduce by statute a lesser compulsory code to accommodate the minority. In advocating this reappraisal I am breaking no agreement.

I have good reason to believe that I am supported by the large majority of estate agent members of the professional societies in advocating the continuance of the existing codes of conduct of the professional societies.[10]

The response to this from Sir Henry Wells, whose family had been associated with attempts at registration since the interwar period, was to accuse ISVA not only of bad judgment but of bad faith:

Discussions prior to and the statement [of October 1967 setting up the EARC] itself recognised that the suppression, backed by statutory powers, of canvassing and unrestricted advertising could not be unreservedly defended on the grounds that it was in the public interest. Parliament, the public, and now, so it would seem, the Monopolies Commission, regard the ordinary run of estate agency (i.e. selling houses) as basically a commercial business. For this reason alone I do not believe that any Parliament would force all estate agents currently in practice to observe those restraints which the members of Mr Kensett's society and others voluntarily accept.[11]

Opinion divided even more sharply in letters from ISVA members in the following issue:

The introduction of a general code of conduct based on that laid down by the Estate Agents Council, while leaving a lot to be desired, has the agreement of the National Association and unattached agents and can only be a step in the right direction. It sets a minimum standard for all estate agents, which is more than we have at the present time, and must, therefore, be to the benefit of the public at large and to the estate agency profession.

The government of the day, whether Socialist or Tory, is interested in the protection of the public, not the protection of professional estate agents! Unless the Incorporated Society realises this, they are likely to jeopardise the profession's chances of influencing the government at all.

Is minimal statutory control any use at all? For the public probably it will be, but for members of the leading professional bodies, not at all. They are not the ones who filch deposits anyway, and the fear of being 'struck off' the rolls of their professional body (after all those exams!) is probably a greater deterrent than the possibility of being struck off the rolls of any statutory estate agents' list.

---

[10]F.J. Kensett, president of ISVA, letter to *Estates Gazette*, 3 March 1969.
[11]*Estates Gazette*, 10 March 1969.

What are we left with? The ludicrous position, unique in the free world, of professionally qualified *house* agents holding back from possible business while their unqualified and uninhibited rivals step in and clean up. What a farce! Perhaps Gilbert (and Sullivan) could have made something of it to laugh and sing about. In the meantime, I do not feel like laughing when I am told (as I was recently) that the reason I did not get an agency was because I did *not* knock on the door. ('This would have shown keenness' said the owner, whom I met later.)[12]

The Monopolies Commission report, which was published at this point, only served to accentuate these tensions. As expected, it strongly recommended the abolition of scale fees as against the public interest, but it also added '... because estate agents with a long tradition of charging at standard rates and of regarding fee cutting as unethical may continue to refrain from fee competition, we consider it important that the proposal that registration should become a statutory requirement should not lead to restraints on entry to the business that would reinforce that tendency'.[13] This was a ranging shot on canvassing and tests of competence in relation to the commercial view of estate agency and freedom of entry and competitive practice. If the government took a strong view of restrictive practices it would come out against restraints on canvassing: if it then went ahead with legislation subsequently it might incorporate such views in statute and undermine the codes of the professional bodies.

Kensett's comment (above) that he believed he had the support of the professional societies was evidently well founded. The EARC found itself in an increasingly tenuous position. Apart from its other difficulties, the block funding agreed by the societies for two years from 1967 would expire in September and the council would then depend on members paying a renewal fee. The council rapidly realised that in practice its survival depended on the recommendation by the professional bodies to their members to register and pay their dues. The first register was finally published only on 27 February 1969. It contained the names of over 10,000 individuals and over 5,000 firms. At the press conference to launch the register Sir Ronald German estimated that about 16,000 people were in business as estate agents. The minutes of the conference[14] do not suggest a very confident performance by the EARC chairman. He conceded that it was still possible to practise as an estate agent without registering, that legislation was still lacking, and of course the figures suggested that a substantial minority had not yet registered. The need for statutory backing was only too evident.

Sir Ronald had ample grounds for pessimism. At its meeting the following month the Nine Societies EARC Committee resolved to accept the EARC

---

[12] *Estates Gazette*, 22 March 1969.
[13] Report of Monopolies Commission on the Supply of Certain Services by Estate Agents para. 261, extracted EAC/37/69.
[14] EAC/38/69.

code of conduct but to delete paragraph 3 (quoted on page 30) and insert the following:

(i)   No registered estate agent shall either directly or indirectly in any manner whatsoever seek instructions for business which he knows, or with ordinary care could have ascertained, is in the hands of another agent; nor in other cases, without definite intimation that if another agent has already been retained, instructions may only be accepted from, and as subagent to, that agent. An agent who seeks instructions to deal with property on which another agent's board or notice is exhibited will be deemed to have disregarded knowingly this injunction. The seeking of instructions by an agent or one of his staff by personal call or telephone or by any communication which in the opinion of the Council constitutes a circular is prohibited.

(ii)   No agent shall offer any financial or other inducement to secure instructions.

(iii)   Nothing in the foregoing shall preclude an agent from accepting instructions from a vendor who without solicitation approaches the agent directly even though the vendor may previously have instructed another agent and that agent may have a sale board on the premises.[15]

Further, the committee resolved by eight to one:

that the Committee should recommend the Councils of the nine societies to advise their members to register with the Estate Agents Registration Council for the year beginning 1st October 1969, subject to the acceptance by the Estate Agents Registration Council of the amendments to the Code of Conduct agreed by the Committee.[16]

The professional bodies were clearly determined to assert control of the EARC in order, as they saw it, to protect standards, even at the risk of a rift that could destroy the EARC and even provoke the government into legislating to frustrate them. The EARC was only too painfully aware that its future depended upon the recommendations to register by the professional bodies and pleaded for their support at its meeting on 13 March.[17]

The dissenting voice was the NAEA, which, given its established position in defending and representing a commercial view of estate agency, was evidently unhappy at this professional dominance and indicated that, whilst it would accept the majority decision on the EARC, it would oppose the amendment to the code of conduct in debate and, if it was accepted, would refer it for comment to the Board of Trade. With this move a clear split had opened up among the nine societies and hence effectively within the EARC. The NAEA put its case forcefully to the EARC in a letter on 17 April:

---

[15]Nine Societies EARC Committee Minutes, 26 March 1969, item 12.
[16]Ibid.
[17]EAC/44/69 item 7.

The EARC's article 36(1) is quite specific. The Council's powers in the matter of rules of conduct are limited to naming acts or omissions which in its opinion are specifically contrary to the public interest, as well as being disgraceful and was specifically intended to be a complete barrier to the attempt by certain societies to impose their private code on EARC.

The letter went on to warn that the Monopolies Commission was due to publish a further fuller report on professional charges in which the matter of canvassing and advertising would probably be considered more fully. It referred pointedly to the remarks of the Under-Secretary at the Board of Trade on the compromise character of the code quoted above. It also quoted the comment on the EARC code by the Consumer Council:

> For victims of inefficiency, the most useful thing is that the rules do not restrict competition among EAC members. There must have been some temptation to include rules restricting competition in promotion and advertising, and on poaching of clients, since the EAC's sponsoring organisations are the nine agents' associations, most of whom have codes of conduct aimed as much at preventing competition as at protecting the public.
> The rules of the Royal Institution of Chartered Surveyors, for example, forbid a member to 'seek instructions for business which he knows, or with reasonable care could have ascertained, is in the hands of another agent'. The EAC's version of this rule forbids only 'seeking instructions in a manner which is oppressive or unconscionable' thus protecting the public from coffin-chasers, but not the dilatory estate agent from his more enterprising competitor.[18]

By the time of the crisis meeting of the EARC on 17 April to consider whether survival was still possible, the RICS had already decided to pull out of the EARC. The 17 April meeting was told by its chairman that there is 'a widespread feeling that the great majority of estate agents already registered with the Council [who were of course members of the professional bodies] would prefer a stricter code'.[19] In the circumstances the Council had no alternative but to accept the amended code as the price of its continued existence, since only by doing so would the professional bodies recommend that their members continue registration. The RICS council at its meeting of 14 April had, however, already resolved that enough was enough, that, amended code or no amended code, the EARC could not survive and that the RICS should take steps to establish a bonding scheme of its own. The president of the RICS wrote to the chairman of the EARC explaining the situation and citing the loss of unanimity among members, the failure to obtain legislation in the short term, and most sharply the position of the Board of Trade:

---

[18] *Focus*, April 1969.
[19] EARC/64/69 item 11.

It now seems quite clear that there is a fundamental difference of philosophy regarding estate agents, and a lack of sympathy in the Board with the aspirations that this Institution had, and still has, for raising the level of competence and standards of professional behaviour of those engaged in estate agency. Since the Board now seems to be primarily interested in safeguarding the public against dishonesty, this can be achieved by much simpler arrangements and without the elaborate machinery of a Registration Council.

It therefore appears that the wider purposes for which the Estate Agents Registration Council was originally set up have been frustrated by a number of factors and that the agreement which the societies and the EARC entered into is consequently nullified. In these unhappy circumstances, it may not come as a surprise to you to learn that my Council decided, at its meeting on Monday, 14th April, 1969, not to take any further steps to urge members of the Institution to register with the Estate Agents Registration Council.[20]

At the same time the Consumer Council made known, in a letter to the chairman of the EARC, its views on the proposed amendments to the code of conduct which it had expressed to the Monopolies Commission. Not surprisingly they were hostile, though the Consumer Council was evidently reluctant to be seen to be wielding yet another dagger, and aware that the EARC was doomed.

The reaction of Council members to these mounting and seemingly overwhelming pressures is interesting. Essentially the evidently strong sentiment among individual members to resist the demise of the Council became articulated collectively in terms of the duty of the EARC to its registered members and to the public and an attempt to assert its independence from its sponsors. One member was reported as saying that:

Council members must now regard themselves as such not to attempt to put forward the individual views of their societies; as Council members they represented registered persons collectively. Whilst he might favour rules on the lines of the chartered societies code, he agreed that the Council's own rules should be upheld at this stage.[21]

The role of non-estate agent members of the Council then suddenly became prominent. Professor Diamond, the distinguished commercial and consumer lawyer, spoke at length in favour of standing firm and expressed the view that the RICS was unlikely actively to discourage its members from continuing their registration.[22] The practical way forward was put by Francis Bennion, the secretary to the Council, whose legal eye detected a lawyer's

---

[20]EARC/72/69 item 6.
[21]EARC/81/69 item 24.
[22]EARC/81/69 items 28 and 29.

hand in the RICS president's concluding remarks about the purposes by the nine societies being frustrated and the agreement hence being nullified. He was able to channel the quite wide desire of the EARC members to continue in existence if at all possible, and the evident feelings of some that ISVA and now the RICS were guilty of bad faith, by suggesting that the original agreement to establish the voluntary Council was, and was intended to be, legally binding and that, contrary to the RICS assertion, it was by no means nullified. The Council agreed that he should seek counsel's opinion to this effect and in the meantime circularise registered estate agents with a sanitised version of recent events and urge them to continue registration. Hence, by 18 votes to two, the EARC voted to continue. It also agreed not to amend the code of conduct for the time being and to approach Mrs Dunwoody again to see what the prospects were for legislation. Subsequently a legal opinion was sought for the next meeting on 15 May.

By that meeting the Council was faced not only with the withdrawal of support for registration by their members by the ISVA and the RICS, but also the announcement that the latter, together with the CLAS and CAEAI were planning a joint deposit guarantee scheme. A meeting with Mrs Dunwoody, the minister at the Board of Trade, gave Sir Ronald German little comfort beyond her continued personal support and willingness to attempt to get the government to accept the Council's plea to legislate, though she held out little hope of this. Members of the EARC were, however, unwilling to give up and pointed out, first, that the response to the drive by the Council to retain the registration of those estate agents already registered was unknown — many might have views closer to the Council's than to the dissident professional bodies, and in any case it was unlikely that the professional bodies would campaign actively against registration, as opposed to failing to recommend it. Further, counsel's opinion was firmly of the view that secession by the professional bodies from the legal agreement between the 10 societies and which underpinned the EARC was quite illegal without giving the required one year's notice. Accordingly letters were sent to the presidents of the professional bodies with copies of the legal opinion, pleading with them not to withdraw their support from the Council.

Alas, politics proved far more decisive that legality. The response of the professional bodies was to give notice of their withdrawal from the 10 Societies agreement, which, even though it implied that formally the agreement would not lapse for a year, politically, in the eyes of the members, it meant that the agreement was dead in the water. At the same time the substitute bonding scheme was announced. The only recourse for the Council was for it to wind up its affairs, and it so decided on 12 June. The only outstanding matter proved to be seeking financial solvency during the period up to 30 September, when the Council finally ceased to exist. The four professional bodies introduced their indemnity scheme in early September.

The end of the Council left considerable confusion in its wake as to how the regulation of estate agency was now to proceed. As the *Estates Gazette* put it '... to many people it appears that it was the Monopolies Commission which held the dagger that ended the life of the Estate Agents Council'.[23] This explains little. More revealing is the obituary of the Consumer Council,[24] which was extraordinarily confused. On the one hand it supported statutory registration, recognition of an EARC and a mandatory code of conduct:

> But even a statutory Council could only be effective if it had the sincere support of all the estate agent bodies. An Act of Parliament cannot in itself generate enthusiasm for the public interest and a willingness to embrace competition as a spur to better service to the public (and better rewards for those who provide it). A mandatory code of conduct which reflected the thinking of the Incorporated Society of Valuers and Auctioneers, for example, would be the worst of all worlds. Moreover, as the Monopolies Commission noted (a comment referred to with distaste by the Incorporated Society in their condemnation of the Estate Agents Council) statutory registration could lead to restriction on entry into the estate agency.

The only way forward was hence a compulsory bonding scheme for all estate agents, the abolition of scale fees and and ensuring that entry to the profession should not be artificially restricted. The implication is that whilst there is a lingering affection for statutory registration, this is seen as a Trojan horse which will only in the end entrench professional monopoly. Hence attacking abuses and securing the consumer's interest piecemeal is the best approach.

Not surprisingly there was remarkably little articulate reflection on what had produced the débâcle. One ingredient was the very fact that estate agency was the last of the professions of the land to attempt professional registration and the related fact that the practice of all the professions of the land was frequently mixed. It was this that produced the diversity of professional bodies of varied size and standing and their constant bickering. When joined with the ambiguous nature of estate agency proper and its conjunction of straight selling with the need for proper care of clients' interests and the difficulties of the agent as an intermediary with duties towards purchasers also, the regulatory problems were likely to become serious. That they became acute was the consequence of the institutional expression of three different strands: the formation of the NAEA to represent the commercially oriented estate agent opposed to professional stuffiness; the rise of consumerism willing and able to give political bite to long-established public doubts about the reliability of estate agents; and the beginning of the attack on the restrictive character of the professions which became rather more agressive under the Thatcher administrations but which clearly began under Wilson. The drive to professional recognition could succeed only if the existing bodies were prepared to make room for estate agency despite its ambiguities and the threat which its sales-oriented side posed to the professional mystique of the senior societies. Once the

---

[23] 21 June 1969.
[24] *Focus*, August 1969.

professions of the land were confronted with a significant counterweight of institutional and political opinion which defended the sales-oriented side of estate agency and consumerism, such an accommodation became impossible. Something else had to take the place of statutory registration of estate agency, but what that was to be was still unclear, and indeed still is. The focus of further attempts at regulation hence continued in ever more ghostly forms to embody the aspiration for a statutory EARC, whilst the reality was a piecemeal targeting of specific abuses.[25]

THE ROAD TO THE ESTATE AGENTS ACT 1979: A PYRRHIC VICTORY

The Heath government, 1970–4, established the Office of Fair Trading (OFT) in 1973, whose experience and responsibilities have steadily grown under administrations of both parties of government to the present day. It was in the same year that the suggestion of licensing by government rather than the registration through professional bodies of estate agency was first aired in Parliament.[26] One of the OFT's early tasks was to undertake supervision of the Consumer Credit Act 1974, the detailed licensing and vetting of which became increasingly complex. With the return of a Labour government in 1974, ministerial interest in estate agency returned and the Department of Prices and Consumer Protection issued a consultative paper on estate agency in 1975. This suggested a licensing scheme run by the OFT which would involve a fit and proper person test based on criminal record, discrimination on grounds of race or sex and the use of deceitful, oppressive or improper business practices, that is, a test of honesty and fairness rather than competence. Bonding for deposits was to be required, a compensation fund to cover fraud and

---

[25]The difficulties, so evident in the EARC episode, of the relationship between the established professional bodies and residential estate agency did not dissipate. The Lay Report on *The Market Requirements of the Profession* for the RICS was commissioned in 1992 to recommend remedies for the perceived sense of loss of professional identity by the RICS and fears of loss of rank, especially to lawyers and accountants. In part this reflected the rise of quantity surveying amongst members, to constitute about one third, and the apparent fission of the RICS into a series of separate specialities. When confronted with the realities of the market in which the financial side of property has tended increasingly to come to the fore, this led away from a perception of members as being specialist property professionals. The recommended solution was hence a more positive public profile based on a wide, but integrated, range of fee-earning services. This, however, led to a hostile view of residential estate agency almost to the point of suggesting that it should be excluded from the profession. This move was immediately rejected by the general council when the report was debated. Even though the rising constituency of quantity surveyors might regard estate agency as grubby and unprofessional, some 13,000 members still obtained some or all of their income from agency. Given this hostile reference it was even more remarkable that the report should have also recommended 'that vigorous efforts should be made in another attempt to bring about the amalgamation with ISVA, despite the failure to achieve this two years ago' (Report, para. 10–18). The failure was on the RICS part; 80–90 per cent of ISVA members approved the merger. RICS sources suggested that, rivalries between quantity surveyors and estate agents apart, there were doubts about whether the ISVA professional qualification was as demanding as that of the RICS. Relations between the two bodies remained cooperative, however, and the RICS took pride in its contribution to the national vocational qualification in estate agency.
[26]R. Card, *The Estate Agents Act 1979* (London: Butterworths, 1979), p. 35.

bankruptcy, and client accounts were to be compulsory. The Secretary of State was to be empowered to make additional licensing conditions.

Standards of professional competence were an immediate ground of dispute over the proposals, with ISVA and the RICS in favour, and the NAEA opposed to them as a condition of holding a licence. The senior bodies suggested that they should form a joint licensing authority, whereas the NAEA welcomed the OFT being responsible for licensing, albeit with the assistance of an estate agents tribunal. Established differences clearly showed no signs of dissipating, and legislative time for what would therefore be foreseen as a contested and complex matter was not forthcoming. The government made it clear that it was open to suggestion as to the way forward.

Negative licensing

It seems to have been in the light of these discussions that the notion of negative licensing arose. Rather than attempt to regulate estate agency by specifying in detail what was required, as the Consumer Credit Act 1974 came to do, why not allow anyone to practise unless they failed to meet certain criteria? Such a strategy was naturally congenial to the NAEA, which supported the next attempt at legislation, the Weetch Bill in 1976. Although this did not get beyond a first reading, it laid the ground for what was to become the Estate Agents Act 1979 by adopting the idea of negative licensing. It envisaged a licensing authority which would exclude those not bonded, those without audited client accounts and those with convictions for dishonesty. The RICS, ISVA and the NAEA welcomed the Weetch Bill, and John Fraser, now Minister of State for Prices and Consumer Protection, stated the government's opposition to endorsing a professional monopoly. With the failure of the Weetch Bill the government had to consider involving itself directly. New proposals were brought forward in 1977 which included the idea of negative licensing, partly as a means of getting round the kind of complexities that had beset the OFT in its responsibility for issuing licences under the Consumer Credit Act 1974. Client accounts were to be mandatory and indemnity protection was to follow. The Secretary of State would be empowered to limit the level of precontract deposits. Estate agents were to be required to declare any interest in a property and to give written notice of the level and basis of charges. A further Bill, the Davies Bill, sponsored by the NAEA, was talked out in 1978 and then adopted by the government. Once again a general election intervened and the bill was only salvaged in limited form by all-party agreement to become the Estate Agents Act 1979.

The Act took on the concept of negative licensing, with the OFT as the licensing authority, with powers to ban or warn estate agents. The previously central regulatory concept of a statutorily recognised professional council was hence entirely abandoned. In its place came a series of specific provisions regarding bonding, client accounts, criminal records and standards of competence, together with a power for the Director General of Fair Trading, with the agreement of the Secretary of State for Trade, to declare specified conduct an undesirable practice and hence the basis for disciplinary action by the OFT.

Because of its unsatisfactory Parliamentary passage, the Act is widely agreed to be ineffective. Local trading standards officers, for example, have powers and responsibilities under the Act to intervene in estate agency, but in practice these are useless and only a few officers take a significant interest in enforcement, necessarily largely by persuasion. In addition the implementation of the Act has been limited. The main sections conferring powers on the OFT, and on client accounts, were implemented in 1982, but the Thatcher administration indicated that it was disinclined to introduce bonding. Section 22, which provides for tests of competence to be introduced which are gradually to be made compulsory for all estate agents, though with experience in practice standing in lieu, was not implemented. Nor was this to be expected even in 1979, since not only are competence tests for all compromised by allowing experience to act as an equivalent, but no enabling schedule was appended to the Act specifying the nature of the examining body, its funding and related matters.

The 1979 Act thus apparently achieved little, particularly given a government since then which has not been minded to intervene in markets unless there is an overriding priority to do so. That priority was present in respect of insurance (Lloyd's Act 1982), building societies (1986) and financial services (1986). On the other hand it might be said that the 1979 Act did reflect a recognition of the changing circumstances of estate agency. Public and governmental opinion have become sceptical of the benefits of professional monopoly, as the legal profession has recently been made to realise. The granting of a new monopoly to an estate agents' council, however widely representative of estate agency bodies, would not be in keeping with this sentiment. The professional bodies in estate agency had felt compelled before, in 1934, to rely upon their own resources to build and secure their reputation for professional competence and integrity, and it would seem that the 1979 Act conveys the same message.

The transfer of licensing to the OFT and the introduction of negative licensing and the power to declare undesirable practices might be said to be in accord with other features of the changed situation. The overt market orientation of the NAEA, which had risen from nowhere to become the most publicly active of the professional bodies and whose membership has grown to around 8,000, has ensured that the problem of regulating market intermediaries has become better recognised alongside the traditional model of professional self-regulation. This implies both the external regulation implicit in the OFT's responsibilities and the limited intervention against specific abuses implicit in the market operator's desire to be permitted to innovate and to do anything which is not specifically prohibited.

Why was the 1979 Act a Pyrrhic victory? Partly of course because it is less effective than it should have been because of its forced passage and partly because of the reluctance of the Thatcher administration to implement its provisions in full. In addition, however, the Act in practice left unresolved two critical issues: if estate agency is a market practice which requires regulation, can this be achieved by limited targeting of abuses? The model of the Financial Services Act 1986 with its sectoral self-regulatory organisation under the tutelage of the Securities and Investments Board would suggest, quite to the contrary, that the professional model is pressed into service for the purposes of regulating markets and market practitioners. Secondly, the 1980s saw the arrival in estate agency of the financial institutions (the corporates), entering the market for their own purposes, with their own powers of self-discipline and their own vast resources. The corporates introduced both new regulatory problems and new possibilities for regulatory control.

Regulatory confusion worse confounded: the coming of the corporates

There is no doubt that the buying up of chains of estate agents by the financial institutions so as to create national networks trading either with the same corporate name or under a new name, but explicitly linked to the services offered by the financial institution was undertaken in order to secure market share by the financial institutions. House purchase is a key opportunity to sell not only mortgage finance but insurance, both life and property, personal loans, and advice on such matters as pensions. The advantage of one-stop shopping as seen by the corporates is that trained staff are in place ready to provide accurate and appropriate advice and, under the increasingly stringent disclosure requirements of the administration of the Financial Services Act 1986, to be explicit about the costs, commissions and comparative benefits of the financial packages offered. For some house purchasers, relatively ignorant of the financial services markets and not already involved in life assurance and other schemes, such readily available packaged advice can be seen as very welcome.

Conflicts of interest are, however, inherent in the situation. In the first place purchasers may be sold financial services products that are not appropriate to their circumstances or are not the best buy: at worst this may involve 'churning' — the more or less coerced surrender of existing endowment policies and the taking out of new ones with companies owned by or linked to the mortgage lender. Secondly, vendors may be disadvantaged by the agent effectively failing to pass on prospective purchasers' offers if they refuse to contemplate taking on financial services from the corporate stable.

The arrival of the corporates coincided with the implementation of the 1979 Act and with a property boom. Booms always bring their share of abuses, including the problematic practice of gazumping, and pressures on the ponderous legal process of property transfer. Booms are also notorious within estate agency for attracting new practitioners, some of whom are neither competent nor scrupulous. The issue of regulation of estate agency hence showed no signs of dissipating following the 1979 Act and the way the issue was posed became considerably more complicated. With the OFT now effectively the regulatory body, it was not surprising that the initiative was, with the support of some of the professional bodies, taken by it. Since the government — for practical purposes the DTI and especially the Minister for Consumer Affairs — indicated that it was not disposed to implement all of the 1979 Act and in particular not s. 22 on tests of competence, the OFT was left with two options. It could attempt to specify the leading forms of misconduct and formulate them into undesirable practices, which the

Director General could then seek to have formalised and use to warn and ban agents who engaged in them. It could also pursue the route that it had followed with some success in other areas of consumer goods and services and seek to obtain an industry-wide code of conduct. The advantages of this route are that it specifies good conduct as well as bad, and that it permits of shades of evaluation rather than focusing on the unacceptable; also it can begin in a voluntary form and gradually be developed and refined into more binding forms by being adopted by professional bodies, trade associations etc., and ultimately be given statutory backing. It would thus give more extensive, sophisticated and flexible backing to the formal declaration of undesirable practices.

Accordingly the OFT issued a discussion paper in 1989 but, despite a quite wide response, was unable to obtain industry-wide agreement on a code of practice. The reasons for this are not entirely clear, but the indications are that the corporates could not agree among themselves, and that they may have been sceptical about the capacity of the independents to enforce a voluntary code; it also seems that in any case they could not agree upon a code covering the sales of their financial services through their estate agency networks which would satisfy the estate agency bodies.

According to one informed source the sequence of events outside the OFT was as follows. One of the corporates, concerned at the image of estate agents that it was buying into in such numbers, commissioned a report from a public relations consultancy into the public's perception of estate agents. This was followed by a meeting of the top 14 or 15 corporates in 1987 to discuss the risk that involvement in estate agency posed to their image. Eleven subsequently agreed to try to establish a code of practice but the issue of restraints upon the capacity of financial institutions to sell their products through their estate agencies proved too contentious to settle, and support for a voluntary code receded in 1988. The NAEA was active during this period also in promoting a code of conduct and representatives went to the DTI to see if government support for a statutory code was possible. At a meeting in mid 1988 with the NAEA, the Minister for Consumer Affairs, John Butcher, undertook to deliver government support for a code of practice. Butcher was evidently willing to go further than his senior colleagues and the issue of a code was put on the government agenda but with a government expectation that it would be voluntary not statutory. Meetings between the corporates and the DTI followed with no satisfactory outcome.

It became increasingly plain that the issue of regulation could not be entirely avoided and that the corporates could not deliver a voluntary code. The way forward was hence left largely to the OFT, which suggested implementing a code via the specification of 'undesirable practices' under the 1979 Act. This fitted with the minimalist sentiments of the government on intervention and the by now established view that estate agents' problems were to be dealt with by specific restraints upon identifiable and agreed malpractice, rather than by a comprehensive and positive regulation and licensing effort which would, *inter alia*, involve tests of competence. The contribution of the DTI was a commitment to reconsider the Trade Descrip-

tions Act 1968 with a view to extending it to estate agency, so removing an
obvious anomaly and meanwhile to initiate public consultation and a review
of the situation, a process which only led the government to confirm its view
that the problems of estate agency were those of ethics not competence.

The OFT review was hence left with the task of specifying undesirable
practices and targeting the worst abuses. Its caution was evident throughout.
In its consultation document in 1989[27] it said under 'The Office's strategy for
improvement':

> In its review of December 1988 the Office did not consider that the level of
> abuse in the field of estate agency called for a radical change in the form of
> regulation. It remains of that view. Nor did it consider that the case is made
> out for introducing compulsory minimum standards of competence
> (implementation of section 22 of the Act). The problems it has identified
> stem largely from unethical behaviour rather than from incompetence.
> Passed examinations or experience on the job are no guarantee of integrity.

This view echoed the views of the Trade and Industry Minister expressed in
November 1989. Mr Newton offered the following by way of explanation:

> I fully understand the support of those already in the industry for
> regulation [i.e., implementation of section 22] but I am conscious that this
> could create something of a closed shop and could hinder entry into the
> industry.[28]

The 1979 Act had been achieved in the light of a recognition of the market
features of estate agency and the NAEA, lobbying for the terms of the Act as
it had lobbied since the Legge-Bourke Bill 1962, had insisted that estate
agency remain open to newcomers without 'artificial' barriers. By the late
1980s, however, things had changed, and all the estate agency bodies were in
favour of tests of competence and sceptical of the government's view. Selling
might be what estate agency is about at its core, but selling houses involves
a complex relationship with the vendor, who retains and pays the agent, and
the purchaser, with whom the agent has to mediate and who will often ask
for the agent's advice. As we have seen, agents will also often gain a
significant part of their income via the purchaser. In a market which had
become very considerably bigger and now involves many who are relatively
ignorant of property transactions and financial services, and in which
financial services have become much more sophisticated and diverse, the
argument is that something must counterbalance the zeal of the negotiator,
who is often young, and the incentives of commissions and sales targets, and
that codes of conduct are not much help unless embedded in a fundamental
understanding of the property and financial services markets and their
operation. Responsibilities cannot be exercised unless they are understood.

---

[27] *Estate Agency: a Consultation Document* (OFT, 1989).
[28] Speech on estate agency, text supplied by DTI.

Should sales negotiators be released upon the unsuspecting public, albeit with oversight by qualified staff, without some training and a test of whether they have benefited from this training and are capable of recognising problems of ethics and best practice matters when they are in the midst of pursuing a deal?

This point was indirectly recognised by the government through its initiative to enhance the skill and training levels of the workforce generally. The Department of Employments' Training Agency has a national programme designed to improve and specify the training standards in many occupations and to improve vocational qualifications. As part of this the Estate Agency Training Group was established to attempt to develop a training programme for estate agents.[29]

The outcome of the OFT review was the identification of a number of undesirable practices and the implementation of regulations outlawing them, which came into force at the beginning of 1991. These cover the requirement to forward all offers of purchase, the declaration of any financial interest in the property by the estate agent; the clear and written specification of fees to be charged and their terms (sole or single agency status etc.); explicit agreement on the right of an agent to offer financial services to purchasers; and the application of the Trade Descriptions Act 1968 to estate agents' descriptions of properties. These deal with the main abuses identified in the review; other matters such as auditing of client accounts were implemented under the 1979 Act in 1982.

The corporates have responded to the failure to agree an industry-wide code of conduct with an ombudsman scheme which offers compensation of up to £100,000 per complainant. The Ombudsman for Corporate Estate Agents was established in July 1990 and the scheme is discussed more fully in chapter 11. It reflects the desire and capacity of the corporates to take advantage of their size and established reputation and to build a reputation in estate agency for service, reliability and fair dealing, using their internal controls to achieve this. The strategy is hence to outflank any industry-wide scheme and in particular to establish a kind of corporate hegemony over estate agency which is all part of making one-stop property shopping the natural way of doing things.

The regulatory problems of estate agency are thus noticeably more complex in the 1990s than in earlier periods. On the one hand, the sustained effort at Parliamentary registration and professional self-regulation with statutory backing has been shown to be unachievable in the light of increasing suspicion of professions as conspiracies against the laity, and of the increasingly marked distinction between the selling and the professional services side of estate agency. The policy solution that has come to be accepted, albeit reluctantly in some quarters, is the piecemeal targeting of abuses, with the OFT acting as the regulatory agency, a policy which quite fails to address the matter of maintaining the quality of professional services.

---

[29]The result of this initiative, the national vocational qualification in estate agency, is discussed in chapter 11.

This, as we shall see in later chapters, is no trivial issue, and poses particular problems for the corporates, whose arrival constitutes a further regulatory problem: are they to be left to regulate themselves? Will orders by the OFT under the 1979 Act be effective in their case? Does the sale of their financial services products in their estate agencies pose further problems of conflict of interest? All these matters will be explored in the coming chapters before returning to a review of the regulatory machinery in the final chapter.

FOUR

Organisation and Structure of Independent Estate Agents

Local and regional variations in the housing market, the size and traditions of individual agencies, and the sector in the market on which an agent concentrates all combine to produce variations in residential estate agency. Five independent agents are examined in varying degrees of detail.[1] One of these, an up-market agency, was sufficiently affected by its traditions and market niche to warrant a separate review at the end of this chapter. There it can be seen how far the self-conscious differentiation of the top people's estate agents resulted in differences in practice. Although there were significant differences between these agencies the focal concerns remain the same. The corporates were all concerned to develop and market a corporately branded image and practice of estate agency, and it is this and the attendant difficulty of integrating the staff and practices of the former independents which were bought out by the financial institutions which will be the focus of chapter 7. Of the other four independents, three were medium-sized multi-branch operations in the North, the Midlands and the South, and the remaining one was a sole practitioner which was observed only briefly, albeit towards the end of the fieldwork when our capacity to identify relevant issues and information was well developed. A brief account of these four is, we believe, worthwhile before launching into the generalising material of the focal concerns, if only to serve to point up the extent to which certain differences were accompanied by powerful similarities. It should be noted therefore that the accounts which follow are intended to highlight the differences, since the material which follows them will accentuate the similarities.

---

[1]Here, as in all our fieldwork accounts, the actual estate agents involved in the research have been disguised using conventional social science techniques. The names we have given to the estate agencies are intended to help secure their anonymity.

LANGFORDS

This agency has been established over 25 years in a North of England industrial area dependent upon declining industries. It has three offices, the most recent of them acquired from another agency 18 months prior to the research. Of the three, Northtown's housing is dominated by old terraced property, with pockets of recently built semi and detached property on the fringes of the town. Westville is a village that has recently expanded into a commuter town. All the major house builders have developments in the area and part-exchange facilities on many estates have had a considerable impact on the housing market. Overall, however, property is varied, with a wide range of styles and prices. Southtown is a suburb of Northtown, with large tracts of mostly postwar middle-class housing. The profile of property on the books at the time of the fieldwork is detailed in table 4.1.

Table 4.1:   Langfords property profile

Office	Northtown	Westville	Southtown
Number of properties on the books (as at 30 January 1991)	40	108	31
Highest priced property (£)	90,000	116,000	198,000
Lowest priced (£)	24,995	26,500	34,995
Price range (£)	65,005	89,500	163,005
Total value of property (£)	1,838,140	6,439,470	2,542,060
Mean price (£)	45,954	59,625	82,002

The business was owned by a husband and wife, but it was the wife who ran it on a day-to-day basis. There were 10 staff, with whom Dora, the owner, had a traditional small-business personal relationship. They were supported by a number of part-time staff. None of the staff was formally qualified, although several had quite extensive experience in the financial services industry before joining Langfords, particularly those who ran the financial services side of the business, which consisted of an agency for three building societies, two large and one small and local, and financial advice provided by a consultant. Staff were nonetheless expected to be flexible and one of the financial services staff would undertake viewings and accept instructions to sell properties and the other would deal with general enquiries and cover for absent staff. Status among staff was determined by specialised skills, effective valuation and the capacity to give financial advice, and by the boss's esteem built up over time as staff were trained by experience on the job and demonstrated their capacity for effectiveness and integrity.

The result of this regime was that Langfords was Dora, and staff had to acquiesce in her well-articulated views about the agency or leave. As a small business woman she was solicitous of her staff's welfare as well as their efforts and, whether by example or resolute management, had contrived to maintain an apparently stable and effective team. This did not in the end protect the business from recession and at the time of fieldwork one office was about to close.

All this provides a context for two themes that characterise the style of Langfords estate agency: its fierce commitment to independence and its decidedly ambivalent view of the public and other estate agents. In sum, one might characterise Langfords and its boss Dora in particular as an embattled independent. The importance of independence was manifested in a variety of ways. Although there was little direct competition in the immediate vicinity of its offices, Langfords was only too aware of the power of the recently arrived corporates. Dora's response was a mixture of awe and revulsion: awe at the vast sums evidently spent on buying up other local agents, refurbishing offices in corporate decor, heavy advertising, and staff training, and revulsion at the huge losses sustained, to public knowledge, by some of the corporates in both estate agency and in their traditional activities, and at the conflict of interest consequent upon being tied as an estate agency to, for example, a building society, or as a building society to an insurer. How could the public possibly get sound advice? It was to give sound advice that Langfords retained its financial capacity and its three building society agencies, besides the fact, of course, that in a slack market they were a useful source of additional income, especially since Langfords, having no qualified staff, conducted little in the way of ancillary professional services such as auctioneering, rating valuation and development advice. It was Dora's passionate view that the only sound and honest advice was independent advice, but that much of the public was naïve and gullible and only too susceptible to the money, blandishments and lack of effective regulation of the financial institutions and their estate agency arms. Being independent both as an estate agent and for financial services was therefore not only right and professional but conferred some market advantage, albeit that many customers might be lost to the marketing muscle of the corporates.

Recession apart, there was a definite sense of structurally produced impending doom on Dora's part. As she noted, the market in some properties was increasingly handled directly by the developers or builders, who were also taking on part-exchanges. The big independent agents would naturally have a fair slice of the market. And the corporates were currently pioneering the corporate relocation market in signing contracts with major national employers to manage the rehousing of their staff when they moved, a service they could offer because they had national branch networks. What then was left for the smaller independent agent? As if this were not enough, another small new agent was muscling into the local market with no background in estate agency, but offering a flat selling fee and no contract with clients other than a handshake. Although such innovators are endemic to the fringes of estate agency, their reputation for price cutting and unscrupulousness was particularly unwelcome at a time when Langfords was hard put to maintain commissions at the $1\frac{1}{2}$ or 2 per cent that was regarded as essential to being able to provide a proper service. A withdrawal fee of £100 had recently had to be introduced to deter vendor clients from hawking around the estate agencies in search of a sale after Langfords had incurred much time and other expenditure.

The sense of being embattled in relation to the corporates was most pronounced in Dora, but the other side of the coin, the naïve, gullible and increasingly unscrupulous public producing pressures upon agents and failing to appreciate the benefits of scrupulous advice and independent service, was testified to by a number of members of staff. To some degree this no doubt reflects the market in which Langfords operated, which, although not uniform, included a preponderance of C1 and C2 clients, many with limited experience of property or financial and business matters. As Dora put it in response to a question as to whether she had to lead people by the nose through the maze of buying and selling:

> Oh yes, absolutely. I have to tell them everything.... It's a pressure. It's nice at the end of it when you see them in the house and you send them a little card or they come with flowers or a bottle of wine.

The negative side of relations with such clients became increasingly evident in the course of negotiating the sale. Staff were clear from the start that applicants were not to be trusted even to tell the truth about whether their own house was sold and claims were always checked with the applicant's agent — though of course there is room for a discussion about what 'sold' means until completion under English law.

Advice about the strength of purchasers' offers was not always accepted by clients — much to the annoyance of the negotiators concerned. In one case a client had spurned a negotiator's advice, choosing to accept an offer from a young couple who had agreed the full asking price, but were not in a position to proceed for some months. Her reason was an emotional attachment to the house and the feeling that the couple would look after it. The negotiator's advice had been to accept a lower offer from a purchaser able to proceed immediately. After some time the client had realised her mistake and decided to switch to the latter offer, and let the negotiator act on her behalf. Following an exchange of phone calls to both parties, a stalemate had ensued, caused by a difference of £100 between the offer and what the client would accept. Clearly exasperated by the obstinacy of her client ('a stupid so-and-so'), the negotiator made a further call to try to resolve the difference. The outcome was an improved offer, provided carpets were included. The client accepted, producing an outburst of triumph from the negotiator, 'Hallelujah!'.

The readiness of clients (and purchasers) to ignore the agent's advice clearly irritated Langfords staff. In the case above, the client had at least allowed the agent to conduct the negotiations on her behalf. In many cases, however, clients negotiated directly with prospective purchasers, thereby depriving the agent of any sense of control over the deal struck. The staff seemed to rationalise this behaviour in terms of a combination of greed, ignorance and unscrupulousness on the part of the public in general, and clients in particular. Whatever the precise cause assigned to each case, the staff were convinced that clients who acted in this way acted against their own best interests. They were convinced of their ability to produce a better deal. As another negotiator, put it:

> People don't realise that we are there to help the client — so many clients do themselves out of money by conducting negotiations themselves.... Many applicants do themselves by telling the negotiator what they can really afford. They might offer £30,000 but say to the agent they 'might go up to £31,000'. The agent then tells the client not to accept the £30,000 because she can get £31,000.

The tendency of both clients and purchasers to think that they know better than the agent and/or to reveal a basic ignorance of the agent's role in the process of house transfer was commented upon by several staff, their views summed up in a comment by the same negotiator: 'This is it. They put both feet in it. They don't listen.... They're thick'.

GUILDHAMS

Established for roughly the same length of time as Langfords, Guildhams is otherwise in substantial contrast. Its network of branches is concentrated in the southern counties of England and it has a presence in West London from which it professes national coverage, for what it claims to be an up-market estate agency for quality property. By this is meant detached country properties in the £100,000 to £500,000 range, for the upper end of which it produces the impressive colour-printed brochures characteristic of leading agencies. Its practice includes estate agents and surveyors, and its publicity brochure offers 'a personal service with the assurance that your business will be handled by a director supported by a specialist team'. Advice to staff emphasises that 'we have never traded on the basis that we are the cheapest', encouraging them to sell the quality of service on offer at 2 per cent or $2\frac{1}{2}$ per cent. In the preparation of property details the worst of estate agents' purple prose is to be avoided, including such terms as: 'character village house', 'unique', 'idyllic', 'blest with an abundance', 'will be found', 'toilet', 'lounge', 'oozes charm', and 'executive'.

Our research was concentrated on an office in a substantial city in the southern counties which had recently been acquired in the takeover of another agency. Staff had been reduced from 20 to five with a Guildhams manager with the style of director introduced, and with supervision from another nearby city in which Guildhams was long established. The director worked with one of the former partners who had been retained as a consultant and seemed to form an effective team conducting valuation visits together. Able, the director, was a naturally outgoing and talkative man from a solid middle-class background — father an architect, public-school education, 10 years' experience, but without qualifications. Roper had started in practice 30 years ago, was a member of ISVA and had been a partner in the acquired agency for 16 years. His style was quieter than Able's and his approach to clients and applicants more that of a confidant than a professional adviser.

These two men dominated the office, which was otherwise staffed by young women of varying levels of experience, who undertook secretarial and administrative duties. Despite its pretensions to quality country property, the office was in practice concerned largely with standard middle-market sales, with half its properties in the city in question, half of them flats priced from £70,000 to £80,000. Although some expensive country properties were on its books, the great majority were in the middle or upper-middle sector, where it was in strong competition with a number of other agencies.

These realities were reflected in the perceived nature of the local market:

> It's different to London, far more commercial, far more wheeler-dealer, far more cut-throat down here.... There's an awful lot of muck and brass down here ... new money.... To get a deal to work you have got to make the buyer think he has got a deal; you have got to make the vendor think he has got a deal (Able, Guildhams.)

Estate agency hence consisted, at least in this office — Able contrasted his experience in the more genteel parts of London as more gentlemanly — in actively negotiating deals. It is significant that the interviewer was prompted by the remark just quoted to say:

> Q: Therefore you have got to appear all things to all men haven't you?
> A: Yes, ultimately, and I am not saying it for the fun of it, you are acting for your client. There is a very difficult line as to where you abuse it.... If I wanted to abuse it I could run riot. If I wanted ... I certainly reckon you could ... with people offering backhanders ... add another £6,000 to your income.
> Q: What sort of backhanders would they be?
> A: The purchaser saying, 'Make sure I get the house, will you'.
> Q: At a certain price?'
> A: £1,000 cash.
> Q: At a price favourable to them or a property favourable to them?
> A: Just make sure you get it. 'Don't mind paying the right price, but I want to buy it.' Or, 'Make sure I get it at the right price'.

This was one of the clearest descriptions of abuse that we came across, and that it should persist even in a slump is an indication of the acceptance of deal making in the local market. Although Able refused to have anything to do with such a practice, the need to broker deals effectively was nonetheless taken to the limit of what he regarded as ethical behaviour. A little earlier in the same interview he reflected on whether it was acceptable to disclose to an applicant that a vendor was under financial pressure and needed the sale. A critical issue in his view was:

the way you word it, the way you handle it. You see, here is a case where, hypothetically, a chap needs to do something with his property. Or he's got the bank breathing down his neck. Now purchasers, they like a bit of a carrot, they like to feel they have got a deal. Now if you can lead someone by dangling a carrot to make them believe there is a deal there to be had, and because of it you sell your client's house for a fair price, where if you had not used that information he might not have been able to persuade them to go and look at it, in my book you are acting in your client's interests. (Able, Guildhams.)

This active deal making contrasts with the agent's ideal image of what a good deal and a bad deal consists in when the agent is clearly much less active. A bad deal arises, he said, when an offer comes in on a property and you do not know whether it is a good offer or a bad offer, for example:

A very difficult unusual house in a village, that was modern and had been designed for the present owner, and therefore its layout ... was about 3,500 square feet, which is double your average executive home, and only had three bedrooms. But that house was built to the highest, highest standards and would cost anyone in today's terms £250,000 to £300,000 to build. That house was on the market at too much money. It started out at £450,000 to £500,000. It never should have done. During the history of about six months' marketing including, I admit, an advert in *Country Life*, we only ever had one viewer and that viewer ... ended up paying £325,000. ... At the time we had no idea whether that was good, right or what. With hindsight, looking at the fact that the market has fallen, it was a bloody good offer.

A good deal ... is when a pretty house goes on to the market with an attractive guide price. We have two or three weeks of pre-arranged advertising that comes out both nationally and locally, good brochure, good presentation, everything works, you have about 30 or 40 people viewing the house in the first three or four weeks and you end up with two or three people who want to buy. Probably have, for want of a better word, a little telephone auction ... and at £300,000 you may have three people who want to buy. One of them is at £290,000 and one is £300,000 and one is £305,000. £305,000 is not a good offer unless they have signed the contract, the £300,000 may be able actually to do something about it. In that case it is a good offer, a good deal and you know that you have got the right price for your client. (Able, Guildhams.)

Most sales evidently require a lot more intervention by the agent, especially when the market is difficult. Able set out to be in a position to exercise influence over vendors and purchasers by a deliberate strategy designed to command respect.

First, he liked to present himself, especially to vendors, as the purveyor of the 'bitter truth' about the market and the fact that prices had fallen sharply in the area. This was reinforced by consciously projecting an image of worldly wiseness in a larger context:

I'm trying to create an image, I am putting over what I think I am, which is as someone who is worldly, has a reasonably good perception of how the entire economy, country and everything is working, so that it is being put into a global context, rather than just look at it as a pile of bricks and mortar and what's it worth.... They won't catch me out. I do actually understand that interest rates are a reflection of the exchange rates, and I do know what the stock market is doing, and I do know what is happening in Russia, and I do understand that what happens in America will have an effect on the UK economy. (Able, Guildhams.)

Such a patter would be lost on Langfords' clients, but at Guildhams it paid off, for example, in a case where a vendor was adamant that £150,000 was his minimum. Able's view was that in practice he probably needed the cash for his business, and expressed the view to the vendor that the property's value was in the 140s and might just reach 150, hence Guildhams might be prepared to put it on the market, but the existing price of £159,000 was too much.

We were able, with that man there, being in business, and I think is fairly determined, but I am not sure he would have taken £145,000 — said directly to him from someone who was younger, because I think he would have said, 'You don't know what you're talking about', where he certainly couldn't say that to Roper, probably couldn't say it to me, because he knows that we do actually have the experience. But he probably knows in his heart of hearts that we were right.

The same pressures and arts of presentation were exercised on purchasers:

We have to win our purchasers' trust ... we spend a lot of time with our purchasers.... These buyers are very important to us because when you go and show them one property and they don't like it, I want to lead them on to another. These purchasers are there to satisfy my client's desire to sell.

But the evidence suggests that this is not how the agents concerned present the situation to purchasers. On the contrary, choice of words and the thrust of the conversation — how 'we' can do something for you — was designed to present the image of agent and applicant working together to get something out of the vendor:

I think you can't stand aloof and say, 'Well, I'm just acting for the vendor, Mr Jones, I'm not really interested in you', because you can't do that. You have got to try and help Mr Jones, and by helping Mr Jones you are also helping the vendor. (Roper, Guildhams.)

Able put this issue more bluntly: 'Nobody made a profit out of being truthful'. We are touching here on a central issue in estate agency: the competing interests of the agent, who only sees any income if deals are completed, his client, the vendor, for whom he is supposed to secure a sale at the best price, and the purchaser who, of course, wants to pay as little as possible, and perhaps is not certain that the property is for him anyway. What is demonstrated by Guildhams is that the ambivalence or the slipperiness of the agent as intermediary is enhanced in a market sustained by buyers and sellers who are themselves slippery customers, deal conscious.

MALCOLM DEVON

This is a multi-disciplinary agency in the Midlands run by two qualified partners, both chartered surveyors. Professional valuations were undertaken for some years for a major building society until, as a corporate estate agent, it took valuation in-house. Malcolm Devon (MD) now values for a range of lenders but has recently acquired considerable business from another large building society which regards the Midlands as out of its home area. The partners confirmed, however, that the work for lenders is now contingent upon reciprocal referrals of mortgage business. This was not difficult in relation to the society which provided them with most business, since they hold an agency for it, but financial services generally were a problem area. They had in the past had brokers working with them, and at the time of the research had a new one occupying office space in one of the three branches, but dependent upon commission for his income. The broker was tied to Commercial Union for insurance but was independent for mortgages, which was just as well in the interests of mortgage valuation business. Although he was evidently able to produce some business, the partners found him generally unsatisfactory and difficult to keep track of. They were unwilling, and in any case did not have the time to become involved in financial services advice themselves, but were clearly under pressure to provide it — requests from purchasers, pressure from lenders as a quid pro quo for valuation work and its attractiveness as an additional source of income in bad times.

Though diversified into repossessions, part-exchanges, valuations, and property management, besides residential sales, the business was clearly under severe pressure as a result of the recession. As one partner put it: 'If we do three sales a week we make a loss, if we do four we are in profit'. The partners were the only qualified staff, backed up by female clerical and administrative staff at the principal branch, a manager at one of the other branches, and an hourly paid representative who showed applicants around vacant properties. The partners would clearly have liked to increase their staffing and accepted that they spent too little time with purchasers, leaving them if possible to sort out deals with vendors themselves.

Our research concentrated, as elsewhere, on the residential sales side of the business. MD also had contracts for the management of commercial and residential properties totalling some 5,000 rents, with a total value of over £1,000,000. Separate support staff were dedicated to administering this. On the residential sales side, work could be classified as conventional private tender, repossessions, sales valuations for dealers, and part-exchanges, the latter three all raising regular issues of acceptable professional conduct, with MD being concerned to keep to the straight and narrow whilst continuing to participate in what was significant business.

Since the latter three types of business tended to come to them and the property management side was already largely established and in-house, it was obtaining instructions in conventional residential sales that was the urgent preoccupation, and one which it was not easy to fulfil — 60 per cent of their list was sold. Handling prospective vendors was hence a priority and one to which their status and expertise was applied, particularly since, in a weak market subject to serious price falls in the preceding two years, only attractive properties would sell, and then only if priced realistically.

MD had adapted their fee system to try to maximise their attractiveness and retain vendors and purchasers once they came in. Fees were negotiable around the 1 per cent mark, ranging up to $1\frac{1}{2}$ per cent where it was possible, but dropping down below 1 per cent and even to $\frac{1}{2}$ per cent in certain cases where a quick sale seemed likely. At the same time advertising costs and the for sale board were charged separately as they were incurred, partly to deter the uncommitted vendor, and partly to make good their 'no sale no fee' promise without the risk of serious financial loss. For the same reason deposits were taken from purchasers. 'They are a nuisance, but they give an early indication of a purchaser doing a runner — they want their £200 back.'

In obtaining instructions the partners took advantage of their professional status, advising clients of how a property would be likely to be valued by a mortgage lender. For mortgage valuation purposes they subscribed to a local monthly property register, the outcome apparently of local initiative and consisting of a compilation of the advertised details and prices of all the properties in a wide area. This provided a more or less comprehensive list of comparables essential to supporting a mortgage valuation, and a useful weapon in convincing vendors to accept a realistic price. Nonetheless they were not unwilling to accept a modest increase in asking price if the property looked to be likely to sell and the vendor seemed serious about selling. Although presented with the same problems as Guildhams in getting across recent falls in property prices and their effect on the vendor's own property, MD displayed none of the bluntness and obvious attempt to demonstrate competence and ascendancy in matters of market judgment. Their approach was more low-key, though when asked for a value directly they would give one without flannel. Their approach to the valuation of a property they wanted is indicated in the following example.

Unlike several of the estate agents observed where it was company practice to establish by pre-valuation inquiry the price a vendor hoped to achieve on the property, MD would not let the vendor predetermine the valuation. One potential vendor was clearly anxious to talk about the property when Devon intervened: 'Don't tell me what you paid for it, I like to start with a fresh mind'. After walking around to get, in his words, a feel for the property, Devon pronounced:

Nice ... a very nice house actually ... it's above average ... it presents itself well and these are the ones that are selling ... it's all great except the market out there which is, you know, rubbish basically.... There are some going. Price is very important ... start too high and you never get anyone round, start too low.... This is directly comparable with the one a couple of doors down which they still haven't sold at 48 and a half.... My opinion on this is about 50. That would be a fair price to ask.

By this time Devon had been plied with coffee. The vendor broadly agreed with the level of valuation and, clearly flattered by the compliments about her home, discussed where she wanted to move to, the house she had seen, how much she wanted to spend, how they would finance the project, her husband's occupation and income and the timing of the move. Sensing the vendor's commitment to purchasing a particular house, empty and sensibly priced, Devon concentrated on the need to put her home on the market, remarking that until it was and a buyer found, it would be difficult to purchase any property. The vendor was uncertain. 'Well, what have you got to lose?' was Devon's encouraging response:

You haven't have you? Everything we get on is as high-profiled as I can get it.... We have sold a couple at 49 and a half ... anyone looking at this will look at the [Mackennas] one, which is why the price has got to be fairly comparable. I'd certainly have a go in the low 50s ... yes I'd have a go at 52, but if you are telling me you would look at 50, I would suggest, especially if you are looking at something else, you go for 50–49,950 — and start at the right price initially and just stick to your guns.... You have got to work out your figures.... So really you have got to have a chat with your husband now and make the decision.
Vendor: Do you think this will go fairly well?
Devon: Yes, because it's nice inside but I am not going to be definite in this market.

After the visit Devon confirmed that his acceptance of the coffee, despite not really wanting it, had been to enable him to chat and attempt to steer the instruction towards MD. Would it sell well? 'Yes I think it would', he replied. 'I didn't want to be too enthusiastic to her.... I thought if I had pushed her we would have got that straight away, but she might have sat back and regretted it. I think that might come. She won't go to anyone else that lady.'

Despite this caution on price, the partners had evidently made some mistakes and vendors were caught by the fall in the market. One semi had been on their books since the previous year, initially priced at £79,950 but recently reduced to £58,950. Whether this situation was exacerbated by lack of staff available to cultivate relations with purchasers is not entirely clear, but the fact that it was shortage of vendors that troubled the partners most suggests not. At all events, purchasers were left largely to their own devices, apart from being shown around by an hourly paid assistant where necessary, and offers and negotiations were handled over the telephone via the office, the partners often being out about their other business. Reliance was clearly placed on getting the right properties at the right prices and leaving the public to recognise in due course that these were worth having.

Repossessions constituted about 10 per cent of MD business, and were a welcome source of income. Attending at repossessions along with the bailiffs and locksmiths could be unpleasant for all concerned. At one that we observed, the elderly mother of the mortgagor, clearly confused and distressed, was evicted. The son was summoned and arrived breathing fire and saying that a month's mortgage had just been paid, a fact which the lender, in a telephone check, denied. The eviction proceeded, with the old woman delivered into the care of the mortgagor's estranged wife, who exchanged abuse with her husband. The partners explained that the attraction of repossessions was the sure knowledge of the fee from a subsequent sale and the likelihood of further work from the same source, but the pressure to get the valuation right was powerful: it had to be high enough to ensure that the lender did not feel that its interests were being risked (other agents would also be used by the same lenders on other repossessions for comparative purposes) and low enough to ensure a quick sale.

Where, as sometimes happened, the lender dumps several repossessed properties into an auction this was less of a problem, though with dealers being the principal buyers at auction, the partners admitted that the scope for abuses was considerable. Those abuses were evident in the work MD undertook for the dealers, mainly Asian. Once again the work had its attractions to the agent. Dealers normally paid cash and could be relied on to come up with it, so that deals did not fall through. Properties included a number that were down-market and might be hard to shift by normal methods. And again there was the prospect of repeat business, with MD regularly being called out to provide valuations. They were regularly offered 'a drink' by dealers who knew them less well, that is, a kickback for providing a valuation a few thousand pounds lower than their true one. Those dealers who knew them better would make no such offers, and used MD as a trustworthy source of true valuations. In MD's view the object of the kickbacks was not just to save cash, but to ensnare the agent so as to be able to put pressure on him in future.

The final source of business was through a major builder forced, in a recession, to accept purchasers' existing properties in part-exchange, the price of the part-exchange being established by an independent valuer, in this case MD. Valuations were done fairly cheaply (£80–£90), and performed the function for the builder not only of pricing the property, but of detecting any structural problems, which MD, as qualified agents, were trained to pick up. They would be instructed to do a full structural survey if they did. In addition, some of the part-exchanged homes would be given to MD for sale at a rate of 2 to $2\frac{1}{2}$ per cent, the objective being that the agent would push these properties to his clients and get them sold and the builder would reduce his overdraft. Most, however, were passed to a local rival agent, owned by a corporate, which was known for sharp practice, including, it was alleged, sales tied to the take-up of financial services. Its staff were also significantly dependent on commission income and hence the chances for part-exchange properties being given priority were greater there.

Although abuse is clearly possible in this market if the vendor is ignorant of current market value, he is unlikely to be induced to complete the deal if he is not offered a reasonable price for his property. MD's view was that the builder was normally happy to take a small loss on the transaction in order to turn over his new property.

FREESTONES

This was the smallest agency that we observed, run by the principal from a single office in the South of England with three supporting staff of varying skill levels. Like Langfords, it was strongly committed to independence, and like them also offered financial services advice, a task undertaken by the principal. The reasons for this were partly a belief in the importance of independent financial advice. Dire tales were related about the quality of advice given by the corporates, none of whom, it was held, could be impartial and one of whom locally was notorious. We had heard similar allegations of high-pressure selling of properties by staff dependent on sales commission from Malcolm Devon in the Midlands, in respect of the same corporate's agency there. Freestones said that they picked up a number of clients from this agency, notably purchasers asking for help and protection from the constant pestering to which they had been subjected to make an offer or to proceed with a deal about which they were unhappy or uncertain. A specific recent instance was also cited in which Freestones rescued purchasers from an unsuitable financial services package provided by the same corporate agency, and effected a considerable saving for them in the repayments.

Financial services advice hence provided an additional source of income and an additional means of putting across Freestones' preferred image as competent, independent agents of integrity. Income from financial services advice was, however, not the prime objective in providing that advice even from a material, as opposed to an ethical or image-building viewpoint. The ability to provide financial services advice was seen as essential to control: 'I know that if I am controlling the thing it has a greater chance of going through'. Thus not only does the agent know that the purchasers are financially capable of proceeding ('qualified' in estate agency jargon), he also knows exactly how the financing of the deal is proceeding, because he is arranging it. 'I will sit here to seven or eight o'clock at night completing forms'. This means both that the deal will go through faster and that problems are identified at an early stage and resolved.

One of the distinctive characteristics of Freestones was their explicit emphasis upon acting as mediators to broker deals — a stark contrast to Malcolm Devon. In part this was because of the negative image of estate agents held by the public, an image which owed much, they believed, to the 'white socks brigade' of the boom years who were 'no more than order takers'. The image of estate agents as incompetent and ruthless, charging large fees for doing little derived from this period, they maintained. It was sustained in the slump by the 'bullying and coercive' tactics of the corporate agency referred to above on the one hand, and by the likes of the 'dog-food saleslady' on the other. This was a reference to a woman who had set up in estate agency three or four months earlier after a career in a quite different industry, and whose capacity to offer anything like a professional service and competent judgments, notably on valuation, was inevitably limited. The solution to this was:

> We have to build a relationship with ... applicant and vendor, and by the time they have dealt with us and it has all gone through, then probably their perception [of estate agents] is completely different.

Getting across a proper appreciation of the agent's efforts and skills was held always to be difficult, however:

> We are professional problem solvers, and having seen a problem and resolved it, you don't phone the vendor and say, 'Just to let you know your purchaser almost withdrew today because he was having doubts about this or that, or the cost, but because I happen to be on your side, I have spent the last hour talking to them, reassuring them, and they have now decided that they will continue with the purchase'. Now that may have happened, but what you tend to do is to protect your vendor. You know they are already in a nervous and high-stressed state.

The agent's role as a mediator, a 'go-between', is hence of vital importance, and central to estate agency.

> Without an agent you can have two solicitors who might be in conflict, you can have a vendor and a purchaser who can very, very easily fall out with each other, because again you have got these highly stressed individuals, and both anticipating that either one is going to let the other side down.

As a result, perhaps 80 per cent of their time was spent with purchasers, because 'If we didn't do it, quite simply the [deals] wouldn't materialise', and in addition, today's purchaser is a vendor in a few years' time. This was recognised to be anomalous in terms of the fee structure, with the vendor paying and there being no fee unless the sale goes through, and a revision of this was seen to be appropriate, at least to the extent of the purchaser paying half the fee. The problems of the conflict between the agent's interest in completing the deal and his client's in getting the right price were only soluble on the basis of the skill, experience and integrity of the agent. Such skill and integrity could only be developed over time, and with the close contact that working in a small agency provides. The corporates were hence seen as having to achieve the same results on the basis of organised training programmes, which were effective in some measure, but were no adequate substitute for on-the-job supervision (though of course this will take place in a corporate as well as in an independent agency).

One might expect that a small independent agency such as Freestones, in strong competition with a corporate locally, and in a difficult market, would display the embattled characteristics which had been found in Langfords. Perhaps because of its location in the South, or perhaps because of the greater resourcefulness of the principal, this did not appear to be the case. The recession was biting hard at Freestones, but deals were still going through and the struggles that were being waged were as much ethical and ideological as economic. Unlike Dora at Langfords, Freestones did not see the public as largely taken in by the blandishments of the corporates; rather their weaknesses and malpractices produced clients who had become disaffected with the corporates, though it did, as we have seen, make gaining their confidence and trust difficult.

Freestones' resourcefulness was strikingly demonstrated in the additional service they offered to clients of chain-breaking, that is, of offering to buy a property from a vendor if it was not sold within a contracted period. We did not come across any other examples of this, though Freestones suggested that the Prudential had offered a similar service at one point, but only provided that the Pru was involved in the sale of at least three properties in the chain. An additional advantage of Freestones' service is that it was quick, with exchange of contracts taking place within a few days. During the boom years the service had been relatively low risk, since quick resales at a higher price were usually obtainable, and in one year Freestones made £60,000 profit from what was essentially property dealing. By the time we saw them, however, the market had slumped and Freestones had used their experience of 10 year's chain-breaking to refine their service so as to avoid loss. The risk, by this point of being left paying substantial interest on the costs of buying clients' properties was obviously significant. The solution was to reduce the percentage of the agreed market price which would be offered for the purposes of chain-breaking, so making a resale at a competitive price easier. In addition, the vendor still paid commission on the sale. Finally, in an astute legal move, only the vendor's rights to sell the property were bought by the agent, not the property itself, so avoiding stamp duty. On this basis chain-breaking was still feasible and, in a difficult market, the guarantee of a sale was an obvious attraction to clients.

Freestones were hence not in the least fearful of situations in which conflicts of interest arise — as arguably they do in chain-breaking in establishing market price, as well as at other points, to some of which we have referred above. Indeed, one of our own conversations began with a discussion of an ethical dilemma to which no clear solution could be offered. If a client comes to an agent having failed to get a property sold elsewhere and the agent says that a potential purchaser for that kind of property is available, how does he demonstrate impartiality, given that he knows the financial means of the potential purchaser. One of the independents, Malcolm Devon, took a lower percentage fee in just such a situation. The question of pricing was not seen by them to be a sensitive issue, partly because they were professional valuers, and partly because the property had nearly sold but the deal had fallen through and hence a price was indicated, if not established. Freestones were full of confidence that estate agents can reconcile conflicts of interest in their practice on the basis of experience and integrity — professionalism — and we saw no reason in our brief visit to doubt their commitment; we were not able to judge their practical effectiveness in doing so. They were scornful of attempts to regulate conflicts of interest:

> [The government] think that buyers are buyers and vendors are vendors, that things are black and white. But vendors are purchasers. And they also think that ... if you come to me and I sold your house and then you buy one through me, that I can't act properly for my vendor. How can I? But the answer is we do, because it works.

Confident though Freestones were about the capacity of professionalism to resolve conflicts of interests, they were of course only too aware that many agents and agencies lacked both the necessary knowledge and experience, and the ethical commitment to professionalism.

A ROLLS ROYCE SERVICE? A TOP PEOPLE'S ESTATE AGENCY

At the start of our research we decided that we would attempt to cover the full range of residential estate agency. Accordingly we arranged our periods of observation to cover the North, Midlands and South, urban, suburban and country areas, corporate and independent agencies, and as full a range in terms of price as possible. We did not know at this stage where the significant differences would be. Probably if we had had the time we could have discriminated some differences between lower and middle-market agencies and rural and urban areas, but our research method meant that the number of agencies we could observe was limited. Our conclusion has been that the principal distinction lies in the arrival of the corporates and the new challenges they pose to estate agency. That apart, estate agency seems broadly similar in its practices and problems in all areas and price ranges and we have sought to reflect that in this chapter, whilst also noting some variations. At the very top of the market, however, which is dominated by about half a dozen specialist agencies, we did find significant differences, though, as we shall describe, in some respects there were more similarities than top people's agents would like to admit. We looked at one élite agency both in its London and its country operations.

The firm dates back to the 19th century and has interests in surveying, land management, sporting agency and residential estate agency. It is run by 25 full and 80 associate partners in 25 branches and employs 500 staff in all. Its historical base as regards residential agency is the country house market, but more recently it has opened offices in the better parts of London. Business in the two markets is different in a number of respects. For one thing it is the only instance in which we found the nature of the agency contract had a significant effect on the practice of estate agency. In the country, sole, or at times joint sole agency, prevailed. This meant that, like other estate agents, there was considerable competition to obtain instructions. Although other top agencies were generally said to behave honourably, touting was complained of from an upper-middle-market agency which was said to be going through hard times (not Guildhams).

It was emphasised that being at the top end of the country market was not to be understood in terms of value, but in terms of the quality of properties. We observed two valuations in rural areas where instructions were declined because the property was not sufficiently attractive to merit being taken on. Clearly Lords and Butler (L & B) are able to be selective about their listing and operate a kind of virtuous circle. The market values tend to be high, perhaps only £100,000 for a country cottage, but running up to half a million pounds for standard properties and much more than that for large country houses. High values mean high fees and in addition L & B makes no bones about charging top rates, 2 per cent sole or 3 per cent joint. This in turn means that L & B's list can be kept relatively small, which in turn means that clients can be given a good deal of attention, though staff in the country branches reported not being able to spend enough time with purchasers. Running a small list means that its quality in terms of the desirability of the properties can be kept high, and hence that they usually sell quite quickly. Public knowledge of the quality of the lists means that purchasers will look to L & B, and vendors will compete to get accepted by them — we observed, as we mentioned, the disappointment of two vendors. Good-quality property also has social connotations — it means the kind of houses that the gentry like, not those which might be more valuable, like a suburban house in Esher, for example. Instructions are also obtained at times as a result of managing a larger estate, where the client or purchaser is a long-term client of the firm. Along with quality and selectiveness and top-quality service, the element of trust based on common class backgrounds is also emphasised.

In London the system is somewhat different. The norm is multiple agency, whereby L & B have relationships with about 50 other agencies of all types on the basis of a 50/50 commission split (at 3 per cent) if an agent manages to provide a purchaser for another agent's property. This means that purchasers become as important as vendors, and much time is spent ferrying them round from viewing to viewing. The object is to cultivate a relationship with the purchaser, with the offer of one-stop shopping because of the multiple listing system, and if possible to obtain instructions for the sale as well. As in the country, L & B insist on maintaining the quality of their list, disdain anything much less than the best, and so maintain a relatively small list. Once again we observed cases of properties being refused by L & B because they were not desirable, though desirability in London depends less on property type than on location:

Prestige is the best, and then prime, and then obviously good and poor. Prime means it is very very good but it is not quite as good on Eaton Square and the Garden Square facing south near the gardens, and the best address must be better than if you were in the street behind it in Eaton Place. You are only one street, but that is different and so that is *prime*.

The same considerations as to location applied to some extent in the country — some villages and parts of villages were more desirable than others — but it is less critical than in London. (Cf. Belloc: 'He now resides in Eaton Square and is accepted everywhere'.)

Running a small list has its consequences for the style of estate agency. As the manager of the London office put it:

The main difference between ourselves and the bottom end of the market, the run-of-the-mill High Street agents, is that they are turnover orientated. They pile them up high and sell them cheap, they have to be because (a) the nature of their costs in running their organisations and (b) their income. You have to sell 50 houses a week or 50 houses a month in order to make the thing work, and the agents involved are all commission orientated. So if you can sell a house this week, it means you have another £60 in your pay packet at the end of the month. We operate on a slightly different basis, where theoretically it doesn't matter if I don't sell a house all year. It may be reflected in a fairly short discussion with my boss but ... my salary packet at the end of the month doesn't rely on the fact of whether I sold one house, 50 houses or no houses'.

He went on to explain that the country house market is restricted to two brief annual sales periods, Spring and September, which further limits sales. In practice he said he probably made 25 sales a year with 25–30 enquiries on each property, a dozen viewing it and two or three offers. The London office we observed expected to have 25-30 clients on their books of whom only a dozen would be active at any given time. Having said that, we noted that sales figures were the first item on the agenda for the next partners' meeting.
In addition, agency staff were encouraged, like their more down-market colleagues to be active in marketing the agency and its properties. A marketing department notice to staff exhorted:

Each week meet five new applicants. Speak to half your 'hot' applicants. Learn something new about your clients ... write a press release. Each month: leave [details of ten] country properties in stategic places. Speak to a journalist. Give out at least 10 business cards. Have a drink with people in the office. Attend lunch with a likely introducer of business. Each year: visit five old clients. Find out who owns every house you would like to sell. Take up a new hobby or sport. Join another association. Deliver a talk at a local event.

Such a programme would not be out of place in the brashest of the corporates. In other respects too, estate agency at the top was the same as further down the system. Asked to define the agent's role, the head of residential agency suggested:

They are there to advise their client, who would normally be the vendor ... how best to sell his property. That's the key to the thing, and assume then they are instructed to act for that person, having given them advice and telling them what their charges are ... is then to go about putting it into practice.... That means introducing a buyer to that house who gets on and buys it.

The role is: 'In the first place advisory; and then selling'. He went on:

> Any deal is better than none and you need something in the deal for both
> sides.... We are there to get the best price but the best price is meaningless
> unless it actually exchanges contracts and completes.... And at the end of
> the day the best deals are the deals which go through quickest.... If you
> get the whole thing tied up and organised ... that is just as important as the
> last £1,000. And if you leave a bit in it so the purchaser feels he hasn't been
> screwed and the vendor is happy, that is how I see our role.

In other respects too the élite agent operates like his humble counterparts.
Valuations are done on comparability, albeit with location more important a
feature than further down-market:

> In a way I always rely on my gut feeling as the most important feeling ...
> and then I substantiate that gut feeling by looking at similar properties ...
> adding up or subtracting down to balance into the same thing.

Successful estate agency, as elsewhere, is seen as a people business, as
selling, and the necessary qualities as being largely innate, a view confirmed
by several sources at L & B. The excitements of the business are also the same
— forging a relationship with vendor and purchaser, doing the deal:

> It's that bit that turns me on, I think it's the bit that turns me all on, doing
> a deal, it buzzes me.

Although the firm's tradition maintained that staff should be qualified,
preferably with the RICS or ISVA, probably only half were, and, as
elsewhere, the emphasis was on their capacity to relate to the public and to
sell. 'A good estate agent is a good salesman.'

Purchasers come to be qualified by agents just as they are further down-
market, though with the provisos that top-market agents have more time,
because they have fewer clients, and that in London purchasers are as
desirable as vendors. Some of the same problems with the public are there as
elsewhere, albeit with a slightly different social flavour. In the London
office applicants and clients were routinely cursed for their rudeness,
and information about their behaviour, requirements and personal
circumstances passed around the agency network:

> Some of them are fairly unpleasant people who you get dumped with....
> 'Listen don't waste my time telling me what I want, just tell me what
> you've got'. You know that sort of attitude.... With women like that you've
> got to be quite tough, because they're real old bags and you need to say,
> 'Look, stop buggering me around'. That's what they need because they've
> been spoilt all their lives.

Further insight into the relationship between agent and client can be
derived from a more extended example:

Mrs S, a South American of some wealth and antiquity, was a tenant on an estate in Knightsbridge. She had taken a dislike to the landlords, notorious, it was alleged, for inefficiency and unreasonableness, and was looking for a suitable freehold property. During the course of the morning we visited three houses. At the first in Chelsea, it soon became apparent that Mrs S knew what she didn't like — 'no character' in this case. The second, again in Chelsea, fared better — light and spacious, but no rear garden, while the third in Knightsbridge, was totally rejected — 'too small, too dark'.

Coping with, even nurturing, such a client, was essential to Rupert. He admitted she was rich, with more money than she knew what to do with, and lazy — she would regularly take a taxi from home to Harrods, five blocks away: 'She buys on emotion . . . she needs leading by the hand'. . . . . Rupert described his relationship with Mrs S as 'like a friend' and maintaining this relationship had become a relaxed exercise in agreement and flattery. 'I can't buy this', Mrs S complained in one property, 'the stairs are too narrow and too steep — I'm a grandmother and I could not cope with these'. 'You're the best looking grandmother I know', was Rupert's comment.

Cultivating Mrs S in her role as applicant clearly held the key to securing her instructions as a vendor client. Rupert was unequivocal both on this and the importance of the fraternal approach:

Q: Is this time spent with her, showing her potential properties, not a free service which she might not in the end pay for because in the end she might buy from another agent?
Rupert: Oh, she might buy from another agent but she will still be our client as a vendor.
Q: How can you be so sure — why will she choose L & B from all the other agents?
Rupert: Because she likes me — I get on with her.
Q: How important is that in this business?
Rupert: Absolutely essential.

Interestingly Mrs S also offered her own perspective on the relationship with Rupert while he was picking up the keys to another property. He was, she assured me, the sort of agent you could trust, a personable agent, who knew a lot of people. He was also, she continued, 'a very, very good salesman . . . he could sell you anything . . . he can get people interested in anything'.

That description gives a flavour of the social differences of up-market agency. How significant were these? As a means of obtaining the business and sustaining the right kind of relationship with vendors and purchasers, participation in the upper-class social world was held to be essential. A striking example of its paying off is provided by a negotiator who attended a charity lunch at the Savoy where he sat next to a member of the Princess of Wales's personal staff. The outcome was a call from a countess who wanted to buy a flat for her son:

A few days later I arranged a tour and went out and met Lord D and as he came through the door he said: 'Hello, how do you do and this is my son the Hon. Rupert C'. I said: 'How funny, I had lunch the other day — I was sat next to someone called Mrs C'. He said: 'That's my wife, that's how we came to you'. They looked at three flats and bought one and that lunch cost a hundred quid, and we got just under a £7,000 fee out of that.

Work, particularly in the London office, involved constant contact with other agents because of the multiple listing system, which was worked into the upper-class social round of functions, dinner parties and receptions. Gossip circulated furiously and names were dropped like confetti. The manager described his business style:

> You like working with people and you latch on to part of them. I am a very musical person and I would meet another musician. Sometimes I spend more time talking about that than actually going to view properties. But that is a link, or you may just find: 'You're not the son of Raymond, I knew him in the City', it could be something like that, some little link. Or it could be a link through a mutual friend, like Rupert has many connections with the artistic world, interior decorators.

Shorn of their upper-class associations these tactics are not disimilar to those further down the system: the objective is to make an informal relationship with the potential vendor or purchaser. As another London manager put it:

> If you happen to have been with their daughter at Ascot last week they are far more likely (a) to listen and (b) to respect the advice that you are giving them, be they vendor or purchaser. If you are saying 'Actually Lady X' and having already established that you were at school with the daughter or son or whatever, they are far more likely to say, this is part of same team, he knows what he's talking about.

Common background is hence vital.

> If you looked at the people we have employed in estate agency across the offices, I suspect 99.9per cent would have been privately educated and of those there would be quite a few schools that would dominate.

The outcome of background and contacts was a kind of knowledge which was appropriate to the section of the public in question and essential to establishing rapport:

> Your man in the Prudential suit down in his show house in the estate, the new town outside Bath, probably isn't, because he has no need to be ... *au fait* with exactly the latest corporate takeovers or the latest directors who are buying and selling shares ... with the owner or breeder of a certain

racehorse.... He can probably list the last 11 managers of Nottingham
Forest, which for his market is very relevant. I couldn't. In his market it's
important that he knows how much a set of alloys for an XR3 costs, because
his market is orientated round what is a return trip to the Costa del Sol....
Likewise at our end of the market you have got to know how to get
membership at Annabel's.

Hence the challenge of the corporates was seen off:

Five years ago we were quite worried because everybody was trying to get
into estate agency and quite a few thought they had better come and have
a go at what they regarded as the old-fashioned fuddy-duddies like
ourselves.... They began making a move to get into the top end of the
country house market, and ... they were backed by a great deal more
money than we as traditional partnerships were. And I think for a while
they might have had an influence with rather more aggressive techniques.
Certainly ... they threw money at the game. On the whole they have all
beat a hasty retreat.

This style is in all respects an anathema to L & B, who think of themselves
as the least pushy of the top agents, definitely gentlemen acting as estate
agents rather than vice versa. This background was taken to be essential in
cultivating professionalism and competence, which derived less from formal
qualifications than from job experience over time:

The main way you acquire your skills is by using your eyes and learning
from your peers, come in as a trainee and you wouldn't expect to do any
valuation work ... for at least two or three years, but obviously more
selling, making appointments, showing them around.

This view by a negotiator is put by his boss more generally:

We can mould them [trainees] and train them.... I would call the moulding
the sort of thing that goes with just being out and about with us and seeing
how other people do it and the training is the sort of endless bumph and
folders that everyone has and all this sort of thing — manuals. It's a
combination.

The object of this in service terms is twofold: a Rolls Royce service and the
establishment of trust, both of which are seen as essential:

We will tirelessly roll out the red carpet for somebody who wants to go and
see a house, loan them a helicopter. They will go and stay the night, we'll
put them up if necessary. We'll chat them up to a pretty high degree. My
personal experience of the bottom end of the market, having been there as
a prospective purchaser, is you are made to feel that you are lucky to have
their time because ... if you spend half an hour on every potential client

you would run out of time. You have got to be looking after 100 to 200 buyers at any one time, chatting to them all once or twice a week.

All this, of course, has to be paid for and the vendor is required to do so up front, with a marketing and advertising budget presented to them at the start. The object is to impress the purchaser and cater to their desire for exclusivity, deference and top-grade service:

They expect to be picked up by limousine and taken down there, x and y are dealt with, lunch laid on and everything done for them. They are impressed when it happens, but they expect it to happen nevertheless.

Business is then conducted in a gentlemanly fashion, with, as one agent was quoted as saying earlier, no attempt to squeeze the last £1,000 out of a deal. This applies to purchasers as much as vendors:

The important thing is that you are not, whilst you are representing your client — the vendor, you are not going to pull a fast one over them [the purchaser].... You are trying to be helpful and give them projective advice ... that's in their interest, because at the end of the day ultimately it's in your interest as well.

Not all of the public can be relied on to respect the gentleman code of business conduct, however:

The worst cases [of abuse] are all by the public against vendors.... One has a genuine regard for a lot of people we act for and to see them being pushed around, forced into corners by people can be pretty upsetting.... There are some creeds or whatever who are very proud to behave badly compared to others ... I have to say, if the money is there and you have got an English buyer and an Arab buyer, the recommendation to our client would be prejudiced by the way we have seen them behave in the past. And it wouldn't only be Arabs either.... There are some firms of Jewish solicitors and their clients, who certainly know how to misbehave. Very unpleasant.

The practices being referred to are for the most part those of hard bargaining and taking advantage of the informality of the English property transfer system. The larger the property and the deal, the greater the room tends to be for haggling to continue. The gentleman's code governing L & B is designed to reassure clients from a restricted background and culture and to protect them from such brash commercial styles of dealing. Paradoxically, the more successful it is in sustaining a closed social world for upper-class estate agency, the ruder the instances of aggressive wheeling and dealing appear when they arise.

FIVE

Estate Agents at Work 1

INTRODUCTION

In this and the next chapter the quite diverse activities that go to make up the work of estate agents are explored, and in doing so the sequence of activities that are specifically concerned with property sales and the dilemmas that some of them raise are identified. We shall be concentrating here on what we found estate agents actually spend most of their time and energy on, their focal concerns, which in turn shape the way they see themselves as practitioners in the housing market.

One issue which perhaps which may surprise — even dismay — the public is advertising, a matter which agents widely found tedious and largely beside the point. As one negotiator put it bluntly. 'Advertising is for clients', i.e., vendors, rather than the prospective purchasers whom it is supposed to attract. All the agents investigated advertised, but, particularly in the weak market that prevailed during the research period, advertising was not seen as an effective means of recruiting potential purchasers. Rather this was achieved by applicants making direct enquiries of the agents indicating definite interest, with the result that the agent could then market properties to them. Advertising was, in other words, an insufficiently active and discriminating means of selling to achieve results, though agents were well aware that vendors regarded it as essential. An additional problem in a weak market is that, apart from the cost of advertising, which has either to be borne by the client directly or comes out of the commission (which varied regionally, locally and by agency), long exposure of the property in the press only serves in time to indicate that it is hard to sell. This fact could be used by the agent where he thought that his client was insisting on too high a price:

> I wanted it on at £150,000 ... It [will] go on £159,000 and I shall do quite a bit of advertising because I want to be able to turn round to him with my

hand on my heart and say to him, 'Look your house has now been out to 80 people who have said they are looking for a house like yours. It has been in the paper three or four times and we have had only five viewings and we have had no offers'.... You have got to go down if you want to sell.

This quotation leads directly into the core group of agents' focal concerns: obtaining instructions and valuation, identifying and qualifying purchasers, and negotiating a sale. These three activities are the heart of residential estate agency and also the source of its most acute dilemmas. They constantly raise the questions of the nature of the relationship between the agent and the purchaser or vendor in respect of differential levels of knowledge and sophistication. The agent is a market insider, whilst they are (usually) outsiders. The agent is resorted to only because of that market knowledge, skill and experience. Yet how can vendors and purchasers know whether their disadvantage is being remedied or exploited by the agent? For the agents the interest at the end of the day is the commission, that is, getting the deal done. An agent may be retained to obtain the best price for the client, but the differential impact of £5,000 or £10,000 on the client is much greater than on the agent, for whom the issue is his or her commission or further work for no pay.

Secondly, in order to broker the deal the agent has to get close to the purchaser, and, in agency language, qualify him or her, that is, establish whether the purchaser is seriously interested in any purchase, potentially interested in purchasing this property — it seems right for him or her — and is financially and otherwise (e.g., domestically) capable of going through with the purchase. The purchaser will be looking to the agent for information and advice, both about the property and the vendor. True, a purchaser can deal with the vendor direct, but the agent may well know things about the vendor — notably how open he or she is to an offer — that the vendor will not tell the purchaser. And once again the agent will probably know the local property market much better than the purchaser. It is this role as an intermediary that we believe gives rise to the slippery image of estate agency. It is a matter which, as we shall see, they are well aware of, but which they believe is a problematic outcome of their necessary work as negotiators and brokers. Its practical solution requires the agent to display and practise professional skills with adroitness and sometimes sophistication if both parties to the transaction are to conclude the deal satisfied. Only if they do will the agent's reputation be secured. This, as many agents emphasise, is the only sound way to long-term business success — repeat business from former clients and the referrals of others by verbal recommendation.

Besides these core activities there are a number of others that come across as matters that concern agents in their day-to-day work, albeit to a lesser extent. Purchasers normally have to have recourse to financial services institutions to complete a sale and there may be additional scope here for income generation by way of commissions when mortgage and insurance referrals by agents result in contracts being signed by purchasers. This is an area of much greater concern to corporate estate agents, the chains which are owned by financial institutions, which are the topic of chapter 7. The concern of this chapter and the next is primarily the independent agents, though where the work of the corporates concerns the same issues — as it certainly does in respect of the core activities referred to above — evidence from the corporates will be included here.

Mention of commissions from financial services referrals raises the issue of reward systems for estate agents, and given that a combination of salaries, bonuses and commissions is the norm and that estate agency is to a substantial extent sales driven, this is not surprisingly a regular, at least background concern. As we shall see in chapter 6, it is a matter which requires careful adjustment by partners and managers according to market conditions if it is to avoid becoming a source of undue sales pressure which can lead to unprofessional and even abusive conduct.

Connected with this is the issue of the individual and the group in the estate agency office. Although individuals are recognised and rewarded for their effectiveness, it was widely acknowledged that teamwork is vital to good estate agency, 'good' meaning effective in achieving sales and ensuring that both purchasers and vendors are satisfied. Recruiting and keeping a team together was a constant background and, in bad circumstances, foreground concern. In this connection the high rate of labour mobility and the recent dramatic changes in the market as a result of the arrival of the corporates and the move from boom to slump accentuated the difficulties.

Two other matters were a source of regular concern and are pursued further in chapter 6. If the public perceive agents as doubtful characters, rather than as the professionals many of them would like to claim to be, agents equally view the public with a mixture of amazement, frustration and antagonism for their persistent, though of course not universal tendency to be rude, fickle, unscrupulous and indeed dishonest. Coping with the public at all levels of intensity of contact, varying from the casual enquirer to the established vendor client, was a constant preoccupation of agents, not just in the senses referred to above in respect of the core activities, but in respect of behaviour that could only be characterised as unacceptable.

Finally, all agents are aware of abuses. We did not expect in the course of our fieldwork to sit in on meetings at which little old ladies were fleeced by undervaluing properties, naïve first-time buyers had properties and endowment mortgages stuffed down their throats and agents colluded with building society staff in mortgage frauds. A variety of abuses were, however, a regular preoccupation of agents, including touting by other agents, the formation of local cartels, and under and overvaluing for the agent's benefit.

OBTAINING INSTRUCTIONS AND VALUATION

The sketches in chapter 4 highlighted differences between the independent estate agents we looked at. We will now provide more comparative and systematic analysis of the principal activities and concerns of estate agents and their work. The core activities are obtaining the vendor's instructions for the sale of property, which also involves valuing it, the appraisal of prospective purchasers, and the negotiation of the sale between vendor and purchaser. All of these may be accomplished relatively simply and quickly at times, but all are in principle, and often in practice, complex, particularly the first and last.

Valuation is crucial in obtaining instructions as well as in the process of negotiating the sale. It consists not of a single figure but of a series of meanings affecting the parties involved, of which the non-agent ones may be more or less unaware. Unlike the price of a retail product like chocolate or soap powder, property does not have a price which can be fixed in advance by the seller; nor in many cases is there a sufficiently strong market for market forces to act properly and determine the price. Properties are unique, even though they have degrees of similarity with each other in respect of size, age, location, construction etc. Even where a number of buyers are interested in the same or similar properties, their circumstances will vary because of the pressures upon them to move, their financial capacities and preferences for properties of one type or another, and so on. There are thus in practice a variety of different values which a property may have. One is its insurance value, that is, the cost of reinstating it following fire, flood, subsidence or other serious damage; another is its value as a security, its mortgage valuation, that is, the price not merely that it would be likely to fetch today, but which could be prudently assigned to it for the reasonably foreseeable future. This may be significantly at variance with its value to actual purchasers, as a mortgage valuer illustrated:

> I have this morning seen a bungalow which has changed hands at £82,000. The people have done everything in it, it has been rewired, replumbed, new PVC double glazing, new PVC conservatory put on the side, and it is a plot of about twice the average size. It is in a little cul-de-sac with other bungalows, quite a lot of elderly people there, the purchasers are elderly. You can't fault it physically. It's only got two bedrooms. What's it worth? (big sigh) ... these bungalows are worth about £68,000 plus something for a corner plot, £72,000, £74,000 on a good day, bigger than an average garage, all right £75,000. It's selling at £82,000.

We shall return to the topic of mortgage valuation later. Here we are concerned with valuation for sale. A point raised by the example is that a property may well be worth more to one buyer, for whom it is ideal and within his means, than to another, for whom it is grudgingly acceptable and a financial stress. The vendor may not be lucky enough to come by the former and may have to make do with the latter.

Estate agents operate with the rough rule that price should reflect a reasonable time, say six to eight weeks, in which the property can be sold. If the price is too high it will remain unsold. This introduces another differentiation: between the asking price and the expected sale price. The two may be identical or may vary by a significant amount. What the difference is will reflect both different areas of the property market and changes in the market over time. The first point is clearly illustrated by Guildhams:

If you are selling a big country house, you will deliberately underprice it to tickle and excite the market. If you are trying to sell a flat along the South Coast in a wheeler-dealer town you will probably overprice it so that the buyer thinks he has got money off it. If you are selling a two or three-bedroom, modernish, five-year-old terrace house on the outskirts of this town, you will probably have the price right within £500. And you will either pay the asking price for it, or you will negotiate within £500. If the mortgage valuation does not come up to what you are paying for it you will renegotiate. Back down here in the middle of the town you will tell the buyer to get stuffed — they always undervalue.

As this agent's colleague expressed it, the art of the agent lies not in getting the valuation right but in the negotiation of the sale. Valuation has thus two distinct features: first, a judgment on what the market should produce as a sale price if it works properly, that is a quasi-objective professional judgment; and secondly, a crucial step in the preparation of the ground for the sale, not only by pitching the price at a level that will attract purchasers' interest but also at a level with additional more or less explicit understandings as to what price the vendor is prepared to accept.

The price is hence negotiated between vendor and agent, and if agreement is reached the instruction to sell is normally obtained — in the language of the agents, property is taken on. Because most agents, even though they may only acquire the right to undertake valuations after some years' experience, are not qualified valuers or accepted by mortgage lenders for this purpose, and because of the negotiated sales advice elements in the valuation, some agents, particularly the corporates, are now reluctant to call them valuations and terms such as 'listing', and 'sales advice' are being used to avoid the implication that the values offered are to be relied upon. What the agent is saying to his client is: I think it is reasonable to put it on the market at this price and you should expect to obtain that price within the period of your contract with me (normally 10–12 weeks).

Two questions immediately arise here: first, how is such a judgment of value arrived at, and second, what are the clients' views of value? The first of these is easily answered: comparability and gut feeling. It should be made clear to the lay reader that they may have been taken in by the mystique of estate agents undertaking apparently extensive surveys of a property and seeming to make elaborate professional evaluations. Market valuation is based almost entirely on comparability, with gut feeling compensating for those areas where comparison is impossible, and frequently being used as the leading basis for valuation. Nor is this confined to valuations for sale. We have observed mortgage valuations by qualified surveyors reached on the basis of a drive-past, even if subsequently confirmed by a tour of inspection for form's sake. The real question is not whether this is unacceptable, cursory and unprofessional, but whether it works. Agents are emphatic that it does, and they appear to be right. It does mean, however, that there is nothing esoteric about valuation and nothing the lay client cannot do as well unaided, and indeed a good many of them do so.

The example of the bungalow sold for £82,000 above indicates the strength of the agent's position in valuing. Every house owner familiar with every idiosyncrasy of their home and every addition and modification they have made, is sensitive to the differences between it and other basically similar properties. It is the similarities in location, facilities, size and construction, however, that determine the basic price, with improvements and alterations inflecting this to a certain degree up to a threshold and beyond that counting for little — central heating and a modern kitchen benefit, a conservatory and elaborate garden much less so. The agent's job in achieving a reliable judgment of value is hence primarily one of market intelligence — keep up with the sales of properties in the area. This may be achieved by a variety of means. A reasonably large multi-branch agency can generate information internally; the property advertisements in the press can be monitored; other agencies can be asked for information on properties; where a valuation appointment is in the offing, a brief blitz on the asking price of other properties with for sale boards in the area can be mounted. In the West Midlands a comprehensive regularly updated directory of all property sales is maintained and circulated among agents (the Green Book); this appears to be local practice only.

Beyond comparability lies judgment: how well properties of this type in this area are moving, whether this property is an attractive example of its type, how effective or obstructive the owners are likely to be in impressing potential purchasers with its merits. Experienced agents repeatedly testified to their tendency to a very rapid judgment on the basis of gut feeling:

> You walk in through the door of a house that you have never been in before and you think £75,000. You walk round it and all you try and do is persuade yourself that £75,000 is wrong. You get to the end and the vendor says: What do you think it's worth? and you say £75,000, because you are always right. A good estate agent is always right. Of course, he is using comparability but ... the experience is right in there and what it does, it transforms to your guts as you walk in there.

This does not necessarily mean the agent always does get it right. The same source quoted the example of a house his agency had valued at £180,000, which a competitor valued at £350,000, though he added with satisfaction that it was still unsold after several months. Another agent referred to a valuation he had done which was confirmed by two competitors reaching figures within £2,000 of his, but then two more offered valuations, one £30,000 less and the other £60,000 more. What are the reasons for such disparities? One is almost certainly lack of experience and insufficient monitoring of the local market. The other is the advantage to the agent in both over and undervaluing. If the agent can successfully undervalue he can probably obtain a rapid sale and his commission. He is unlikely to be able to get away with this, however, since most vendors ask for several valuations. Much more common is overvaluation. Here again the interests of the agents and those of the vendor compete, if not conflict.

Although the agent's interest lies in achieving a sale within a reasonable time, and he is particularly alive to the costs of marketing properties which do not sell and for which he is therefore not paid, the agent also wants to maintain a good stock of properties on his books in order both to advertise his presence in the locality with for sale boards and to have something to offer potential purchasers who make enquiries of him. Ideally properties should flow in as instructions, create interest, agree a sale and complete in a regular process:

> We in this office, on average do six or seven valuations a day I suppose, and of those six or seven you will certainly get half of them on. So you are looking at three or four new properties coming on every day. Now if you are keeping a constant flow like that, you have always got more property coming on the market. If you feel the prices are going up, then obviously you would advise your client that prices have started to move up. This is the price that you should be able to achieve on this property; now in our opinion that is the price we would be happy to take it on for. As long as you keep your momentum going, then that's okay. As long as you keep your stock level going. At any one time this office has probably got 200 properties for sale, roughly speaking. Now if it falls below 150 I would start worrying about that seriously. If it rose above 220 again I would worry about it because I don't think we could service any more really.

If stocks get too high, vendors will come under pressure from agents to reduce their prices; if they fall too low, agents will be looking to obtain more instructions and be more willing to take on properties at prices higher than their honest judgment of value indicates. In the weak market in which our research took place, with often few properties on the market and few purchasers, the tendency of agents to overprice to obtain instructions, particularly with optimistic anticipations of a recovery in the housing market, was endemic. The problem was exacerbated by the fact that prices had fallen sharply in most areas and vendors were reluctant to accept this, and by competition and overcapacity of agents, where, with too many agents chasing too few properties, the only way to obtain instructions was to go along with the vendor's valuation and allow time to whittle them down.

It should be interjected here that vendors were not unaware of, nor unwilling to negotiate about terms and conditions — agency fee, withdrawal penalties and the like, but these were clearly not the central issue. Negotiation on such matters was likely to make at most a difference of £1,000 or so, where it was only too evident that prices could vary by a considerable multiple of that. Agreement to instruct an agent hence revolved constantly around price, both from the agent's and the vendor's viewpoint. Some of the leading factors affecting the agent, besides wanting to have more properties for sale, are that the property is of the type and location that the agency specialises in, that there are applicants with an expressed interest in that type of property and that the property is an attractive example of its type, all of which will inflate the acceptable starting price. A desire for a quick sale will of course deflate the price. The nature of the property itself, its state of repair, 'presentation', the neighbourhood, access to amenities and disamenities such as noise and pollution, will affect the property's attractiveness. The state of the market for that type of property will also be a concern — different sectors may have quite varying levels of activity at a particular time. Finally the circumstances of the vendor are vital. Does he or she have to move for a job or for domestic reasons or is this purely discretionary? Is the vendor already keen to buy a specific property? If so, how tight are finances? On the other hand is the vendor not really contemplating a move at all, but just seeking a free valuation? How reasonable and congenial a client is he likely to prove in the course of future negotiations? All this information, and more, has to be extracted by the agent in determining how interested he is in the property, and how close he is willing to go to the asking price which the vendor hopes for.

On the whole, in an adverse market, the task of agents during our research was to get vendors to be realistic about price and to accept that the agent was not undervaluing and would offer an effective service in marketing the property and locating potential purchasers. It was not uncommon to find vendors transferring to another agency because marketing had been ineffective and plainly poor. How did this cocktail of interests and aspirations work out in practice? By no means straightforwardly: what stands out in the fieldwork is the complexity and variety of vendors' circumstances, sophistication, aspirations and the range of styles and competence of agents. At the same time, however, the central concern of vendors is quite clearly the twin issues of sale and purchase and, in that connection, the price. Vendors, if they already have a property in mind to buy, normally need to achieve a certain price on their own sale to do so; even if they do not, they are anxious to obtain the best price for their own property, and if there is a fall in the market are often reluctant to be 'realistic'. These and other conditions such as whether advertising is included and sole or multiple agency and withdrawal fees may at times be a point of negotiation, even to the extent of instructing one agent rather than another, but price is the critical negotiating point.

Thus, even in cases where costs and commission are apparently central, it is often in practice the issue of a successful sale and purchase which is the real issue, as in this example:

I went to see a large house on X Road and I know that there was a client who had missed out on a purchase of a similar property. I said to her, I will agree 0.5 per cent with you if I get this person in. No advertising costs, this, that and the other, and the sale would run. If it didn't I would go for the full 1 per cent of the price, which was over £100,000, plus costs. In the event the sale went through to our client. It suited me because I could see him losing his own sale because he had got a purchaser pushing him. It was what he wanted. It also gave me a fee very easily and very quickly. So I said £500 to £600, I would do it rather than for £1200.

Here the agent is glad to offer a cut-rate package because of the prospects of rapid turnover, and the benefit to the instructing vendor is not just a reduced cost but the prospect of a speedy and satisfactory sale and purchase. This is an atypical transaction, however. Here is a more typical one where all the main elements are present, and where the agent ends up being instructed against her wishes:

The house, a two-bedroom semi, was in fairly poor condition, savaged by 'a playful dog' (fortunately confined to the car during the duration of the visit) and backed on to an extremely busy motorway. Both husband and wife were present. After the viewing, Anthea, the agent, suggested upper 50s perhaps £60,000. The owners became quite agitated at this and again displayed their encyclopedic knowledge of local property prices, which were all far higher than this valuation. At this point Anthea went through what became a fairly standard repertoire — you have to compare like with like, differences in location and accommodation are important, and the usual statement that they could 'try anything they like — within reason'. Gradually the atmosphere became less hostile, although by this time it was clear that Anthea was itching to get away. After some pleasantries about the danger of holiday flights, property in the Northtown area, family in the Northtown area ... the husband said, 'Well all right then, will it be on the market this Saturday?' This instruction was not accompanied by any enquiry about either the fee or contract — their sole concern was the price and the speed at which the house would go on to the market. The take-on duly took place on Saturday — the owners indicated that they wanted £62,000. It was fairly clear that the decision had been motivated by a desire to secure a property the clients had already seen at £62,000 in Northtown. Back in the office where the house received an inside categorisation as 'grotty', I asked Anthea whether she thought they might withdraw the property if they lost the house in Northtown: Anthea said she didn't know. Her colleage inquired as to whether they had been told about the £100 withdrawal fee. The answer was no.

Anthea was, in the event, insufficiently firm in her true valuation and prepared to accept an undesirable property at an unrealistic price, no doubt in the hope that the vendors would be more realistic when it failed to attract purchasers at that price. It is questionable, however, whether she was doing them a service, if their aspirations to the property they wanted to buy were contingent upon the sale of their own home taking place at the price they nominated. It was likely the entire enterprise would fall through. Not all agents were as weak as Anthea, however. Here is an example where the agent is determined to educate the vendor:

The location was a top-floor flat, a conversion of an Edwardian terrace overlooking the sea. Recourse to her records prior to the inspection told Janet, the agent, that she had valued the property a year earlier at £50,000. With prices having fallen further since then, Janet told me the valuation would be difficult, since client expectations were bound to be unrealistic. Predetermined in this course Janet hit the owner, a single male, with shock tactics to prepare for a low valuation. During the tour of inspection, the lack of gas supply, parking, and a properly formed management company were introduced as disincentives to potential purchasers. Seated in the living-room these were translated into value by open reference to comparable properties, each superior, yet currently asking lower prices than the valuer had previously placed on the flat only a year ago. This meant, Janet assured him, that 'The value here is £40,000, perhaps asking £42,500; you might ask £45,000 but your chance of getting anything over £40,000 is a bit slim'.

Visibly reeling from this onslaught, the owner recovered sufficiently to counter that a similar flat over the road was on the market at over £50,000. Undaunted, Janet returned to the attack with further criticism of the flat: its split level and the lack of a separate dining-room. After asking the owner if he had any questions, a rather perfunctory exercise, and promising to write confirming her valuation, together with a realistic and optimistic asking price, Janet took her leave. Later Janet admitted that she was not interested in taking on a property of that type unless it was realistically priced, and her approach had been explicitly designed to impart the new realism of the property world to yet another greedy (and immature) owner. This was the dominant style in its most extreme form: honest to the point of being brutal, with no apparent tact or empathy. Concern for the instruction was clearly a secondary consideration to educating another owner. 'It's not the property that is difficult,' Janet later confided, 'it's the people; the property is easy to deal with, it's not awkward, it doesn't answer back. People are and do'.

Janet did not want the property on almost any terms — it was not an especially attractive sales prospect, even if the price was realistic. In other cases the agent may see mileage in a property, provided that the vendor accepts the valuation, and they make some effort to achieve this. Here is an example where there was no agreement in the end despite attempts at negotiation, and where the agent's underlying reasons for refusing to budge are of interest:

Able and Roper went on a valuation of a detached stone-built house in a favoured area of villages. As he drove past the property Able remarked, 'There it is, that's quite a nice house. That's worth £120,000'. By the end of the tour and after a consultation with Roper, he had seen nothing to substantially change his opinion.

Able to Roper: I've gone up a bit.
Roper: £125,000?
Able: £125,000, yes. We ask £130,000. It would cost you £85,000 to build this today ... the plot value is about £45,000.

To the owners Able prefaced his valuation with reference to the market:

The bitter facts are that this market is very tough … the important thing to remember is that whatever you get for this at the end of the day would be its market value.… We both came up with the same figure.… There are a number of figures today, there are the figures for the bank, there is the figure we feel you should obtain for the house and there is the asking price.… We would think that today you should be able to get, for a house like this, somewhere in the region of £125,000.

After some prompting from Able, the owners admitted they were hoping for somewhere near £150,000. 'I just don't think that's obtainable at the moment', retorted Able, but then offered the small carrot of a guide price in the region of £135,000, not enough in the event to secure the instruction.

Why had Able refused to shift sufficiently to give Guildhams at least a slim chance of obtaining the instruction, particularly given the fact that Roper would have been inclined to have a go, and in the end the house probably would have sold? Travelling to the next appointment Able talked about it being bad advice to overvalue. Eventually however he came to the real reason: the vendor's circumstances. 'I'll tell you what would have made me take it on', he continued. 'If I was meeting them, and it was a family house with someone who had died, or if they had bought another house, or if they were in financial trouble and they just had to move — for one reason or another they had to sell the house … they weren't in that position'.

Here by contrast is a case in which there was more in the sale for the agent than was evident in the valuation negotiations, and hence the vendor was allowed to influence the asking price well beyond what the agent believed was a realistic price:

Prior to leaving, Dan had checked the files and found that the house, a three-bedroom estate box, had been valued two years previously at about £89,000. Unsold, it had been withdrawn from the market, but was currently being offered for sale again by GA Property Services. According to Dan, price was going to be the problem with this property; the main comparable was an equivalent house on the estate recently offered for sale at £79,995 but sold at £76,000. At the property, Dan asked the owner how quickly she wanted to move and how much her current agents were asking. The answer was that there was some element of urgency as she had found a house somewhere nearby and did not want to lose it. GA had put the house on the market at £81,500 but 'I'm taking it off them — they valued it three or four weeks ago and we haven't even had a set of details off them yet'.

Armed with this information, Dan set off without the owner to tour the property. During the tour he confirmed his original comparable at £76,000, but that had a garage and a downstairs cloakroom in its favour. Another similar property was on the market at £82,000, much too high. The answer, he assured me, was to get his client to think in terms of asking £79,500, and to take £78,000. The trick would be to convince the client of this. He failed. In the living-room Dan talked about the comparables and suggested asking £79,995 in order to move quickly. The client was singularly unimpressed, but not very articulate; she wanted £80,000. Dan responded immediately with a suggestion to 'try it at £81,500 and see how it goes'. The client nodded her acceptance and Dan pulled out an instruction form that she read and signed. Why had Dan apparently disregarded his own framework by taking on the instruction? The answer was in two parts. First, the client's behaviour was far from conciliatory — price was the overarching consideration, for when Dan had tried to use the need for an urgent sale, hence 'a sensible' asking price in the 70s, the client blocked what he was trying to do, 'She blocked me by saying, we can't afford to move if we don't get £80,000'. Dan knew that he would not be able to overcome this particular client's objection to price and secure the instruction. Rather than lose it, therefore, he had decided to take it on at the price indicated by the client. 'But if we do get problems', he admitted, 'we can negotiate the price later'. This merely postponed the need to overcome the client's objections, but it enabled Dan to do so at a time when the client would be much more amenable to pressure. That would be when negotiating the purchase of the next house. The latter was the second part of the equation for Dan; a colleague was involved in the sale of that property and Dan knew that he would be able to make use of the information secured as part of the vendor-client relationship in that case to ease the passage of the sale in his own case.

Should the agent have disclosed his interest in the linked sale when obtaining instructions? The information would be likely to come out later, though its significance might not even then be evident to the vendor. In this, as in previous examples, the agent felt that a long-term strategy was essential to getting the client to be realistic on price, and that this was essential if the business was to be obtained by his agency. It is not always so. The next example demonstrates that by judging the vendor correctly, business can be obtained on an up-front basis, even when citing, in Able's terms, 'the bitter facts' of the market:

A guy rang up and he was very obnoxious on the phone and it was very quick. He said, 'I want someone to see me immediately'. I thought, oh God we've got a right one here. That sort of guy you deal with. Bang. I said 'Right, I'll be there in 45 minutes, I'll see you at 5 o'clock'. Bang. 'Can I just ask you . . .?' 'No, I'll talk to you then. Bang'. Gone. So you turn up and say, 'Right, what's the situation?' 'Oh, I just want a valuation'. I go round the house and say, 'Why do you want a valuation, because if you want it to be high I can do it, how quickly do you need to sell? What's your situation?' You start to go through it and say if you want the honest truth. Obviously with that sort of person, who is abrasive like that, wants to know the bare facts. Says right my honest feeling for this is that, I can bullshit you and tell you it's £95,000, my honest feeling is that because of the situation, because of this, because of that, it's only £75,000. Oh right, we have got someone here who's being honest, because he has had somebody else in who has said, oh well it's beautiful, it's magnificent, it's £95,000. Here's somebody telling me what he really feels, and then he came and I think he had three other people round, a couple at £95,000, one at £95,000, one at £85,000, we were at £75,000 and we got it. Because he felt I was telling the truth.

Q: That's a lot of difference isn't it, that's £20,000?

A: Yes, but I gave him the comparisons. That one over there hasn't sold, we have got one over there ourselves, we haven't got anybody around, that realistically should be on the market for £75,000, that ...

The reader will have noticed that the examples of estate agents in action here, and in the earlier sketches of the independent agencies have a dominant even domineering style in relation to their prospective clients. In part this is a reflection of their difficulties in a market where prices had fallen and vendors were reluctant to accept this. Many were explicit that in the previous boom market they were willing to go along with vendors' views because prices were rising fast and steadily enough for the outcome to be no more than a delay of a month or two in the sale. It is also true, however, that agents, especially the older, more experienced and qualified of them consciously sought to achieve dominance over the prospective client when seeking instructions. This, of course, would make it more likely the client would defer to their professional knowledge and accept their valuation and further guidance. Although the resistance and abrasiveness of individual clients and the adverse market meant that at times this came out as an almost brutal frankness, agents were well aware that the object was not to alienate vendors but to gain their trust. As the well-established and qualified valuers at Malcolm Devon put it, if they are going to instruct you they have to like you.

The closeness of the relationship between agent and client varies enormously, of course, with the sophistication of both parties and the inclinations of the client. The experienced client may want no more than a very limited business relationship. The unsophisticated may want constant help and guidance on every aspect of property transfer and moving home. Obtaining instructions and, in the jargon, qualifying the vendor — establishing the vendor's circumstances and the extent of the real need or intention to sell — did not, however, have to be achieved by a demonstration of superior professional knowledge accompanied by client deference or at least respect. This style, which we will call 'dominant', may have been the most common, in part we suspect because of agents' constant frustrations at the ignorance, pig-headedness and rudeness of the public in property matters — a matter we shall return to more fully in the next chapter; it was not, however, the only possible style. Another which we call the 'supplicant', was characteristic of the younger, less experienced agent. At times it was associated with limited capacities and incompetence but, as we shall see, this did not prevent it resulting in obtaining instructions and the information necessary to qualify the vendor. Nor was it seen as inappropriate by clients — rather the reverse. Here is an example — independent agents will be glad to know it is from a corporate agency, though whether James was wearing white socks is not recorded — in which incompetence clearly had its charms and its rewards:

Having inspected a property in Chessington, recording the details on tape as he went, James, the office manager, leant heavily on the agenda set out in the Ash Property Agency's (APA) glossy sales literature. Reading from the same, James asked his potential client 'How do I know the price is right?' Pre-empting any reply he assured her: 'We don't just pluck a figure from the sky', and went on to explain that it was basically on a comparable basis. Thereafter James plodded remorselessly through the agenda, dealing in turn with 'What's really involved in selling my home? Communicating effectively through our corporate resources (advertising); our home marketing plan; distinctive boards', and so on.

Far from negotiating status with clients, my impression was that James risked boring them to death; on one occasion he was espousing the benefits of APA specialist mortgage advice to a client who did not require a mortgage. But it was all done with a considerable degree of earnestness and could produce the kind of reassurance sought by some clients, especially for the elderly lady who, having admitted her ignorance of the property world, warmed to James when he promised to lead her by the hand through all its pitfalls. Significantly, however, James was altogether more circumspect when the real reason for this client's obvious preference for instructing the APA became apparent. Somewhat frustrated by the agenda imposed by James, the client interjected with her fear that the bungalow she 'had set her heart on' was also being sold by the APA and although the vendor had assured her that it was hers (the full asking price had been offered), she wanted James, in effect, to act as the guarantor for the deal struck. James carefully avoided giving any promises, advising the client that until she had sold her own property 'he was afraid that' the bungalow would have to stay on the market and people sent to view. With the client still looking for some form of assurance that her place in the queue was secure, James confirmed that, if an offer was received from someone able to proceed on the bungalow, she would be informed and given every opportunity to proceed herself. Reassured and, presumably convinced that placing her own house with the APA might secure a better guarantee of the agent's attachment to her cause the instruction was given to James.

Arguably James was hampered as much as he was helped by the patter he derived from his sales training. Patter is not the issue here: many dominant agents had a patter, although usually a flexible and sophisticated one. As another more experienced but still young agent acting for another corporate put it:

I think ... you tend to come out with perhaps similar phrases. ... I try not to go in with a set speech. You try and talk with the people. A lot of the time I turn round and I feel, have I actually had a conversation with them or have I told them something.

This more relaxed supplicant style and its appropriateness and effectiveness both in getting results and in covering up the agents' weaknesses can be seen in this final example:

Her usual procedure was to enter the property and ask to sit down and 'have a little chat with you before looking round'. It was at this stage, Claudia openly admitted, that she would try to make friends with the clients, associate herself with their concerns and provide reassurance where necessary. Thus, in one property it became clear that the owners believed that they would be foolish to put their house on the market until they had found another to purchase because if they sold they would have to leave with nowhere to go. Claudia invoked the benign power of the name 'The APA' to protect and shield them from the harsh realities of the property world; the APA would make it clear on their behalf that any offer would only be accepted subject to them finding a suitable new home.

After accompanying Claudia on several inspections it was difficult to escape the conclusion that fraternising with potential clients, being herself and thereby projecting an image of a friendly and caring person, created a situation in which any gaffes in her presentation, which could dent her image in the eyes of some clients, might be overlooked. For example, on two occasions Claudia was asked what the fee was. On being told 1 per cent plus VAT, both clients asked what that meant: how much would they have to pay? Although Claudia confirmed that it was a percentage of the eventual sale price, she was unable to calculate the actual cost to the client since she had forgotten her calculator. Far from being dismayed, both owners sympathised, admitting that they too were unskilled in mental arithmetic. On another occasion Claudia blatantly misunderstood the (relatively simple) context of the potential client's circumstances, assuming that she had been brought in under false pretences to provide a free valuation for a sale. Only in the later stages of the inspection did she realise that she was at cross purposes with the owner and there was every chance of securing a genuine instruction. Presumably reassured by the strength of Claudia's friendliness rather than her powers of comprehension this owner was to give her the instruction the following day.

Claudia was keen to emphasise that the expectations and culture of the community determined her approach to valuations. She claimed that people in the locality, an area of predominantly low-cost, high-density housing, expected her to be friendly, almost familiar; they would react unfavourably to any hint of stand-offishness. But all the supplicant agents deployed friendliness not just to negotiate status with potential clients but to qualify them and ensure that the instruction was secured on terms favourable to the Ash Property Agency. As James put it, 'Are they serious about selling?'

QUALIFYING PURCHASERS

Once the agent has been instructed and details of the property prepared and advertised, his or her prime task is to locate a likely purchaser. This is the key service provided to the client, and the agent sees it as an important element of it that expressions of interest in the property are carefully winnowed to eliminate those incapable of making a purchase, along with those who have no real intention of doing so. Ideally the object is to come up with two or more keen purchasers who can then be induced to bid against each other to maximise the price. This, however, takes us up to the next stage, negotiation. The agent's problem initially is to discriminate capacity and intention broadly, whilst at the same time stimulating as much interest as possible in the property. That interest may arise in response to advertising, as a result of the regular mailing of selected property details to applicants who have registered their interest, or as a result of casual calls, either directly on the agency, or on the agency having seen a sale board.

As with potential vendors, the agent's first concern is to discriminate the serious purchaser of some property from those motivated by little more than curiosity, or time wasters. Because the agent derives income from commission from the vendor he is vulnerable to the demands of prospective purchasers: he needs them, but they know that they do not pay for his time. This can be the source of considerable frustration by agents, most of whom have a fund of anecdotes about the capacity of the public to string them along. At the same time, agents know that house purchase is a slow and often fraught business, and that it will pay in the long run to cultivate those serious about buying, even if it takes them time to settle on a property. The danger is that the agent will not be able to provide what they want, and here we move into the deeper levels of the agent's relationship with the purchaser, at which he attempts to persuade the purchaser to accept what he has on offer. At this stage qualifying the purchaser starts to become negotiation.

Initially the agent will want to know the circumstances and level of intention to purchase. Is this an initial prospecting of the local market or has the applicant had it under review for some time? How soon does the purchaser want to move and what pressures are there to do so? Is this a purely voluntary move that might in the event never take place, or is it, for example, the outcome of a job move or a divorce? Has the applicant a property to sell, and if so has it been sold? If it is sold what does that mean — a sale agreed, contracts exchanged or cash in the bank? What are the applicant's means — how much does the applicant want to spend and how much can he or she spend if pushed? Is there money in the bank or will a mortgage be required? If so, what are the applicant's income and commitments? All these constitute the elements of a basic profile of the applicant. Most agents will classify them as a result as more or less 'hot', that is, ready, willing and able to proceed immediately. Attention will then be given to them in proportion to their 'hotness', often with a special file or 'hot box' for the most eligible, who thus constitute the polar opposite of the time wasters.

Some of this information can be elicited by direct questioning to which most applicants will not object. The agent will ask what type of property is sought. This may be seen as central by those entering the market to buy, and at times they may stick to their views, but agents are sceptical in many cases that applicants really know what they want. The important issue for the agent in qualifying a purchaser is that the purchaser is strongly motivated to buy and has the means to do so. If these two features obtain, the agent is in a good position to do his job for his vendor clients, namely to sell their property.

Some of the information the agent wants will be less easy to obtain, at least by direct questioning, and here, as with vendors, the agent's skills in relating to the purchaser are crucial. A senior and experienced agent puts it like this:

> You see it isn't always invasive, David. I say to my staff, look it isn't a question of you saying why are you coming to [this area] and what job are you going to take up, it's a question of conversation, and initially, yes you ask them questions when you take the first information. After that when you are showing them round property you converse, and I will tell them about the facilities we have got [here] and might say, where do your interests lie, so I can tell them about the facilities we have got in [this area]. And I would make conversation about, Do you need to know about schools?, because I then find out what children they have got and what sort of age they are. I might sort of talk about what sort of industry we have got here, and what sort of jobs. And you would find out not so much by asking direct questions, but by general conversation, because people like to talk. Generally speaking people like to talk. If you encourage them they will tell you without you asking. You have got to start with a liking for people. The property is not important. Most people find going round houses interest-ing, and the houses don't change, they have all got something that is nice about them, I don't care what anybody says. I have seen the most grotty properties and I can still find something that is nice about them. But the people are the things you need to have skills with, and that is getting the information from them. I find a relationship with them, tension eases and you have a nice relaxed way of dealing with them, and this again is another that I think is important. It is stressful moving house, I think that life is stressful and I think that moving house is stressful and quite often there are other stresses in the background like bereavement, like divorce, like uprooting the wife because the husband has got promotion and she doesn't want to be uprooted because she has got a nice way of life. And you have to make the whole process as pleasant as possible, which is why I try and make people laugh.

Where the information is of a verifiable character, such as a house sold or a mortgageable limit, this is often checked through the other agent involved, the applicant's solicitor and, especially in corporate agents with a financial services arm, an interview with a financial adviser. Much of the information, however, has to be taken as trust, and its validity evaluated in the context of the overall relationship between agent and client. At times this can lead to frustrating results, as in the following example:

Applicant: I want a Victorian house — up to £70–75,000.
Wayne: Can I have your name, address and telephone number?

The formalities completed, the applicant was given details of several properties and departed. He returned an hour later asking to view. This time Janet dealt with the applicant. Without hesitation she went with the applicant, in his car, to view. She returned over an hour later extremely agitated because she had not known anything about the applicant's circumstances:

Janet: Did you put him on an applicant's sheet?
Wayne: No, I put him on the pad — I've just put him on the form now!

This admission produced a sharp telling off for Wayne for it emerged that the applicant still had to sell his house. A week later he telephoned to say that he was not moving to [the area] after all.

Other applicants present a radically different prospect calling for a quite different response from the agency. Another agent in the same office described the typical first-time buyer:

They walk in and they will usually be very quiet, look at you as if to say, 'Please help me, please come towards me because I don't really want to walk up to your desk and say I am looking for a house'. Usually you have got to be very gentle with them really. Explain basically what the house process is because they don't understand quite what's in it ... they look nervous when they come through your door. So somehow we try to overcome that and make them welcome.

Such an applicant provides easier access for the agent to demonstrate one of his distinctive skills, namely marketing. A senior agent describes this:

A salesman would be pushing those particular houses that they have got and saying, 'That is a brilliant buy, you must go and have a look at this, it's brilliant. Whether you like it or you don't like it, I am going to get you round that house.' A marketeer will sit there and say, 'Well what are you looking for?' You will say, 'I want four bedrooms.' 'Are you sure you need four bedrooms, you have got a couple of kids?' You start talking to them, 'We would like really a separate lounge and dining-room and ideally we would like an acre, but we could settle for a good size garden'. 'What can you afford to go up to? What would your maximum price be?' Get all those details and then say, 'Right we have got a selection here. Have a look at that, that and that' — see their reaction. And they would turn round and say, 'Yes, I like that'. 'Why do you like that? What's appealing?' 'Well it has got the right sort of bedroom accommodation, it looks nice, it looks pretty, it is pretty, it's beautiful.' You pick up on what they are saying about it, and expand a little bit further, and get them interested. It is that method of marketing just person to person, rather than the heavy sell! So you are not actually a salesman there. And likewise all we can do for a client is advertise and make sure that anybody that is looking for that particular house has got the information about it, and it is put in front of them. We can never force anybody to buy anything, because at the end of the day you make your own decision whether you like a house or not. *But* you can very cleverly say — I mean a lot of people have walked in and said, 'We have got a list of 10 points that we must have in a house'. I have on several occasions sold houses to people who have got only six or seven of those points on, by saying, 'Look, that house there actually fits seven of those points. The other three points, they are not desperately important to you are they? Or are they?' And if they are not, you say, 'The house that you are really looking for, with every single one of those 10 points, doesn't actually exist, this is the nearest thing that you are going to get to that'. And they look at it and say, 'You are probably absolutely right, we have looked at everything', and it is getting them to agree that that is the house they want to buy.

The agent's view, clearly, is that he is drawing out of the applicant what kind of property the applicant realistically wants to buy, i.e., in the light of his or her real needs, means, and what is on the market, and in doing so dispelling at least some of the idealised dream of perfection. It may of course take quite a while and the viewing of numerous properties to achieve this. In the course of this the agent may build quite a substantial relationship with the applicant — as we have seen, a relaxed, friendly and trusting style is sought. As a result the agent may very well be helpful, both as a sounding-board for the applicant in clarifying what he or she wants, and as a source of advice as to what is available and on what terms. This relationship also, however, results in the applicant divulging a great deal of personal information to the agent, who is of course paid for and retained by the vendor. The agent's job is to find a purchaser and see the deal through at the best obtainable price. To a significant degree the agent's interests and those of the vendor coincide. The agent's interests coincide far less with the applicant's. True, if the agent markets rather than sells, this may help the applicant make a choice he or she will be happy with, but when it comes to the next stage, negotiation, the applicant may well find that the agent has acquired information, notably about financial capacity, which can be used to the applicant's disadvantage.

Most of the agents we investigated combined the qualifying of applicants, which is essential to all agents, with the marketing approach, which they contrasted with the unprofessional habits of unqualified or inexperienced agents who merely list properties, that is, advertise and circulate details widely, but leave appraisal and decisions on whether to make an offer entirely to the applicant. It is interesting that the agents at Malcolm Devon spontaneously expressed caution at getting too close to purchasers. Although they said that lack of staff time was one problem, and that applicants very often preferred to view properties unaccompanied (not the entire point in any case) it was also remarked, 'If negotiators knew the purchasers better than the vendor, I wonder whether that might lead to problems.'

In our view this is one of the central problems of estate agency. Agents very widely see their job as lubricating the market, getting deals done, bringing vendor and purchaser together, and express satisfaction when this job is well done and both parties are pleased with the result. All are aware, however, that it is the vendor who pays them and that their relationship with the purchaser is a means to that end. The purchaser's interests are hence protected only by the agent's integrity and sense of professionalism, a phrase which elicits a hollow laugh, at least among certain members of the public. This is an issue which becomes critical when we move to the next stage in the property sale process, negotiation.

NEGOTIATING SALES

Negotiation is the key phase of the residential agency cycle, since it determines whether a deal will go through, and hence whether the agency generates any income. The position of negotiator is therefore one of recognised importance. Although agencies vary in their division of labour, and in most cases vendors and purchasers will speak to staff other than the negotiator during this phase, the negotiator is usually in charge of the process, from the soliciting of the offer, or certainly the acceptance of it, and its negotiation, to an agreement of sale with the vendor, and including the verification of finance, dealing with solicitors and the monitoring of the progress of the deal past the mortgage lender's report through to at least exchange of contracts. The intensive part of this phase is bringing the applicant to the point of making an offer and then managing both parties to the point of agreement. Agreements can fall apart and may need renegotiation in the light of the survey, the true state of the applicant's finances, or the applicant's interest in several properties at once. In these circumstances the negotiator's job is to keep the purchaser committed, and of course preferably to know enough about the purchaser already to ensure that he or she is ready, willing and able to complete the deal. It is on that basis as well as on the size of an offer that the negotiator advises the vendor client.

None of this is easy. The relationship between vendor and purchaser is adversarial to the (usually significant) extent that, in the first place one is attempting to minimise the purchase price and the other to maximise it, and in the second, the purchaser is doubtful of knowing all that is necessary about the property, though the survey is supposed to help here, including providing guidance on overall value. The vendor is uncertain both about the purchaser's capacity to go ahead in good time, and as to whether he or she may not have a parallel interest in another property. This system is reinforced by the retention of solicitors by the two parties.

In the view of some agents, the market since the end of the boom in 1988 has become tough, with purchasers becoming more assertive in making offers well below the asking price on a number of properties. In a market in which offers are few and far between, this puts the agent in a difficult position. Here are two examples. In the first the agent knows that it is in his client's interest to accept the offer, but he has to use all his skills to get her to do it and avoid putting the purchaser off:

> You probably heard me talking to the lady at Douglas Road, where she had an offer of £58,000 on the property, and she wasn't going to accept it. Now I didn't want to go and frighten the purchaser. And we have sold two houses like that this week, both at £55,000, and one of them a much nicer house than that. And we haven't sold any of that type of property at anything like that sort of money for a long, long time. So £58,000 was an incredibly good offer and she wouldn't accept it, she wanted £59,000 so I didn't want to frighten away the purchaser, because he was a cash buyer, and you give them 48 hours to make a decision anyway. I didn't want to frighten him away, but at the same time I had to go back to him and tell him that it wasn't accepted. If you dither there — I went back to him and said the offer isn't accepted, but the vendor has told us she wants £59,000. Now if you can raise your offer at all, I said, even if you can't quite reach £59,000, if you can raise your offer at all, I will go back to the vendor and see if I can persuade her again, but at the same time you must understand that we are trying to get the best price we can for the vendor. Now in that instance he went up to £58,500 and met her halfway. But if I had gone back to him in a strong way and said look she isn't going to sell for anything less than £59,000, if you don't come back with an offer of £59,000 forget it, he might have gone away altogether.

The second case is more difficult still, because the agent does not know either just what the sale price should be, because of the weak market, or how far he can push the purchaser; yet his job is to extract the best price for his client:

> Prior to instructing APA the vendors had received several valuations, with a high of £150,000 and a low of £110,000. Wayne, who handled the negotiations, had advised asking £125,000, on the grounds that the property required renovation, although the vendors had instructed at £135,000.
>
> After several viewings an offer of £105,000 was received, which Wayne advised the vendors to reject. With these purchasers Wayne discussed the property: what needed upgrading and how much they were prepared to spend. On the basis of this conversation the offer was increased to £112,000, a figure which, in view of the general condition of the property, Wayne thought was 'getting reasonable'. The clients were unimpressed and rejected, an action which prompted the purchasers to increase their offer by a further £3,000. At £115,000 Wayne telephoned his clients to urge them to accept, but he failed to make progress. The following day the offer was increased to £118,000, a figure the clients accepted.

Was the agent guilty of thinking more of his commission and getting the deal done than his clients' concern to maximise the price — remember that 2 per cent of £115,000 is a healthy figure in commission in comparison to 2 per cent of £3,000? In this case the fieldworker thought that his view on price was genuine; his failure was in identifying the purchaser's limits.

Purchasers are said to have become more assertive in other ways too. Another qualified agent commented:

> People know the market is at rock bottom and they are looking to take command of it. They are coming in saying, 'Yes it looks worth 50 but I am only going to pay 45'. They then have the report and it's worth 45, but they say, 'Oh, they told me it needed a damp-proof course and it needed rewiring'. So they want another £3,000 off for that. It's much tougher to sell nowadays than it ever used to be.
>
> A lady phoned me up this morning and she said, 'I want you to be hard on it (i.e., the mortgage valuation report) because I want your report to get the price down'.

Of course agents have techniques for stimulating better offers. One explained to us that a poor offer would not necessarily be transmitted direct to a vendor. Instead, after a delay, the applicant would be told that the offer was not acceptable and, in confidence, that the vendor would not accept anything under a certain level, which was a pity because the applicant clearly could not afford that. Nothing was more calculated to improve an offer, it was said, than an expressed assumption that the property was beyond the applicant's means.

By no means all applicants are assertive, sophisticated, or even equipped with a basic knowledge of the situation:

> You also get the people who are genuinely naïve, you get first-time buyers that come in and they say, is it customary for us to make an offer? Or are we meant to offer the asking price? Or what do we do? They have absolutely no idea. And you say to them — it's difficult, we have to say, 'Look, you must understand we act on behalf of the vendor. At the end of the day we must get the best price we can for our vendor. Any offer you wish to make we will put that forward, but if we consider it to be a silly offer, we will put the offer forward, but we will advise our vendor not to accept it.'

It is hard to imagine that first-time buyers are not sometimes exploited, though we suspect that they are more at risk in respect of financial services arrangements than house purchase. The agents we observed seemed to respond supportively to the plainly naïve. This did not mean that they were not reluctant to extract as much information from purchasers as possible, to spend a considerable amount of time gaining their trust and then use both the information and the relationship to the advantage of their client, the vendor. Sometimes, this may amount, apparently at least, to little more than lack of prudence of the part of the applicant:

> What gives me great pleasure is for somebody to make an offer of say £70,000 for a £90,000 house — you talk to the client and he says, 'Right well

it's a bit low'. You are having a chat and say, 'Well what would you accept?'
He says, I will come down to £80,000', and you then talk to the purchaser,
or potential purchaser, and really get their confidence, and get them to talk
to you and say, 'Well, what do you think of this house?' 'I really do like it,
and as a matter of fact I am prepared to go to £85,000.' Although the client
has told you he would go to £80,000, you are actually getting him an extra
£5,000 and he turns to you and says, 'That's brilliant, I only wanted
£80,000, but you have got me £85,000', and that gives me a buzz, because
you have paid for yourself and you have put a little bit of money in his
bank. Then he thinks you are brilliant and will pass the word on.

A number of agents remarked to us that in a thin market with fewer
purchasers and sometimes not many vendors either, agents have much more
time to build up a relationship with both parties. It is also fair to say that, in
our experience, there are three things that are a source of gratification — a
buzz or turn on, an emotional high — to agents. One is bringing off a deal.
Another is the intermittent fever of activity in the office as telephones ring,
clients and prospective clients walk in, and everyone is busy, most of them
in the attempt to secure instructions or sell property, and in so doing to relate
to vendors, applicants and their representatives. The third is making effective
contact with a vendor and obtaining instructions. The capacity to relate, a
need to like people and to talk to them was widely remarked in this
connection. Behind the elation lay not just that it was doing business, but in
the first place, as we have noted, the achievement of a certain ascendancy
over the clients, coupled with a sense of being of service to them, of being
able to use knowledge and skill for their benefit. When translated into the
sales training of the corporates this can become a blatant recipe for
dominance and manipulation both of the client and the purchaser:

A: There are six questions used in sales, which if I remember, are which,
why, who, how, where, when. If I asked you a question with one of those
words with it, I could guarantee that you wouldn't be able to say yes or no
to them. It would sound silly if you replied yes or no to one of those
questions.
Q: You are getting this information flow going. What's the purpose of
that though?
A: Basically by doing that we can swing, especially if we take control of
the conversation, if you like, and by doing that we can be in a more
dominating situation, but we can be more aggressive — aggressive is the
wrong word — as well. It puts you in a position where we know as much
about the person as possible, so, if we were to put something to them, they
wouldn't have as much to fall back on as they may like, basically. So it puts
us in a position where we can do the talking, and at the end of it they need
to say yes. But it's not necessarily hard selling — it doesn't always
come over that way. It's very much linked to personality and the way you
do it. If I started asking the wrong questions, then I would be in deep
trouble.

Q: From that information presumably you can begin to establish what, in some respects, the vendor will want to hear in terms of the likely sort of price they want for the house, how quickly they want it.
A: Yes. And we can use that information to our advantage and cut out all the things that we don't need to say. It can work on the purchaser's side.
Q: It's more difficult on that side isn't it?
A: Not really no, it's just a different way of doing it. For example, if someone came up to me and said how far is that from the schools I could turn round and say how old are your children? They say well we don't have any children, and I can tell them that it is quite a distance from the school but you don't get much trouble with the children, because if they don't have children and they are asking that question, then they don't want too many children to-ing and fro-ing past their house. If I said to them how old are your children and they said 17 and 15, I could say it is x number of miles, but there are bus routes towards it. . . .
Q: So you are providing them with a reassurance that they are essentially looking for?
A: That's right. You can use it so you don't give the wrong information to put them off, if you see what I mean.

Such deliberate tactics are by no means always necessary. Another agent remarked that purchasers would not infrequently reveal intimate details of their domestic lives:

The mother was telling us how her daughter gets locked in by her husband, gets beaten up, all this sort of thing. . . . And there you are put in a bit of a spot, where you think, what should I do about this now that I know it? But you can't really betray a confidence.
Q: But what happens if you get information which tells you something about their ability to afford a house, to raise their offer. Is there an ethical difficulty there?
A: Not really. You see, quite a lot of people, say for a house at £59,000, purchasers put in an offer of £55,000 — he will say can you try that for me? I will go to £57,000 but can you try £55,000? You know he will go to £57,000 so you put the offer of £55,000 to your vendor and you say to him, 'Well I think I can get him up again, probably get him up to £57,000'.

That there is a problem here is recognised by some agents:

Very often the purchaser is actually unaware that you are not actually acting for them. You build up the relationship to an extent that they come to trust you — which is good, which is what it should be. And I hope that with my staff that you could rely on that, that you wouldn't be pointed in the wrong direction. But sometimes that relationship — you are right, and the relationship with the client — it becomes a little bit clouded. Not to us because we know who is paying our fee, but to the person in the street who is buying the house. And we do very often build up very close relationships with somebody over a very short period of time whilst they are going through the purchasing process, and we try to be as caring as possible and help people with their moves. We may go all the way through until they are actually in the house, and not just drop out when the contract is exchanged. That may be a period of four to five months from the time they first start looking.

When it was put to him later that this was surely a conflict of interests he responded:

You are making us sound all-powerful. I don't think we are. The client inevitably has a price in mind that they wish to achieve. Sometimes it is based on our advice, sometimes it is not based on our advice, it is based on something they have conceived, like the house in Surrey that they have got to buy, therefore they need a certain price to be able to do the transaction. And somebody here, who has got to be capable of setting themselves limits. OK I know I can afford a £100,000 mortgage, but I don't want a £100,000 mortgage, I think that would be stretching me, I want to keep my mortgage not above £65,000. All right, I get into a situation, I set myself that, and they set themselves that. In comes the estate agent. Now as well as that person possibly paying more than they intended, or a larger mortgage than they intended, that person may actually take less than they originally intended. It's the art of negotiation between the two parties. Now the market forces also come into it, and at the moment I am a buyer, and if I have got cash I am more likely to get him off his price than he is to get me off mine. And at any time you can say stop! The individual doesn't lose control, you make it sound as though we are inflating it all the time, and they lose control of their own destiny. At any time they can say 'I'm very sorry I don't want to give you that information' — they are perfectly entitled to do it.

There is a certain amount of bluster in this reply. The only solid suggestion we elicited in response to our repeated enquiries as to what safeguards the interests of purchasers was that the lender's valuation survey will provide an independent judgment and a reminder to the purchaser that he or she may be paying too much. This is a slim defence indeed, particularly given the pressures upon mortgage valuers during the boom to produce reports concurring with an agreed sale price, to ensure that lenders obtained the business (see further chapter 11). This apart, the relationship with the purchaser goes beyond the issue of price in isolation. The plain fact is that the agent deliberately cultivates a relationship with the purchaser in order to take advantage of it for the benefit of his client, the vendor. This is not to say that agents are without merit when they argue that their job is to get the parties to agree, that they will not pressure their clients to agree, that their objective is to do deals that leave both parties happy, and that only in that way will they secure their good name and future business. There is no doubt that many agents derive their greatest satisfaction from achieving sales that both parties are happy with at a price the agent regards as the fair market price.

The point is that agents are paid by vendors, and that no one acts in a similar role to protect the purchaser. From this conflict of interest derives, we believe, much of the poor image of the estate agent, his or her slippery character, for they are all things to all men, and deliberately so. They may in some cases use experience and integrity to try to achieve something approximating professional judgment and detachment in their dealings but we doubt, first, whether the inherent conflict can be reconciled in all cases, and second, whether many agents have either the inclination or the training and experience to achieve professionalism. We shall return to this issue again later, but it should be evident that it is not something capable of being resolved easily, for example, by drawing a purchaser's attention to the fact that agents are paid by vendors. Many agents already do this routinely. It is water off a duck's back if the purchaser needs advice and support and the agent is the only person available to provide it and has a powerful motivation to get close to the purchaser. Just how far purchasers can be their own worst enemies is illustrated in the following example. Note the way in which the agent, despite his desire to protect the purchaser from her own folly, in the end relies upon an independent source, the survey, to resolve his conflict of interest:

A: The vendor is actually buying through us in X office, so we are involved and I have been involved with this girl for quite a long time, and we have got to the stage now where in the ordinary valuation report the surveyor has picked out all sorts of problems, and he actually asked for a structural engineer's report, purely for the valuation. We have actually had a structural engineer's report done, but the surveyor also asked for a survey for rising damp and woodwork. That's from an ordinary valuation report — not a survey, and there's essential repairs. Obtain a damp and timber specialist's report, evidence of some damp in entrance hall, that's very odd. Evidence of some historic crack down the left-hand party wall … subsidence problems, and that is just from a normal valuation you see. They haven't even paid extra for that. So it's all there. Now we have actually got, the vendor has paid £350 for a structural engineer's report, which we have there. Now the [first] insurers have refused to insure the property and we have been hunting around for two or three days, trying to get somebody else to do it, and I actually had the girl in here. Unfortunately for her, she has got very, very friendly with the vendor, to the extent where they have come looking for curtains together for this house she is buying off her. They go out drinking at night, go for a drink together, so they have established a terrific relationship and I had … the purchaser in here the day before yesterday and said, 'Look I don't think you ought to be buying this house. I really can't see why you are trying so hard to buy something that has got inherent faults in it', I said, 'Why?', She said, 'I am coming round to that way of thinking'. I said, 'You have made it very awkward for yourself because you have got too friendly with the vendor now. You are going to have to ring her and say, "I don't want your house" if you decide to follow my advice.' And that is affecting our sale at the same time, because the girl who is actually selling it is actually buying from us down there. I told the manager last night. He wasn't very happy. But I said, 'Look no way would I buy that house. For God's sake, forget it. Every time you sit down in your lounge if you hear a little crack somewhere you are going to be frightened to death. Why take the risk?'

Q: The survey provides some safeguard?

A: There's quite a lot of safeguard, it takes the pressure off me really. All I have got to talk to them about is the cash, 'Can you afford it and do you want to spend an extra £24 a month to pay £2,000 more for this house'. And that is the only pressure I can put on, because with house buying it is a very, very emotive thing, it is a very personal thing. You either like a house or you don't. If you particularly like a house it's probably worth £50 to 60 a month more to you if you can afford it.

MARKETING FINANCIAL SERVICES

Most purchasers will need a mortgage, and we have seen that qualifying the purchaser includes an attempt to verify his or her capacity to complete the deal. Estate agents have traditionally had formal relationships with financial services institutions, notably as agents for building societies, as well as informal ones in established contacts with banks, building societies and insurers (as well as solicitors). In some instances then the provision of financial services has been part of the business, where in others it has been no more than the outcome of repeated requests for advice by purchasers and vendors, although it may also in that case have led to extra income, both through formal commissions and through informal gifts and reciprocal introduction of business. In recent years many estate agents have been bought up by financial services institutions and this is the subject of chapters 7 and 8. We confine ourselves here therefore to a few general remarks and to some comments on the place of financial services among independent agents, at least as we found them.

We have already seen that there is a widespread perception that many purchasers — and vendors for that matter since it is not confined to first-time buyers — are uninformed and poorly organised about house sale and purchase. The same view was widely held of the financial services associated with house purchase: mortgage, bank transactions, buildings insurance, mortgage indemnity insurance, and endowment and mortgage protection life insurance. This was not simply a matter of total ignorance and willingness to be guided by anyone offering to do so, though this was not infrequent, but damaging ignorance even by those with some grasp of the situation. One agent, for example, asked a purchaser, whom he reminded to sort out his mortgage, if he was to be able to complete, and was told that he could do that in three days. In the event the purchaser signed up rapidly with a building society on his own initiative, but failed to notice that if he redeemed the loan within five years, which as a youngish man was not improbable, he would pay a three-month interest penalty.

This purchaser, who owned his own business, was clearly reluctant to be drawn into the financial services advice offered by the estate agent, no doubt wary about the potential conflict of interest inherent here. That such conflicts are unavoidable is indicated by two examples, one by a regional manager of a corporate estate agent, the other by the financial advice service of an independent agency. When the corporate agency manager was asked to comment on the potential conflict of interest in providing financial services to purchasers, he replied that his organisation had never discriminated against purchasers going elsewhere:

> The individual has that freedom at any time to say: 'I don't want your product but I want the house and, no I won't tell you what I earn'. There is nothing we can do if they decide to take that route. But when we go to the client and say 'There is an offer of £75,000 from Mr Bloggs', and they say 'What do you know about him', and we say 'Nothing, because he won't tell us anything', an element of suspicion creeps in. An element of doubt of how substantial that offer is creeps in, because we can't make any recommendations. We just put it forward as an offer.

Explicit conditional selling is recognised here to be out of the question. Instead, the financial services sale is linked to the need to qualify the purchaser. The latter is an obvious necessity but one which is actually confused by the presence of a financial services arm to the estate agency. The presumptive reason why the purchaser will not disclose his income is that he wants to avoid being hard sold a financial package. There is evidence that purchasers are uneasy at this prospect. Another agent (as it happens working for a different corporate estate agency, but as a negotiator) pointed out the dangers of linking in financial services too explicitly. His client looked like taking a £10,000 loss on a property bought two years earlier for £62,000. The move was forced upon him because of redundancy. The vendor called in several agents, including one from an office which was the financial services area office for another agency and whose representative, besides doing a valuation, began to discuss his financial position at length. The vendor instructed the agent we spoke to referring to the competitor as an insurance salesman: 'I invited him round to look at the house and he started selling insurance to me. That wasn't on.'

Clearly this vendor intended to determine how he would resolve his financial difficulties in his own way. Others may be more at a loss and welcome the prospect of financial advice. In this example, also of a corporate agency with a financial services arm, the name and reputation of the financial institution and the offer of help was instrumental both in obtaining instructions and negotiating an immediate drop in asking price to a 'realistic' level. The property had been with another (also corporate) agency for the term of a contract (three months) without attracting interest. The agent we observed was aware that the vendors had already contacted his financial services adviser and commented on this after his inspection. This opened the floodgates. The couple had originally borrowed from a major building society and added new loans and then a remortgage with a centralised lender to pay for modernising the property. Their objective by the time of interview was to sell, redeem the mortgage despite the penalty and trade down to a cheaper property in the district. The agent was in no difficulty in putting himself across as a worldly professional and expressed incredulity at the terms of the remortgage. 'They keep talking till you sign', was the reply. But since a refinancing package via the corporate's financial services parent would save them, the vendors were glad to instruct the agent forthwith at a 10 per cent drop in price. There was no reason to doubt that this would be a sensible and effective course, as well as good business for the corporate agency.

It will be remarked that, having deferred corporate agencies and their financial services to later chapters we have nonetheless used them as examples in this one. Apart from the fact that a good deal of our research was with corporate agents, the reason for this is that the corporates now have a dual aspect in the high street. They are both more or less integrated estate agency and financial services entities, as was evident in the example of the vendor who resented being sold insurance, and continuing sources of financial services and advice, which is the guise in which they appear in the last example. One can, for all that, still buy a house through Ash Property Agency, obtain a mortgage through the Woolwich and insure with the Prudential. The question is whether this is any longer very likely, and it is that which we will defer until later. The choice for agents is how they respond to the need for most of their purchasers for finance and financial advice. Two of the independents we observed exemplify in particular the choices to be made.

Langfords, as was described in our sketch at the beginning of chapter 4, had a financial services side which, like the estate agency, was fiercely independent. It was an agent for three building societies, which meant that mortgages generated income but was not tied to any financial institution, unlike all the local competion. All the staff believed in the morality of independent advice, in part because of Dora's almost missionary faith in independence. This outweighed the financial disadvantages to her business in terms of lesser commissions, the costs of membership of the regulatory body, FIMBRA, and the lack of the massive financial backing in terms of training, equipment and office refurbishment that the corporates have. Nonetheless, she claimed that there was a competitive advantage to being independent which people would readily recognise — that you could provide the right product for the individual customer, rather than just those of one company, even though she acknowledged that the public are very ignorant in financial services matters. The financial services unit provided important additional income, which was certainly helpful in coping with a recession severe enough to necessitate the closure of the founding branch of the agency, and the unit probably served to promote the agency's independent image to the local public. The financial services consultant was in no doubt that regulation was effectively lax, especially in the arrangement of life insurance. He had worked elsewhere with people whose practices were sharp, to say the least, and quite willing to push products generating the highest commission. He was evidently unhappy with this, which is why (in part) he moved to Langfords.

All in all the example suggests that financial services are a double-edged weapon for the independent, who must struggle to compete with the corporates and is still not free of the pressures inherent in a weak regulatory system to pursue commission income and, of course, vulnerable to the gibes of the corporates, to the effect that a client is better with them being straightforward about their tied status than with an independent whose competence is unknown and whose pursuit of best advice may be hampered by an inclination to maximise commission.

Such was the conclusion of Malcolm Devon, which adopted the opposite strategy to Langfords, eschewing all financial advice; just as they were wary of getting too close to purchasers for fear of conflict of interest, so with financial advice. Their business was selling houses and providing valuation and other professional services. Evidently purchasers who asked for help were given it, since commissions did provide 'a little bit of icing on the cake', but this was via referrals rather than through a financial services arm of the business. As one of the partners put it:

> We have been asked by some companies to come in with us, and when we have found out their background it wouldn't have gelled with us. They were going to be the hard sell and we pulled away from that.

Other firms, they pointed out, had reached the point of advertising the fact that they were estate agents only and that they would not try to sell vendors or purchasers anything but property. Whether it is just 'the hard sell' which is the problem, or whether the conflict of interest is more fundamental we leave until later. For the present it is enough to observe that estate agents in the traditional mould continue to prosper and that there were not a few who made it clear to us implicitly or explicitly, that financial services, whilst they might be an alternative source of income, were essentially a diversion from estate agency proper, and as such something in which they took little interest. It was better that someone else suitably qualified and experienced should do it and leave the agents to get on with what they enjoyed and were good at: selling houses and brokering deals.

Having said this there is no doubt that there are substantial advantages to the agent in being able to offer financial services advice. One of these is the additional income generated, but a more important one is what was put plainly by Freestones in chapter 4: control. In its weak form this involves being able to assist purchasers who are unable or unwilling to take the initiative in making their financial arrangements and hence cementing a relationship with them. In its strong form it means knowing everything about the deal as it unfolds and being able to prevent it unravelling in the latter stages because of a hitch in the financial arrangements. As Freestones pointed out, competent independent financial advice for the purchaser is invaluable. Incompetent or restricted advice can impose a severe long-term financial penalty.

SIX

Estate Agents at Work 2

This chapter examines key structural features of independent estate agency. We describe the recruitment and training of agents, the methods by which they are remunerated, and the ways in which they view members of the public, and we describe the kinds of abuse to which estate agency is subject.

RECRUITMENT AND TRAINING

The workforce in estate agency is volatile, even though a successful agency is widely seen as requiring a stable team. A number of factors contribute to this. The housing market is cyclical, and this has an impact both on the number of branches and agencies and the staffing of them. The boom which ran until August 1988 was particularly long and strong and led to great expansion in staffing, with properties selling at great speed. It was also the period in which the corporates began to buy into estate agency and this has had a very disruptive impact on the labour market. The corporates quickly began to rationalise their branch networks, eliminating duplicate branches and opening new ones in promising locations. This in itself forced staff turnover, and the tendency was enhanced by the impact of the new corporate culture, links with financial services, new procedures, refurbishment, even uniforms, all of which alienated some established staff, who left. The takeovers were rapidly followed by the ensuing slump, which soon necessitated staff redundancies and further rationalisation of the branch networks. The interaction of the sudden moves from strong boom to severe slump and the arrival of the corporates probably constituted the greatest turmoil in the labour market for generations.

Those recruited in the heyday of the boom, especially by the then gung-ho corporates, have acquired a particular and widespread notoriety in estate agency:

They were working 15 hours a day, six days a week — they just burned themselves out. Average age 19, the white socks and earring brigade as we call it, the people who really did our business an awful lot of harm because they were just manipulating the sale of those 1988 houses.

At this point houses were selling in days, sometimes hours, and prices had been rising steadily for years. It seemed that estate agents could not go wrong, and commission income flooded in. Quality of service was, as the above comment implies, poor in part because of pressure of time and in part because of lack of experience and motivation; and it has also to be said that such young unqualified staff were and are not required to achieve any standards of competence before being released on to the public.

The white socks generation have now either shed their 1980s image and acquired more experience or, more likely, left the industry altogether. Labour turnover still shows a tendency to be high, however, and keeping a team together is seen as particularly important. In the independent agency this is conventionally achieved by the personal relationships between staff and the boss, as was evident in Langfords where, as Dora put it: 'The staff that I have, I have had for quite a long time. They know what I want from them.' This meant that her staff had settled into an acceptance of her style of estate agency, which emphasised integrity, service and the virtues of independence. Asked what she would do if she needed to replace staff she replied: 'I would contact people I know within the [area NAEA] branch and find somebody that I knew'. This comment conceals several features of estate agency staffing. First, the standard and for the recruiters most satisfactory means of obtaining staff is through the estate agency social world. It was regularly emphasised to us that agents, even though in close rivalry for business, are everywhere in regular social contact with each other, formally through professional bodies as above, semi-formally in outings, parties, sporting competitions and the like, and informally in the local pubs and restaurants. Gossip constantly circulates about the state of the market, new initiatives by agencies, and potential or actual job vacancies.

In its standard form this social networking acts as an employment exchange of a quite critical and effective kind since all aspects of the jobs are discussed in advance and an agent seeking to recruit may not only ask around quite widely and obtain various opinions on a good candidate, but be subject to the same process simultaneously by the candidate. In its tougher form this process can become head-hunting or poaching, whereby the best staff in the town will be targeted, perhaps over a quite extended period. Here is an example of a successful operation:

About a month ago, we had a five-a-side football competition, where a lot of the agents get together, and talk and generally they all get on very well, believe it or not. You generally get to know who is out there and who is not, who is worth having, and who is not. When I was down in [one of our other offices], Dot was working for Black Horse and I never came across her as a valuer, in fact by her own admission she will tell you she is not very good at going out and valuing houses, but she is red hot when it comes to dealing with sales and dealing with solicitors and that in the office. She is very good at that. And with vendors, they get on with her great and she gets on with them great.

That came across to me. I had gone out and spoken to purchasers and vendors and they would be saying, 'Oh, also we are dealing with Dot ... she has told us this, and she has told us that'. And at the end of the day she was almost becoming a pain in the arse to you, I'd get earache from Dot. And I thought if she is having that impression she must be good at her job. I had spoken to Bill about taking on this office and I said I needed more staff. He said, if you feel the justification we will do something about it. I said, 'Well, I have got somebody in mind'. I just rang Dot up and said, just general chit-chat first of all, and then I said, 'How are things going down there, are you happy with Black Horse?' Her answer was yes. But I said, 'If you ever feel that things are not going the way you want them or whatever, have a chat with me and I will have a position here for you, I am sure. I would certainly like to have a talk with you anyway.' And I think that's how it started. Then about a couple of weeks after that I rang her and said, 'Look I will have a position available soon. I know I spoke to you a couple of weeks ago, but I would like to have another chat with you, is it possible that we can meet one lunch and I will talk to you about it?' Which we did. I told her about the position that was going here, what the responsibility and what the strength of the position was. She was interested. I rang her a couple of days later, offered her the job, told her she could have the job. She said that she would consider it, talk to her boyfriend, came back and said she didn't want the job. I asked her why and said, 'Can we meet again', which I did. And then managed to convince her into coming with us. But it was a bit of a long-drawn-out process. If somebody is good and they are with a company, that company will want to keep them, and they are difficult to get. You have got to either offer them a pretty good incentive with money, or have a package of a car or whatever, or you have got to have a considerable edge over the person they are working for. Although we couldn't offer her a great improvement on her income, we were obviously doing substantially more business than the company she was with, and we had a lot more potential than the company she was with. Consequently she had more potential with us, which she has proved, and over the last two years she has grown in strength and seniority and her salary has gone up.

This is not the only way to recruit good staff. The same agent referred to two of his team who had been recruited as juniors through YTS and had demonstrated their commitment and ability over 18 months or so and been offered permanent positions. He admitted, however, that he had been lucky, and this leads us on to the issue of training and its relationship to recruitment. There was a widespread view that, to put it simply, estate agents are born not made. Training in various forms is available and we shall return to the topic in a later chapter, but the point for the present is that it is widely regarded as somehow beside the point in comparison with experience and ability, the possession of the appropriate qualities to be a good estate agent. Besides the courses run by the corporates, which have the dual function of training for estate agency and training in the corporate culture and bureaucracy, and on the other hand the professional qualification of the RICS and other bodies, there are briefer training courses run by the NAEA, and from 1992, the national vocational qualifications in estate agency are coming on stream (discussed in chapter 11). The widespread attitude to training is well expressed by this agent, now a manager for a corporate agency:

> Before you get an introduction to see a house, the very first thing you have to sell, as soon as you ring the doorbell, is yourself. I firmly believe that most people who instruct, they don't give a damn whether it is for the Royal or the Pru, the Halifax or Joe Bloggs and Co. in the High Street. It is purely a relationship between you the client and me the agent. If you like me then I have got every chance of getting the job.

Hence:

> The successful agents of the past have been very much people who have learnt from experience rather than learnt from training. There was virtually no sales training in what is essentially a selling job. I never personally qualified. I started doing the old chartered auctioneers' exams and I failed them three times and gave up.... I firmly believe that if you want specialist knowledge on detailed subjects, there are always people whom you can employ, or experts in that particular field who can deal with it....
>
> I can take someone who is an unsuccessful estate agent.... I can put them through an intensive training course and attach them maybe to one of our better managers for a period of time and then let them loose again. Obviously they might be practically better than before, but they won't be really good. So I think you need to have certain basic qualities to start with, and then I think you can build on those.... But if you are a shy retiring introvert, then it is my belief that you will never be a successful estate agent.

Another, by common consent, star branch manager took this further:

> [Clients] want you to know everything about them and that's what it's about. It's a very personal thing estate agency. And it's the same with the purchaser as well, you have got to build up a good relationship with your purchaser in the hope that they will come back to you. And they will feel so secure and safe in your hands ... that they want to come back to you and buy a house through you. We have had people that have come in our door and they have seen other houses they wanted to buy but they have not bought them because they wanted to buy a house from Sycamore and Elm and we have eventually sold them a house.

Whether a significant sector of the public, as either vendors or purchasers, share this view or not, it is quite widely held as an ideal by agents. According to it estate agency is fundamentally about building positive relationships with the public as customers and clients and providing an attentive and competent service within those relationships. Learning to achieve this involves long exposure to established practitioners, and hence training normally takes the form of a slow acquisition of recognised competences, beginning at a lowly level on the office duplicator and rising gradually to dealing with inquiries in the office, going out on valuations and learning to do them and finally involvement in negotiations. The successful, however, may progress very rapidly through the system, and the team run by the branch manager above, which was very highly regarded and kept the area manager in constant fear of having them poached, were all in their early and middle 20s. Indeed there was a view that constant contact with a demanding public meant that the number of agents in front-line work doing valuations and negotiations fell precipitately beyond the age of 40. Coping with the public was rewarding if it was successful, but it was also very stressful, as we shall see in the next section.

The implication of this account of successful agency, then, is that effective teams, especially in a disturbed market, will not be the norm and this will contribute to labour turnover. It will be the objective of every agent responsible for recruitment to build such a team, which means both people capable of hard work and effectiveness as individuals, and capable of working well with their colleagues and of recognising complementary strengths. Success, however, will constantly bring the threat of poaching and major increases in income are often — we are tempted to say normally — achieved by job moves. Training has hence a modest role in this view of the occupational world, since it cannot substitute for ability, and the object of recruitment is to catch at least a few able practitioners capable of energising the branch. This is, it goes without saying, quite the reverse of a job that can be done effectively by following set procedures. It requires knowledge and competence and attention to detail, but especially, in the old adage, inspiration and perspiration.

Whilst some of the necessary knowledge and competences are general to estate agency, much of it is local. Literally knowing the town or district street by street and the history of the prices at which properties have sold is essential to building up the capacity for intuitive valuation — knowing not only the rough value of a property, but how difficult it is likely to be to sell and the peculiarities of its submarket. And, of course, a detailed knowledge of the local economy, which also takes time to acquire, is valuable. The penalties of being cut off from this local knowledge can be dramatic, as the following example indicated:

> Ronald used to be based in [an adjacent town] ... very very successful there ... in terms of selling the stuff.... And he obviously had a great deal of local knowledge there. Then once we became part of the Beech Insurance Co. he didn't like the guy who was his immediately superior,

who came in above him ... and he said 'Get me out of here, please!' and we put him into [a branch] 40 miles away and he was there for ... maybe 12 months. It was a disaster.... The reason we put him there was so he would build it up, but he just wasn't able to. Without local knowledge, local contacts and a name which was new there ... he couldn't do anything at all. So eventually we took the view we would close the branch, which we did. We moved him to [a bigger town], where after a comparatively short period of time, because he had a much better surface knowledge of the area, and because the name of the company ... was well known ... and perceived to be one of the top three ... he was able to develop in a satisfactory way.

It is the coordination of this local knowledge with acquired competence and skills and enthusiasm about the job and putting oneself across to the public that creates the successful agent, at least in the view of agents. As one put it, 'If you don't enjoy it, if you just come to work and do your job and don't particularly enjoy it, you won't be a good estate agent'.

SALARIES, COMMISSIONS AND BONUSES

Almost all estate agents, usually up to a quite senior level if there is a management hierarchy and, of course, as partners, are paid on a combination of basic and performance-related pay. The latter may take the form of commission on sales, monthly or quarterly, bonuses based on the achievements of the individual, the branch or, in some of the corporates, a larger unit. In some instances, mostly in the corporates, small commissions were paid for financial services leads and obtaining instructions. Commission rates could also vary and increase once an individual had achieved a certain threshold of commission income for the business in the course of a year. In addition more senior staff and negotiators, and perhaps others too, would have a company car.

Pay — by which we mean here actual income achieved — varies considerably in estate agency from company to company and may also vary greatly as between individuals. The corporates have introduced pay scales and a more overtly structured personnel policy in all respects, but we still found that there could be differences approaching 100 per cent between corporates in the same town and that rates were often under the control of regional managers as part of their overall budget, rather than dicated by head office. Traditionally estate agency is sales driven and individualistic and this is reflected in payment systems. The classic model is of the individual starting business on his own with minimal support and expanding gradually by effective service and sales success. The staff then recruited are hired on an individual basis and are expected to work in the same way — though as we shall see below teamwork becomes increasingly important in larger branches. In good times — notably the boom period of housing construction and affluence and steadily rising prices from the late 1950s to the mid 1970s — estate agents have come into the market from a variety of backgrounds, qualified and unqualified, and made good.

It is perhaps because of this entrenched individualism and emphasis on results that there is no market monitoring of pay levels. The RICS initiated one after the slump in 1988–9 began to put increasing numbers of their members out of work, but these figures relate to the minority of agents with the top level of qualification, where most have none at all. We understand that *Estate Agency News* went some way to starting up a similar monitoring and reporting system, but abandoned it because of lack of support. Agents, although obviously they compare themselves with others in the same town, and most participate in quite extensive socialising and gossip networks, do not see their rates of pay by reference to externally identified scale-type yardsticks, we suggest. Rather they look to their evaluation within the business and whether they are being rewarded appropriately. If not, they will feel it right to point this out and, if the response is not satisfactory, to begin to look for a move. Pay is hence linked to the high mobility of labour in estate agency.

The other thing to be said here is that payment systems in independent agencies are constantly revamped, both by reference to the individual's performance and by reference to the market. Thus, when times are good, the commission element predominates and staff are expected to achieve a good income through sales. When the market slumps, however, it is impossible to achieve a reasonable income on a commission basis and the basic salary component is increased. One of the criticisms that we heard of corporates is that their payment systems tend to be less reactive to market conditions.

Finally it is worth recording our impression that if a general judgment on pay levels is to be attempted, it would suggest that they are not very high. There is a good deal of front to estate agency: the pleasantly furnished office, the besuited staff, the polished and, in the case of more successful staff, quite expensive cars. Behind this, however, lie income levels that do not compare favourably with, for instance, the staff of a solicitor's office, albeit that more of the latter are formally qualified. Incoming staff and front-line clerical and administrative staff may earn no more than £5,000–6,000 p.a. (at 1991 levels) and negotiators perhaps £11,000–15,000, though with more room for enhancing their earnings by commission. Partners and managers may, in the case of large agencies, take a considerable sum, especially in good years, but in some of the small agencies probably only £25,000–35,000, and in some cases less. Estate agency is, then, not, for the majority, a means to either wealth or great security. Downturns in the market result in severe labour shakeouts, the closing of branches and the ruthless thinning of staff in those remaining. The attraction of estate agency is hence in the nature of the job, the buzz of getting deals done, and a satisfaction from service to clients, rather than from the prospect of large incomes. Of course those agents who are successful and end up with three, four or a dozen branches, are modestly wealthy, though precariously so. A downturn in the market can easily decimate branches and greatly reduce the goodwill component in the value of the business. For this reason estate agency has always been subject to cyclical competition: new entrants arrive during booms and are weeded out in the ensuing slump, particularly if they have been unscrupulous and failed to establish a reputation for service and integrity.

PERCEPTIONS OF THE PUBLIC

Talk to any estate agent about the public and he or she will regale you with a stream of anecdotes about how obnoxious some of them are. One of the first that we were treated to as researchers was an account of the habit of some people doing a tea circuit on a Sunday afternoon — making appointments to view or just turning up at the properties and asking to see round for no better reason than that they had nothing better to do, liked nosing round other people's houses and usually got a cup of tea in the process. Such people had no intention of buying a property, we were told. Such stories may be unfair to the public of course. The people in question may indeed be less than committed to a purchase in the near future, but such prospecting may be an essential part of deciding where they are going to buy and what kind of property. From the agent's point of view, however, they are time wasters totally unappreciative of the value of the agent's time and often rude to boot.

Time wasting is an inevitable consequence of the system by which agents are paid, which forces them to cultivate purchasers as the means to earning their commission, but places no constraints whatever on the purchasers whom they are prospecting. Perhaps this is one reason why agents generally feel happy about using their relationship with the purchaser for the benefit of their vendor clients. The other problem, rudeness, we find more perplexing, but it is evidently widespread. Perhaps it derives from the confusion of the public in the face of the enormity of buying a property, the insecurity in the face of the agent, who seems to know what is what and is obviously in business to make a sale. We did, at any rate, find that the public can be abrasive, inconsiderate and downright rude for no expressed or obvious reason. There is, however, a sense, behind their irritation, among some agents that it is the public's fear of being taken advantage of that leads to rudeness:

People will come in, they won't acknowledge your smile or your greeting. Whether they are naturally rude or whether they are slightly nervous and they have got it into their heads that we are going to trap them into signing something . . . I think it's just a lack of manners basically.

It is that much easier to handle the whole thing because at the end of the day we are pulling for the purchasers all the way along because if they buy they earn their fees and we are there to make sure that the sale goes through without any problem. So really we are very keen for them to buy, we are very keen for their mortgage to go through without any problems and yes, we don't want some other estate agent importing our mortgages.
Q: So really you are the friendly face for the purchaser?
A: Yes, we are, but they don't all realise that. They all think we are trying to con them. It's really quite interesting. I suppose perhaps some people are. . . . We actually work for a building society. If I tried anything like that I would be out tomorrow.

These remarks from a manager in a corporate estate agency betray an awareness of and simultaneously a self-delusion about his relationship with his customers and clients. He openly admits that he wants purchasers to buy his properties and his mortgages and thereby double the organisation's business. His customers are pehaps wrong in believing he is trying to con them, but he is certainly trying to sign them up for enormous commitments as smoothly as possible, and is not about to give them objective advice on the merits of either his mortgages or his properties. Aggressiveness and hostility may well derive from the ambivalence of the estate agent's relations with purchasers and vendors described above, precipitated by the agent's eagerness to put him or herself across to the public and form a positive realtionship, a relationship which is perceived as being intended to ensnare rather than to enable. The secure and confident member of the public may be able to manage this with cordiality, whilst preserving inner reserve, whilst the less confident and organised may seek security in antagonism. The following example seems to illustrate this:

> The other day I was sitting writing and Marina was dealing with a woman whom I could see was trouble when she walked through the door. And she was really giving Marina a hard time. I think because Marina was young and flushes and hasn't got quite the experience yet to be able to be firm but polite. In the end I thought I've got to intervene. The woman said, 'This girl doesn't seem to know what I am looking for'. So I said to Marina, 'I'll deal with this lady. I wonder if you'd mind telling me what you're looking for.' 'Well anything.' 'Shall we start with the price?' 'Any price.' So I said fine, I went to the bottom drawer which is the most expensive and I said, 'We have got a really nice house here for £250,000'. 'Oh, I wouldn't spend as much as that.' So then we started to get down. But she was still very ungracious and when she went out in the end I heard her say to her husband 'You won't get much help in there'.

This agent admitted that politeness was more normal, and that this case was exceptional in its rudeness. It is notable, however, that no attempt was made to retaliate or even to draw attention to the customer's outrageous behaviour. It seems to be a universal maxim among agents that however offensive the public is, the agent continues to respond with politeness and decorum. The repeated experience does, however, produce some choice invective when agents are given the opportunity to vent their feelings, for example:

> The general public of this country are by far the most devious, fickle, unbelievable set of people you can ever come across! ... Why do sales fall through? Twenty-five per cent maybe just change their mind.... People just suddenly wake up one morning and say we are not going to move.

Another agent put it more kindly:

> There is nothing more frustrating for the agent than doing all the back-breaking work of getting the property on the market, showing people

over it, getting the offer in ... and then finding just before exchange of contracts the vendor or purchaser have changed their mind and then you have lost it. Because you have put all the work and effort in by then, you have put a lot of time into it. That's where our money is involved, that's where our expense is.

Thus although estate agents may express hurt, resentment and anger at the public, — 'It's not the public that need to be looked after by these [regulatory] bodies it's the estate agents who need protection against the public' — and although a general increase in consumerism in recent years was widely remarked upon; although the public's standards of morality were widely seen to have declined recently, especially in the 1980s, with people failing to honour agreements, whether to sell, to buy, or simply to keep an appointment to view; despite all these features of the changing world in which estate agents operate, much of the problems they have with the public can be seen to derive from structural features of their relationship with them. The agent is paid only by the vendor and only at sale. It is scarcely surprising, then, that their time and services get taken advantage of by purchasers, and by vendors who want nothing more than a free valuation for the purposes of a private sale — a habit widely complained of. Given the ambivalence of the relationship with vendor and purchaser and the conscious attempt to form a bond with both parties, and to achieve ascendency in managing the situation and brokering a deal that we have described above, it is understandable and indeed desirable that the public should be cautious, particularly given widespread ignorance and lack of experience. In addition the English legal system of property transfer, which is adversarial and delays commitment until exchange of contracts, provides ample space for backing off and messing up. Finally, as agents recognise, moving home is an emotionally fraught experience for many people, the financial consequences of which, as recent years have seen, can be quite devastating if they go wrong. Recent estimates are that about two million households have negative equity in their properties after buying at the peak of the boom, and repossessions are now a matter of public concern.

Not all agents are insensitive to these points or to how long-term business reputation can benefit from being sensitive to the customer:

I try to give the best possible advice, even though it might not be the best financial advice from our company's point of view, in that, if somebody turns round and says 'Look, I want to put this on the market, I want to sell it', and then their circumstances change and you can see that they really don't want to sell it any longer, I have turned round to some clients and said, 'Look you don't really want to do this do you?' And they have said, 'No'. So I said, 'Well, why don't we just take it off the market?' 'It's worried me that you have done all this work and you have spent all this time with me and I was worried what your reaction would be. I am glad you suggested it, I would like to take it off.' That's fine, because it's good PR, and if they ever come to sell again they'll be more confident to come back to me and say, 'Look you advised me correctly, and I was happy with that'.

Perhaps the most pointed case of each side accusing the other of malpractice is gazumping. Although this was not a problem during the research period, mention of abuses almost invariably prompted a vehement account of how it is vendors who gazump and agents who get the blame:

> When I started work people's word was their bond; now people's word means perhaps £250. They will change houses, transactions, for as little money as that, regardless of what I or any one else says to them. And of course the agent representing the vendor is bound by law to get the best possible price for a property and *has* to report to his client any offers that are received. We can *advise* the client on how to deal with those offers, but at the end of the day it is the client who, usually, these days, tells us what he wants to do.... I have always taken the view that you must at least give the first party the opportunity to match or better that bid ... but it is surprising these days how many clients will not even do that.... They then use the agent as the person to blame, because the first party obviously plays hell with the agent and the client will say, 'Oh, the agent told me to do that'.

Gazumping is a difficult problem, which has its costs in the delays before the vendor is committed under English law, though it can be minimised by good practice as suggested here; and as other agents pointed out, it tends to be self-denying anyway, because in the rising market that makes it possible, the cost of the property to be purchased may well also rise during the delay to take on the new purchaser.

The only real abuses by the public that we came across, other than attempts by dealers to obtain properties at less than their value described by Malcolm Devon, were those described in the sketch of Guildhams, the backhanders or 'drinks' offered for the agent's undertaking to secure the sale of a property to a keen purchaser. Sometimes this could involve the agent in undervaluing:

> If it was on at £45,000 they would come in and say, 'Well I will buy it and I'll give you £42,000 and there's a thousand in it for you'.

The abuse here appears to occur in the Midlands as well as in the South of England. A related form of deviousness was cited by Guildhams:

> Perhaps a chap is going broke and selling the property for £100,000 and he owes the bank £110,000. Rather than, as the money comes through it goes straight to the bank, the guy says we'll put it through the books at £105,000 and I'll give you five grand so that you can put that in your pocket to get you going again. And that might stitch a deal together at a slightly lower price as well.

The agent here made it clear that he turned a blind eye to such practices.

Probably the best overall judgment on the public as a source of trouble for agents came from this senior agent in the North of England:

The problems are, I think, twofold. A lot of the problems are at the very bottom of the market where it is ignorance of the law, ignorance of the procedures and therefore in part it is probably our fault for not imparting the knowledge. Although it is very difficult because, as you know, you can actually tell people in the house exactly what's going to happen and how much of that do they retain? You can tell them and give them a leaflet and you might double that, but there is still 60 per cent which is going to whistle out of the window. And when you are dealing with some of the inner city stuff I think the leaflet you gave them probably goes straight in the bin.

The other problem is right at the top end of the market, where you are dealing with some equally astute and sharp people who are up to every trick in the book, because that is how they have got there in the first place. So that's where you can expect problems sometimes. The chap living in this semi in suburbia has probably moved from a terraced house originally, so he has moved once or twice, or maybe even three times. He knows what it is all about, he knows the procedures, he knows what to expect and what we do for our money and what we don't do for our money. As he, in the past, has probably been the bulk of the business it has not been a problem.

ABUSES

We have made it clear earlier in this book that we did not conduct our research with the objective of tracking down instances of abuse. Rather we have sought to understand the circumstances in which estate agents operate and their view of their work. It is this that we have attempted to convey to the reader in this and the previous chapters. We detail below information on some abuses that came to our attention during the research, though, as expected, we did not observe any of them taking place directly. The principal area of abuse that we did identify and which agents were ready, and indeed eager to discuss as a problem, was that arising out of competition. What is of interest in this connection is that estate agency appears to be structurally unstable, such that whatever the solution attempted to dealing with competition, there are pressures to one form of abuse or another. We can explain this as follows.

Nearly all estate agents emphasised that their objective is to give good-quality service to their clients, which means also some expenditure on advertising, boards, preparation of details and mailing, together with time for the agent to market the property actively — to ring potential purchasers and suggest they view, call back viewers and get their reactions, report back to vendors and so on. This in turn means that the staff of an office can run a list of a given size which they can service adequately and which should, as a result, turn over regularly. In an ideal world most agents would like to compete solely on the basis of quality of service to clients, which they identify as their professional contribution, and to be able to rely on the reputation which that generates to maintain the flow of new instructions. A number of agents reported to us with satisfaction stories of clients returning to them because of satisfaction with service provided in the past.

Difficulties arise in several respects, however. An agency which begins to lack an adequate list of properties is in danger of serious disadvantage; that agency's presence in the street through for sale boards is less evident; its press advertisements look thin, and enquirers cannot be offered much of a choice of properties within their price range. The usual remedy for this problem is to seek more introductions by overvaluing properties. Even though some clients will respond to a reasoned and accurate valuation, where evidence of comparability is offered and warnings given about a property failing to sell if it is overpriced and acquires a negative image in the market, many vendors are tempted by a confident overvaluation. Since valuation is an art not a science, and is accepted to be accurate only within a range of plus or minus 10 per cent , even when undertaken professionally rather than, as here, as marketing advice, there is no remedy to overvaluing. It is, however, an abuse of the client undertaken to serve the agent's interest in building up a list and with the clear expectation that the vendor can be pressured over time to drop the price. In a falling market, with vendors reluctant to acknowledge the extent of price falls, and agents under pressure from them to overvalue, the agent who is looking to increase a list is particularly prone to this abuse. We found it to be very widespread and as characteristic of the corporates, where it was clearly deliberate policy for a period to increase listings, as it was of independents.

The alternative means of increasing competitive advantage is of course commission cuts, but here agents were very aware that they were in danger of cutting their own throats. Overvaluation is a hidden issue since unless the property has been inspected, an inflation of 10 per cent or so in the price, enough to obtain instructions, is not evident immediately. A reduction in commission is normally across the board and only works if it is publicised. Rate cutting, however, means that more sales have to be made to generate the same income, which in turn means less attention to each client and a less professional service and so lack of satisfaction all round. Once again rate cutting can be countered with reasoned argument, and some agents took advantage of their strength and reputation — Guildhams has been cited earlier as an example — to say plainly that they are not the cheapest but that they do provide a good service.

Over time changes in the state of the market stimulate rate changes and all agents accepted that the faster properties in general sell the lower rates will go. For this reason a number of agents expressed unhappiness with the boom period, when rates fell to 1 per cent and lower, because competition for rapid sales was strong, client pressure was strong, little time would be given to clients and purchasers and everyone was frantically scrambling for money. Some even suggested that income was no better or worse during the boom than in the slumps because of this. By the time of our research, rates had settled around the 2 per cent mark, though with considerable variation, up to 3 per cent and down to 1 per cent in localities, as a result of rate cutting by some and as a reflection of differing forms of contract — multiple as against sole agency for example. In any given locality, however, there was nearly always a central or normal rate which reflected the level of activity in the local market. Unusual properties might attract a special rate and this was accepted. The corporates, in particular, would offer discounts if a purchase went through them as well, because of the additional chance of financial services commission. The central standard rate, however, was usually well recognised and there was clearly a powerful incentive to stabilise it as much as possible, to maximise income and to ensure the ability to offer a service of adequate quality. This amounts, of course, to saying that estate agency tends inherently towards local cartels, and indeed we believe this to be the case. Curiously it is the one form of competitive abuse that has been attacked seriously, with court action having been taken against some estate agents by the OFT for operating local commission agreements.[1] The OFT confirmed to us that it does receive complaints about estate agents organising local commission agreements. Apart from the difficulty of proving the existence of such an agreement, the Office's experience is that local cartels are normally abandoned as soon as members become aware of the OFT's interest.

Evidence of the tendency to local cartels was widespread in the local recognition of a standard rate and in the concern of agents not to be drawn into a rate-cutting war and hence a desire 'not to rock the boat'. Agents' perceptions were that part of their poor image with the public was that they were often thought of as getting a lot of money for nothing, that the public realise neither the extent of an agent's efforts on behalf of a client nor the fact that income only comes from sales commission paid by vendors which, hence, subsidises both purchasers and vendors who withdraw their properties. The public was hence likely to be attracted, at least to some extent, by rate cutting, especially if accompanied by judicious over valuation, even though neither were in the client's interest, since they would lead to properties being less effectively marketed.

The establishment of formal cartels is less common, but by no means unusual. We came across one case where it was striking, not that the cartel existed and that we got to know about it, but that agents were quite open about it and discussed it solely in terms of the difficulties of making it work: 'We have got an agreement at the moment throughout the agents that we stick at 2 per cent , but all it takes is one person to start deviating from that'. The speaker worked for a corporate estate agency and it was clear that all seven local agents were party to this agreement, corporates and independents. It is the fact that all our contacts were open that leads us to conclude that such arrangements are not seen as exceptional. As explained already, cartels are seen as a means to maintaining quality service not an abuse of the public. In this case one agent was breaking the agreement by offering 1.5 per cent and it was made clear that where evidence of this was uncovered the matter would be pursued and complaints made to the agent to enforce the agreement.

---

[1] See *Estate Agents Act 1979: A Review by the Director General of Fair Trading*, Office of Fair Trading, December, 1988, para. 1.8, p. 3.

This locality also pointed up the status of cartels because the agents were subject to competition by an outsider engaging, in other agent's views, in far more serious abuses, though his practices were probably not illegal. This interloper, a one-man operation, was not merely cutting rates sharply to 0.9 per cent , which the others said was simply uneconomic, but also touting for business by calling on vendors identifiable by for sale boards, and offering to sell their house for £500 flat rate. He also had a habit of knocking down the boards of his competitors and paying people on main roads £5 to put up a for sale board to increase his presence in the locality — all time-honoured touting abuses. He was also said to put undue pressure on vendors and purchasers to reach an agreement. In this case one of the agents subjected to touting took his revenge:

> One of the agents went round with a form saying 'I will sell your house for £500', and put it through all the agents' doors with a board. That certain agent arranged to get hold of one of these copies which said 'I will sell your house for £500' and put it back through all the letter-boxes of the agent who started it.

The interloper was hence forced to offer his special terms of £500 even to his existing clients whom he had signed up at 0.9 per cent .

A similar problem of aggressive touting and fee cutting was complained of by Langfords, where an ex insurance salesman was said to be offering a fixed fee of £250 + VAT, calling on houses with boards up and attempting to ensure a sale by undervaluing. Touting in these extreme forms was seen by established agents as thoroughly reprehensible, because such cost cutting could only lead to success if accompanied by abuse of clients. Touting itself is, as we have seen in chapter 3, a form of competition between agents which is seen as the most serious form of unprofessional conduct.

Competitive pressures mean that touting is not confined to those attempting to get a foothold in estate agency. The manager of a corporate agency in the area with the cartel complained that the manager of another corporate agency, an RICS member and former partner in an independent bought up by the corporate, had been sending touting letters to the clients of other agents. When he complained and pointed out that the letter contained no disclaimer, as required by RICS rules, to the effect that if another member agent had already been instructed please disregard the letter, the agent responded that 'I am ashamed of myself, but I have to do it on a three-month trial period' as a result of a decision by the corporate management to increase the agency's listings.

Whatever else may be said about these various abuses arising from competition, we think the following two points bear consideration. First, competitive pressures seem clearly to make local estate agency unstable in its practices and to detract from its aspiration to provide good service. Second, these destabilising effects evidently divert estate agents' attention from what they should be doing — servicing their clients. This is not a simple plea for cartels but it is a claim that the consequences of cartels are by no means entirely negative, particularly in comparison with the alternative means of arranging competition.

What of other abuses? We came across four or five, some of which have been referred to earlier in this chapter. Two effectively involved dealing in properties whilst also acting as an agent, sometimes personally, sometimes with a builder. In one instance a corporate agent said he knew that an agent in the area was dealing: 'Buying properties yourself when you have taken on the property, you have valued it, you have put the price on it and then you buy it'. Whilst she found this outrageous, she had no hard evidence with which to make a complaint and also seemed at a loss to know to whom she might effectively complain. A similar abuse appeared to have been un-covered by another corporate agency, where a financial adviser looked as though he was dealing in properties using the resources (mortgages) of the corporate. He was dismissed after an internal inquiry. How widespread self-dealing is we are unable to determine. It is an abuse that has long been complained of and is clearly now recognised as such and hence driven underground.

Rather nearer the surface is a related abuse, where an agent works with a builder to sell a property at below value. Here, because a genuine third party is involved, the need for subterfuge is less, though the damage to the client through undervaluation can be just as severe. Instances of this were confirmed by staff in two corporates in the North of England in different areas:

> There are firms that will knowingly undervalue a house and ... work with a builder, because they know that the builder will buy it at a cheaper rate. They know that the builder will then spend x pounds on it, but they also know that there will be a chance that they will then be instructed by that builder when the house is improved.

The other source gave an example of just this taking place to the clear disadvantage of the client.

Another abuse of which we had a single example, but one illustrative of how the vulnerable can be taken advantage of, was the result of over-valuation. It involved an elderly couple and a property initially listed for £103,000 but dropped to £95,000 later, though our informant had seen it and valued it at £85,000:

> These people offered £93,000 and were literally conned into it, because they were desperate, because he was not well and there was all sorts of things. They must have a bungalow on the level, so they sold up their home and they [withdrew] ... all their savings and took this bungalow.

It emerged that the couple had been pressured into making their offer by a false claim that there was another bidder in competition with them. Such stories, which clearly distressed our informant, exemplify the vulnerability of purchasers if they are not knowledgeable and robust.

The abuses revealed by Guildhams have already been described and are primarily the responsibility of clients and purchasers rather than the agents, though as one of the agents, Langfords, remarked of the offering of backhanders to the agent to fix the sale of a property, if people keep offering the bribes, there must be takers somewhere. That Guildhams themselves were willing to allow the wheeler-dealer attitude to lead them to connive at illegality is demonstrated by the attitude to a fraud upon the creditors of a bankrupt. As described earlier, they came across cases where deals were booked at a lower figure when the proceeds of the sale would go to the creditors and the difference transferred in cash to the bankrupt vendor: 'So you can put that in your pocket to get you going again'. When asked what their attitude to this was, the reply was:

> I don't want to know, don't want to hear ... let them get on with it. ... I am not going to risk my client's deal. I'll just charge a fee on the amount that officially goes through the books.

Whether such attitudes were developed as a result of working in a wheeler-dealer culture with a good many 'foreigners and Jews' whose business habits they clearly held in contempt or whether they were present from an earlier time, we cannot tell. What was evident was that it was not just the public who could be characterised as wheeler-dealers.

SEVEN

The Corporates and Estate Agency: Issues and Conflicts

In a number of readily evident ways the buying up of more or less extensive networks of estate agencies by financial institutions in the latter 1980s has transformed English estate agency. This will be documented here and in Chapter 8. We evaluate some of the implications of the changes and assess how radical the transformation is likely to be in the longer term. We also question the compatibility of the financial institutions, as vast corporations, with the practice of residential agency, and in doing so further highlight what we believe to be its essential features. In undertaking this analysis we shall also identify the conflicts of interest that the coming of the corporates has occasioned and the regulatory problems these pose, as well as the potential for better standards of conduct that may arise.

The broad outlines of the corporate takeovers are dramatic and well documented by Hennebury and Khan (Working Paper 5). Table 7.1 shows the position in 1982 before the takeovers began. Although it was not unknown for outside interests to own estate agents before this date, it is clear, first, that existing holdings were modest, at least in 1982, and second, that the size of estate agency chains was relatively small, with only two exceeding 40 branches. Black Horse agencies (Lloyds Bank) began buying the following year and immediately took the head of the field with 104 branches in 1983 and 160 in 1984, 218 in 1985 and 219 in 1986, when it was joined by Hambro, who took the lead with 350 agencies. The following three years saw what is now recognised as a gadarene rush by the other financial institutions to produce the outcome presented in Table 7.2. By this time only a few independents remain, notably Connells, itself since taken over by Scottish Widows Insurance in September 1990, and enhanced by the acquisition of 99 of the Prudential's western region offices in February 1991. The growth in Connells during the period is itself worthy of note: a network of 135 branches in 1982 would have made it by far the largest agency.

Table 7.1 Twenty largest residential estate agents in 1982

Position	Agent	Type	Number of offices
1	Mann & Co.	Independent	91
2	Fox & Sons	Independent	62
3	Andrews & Partners	Independent	37
4	Reeds Rains	Independent	35
5	Gascoigne-Pees	Independent	34
6	Bairstow Eves	Independent	32
7	William H. Brown	Independent	31
8	Allen & Harris	Independent	30
9	Connells	Independent	28
10	Whiteheads	Independent	27
11	Pearsons	Independent	22
11	Whitegates	Independent	22
13	A.C. Frost & Co.	Independent	20
14	Entwistle Green	Independent	18
14	Oystons	Independent	18
14	Watsons	Independent	18
17	James Abbott	Independent	16
17	Bridges	Independent	16
17	Cubitt & West	Independent	16
17	Brian Morton & Co.	Independent	16
All			589

Source: J. Henneberry and F. Khan, *The Restructuring of Residential Estate Agencies*, Working Paper 5, Centre for Economic and Social Research, Sheffield City Polytechnic, 1990, Appendix A, drawing on *Chartered Surveyor Weekly*.

Table 7.2   Twenty largest residential estate agents in 1989

Position	Agent	Type	Number of offices
1	Prudential Property Services	Insurance company	805
2	Royal Life Estates	Insurance company	803
3	GA Property Services	Insurance company	612
4	Halifax Estate Agencies	Building society	564
5	Black Horse Agencies	Bank	551
6	Nationwide Anglia	Building society	520
7	Hambro Countrywide	Bank	510
8	Abbey National Cornerstone	Building society	388
9	Hamptons	Financial services company	160
10	TSB Property Service	Bank	144
11	Connells	Independent	135
12	Property Leeds	Building society	127
13	Hogg Robinson	Insurance company	115
14	Whitegates	Financial services company	102
15	Park Estates	Independent	74
16	Bristol & West	Building society	63
17	Hanover Druce	Financial services company	60
18	Parkers	Independent	52
18	Pioneer Mutual Estate	Independent	52
20	Consolidated Term	Independent	52
All			5,889

Source: Henneberry and Khan, op. cit., drawing on the National Association of Estate Agents

Table 7.3 Branch offices controlled by the 20 largest residential estate agents 1982 to 1989

Branch offices controlled by residential estate agencies by type of company: number and (percentage)

Year	Independent	Bank	Building society	Financial services company	Solicitor	Insurance company	Row totals
1982	589 (100)	– –	– –	– –	– –	– –	589 (100)
1983	718 (84.86)	104 (12.29)	– –	24 (2.83)	– –	– –	846 (100)
1984	860 (84.31)	160 (15.68)	– –	– –	– –	– –	1,020 (100)
1985	958 (77.69)	218 (17.68)	– –	57 (4.62)	– –	– –	1,233 (100)
1986	644 (43.51)	569 (38.44)	– –	95 (6.41)	– –	172 (11.62)	1,480 (100)
1987	730 (21.93)	812 (24.39)	638 (19.17)	263 (7.09)	– –	912 (27.40)	3,328 (100)
1988	858 (16.88)	1,119 (22.01)	1,414 (27.82)	299 (5.88)	– –	1,392 (27.39)	5,082 (100)
1989	480 (8.15)	1,205 (20.46)	1,662 (28.22)	322 (5.46)	– –	2,220 (37.69)	5,889 (100)

Source: Chartered Surveyor Weekly, *League Table of Agents* 1982–1988; National Association of Estate Agents, *League Table of Agents* 1989 in Henneberry and Khan, op. cit., Table 1

We did not have time to conduct detailed research on the takeover process, which was largely complete by the time our work began. Table 7.3 identifies the distribution of acquiring networks by type of financial institution. Certain facts were widely acknowledged about the process, however, even by those who had cause to rue them. The objective of the takeovers was to secure market share for the sale of financial services products by routing sales through estate agencies and picking up mortgage and endowment and other insurance business. At the same time it was held that the agencies themselves were and could remain profitable and hence constituted a sound investment. Many of the buyers were demonstrably wrong on both counts. It has proved much harder to obtain additional sales through estate agencies than anticipated by the financial institutions, and the venture has led to antagonism at property transactions being made conditional on financial services packages being taken up — a practice which is now outlawed by the OFT. The wider concept of 'one-stop property shopping', which seemed to be in prospect with proposals to liberalise the regulation of conveyancing and to allow the institutions to offer the service in-house has been set back by the government's failure to enact the necessary reforms, and by solicitors' response to the challenge by specialisation, cooperation, and improved efficiency and pricing.

At the same time the institutions failed to recognise the cyclical nature of the property market and were hit doubly hard by the slump after 1988. In the first place they found themselves with more branches than they could do profitable business with, and in the second they realised that, in the rush to buy, a good many poor agencies had been taken on including, in some cases, branches which had only been opened a few weeks earlier in order to increase the value of the sell-out. Heavy losses were thus sustained both on a capital and trading profit basis. As is widely known, a period of retrenchment started in 1989–90, exemplified most dramatically by the Prudential, which sold its entire chain, producing the result outlined in table 7.4. By this time there were a few large buyers still in the market, but most of the corporates were still shedding branches. Such figures on results as the parent bodies were willing to divulge showed a continuing pattern of losses. An indication of the level of losses sustained by those who would not divulge the information publicly was provided by Harry Hill, head of Hambro Countrywide: 'It is fairly well accepted that every other major group has lost in excess of £100m in the past five years' (*The Times*, 10 May 1993, p. 20). A specific example is provided by the Abbey National. It bought into estate agency in order to secure its position, given that half its mortgage business was introduced by estate agents. As a latecomer in the rush it paid premium prices for a large number (112) of businesses, which it rebranded into Cornerstones estate agents. They never produced more than 5 per cent of the Abbey's mortgage business before the 347 branch network was sold for £8m in 1993 for a loss of £250m since 1987. The Abbey National was joined in ditching estate agency as a mistake by the Prudential and the Nationwide by 1993, but others with major national networks such as the Royal, the Halifax, General Accident and the Woolwich remained committed. Even in these cases, however, severe retrenchment involved the disclosure of evident

Table 7.4 League table of residential estate agency offices

League rating 1991	1990	Estate agency group	Number of outlets 31 December 1991	Change over year	Pre-tax result (£m)
1	(2)	Royal Life Estates	584	−34	−20.0
2	(1)	Halifax Property Services	565	−57	−6.6
3	(4)	Hambro Countrywide	486	+13	−8.3
4	(3)	GA Property Services	434	−66	−17.8
5	(5)	Black Horse Agencies	397	−53	−1.4
6	(7=)	Nationwide Estate Agents	378	−22	
7	(6)	Cornerstone Estate Agents	373	−54	−19.0
8	(7=)	Woolwich Property Services	314	+194	−30.9
9	(9)	Legal & General (including Whitegates)	270	−68	−6.3
10	(14)	Connell Estate Agents	171	+68	
11	(12)	Bristol & West (including Hamptons)	158	−15	
12	(11)	TSB Property Services	144	−39	
13	(–)	Arun Estate Agents	115	+115	0.0
14	(13)	Property Leeds	100	−12	
15	(16)	Reeds Rains	99	−1	
16	(17)	London & Manchester Agency Services	93	−2	
17	(15)	Alliance & Leicester Property Services	92	−8	−7.8
18	(19)	Chancellors (formerly Hogg Robinson)	88	+13	
19	(18)	Northern Rock Property Services	79	−8	
20	(20)	Birmingham Midshires Property Services	71	−1	

Source: *Estate Agency News*, UBS Phillips & Drew

Table 7.5 Interrelationship between branch office distribution and housing market structure (large agents)

Region	% Branch offices large agents	% Owner-occupied housing stock	% Market value of housing stock	% Residential conveyances	% Value of transactions	% Building society loans (number)	% Building society loans (value)
North	5.39	5.38	2.89	4.63	2.59	7.18	5.24
Yorkshire and Humberside	6.13	9.35	5.35	7.29	4.60	11.34	8.21
East Midlands	6.13	8.09	5.44	7.74	5.41	8.84	7.17
East Anglia	4.28	4.23	3.97	3.95	3.68	4.37	4.40
South East	40.93	34.72	58.70	40.73	56.83	32.15	44.13
South West	13.70	10.50	10.40	11.02	11.23	9.89	10.19
West Midlands	9.13	9.86	7.86	9.04	6.10	9.89	8.09
North West	19.40	12.43	7.26	10.96	6.80	11.86	9.15

Source: Hanneberry and Khan op. cit., Table 6 and Appendix C.

Note: Data on housing stock are for England and Wales but those for estate agents are for England. Wales has been omitted from this Table.

failures. The Royal bought 25per cent of a Midlands chain in 1986 and injected capital to expand it from 62 to 250 offices. In 1988 it decided to take full control, spending about £300,000 per office and a total of £90m. In 1993 the original owner of the chain went into partnership with another agent who had also sold out to the Royal and with the backing of Provident Life, a new player in the market, bought the Abbey's Cornerstone chain for £8m or £23,000 per office (*The Independent on Sunday*, Business, 22 August, 1993, pp. 6-7). Some of the financial institutions have thus decided that estate agency is not for them, others have rationalised their networks and have expanded; others still have entered the market for the first time recently. The process of adjustment is likely to continue for some years yet.

Of the initial strategy, however, there is little doubt. As table 7.5 shows, the buying patterns of the corporates were closely associated with the stock of owner-occupied dwellings, the market value of housing stock, the number of residential conveyances, the value of these transactions, the number of building society mortgage advances and their value, and the distribution of all these regionally. These factors are of course themselves closely connected. What they demonstrate is that within the broad objectives of establishing national or major regional networks, the corporates went where the action is. It is our view that when they took stock of the results of their buying spree they were confronted with a series of issues that they had not properly reflected upon and with which they were still grappling at the time of our research. We looked at several branches, and in one case two regions, of three corporate agencies and talked to senior management in these and other corporate networks. We were thus able to identify how the problems arising were being dealt with and the strategies and tactics adopted in each case and the response to them at front-line and more senior levels. We shall review the three corporates, two with national networks, one insurance based, the other building society based, and the last building society based with a regional bias, in chapter 8. First, however, we will outline some of the main issues that the corporates confronted following their rapid acquisition of estate agencies. We begin with issues which are clearly those of transition, move on to those that have to be addressed but are likely to be resolved eventually, and conclude with those that are most intractable. We shall then present a simple model of the options available for the relations between financial institutions and their estate agencies in order to bring into focus an analysis of the situation of where the corporates now find themselves. With this as background we shall then go on in chapter 8 to look at each of the corporates we researched, to see how it has addressed the problem and opportunities, and with what success.

As we shall see, the way in which issues have developed for the corporates has given rise to a series of dilemmas and responses, some of them reflecting the history, strategy and tactics of the individual corporate. We think it is helpful therefore to begin by reviewing the problems facing the corporates generally as a result of going with estate agency. This will have the added benefit of pointing the way to the principal dilemmas of corporate estate agency and the alternative solutions to them, which will provide a context in which to understand the practice and experience of individual agencies. The following account of the issues makes no pretence to being definitive, but it does provide a guide to understanding the experience of the corporates.

The period of acquisition, although relatively intensive for most of the corporates, spanned two or three years. It was accompanied by a number of cold starts of new branches in a good many cases, all of this taking place during a sustained boom in house prices. As a result the number of estate agency outlets rose from around 15,000 offices and 60,000 employees in 1986 to 19,000 offices and 100,000 employees in 1989. The purchase price of outlets' goodwill was £150,000–500,000 during the boom, but this collapsed subsequently to as low as £20,000 in 1991. Strategy at this stage may be identified as (a) keeping up with the opposition and doing whatever they do for fear of being left behind, on the assumption that long-term market share of their primary products (financial services) was at stake; and (b) attempting to transform estate agency into a corporate product, taking advantage of established corporate identities and creating national or strong regional chains. The ultimate objective here was to marginalise the independent sector and in doing so transform the image of estate agency which, the corporates recognised, was widely held by the public to be dubious. The critical period of acquisition was hence likely to involve considerable turmoil. The market was hectic, the corporates were generally seen as having deep pockets and substantial ignorance about estate agency, and were derided for their willingness to buy up less reputable agencies as well as those with good names.

The latter 1980s seem to have been a very confused period for the corporates. The real skills of estate agency were largely unseen, as properties sold very rapidly at ever-increasing prices. The corporates could therefore afford to recruit new, inexperienced staff who could still process houses and sales, and could also comfort themselves that, since the agencies were all profitable, the extent of successful sales of financial services was not an immediate issue. Besides, there were few constraints on making take-up of financial services a condition of buying the property. Pressure was exercised by staff from the corporate parents, staff from the estate agencies acquiesced and newly hired staff complied eagerly in what became derided by career estate agents, especially in the independents, as the white socks and earrings period, a reference to the unqualified brash young staff hired by the corporates, who were viewed as neither competent nor scrupulous.

Adjustment would clearly be necessary regardless of the state of the market. The takeover of several chains in a locality produced inevitable duplication and branch rationalisation was called for. Estate agency has a high labour turnover which was bound to be raised by the advent of the corporates — not all staff relished the prospect of a corporate hierarchy. Where partners in the acquired agencies had been integrated into the corporate agency, they needed training and time to adjust to the corporate culture and practices. Decisions on branding and the identity of the corporate chain had to be taken: was the name of old and respected firms to be preserved, was all to be submerged under the corporate brand image, or was there to be some compromise?

The downturn in the market in 1988–9 increased the speed and vigour of the shake-out, leading ultimately to the withdrawal of some of the corporates. Corporate managements were rapidly jolted out of their complacency and forced to retrench, closing branches, purging staff and introducing strict cost controls. This only accentuated the pressures consequent upon the second of the two general strategies, the creation of something distinctive in corporate estate agency. A series of issues had rapidly to be confronted in the early 1990s, all bearing upon the relationships between a financial institution and its estate agency arm. Such matters as contracts, personnel policy, training, promotion, salaries and bonuses were all established for the parent body, but could not be applied wholesale to estate agents, whose work is different and who traditionally had little or any of this in a formalised way, each employee constantly negotiating his or her own position, by moving to another agency if necessary, and with a career peak as a partner in an agency. The corporates were aware that this had to be dealt with, but had no clear idea of how — or rather industry mythology now has it that one, the Prudential, did have a clear idea, and it was wrong.

The Prudential — how fairly we cannot say, but it was a widely asserted criticism — made the mistake of overcentralisation and heavy branding, the imposition of standard procedures for everything and little local autonomy. The object was to produce a standardised service which is reliable (from the public's point of view), marketable as such, and checkable and trainable (from the corporate's point of view). This underestimated the distinctiveness of estate agency and its localism, and the individualism of estate agents. This point was widely reiterated by corporate management in the phrase that 'of course estate agency is a cottage industry'. This blurs two points, first that estate agency services are delivered in their totality at local level, unlike financial services; and secondly that estate agency services are dependent on the needs and interests of vendors and purchasers and the idiosyncrasies of properties, and are not very amenable to standardisation. Indeed recognising and responding to the distinctiveness of each situation might be identified as one of the chief qualities of the competent agent.

How then, from the vantage point of the corporate parent were staff to be selected, evaluated, rewarded or trained? How, if at all, were their careers to be related to those in the parent bureaucracy? One attractive option was to seek to identify appropriate training and standards of competence, which would have the simultaneous benefits of clarifying what corporate estate agency is and requires, so indicating to those who want none of it that they should leave, and of providing a route for integration and advancement for those who wanted to adapt. Further, it should serve to secure the reliability and standards of service that the corporates generally saw as the substance behind the powerful brand image. For this reason the corporates have devoted considerable effort and resources to internal training and have been active in working with others, including the professional bodies, to develop the national vocational qualifications in estate agency which began to come on stream in 1992. In addition, the corporates created the OCEA Ombudsman scheme, guaranteeing compensation of up to £100,000 to complainants, as a token of their commitment to high standards and as a means of controlling staff, since failure to meet the standards required by the OCEA code can result in disciplinary action (NVQ and OCEA are considered fully in chapter 11).

It soon became clear, however, that achieving adequate training, competence and compliance presupposed that the corporates knew what their objectives were, that is, had a clear understanding of the distinctive character of corporate estate agency. The problem was and is that they do not. The example of the Prudential stands as a warning against over-assimilation, yet equally the corporates were unwilling simply to see estate agencies as investments to be run at arm's length — they might get up to things that would tarnish the good name of the parent, and in any case one principal object was to use them to market the financial services of the parent. In practice two other mechanisms became more powerful levers for achieving the necessary purchase upon the new acquisitions: targets and accounting controls.

Accounting controls have become familiar both in the private and in the public sectors in the 1980s as a means of containing costs in an inflationary environment. Because they require the identification of appropriate cost centres within which to allocate a budget, they acted in the corporate estate agents to stimulate further the process of creating a structural relationship between the parent corporation and the estate agency business, and in establishing uniformity of organisation with estate agency. The advantage of accounting controls, given the uncertainty of the corporates as to how far to attempt to integrate estate agency, is that costs can be contained by allocating an overall budget, whilst allowing considerable local autonomy in its expenditure. In practice this autonomy was secured, in the examples we investigated, by the establishment of the very rough equivalent of local estate agency chains, which were constituted as budget centres and which formed part of the regional structure. In all three cases that we looked at, this structure was achieved only as the outcome of painful experience and forced recognition that 'estate agency is different' and essentially local in its operation. Centralised control even at regional level tended to be too distant and impersonal. Once local budget centres were set up, the relationship of branches to them could be negotiated — some branches were larger and busier than others, some took more responsibility for financial services; they were in turn allocated budgets.

We did not investigate the accounting systems used in detail, taking them rather at the level at which they impinged upon front-line staff and first-level management (although we also spoke to senior management about the problems of implementing the changes). It was widely remarked that one of the errors made by the Prudential was suddenly to ban local press advertising and insist on the use only of the Pru's own property paper. This was an example of overcentralisation and budgetary intervention which was wrong, it was said, not because it was necessarily inappropriate, but rather because it was bound to be inappropriate to some local situations. Local management needed the freedom to respond quickly to local conditions —

indeed this freedom and flexibility, together with considerably smaller overheads because of the lack of an infrastructure involving a corporate parent, were seen to be the principal competitive advantages of the independents.

Whilst global budgets and 'the bottom line' might be the ultimate bases for decision-making and profitability, they were seen to be too crude for month-to-month decision-making. They failed to recognise the difficulties of local branches or areas — the property market is notoriously local in its variations, with a few streets or a village becoming fashionable and other patches declining, besides the wider impact of the arrival and departure of major employers in an area. Further, global budgets failed to take account of individuals, both as achievers and as fixed costs. As fixed costs it might be, for example, that a branch had a poor apparent profit record because it had a staff structure that was expensive and effectively serviced other branches in the area, whilst one of the smaller branches had a more favourable staff structure, dominated by part-timers, and young full-timers which made it easy to seem profitable. When put in the context of a constantly changing market, and a long-term strategy of building a brand image and a local reputation which would secure repeat custom, profit and loss in simple accounting terms could seem a hard discipline, exercised by impersonal bureaucrats far away.

Accounting controls also fail to identify and reward individual skill, effort and achievement, especially in an adverse market where a person's contribution to running an effective team may be more important than an individual record of sales. Some purchase upon individual achievement other than the qualitative judgment of management was felt to be essential by the corporate parents, and all resolved the problem by having detailed targets, usually set at branch and/or budget centre level primarily, but with individual targets also clearly identified and rewarded. The prime target was of course sales, but such was the competition to sustain a strong high street presence and the awareness of the spin-off into sales of financial services, that obtaining instructions, even viewings, as well as agreements to buy and financial services referrals were all subject to targeting, and to payment for achieving targets, both through group bonus schemes and by individualised points systems where, for example, a referral for a financial services interview would be rewarded with a few pounds.

It was targets that were the principal form of pressure on front-line staff, therefore, with budgetary controls looming larger for branch and more senior management. Through targeting, the region and the centre could effectively alter local policy. If financial services income was inadequate and it was felt the opposition was doing better, targets could be emphasised in this area; if the list of properties under instruction was too small, valuations and instructions could be targeted. Targets hence altered quite often at the trivial end — points systems — but were set on an annual or semi-annual basis for sales. Target setting was inevitably a somewhat arbitrary business given the housing market, and here the relative autonomy of regions and budget centres was important in introducing a qualitative judgment, particularly in respect of achieving targets. In this respect it was seen to be important to have management with an estate agency background in charge, not only of budget centres but also of regional operations. In practice at the latter level there tended to be continuing lack of clarity and in some cases differences in structure between regions, as the corporates continued to evolve their structures at the time of our research. The financial services side of the corporates was also represented at regional level, usually on an equal footing with estate agency, and other managerial posts also existed such as operations director and sometimes an overall regional manager.

These arrangements gave rise to the tendency to various kinds of abuses, though we should say that we did not find them to be gross in the cases we investigated. It is worth adding at this point that we strongly suspect that the corporates we looked at had certain benign qualities in common in comparison to some of the competition. In the first place all were committed to estate agency long term, and were not about to withdraw and concentrate upon their traditional business: their central concern was to get corporate estate agency right and to sustain a national or major regional presence which was compatible with and mutually beneficial to their established financial services business. Secondly, the corporates we investigated were aware of the dangers of an overemphasis on short-term results, especially given the turmoil they had all come through, which involved heavy staff turnover (in excess of 50 per cent). All were grappling more or less deliberately with the distinctiveness of estate agency in comparison with financial services retailing and were aware of the dangers of the hard sell in reproducing the negative image of estate agency. Staff, particularly front-line staff, regularly referred to their competitors among the corporates by identifying a much greater degree of ruthlessness and a much greater managerial pressure to achieve results or face dismissal. In some cases staff we talked to had worked for the competitors and had left to avoid the pressures. Two major national networks were repeatedly identified as hard players, and it is probably significant that one of them refused consistently at all levels throughout our research to respond positively to our requests for information. We talked to senior management at a number of corporates before gaining access to do fieldwork with the three we investigated in detail. We also sent a questionnaire at the end of the fieldwork to all the corporates requesting basic information on structure, policy and experience, but this produced only a very patchy and limited response and the results are not usable.

Some of the potential abuses are notorious, the most obvious being the conditional selling of houses. Although some informants said that this did indeed go on in the boom years, after 1988 the adverse market exerted a pressure to eliminate any conditionality in sales, besides which the publicity and the intervention of the OFT seemed to have been effective in eliminating it. We found no evidence that staff would contemplate simple conditional selling: if you want this house, take our mortgage and our endowment policy. It was clear that company policy was established outlawing this and it did not feature as part of the professional repertoire of staff. This did not mean that the dangers of linked selling were entirely absent. Staff were under pressure to achieve targets for financial services referrals, something established estate agency staff often resented, at least initially, as irrelevant to their proper function. The problem that arose was not forced tie-in sales but the structural conflict of interest once a purchaser was drawn into financial services advice.

This takes us back to the concern voiced in chapter 6 about the exposed position of the purchaser in the property purchasing process. The agent needs to get quite close to the purchaser in order to negotiate the sale and to ensure that it goes through, but the agent acts for the vendor. Where there is the prospect of a financial services sale which may generate as much or more than the vendor's commission, the interest of the agent in getting the deal done becomes proportionately greater. We did not find much evidence that this resulted in purchasers who were willing to take up financial services being given surreptitious preference, though that danger must exist. Rather we were concerned at the even more exposed position of the purchaser, who not only had the agent acting for the vendor to extract as much in the way of a purchase price as possible, but also the financial services representative selling him or her a mortgage, insurance etc. An independent financial adviser would not only ensure that the purchaser's best interests were served as regards the financial services product, something that the tied status of most corporates precludes (though this is not to say they do not provide sound advice, since most of the ties are with leading institutions), but should also ensure that the purchaser is not induced to overextend or pay too much for the property. The only formal safeguard against this is the mortgage valuation survey, which is increasingly being undertaken in-house by the lender, who may also be the corporate parent. In sum the danger is that the unsuspecting purchaser is greeted with smiles all around and told yes, yes, yes, this is the price, here is the finance, here is what the vendor will agree, only at the end of the day to realise — if indeed there is any subsequent reflection — that a considerably harder bargain could have been pushed for with the vendor. We do not wish to say that this was an obvious and gross abuse, but that the structural conditions conduced to it and that there are no real safeguards; and when one is dealing in sums often exceeding £50,000, leeway of even 10 per cent involves £5,000 to be paid for over the next 25 years.

The interest of the corporate agency in getting the deal done could work in both directions to disadvantage purchaser or vendor. Information available as a result of financial services interviews could result in the purchaser being pressured to make a better offer, often because the agent got to know — as we often observed that they did — that the purchaser could afford it. Where a sale did not look in prospect at the vendor's acceptable price, but was likely if the price fell to what a prospective purchaser could manage, the pressure could fall on the vendor to reduce the price in the interests of a sale. Because the agent had an interest in the purchaser, and in any case the agent's own interests are in the sale rather than the last achievable £1,000, since he only takes 1–3 per cent in commission, the vendor stood to be compromised. In a falling market with negative equity looming for many vendors, a powerful climate among agents existed in which clients were to be induced to be realistic, and indeed some of the corporates we researched had actually targeted price reductions for a period, and all were keen to get clients to drop prices to achieve sales targets. Since most house sales are discretionary on the part of the vendor (not, e.g., job related), this means that vendors may be induced to sell at a price that is not unequivocally in their interests.

Finally, a feature of the corporates which made this situation, more complicated is the issue of listing. The corporates competed hard for high street presence and were concerned to maintain a full list of properties. Given vendors' reluctance to accept how much prices had fallen, this resulted in a tendency to overvalue in order to obtain instructions. This was recognised to be, in one sense, foolish, and senior management made regular attempts to curtail it, but if the competition was overvaluing and there was any sense that the local market was becoming more buoyant, the temptation to raise a valuation to near what the vendor expected became irresistible. Although the practice is explicitly outlawed by the OCEA code of conduct, we found this habit to be endemic and widespread. Agents frequently complained that overpriced properties do not sell; on the other hand instructions would often be targeted and there was a keen sense that 'if we do not have it the opposition will. Far better for us to get it on and then negotiate a hefty price reduction in a few weeks. After all no one expects properties to sell overnight in the present market'.

The effect of overvaluation was to produce a much more confused market as regards price. In a weak market with few transactions, listed asking prices might be within 5–10 per cent of what was expected and achievable or 25 per cent above it. Information about prices actually achieved was of course much less widely known, especially to vendors and purchasers, though it is part of the agent's job to find out and this information can then be used to negotiate overpricing downwards. The overall consequence was that overpricing sustained a lack of realism in a difficult market and, more to the point, contributed to the difficulty of vendors and purchasers knowing what they should be expecting to pay or receive for their property.

We are not then claiming to identify dramatic abuses, but rather to identify structural conflicts of interest which weaken the protection which vendors and purchasers should have in the property market-place when dealing with those with market experience, in this case the corporate estate agents and financial advisers. We have seen when considering independent agents that this is an intractable problem, particularly as regards purchasers. Financial services sales introduce an additional conflict of interest and enhance the agency's interest in pushing deals through whether or not they are in the best interests of clients. Can these conflicts be prevented from becoming mani-fest? Corporate management naturally believed that they could though none could offer a clear and satisfactory way of containing them structurally. Rather the approach is through selection, training and control of staff and through the development of a distinctive kind of corporate estate agency.

As we have seen, the corporate parents have sought to achieve control over their estate agents by accounting procedures and targeting and to back this up qualitatively with training programmes which were under active development and implementation at the time of our research. Career structures remain less clear and constitute one of the areas of evident conflict between the parent, with its bureaucratic structure, and the estate agents, with their localism and emphasis upon the individual. The final means of control, apart from simple hiring and firing and the bonus and pay systems which were linked to targets, is the administrative system. Once again, estate agency posed problems for the corporates. One of the errors the Prudential was held to have made was to require the proceduralisation and standardisation of everything, with the result that individual and local discretion was all but eliminated, yet some conformity of procedure is vital to the corporates for several reasons. In the first place common reporting systems are essential if adequate information is to be collated at the centre. Information has therefore to be collected, recorded and reported in a standardised form. Only if this happens can budgets, targets and performance be appraised on an adequate and equal basis. Because the centre is far removed from the local agency, much information that in an independent may not be recorded at all has to be collected and reported. Reporting systems, then, have not only to be standard but to a significant extent started from scratch, to the irritation of front-line staff, for whom all this is paperwork, not real work dealing with clients. Yet only if they do it can they get the rewards from successful dealings with clients. Further, getting the right kind and amount of information flowing to the centre in respect of a new and unfamiliar activity, estate agency, was not easy to achieve. All the corporates seem to have gone through a series of stages, alongside the structuring process which we referred to above, which led to the establishment of reporting systems.

Reporting systems are linked to another critical feature of corporate estate agency: proceduralisation and the maintenance of quality of service. The corporates generally saw the provision of a reliable service to customers as their principal selling point. There was usually a link between this and their established image as reliable, customer-friendly financial services institutions. The object in relation to estate agency was to eliminate the tarnished image of the estate agent as devious and unreliable and to substitute one of pleasant demeanour, open dealing, strict rectitude and efficient service, so that customers would feel relaxed and confident, would return as subsequent clients, whether as vendor or purchaser, and be more amenable to accept financial services advice. This approach was bolstered by the emphasis upon corporate appearance in office furnishings, stationery, telephone manner and, for women, uniforms. Despite considerable circumstantial evidence that much of this effort was wasted on customers, whose main concern is achieving a sale at an acceptable price, the corporates were not to be deflected. The reasons for this go to the heart of the corporates' aspirations to constitute a new form of estate agency, in chains which will be nationally known and relied upon, just as their parent bodies are for mortgages and insurances.

One feature of this approach which was perhaps better judged was its emphasis upon openness and transparency, a move very much in accord with the times, with the OFT requiring explicit written contracts and clear disclosure as its strategy for improving estate agency, using its powers under the Estate Agents Act 1979. The customers of the corporates were predominantly at the middle and lower end of the market, including a number of new, young first-time buyers and many with limited, if any, experience of the property market and financial services. This had a number of consequences. First, it meant that volume of business was essential to profitability. Having brochures and procedures which set out clearly what is on offer, what everyone's responsibilities are, and what the stages of the property sales process are is helpful if staff time for each customer is limited. Secondly, it meant that there was a reasonably good chance of getting financial services take-up — older, more affluent customers would be more likely to be already committed to insurance policies and have established preferences for advisers and mortgage lenders. Thirdly, it conduced to an atmosphere which is closer to that of a shop than a lawyer's office, where people are just ordinary people selling a retail product and not expected to be verbally sophisticated or have a wide knowledge of the workings of institutions, not highly educated and lower-middle rather than upper-middle class.

Proceduralisation is hence a natural means for the corporates to maintain quality of service, ensuring that each customer is treated alike, that each is subjected to adequate enquiries, that each is kept up-to-date with developments following instructions, and that each is aware of at least the basic elements of the sale process. Record keeping, job descriptions and clear division of labour all assist here. There was reason to suppose that, in principle, staff, management and customers saw a shared advantage in these arrangements. Practice, however, is different. Properties, even houses on modern estates, are all different, as are clients and purchasers, their circumstances, personal and financial, their personalities and their predispositions. Every property sale is a unique mix of properties and people with, as we have seen, the agent's function being to bring them together with a harmonious outcome. In this sense every transaction is a one-off, not a repeat performance, and, as we have seen, it is precisely this which both provides most intrinsic rewards for estate agents and is the basis for most significant difficulties, betrayals and abuses. It is here that the corporates had their greatest problem, for they had a natural tendency to see estate agency as merely local operators providing essentially the same kind of service that they did as, for example, insurers. After all, insureds are individuals with their variations and idiosyncracies but, within fairly generous and readily understandable limits, they are offered the same terms of insurance and accept standardised packages, which are created, maintained and distributed very effectively by corporate headquarters. The corporates found it very hard to recognise, and even harder to accept as a practical proposition, that estate agency is not retail selling but the negotiation of a series of individual deals — deals which call for the delicate exercise of judgment continuously to bring them off, so that not only are all parties brought to agree, and to agree on fair terms for all, but also to feel that they have agreed to the right deal on the right terms. It is, to say the least, open to question whether this can be proceduralised.

This problem becomes the more pressing when translated into the culture and careers that estate agency has traditionally generated. At their worst estate agents are deal makers in their own interest, ruthlessly exploiting the two other parties. Such agents rapidly acquire a bad name, however, and whilst practices which are pretty sharp may survive in quite successful chains, they must be kept carefully hidden. The better estate agent aspires to a long-term reputation for good service and honesty and to derive a secure income from repeat business. In the short term an agent takes satisfaction from bringing off a deal which satisfies both a personal sense of integrity as to its terms, and which leaves vendor and purchaser content. The small gestures of appreciation, a card, flowers, a bottle of wine, from satisfied customers were repeatedly referred to as part of what makes the job worthwhile — and compensates for the contrariness of some members of the public. To achieve this requires the exercise of discretion — freedom of movement — and judgment which is in principle professional, albeit without the extensive training characteristic of the full profession.

Estate agency places a strong emphasis upon practical experience over time as essential, and qualitatively different from academic learning in acquiring the competence, not only to make professional judgments — that is, judgments that are right given all the circumstances — but also in identifying when such judgments are called for. Above all it calls for a capacity to manage clients and customers adroitly and with knowledge — that is to say without misleading them through ignorance. Training, transparency, supervision and procedures are geared to dealing with standard circumstances and are indeed a means to standardisation. To that extent they are a protection, but if every case is to some extent an exception they are of little avail. From the point of view of the agent standardisation and proceduralisation then becomes an affront to his or her professional capacity and a burdensome restraint. This is enhanced in the case of estate agents by the existence of a culture in which individualism is emphasised and careers are traditionally made by building up a personal local reputation, knowledge and client base, and ending as an owner-partner of an estate agency, probably with an income deriving only in part, albeit the major part, from property sales. Subject such a person to the hierarchy, budgets, targets and procedures of the corporation and the outcome is mutual antagonism. The estate agent perceives the corporate management as remote and ignorant, and their requirements as pointlessly burdensome at best and probably an actual constraint on doing good business. The corporates experience the agent as administratively feckless, insubordinate, not a good company person, variable in achievement and a constant source of anxiety.

Such a contrast is overdrawn for expository purposes, but is undoubtedly present and we shall comment on it in respect of each of the corporates we studied and refer to it by the general term 'culture clash'. It obviously poses a long-term difficulty for the corporates in integrating estate agency into their mainstream business, and, when associated with higher staff turnover, which implies a constant need to socialise new staff into the corporate culture, it is a source of considerable anxiety. Most of the corporate management recognised the problem; none had really resolved it, and the corporates were all in the process of attempting to deal with the matter in the structural context of the greater or lesser integration of estate agency into their mainstream business.

This cultural issue is, however, distinct from the separate point made above as to the development of a distinctive corporate species of estate agency which is consciously different from that espoused by the professional bodies and reflected in the better practices of independent agencies, which we will refer to as professional estate agency. The question which arises here, to put it at its plainest, is whether the distinctive problems of estate agency transactions are capable of being managed successfully on the procedural model envisaged by the corporates, or whether professional judgment, and with it professional autonomy, is the only at least possibly viable solution. Given the conflicts of interest we have referred to above, which exist in the corporates, is there not just too much of an in built tendency for the company to send its trained battalions to ride roughshod over the public, albeit in a perfectly orderly and publicly explicit fashion? Are we not in the world of the professional conjurer who pulls up his sleeves to prove that nothing can be hidden before pulling off his greatest trick?

The practical manifestation of these difficulties lies most obviously in a hard choice which the corporate has to make as to just what its relations are to be with its estate agencies: how tight is the embrace to be? It is important to recognise that the choice is a qualitative one. It can be conceptualised as identifying an optional point on a continuum shown in figure 7.1.

It is evident that maximum independence is not a serious option, for here estate agency is no more than an investment, run completely separately from the parent, with no corporate identity, and merely a vehicle for increasing group profits. This arrangement conflicts with the aspiration to use estate agency to sell financial services products. If these products are to be sold, the corporate name is involved, and hence it is likely to be used for the estate

---

Figure 7.1   Estate agency relation to corporate parent

Complete integration < --------------------- > Formally independent subsidiary

more — degree of integration — less

---

agency also. Corporates have taken varying decisions, however: some agencies, especially those with good reputations, have been allowed to continue to trade under their old names; some have introduced the corporate logo alongside the existing agency's name — a practice adopted by the Royal; others, notably GA and the Halifax have imposed the corporate name and colours universally; the Abbey introduced a new name, Cornerstone, for its estate agents, as did the first in the field, Lloyds Bank, with Black Horse.

At the other extreme complete integration of the agency into the corporation remains an objective for a number of corporates, including some that we researched, though there is caution about how to go about doing thi s, since there is now general recognition that estate agency is dissimilar from mass retail financial services. The problem of developing a viable form of corporate estate agency hence becomes expressed through the issue of integration. A degree of integration is essential to maintain control and to market financial services; substantial or complete integration presupposes overcoming the problems referred to above in creating a new corporate form of estate agency. None of the three corporates we looked at had achieved complete integration, and only one retained it as a serious aspiration. The other two were content to sustain varying degrees of autonomy for agencies, whilst continuing to struggle to achieve profitability (or at least limit losses), to evolve a *modus vivendi* with agencies and create a stable and corporately trained workforce.

There was a quite widely held expectation that further corporates would follow the Prudential, the Cheltenham and Gloucester and the Northern Rock and withdraw from estate agency, which will, of course, put pressure on those remaining to contain costs; it is one thing to lose heavily if all your competitors are 'seeing it long term', but quite another if they cut their losses and revert to their core business. At the same time other corporates, notably the Woolwich and, in a more limited way, the Norwich Union, have entered estate agency. The precise structure of the corporate estate agency market is not our concern. It is relevant, however, that it seems likely that at least a significant number of corporates will have estate agency chains in 10 years' time, and hence it is significant in what ways and with what success they deal with the problem of integration and the creation of a new form of corporate estate agency. We suspect, however, to anticipate the evidence to come, that, whilst it is possible that corporate agency will emerge as a lasting phenomenon, it will not, as the corporates widely anticipated, sweep traditional agency into a marginal position. The analysis above suggests that there is a basis for the professional bodies who have supported independent agencies for the past half century and more to demonstrate that there is at least as good a model for the provision of an adequate public service as the corporates. This is a matter to which we will return in a later chapter.

EIGHT

Corporate Strategies and Tactics: Three Case Studies

This chapter examines how the corporate sector has addressed the problems arising from their entry into estate agency, the strategies and tactics adopted, and the solutions proposed. This is approached through an examination of three corporates, two with national networks, the other regionally based. It is not claimed that these case studies comprehensively describe how the corporate sector as a whole has confronted estate agency, but they do elicit the ways in which major financial institutions have sought to manage the problems and conflicts described in chapter 7.

BEECH INSURANCE COMPANY

The move into estate agency took place in the mid 1980s with fairly rapid expansion to the present position, which makes it one of the largest corporates. Estate agency was part of a wider campaign to secure its insurance business and was accompanied by a move into direct marketing and selling and ties with a number of brokers and agents. Although initially only limited stakes were taken in estate agencies, this altered to outright takeovers with many partners — 250 at the time of the research — brought into the Beech and 80 per cent of them remaining with it. The structure was changing during our research period in 1991 from three to five regional divisions, each with considerable local autonomy, and with only a small headquarters staff. We looked at two rather different branches in a northern region which had in all around 100 offices assembled from 30 or 40 buy-outs and some cold starts. The managing director was an estate agent by background, a fact which found favour with front-line staff but it was explained that he had been appointed recently only after a period of considerable confusion and several strategy reviews, with other management saying that the Beech did not understand estate agency and that constant policy changes demotivated staff. The new director, Jim Hodgson, was the former owner of a medium-sized chain of middle to lower-market agencies in the region, and described himself as hard but fair. He was brought in with a remit to contain costs in a difficult market, a task for which he had a formidable reputation — 'as tight as a camel's arse in a sand storm' in the words of one of his colleagues.

Despite the difficulties of the market and of adapting an insurance company to estate agency, the Beech clearly remained committed to estate agency. It had recently changed the formal reporting system for the estate agency business to refer directly to the parent insurance company rather than a subsidiary as before, and when forced by the recession to shut down branches in the region, it mothballed them with a view to reopening later rather than liquidating them. Policy on branding was mixed. On the whole the insurance logo was added to the masthead of the existing agencies' names, though with variations in prominence. In the case of one quite large chain in the region with a decidedly doubtful reputation the corporate name was entirely substituted, but at the time of our research the name of one of the other acquisitions was being used to add to the corporate logo. This reflected a general sense among the staff we spoke to that the Beech had accepted that estate agency is distinctive and needs a certain independence to run effectively and that the presence of estate agents in middle and senior management at regional level is necessary to secure this.

The two offices we looked at presented a considerable contrast. One, in a prosperous suburb of a major city, had the appearance of a standardised corporate with 4.5 staff catering to the middle market. In fact the office had been acquired by the agency with the poor reputation and been rebranded as the Beech. The staff were all new, the longest serving less than two years and several had previously worked for the Prudential or other corporates, which they had left because they disliked the restraints and pressures. Competition was intense, with six other agencies located alongside the Beech.

The other office was located in a prosperous market town and tourist centre where it had a venerable reputation. It had 36 staff and was one of the leading offices in the region. The business was a family one with the present manager the former owner, who at one time had his father, brother and brother-in-law working with him. The business had been built up by amalgamation, crucially in the 1960s and early 1970s, when the business acquired a very considerable range of expertise in all areas of estate agency work and 12 offices. This gave it strength, with, as the manager put it, a rise in one market being balanced by a fall in another. The takeover by the Beech provided a culture shock and Davies, the manager, remarked that the top end of the market business, which the office used to dominate in the area, had declined dramatically during the period that he was drafted elsewhere in the Beech after the takeover. Davies was, however, remarkably confident that things would improve now he was back in charge and the Beech had accepted the need for estate agency autonomy. In contrast to the other research site, therefore, this office was large, established, self-confident, and willing and able to resist what at any rate it perceived as the excesses of corporate culture.

This office hence provides a prime example of a defence of what we called earlier professional values in estate agency, with Davies, in particular, able to contrast them with the weaknesses, as he saw it, of the corporate approach to estate agency. He regretted the increasing emphasis on volume and through-put since the takeover and the inevitably greater emphasis on financial services sales, which were much more likely to be attractive to younger, less affluent customers, because older wealthier ones would have already made their financial arrangements and have established advisers. The business had a financial adviser before the takeover, who was paid on a turnover basis and the arrangement was amicable, but there was not a great deal of business to be done in that area. In the past business was sustained by a reputation for honesty and service and by regular contact with the business and profes-sional community, both those immediately relevant — solicitors, account-ants, other estate agents — and more widely: 'I would have a lunch here at least once every two months and I would invite maybe the local paper, maybe a couple of accountants and a couple of lawyers and a couple of heads of business, somebody from ICI, say personnel departments, and have an informal sit-down and a bit of lunch ... and you develop those people'. This is very much the way in which the law and accountancy professions traditionally develop business contacts.

The actual business of selling properties must be founded upon the careful nurturing of relationships with vendor and client and meticulous attention to individual needs and preferences as Davies put it:

The ideal is the person who is dedicated to finding out what people want and what they like and looking after people. So many estate agents just have an answering service, what do you want? Four bedrooms, two bathrooms and you want it in X or whatever.... That's not satisfaction in my opinion, that's what I call blowing out of the door. You have just got rid of somebody who said what they wanted and you didn't actually sit them down and talk to them and find out what they wanted.

Self-selection was one of the biggest downfalls in our industry.... It meant that people could walk through our door and go 'I would like details of that and that' and they would walk out of the office. Nobody would explain to them what that house was like or what its location was like. They would look at the picture and they would throw it in the bin if they didn't like it. But probably it could be the house they would buy at the end of the day.

It's generating ideas in people's minds that sells houses. 'Would you go to Bishopston? Churchtown is right next door to Bishopston. Have you considered Bishopston?' 'No, we haven't, but yes we would.' So OK you widen the scope of the market place for him as an individual.

We have seen the concern to get close to clients and customers before, but in this case the emphasis upon service and honesty is consistent and there is no hint of any need to manipulate. The solution, it is maintained, is honesty, dedication and openness. Given this, relations with purchasers are as important as those with vendors — after all purchasers produce the agent's fee:

> As long as the estate agent is totally and utterly honest, then there is no reason why he should not have a good relationship with both and there is no reason why the vendor should not have a good relationship with his purchaser. That's really the ultimate, to have a good relationship between the three parties. I think it's important that the three parties are kept at arm's length and if there is a problem emerging the estate agent can rectify that quickly.... That will normally occur through a problem with the survey or just the actual deal itself hasn't been struck correctly and everything has not been crossed and dotted at the right time. If everything has been done there shouldn't be any problems but if something has been left out, and if there is a niggle on one side that you haven't resolved, then that is the seed that the estate agent has started through not doing his job properly and resolutely qualifying everybody, obtaining everybody's agreement that they are satisfied with what has been struck as a deal. If they have left that seed there to grow, then it will grow and sometimes it grows rapidly and it bursts.... You have to overcome the objections ... people's objections are the most difficult thing to deal with as an agent. We find our negotiators have difficulty in understanding it because every situation is different. You can't just train them, you have to say to them. 'Look into that man's eyes, look into his problem, try and prejudge the situations to resolve them, don't let things happen....' I have got a girl downstairs now who desperately wants to negotiate, but I won't let her do it because I know that she has not got the right attitude.

It is interesting to contrast these views with some of those of the regional managing director, the former owner of a middle to lower-market agency. His notion of professionalism is slightly different:

> People do expect a much higher standard in everything today, rightly so. The days of the horse trader, whether they be in the car field or the estate agency field have got to be long over. It has got to be done in a professional manner. Now when you are dealing with emotive things such as people's life savings — and that is what a house really is, isn't it — you are always going to have problems.

For these reasons regulation, by government or self-regulation, is to be welcomed and licensing would be beneficial. What does professionalism consist in however? Hodgson is in agreement with Davies:

> The relationships we try to build up between ourselves and our clients by means of regular contact is paramount. We have been guilty in the past on a lot of occasions of actually doing our job, but not telling people what we

are actually doing and therefore they think they are paying this vast sum of money for absolutely naff all.

Estate agency is not a relationship with a business, corporate or independent. 'It is purely a relationship between you, the client and me the agent. If you like me then I have every chance of getting the job.' This relationship, however, is not based on the professional idea of service, but on selling. Hodgson regretted that in his early career, 'There was virtually no sales training in what is essentially a selling job'. His view of the public is 'the cynic's view that by the time they have reached 45, estate agents are fed up with the public, they have had enough. The public are very demanding on one's time'.

This view of the public was expressed forcibly by the staff at the other Beech office in the phrase 'Buyers are liars'. The atmosphere here was far less genteel and secure and the need to meet targets, control costs and manage staff vigorously was almost abrasively evident. Control was exercised less by attention to professional development than by an emphasis on management's basic rights to hire, fire and promote. The willingness of the Beech to allow local autonomy is decidedly two-edged:

> If you are running your office and it is all hunky-dory you never see the boss. If you are behind target and things are going wrong ... he would come in and virtually start running the office.... I have got rid of our weekend person because [the staff] all moaned about him. John ... has got somebody who is quite hyped up about sales.... I met her last week and said, 'Right, I want her on board', and she starts on Saturday.

> If Fiona was being paid a lot more than Mike and Mike knew it and Mike was doing all the work, I would say I want to give you £500 bonus per annum, just increase your salary and make Fiona know about it.

We will say more presently about pay and targets but before doing so it is important to put in place the major administrative form of corporate control known as paper flow. This is in essence no more than a uniform information recording and reporting system. As the person responsible for developing it pointed out, it does not so much generate additional information as 'put all the information on one piece of paper', the control card. Achieving this common system in the region nonetheless took some time. Earlier when estate agency was controlled more directly by the parent company, confusion obviously reigned for some time, since decisions had to be referred up the corporate hierarchy — 'the bureaucracy was unbelievable, trying to get a decision' — and there was no common information-recording system. It took the decision to grant estate agents regional autonomy, the hiring of outside consultants, and several months' work with regional management to develop paper flow, and then a training team of nine or 10 people, 18 months to implement the system and overcome resistance. Staff turnover at sub-manager level was heavy — 50 per cent — which inevitably slowed the process down. All this is indicative of the difficulty an established financial services company has in digesting large numbers of estate agents.

Paper flow was not created merely to enable the regional administrative system to function reasonably smoothly, however. As one manager put it: 'The main objectives were to ensure that customers were treated with the same level of service and could expect a certain level of professionalism from every office they went into which had our banner. We also wanted to cut down costs in relation to the different sorts of paperwork that we had in different areas . . . and put our heading on everything'. At the centre of paper flow is a standardised control card on to which are entered the details of every property offered for sale, which is progressively updated as the property moves through the various stages from valuation to sale. Included are not just the mundane details of the property but various assessments, notably whether in the valuer's opinion the property would sustain a 100 per cent mortgage application, and cost sections for boards, advertisements, photographs etc. Forms registering customer requirements for the mailing of property details supplement the control card, together with a hot box priority card system which identifies those able to move within eight weeks. The hot box was the object of meticulous attention in both offices.

The consequences of the control card and paper flow system are critical to the Beech's view of corporate estate agency. 'Professional standards' and reliable uniform 'service' are to be verified by entries confirming that certain procedures have been undertaken: uniformity not idiosyncrasy is sustained, and the quality of effort and skill with which the procedures are carried out is left unevaluated. Such a system provides a basic level of security of service, preventing clients being forgotten about entirely, but is far from the views of Davies quoted above on the matter of professional service.

It is noteworthy that the training officer responsible for developing paper flow should respond to the suggestion that such a system would be likely to inhibit the freedom of action characteristic of the independent estate agent and hence perhaps alienate and demotivate some staff responded by saying that although there had been resistance to it, the changes 'weren't as bad as they thought they were going to be'. In addition 'there are one or two characters — they can't do their admin, say, but they can bring houses on and they can sell them'. Such a marginalisation of independently minded but effective agents as mavericks epitomises one dilemma of corporate estate agency: total absorption into the corporation may be incompatible with the freedom of action necessary to successful estate agency. Like the other corporates we observed, the Beech had recognised this to a significant extent in granting estate agency regional autonomy and in putting estate agents in senior management positions, but the requirement to exercise control and contain costs could not be bucked. Agents could comfort themselves that at least they were better off than at the Prudential according to the recollection of a former employee, where staff were told:

You will sit down and talk to them for five minutes . . . and go through your presentation, go through the folder with them, explain what we do with the photographs, what we do with that, building desire, building this, building that. You were just a crowbar.... I said, I am not going to do it. I can't get houses on if I am going to do that because my area doesn't work like that.

The other major contribution of the paper flow system to corporate control is that it provides a record of individual staff output — who did which valuation, wrote letters forwarding offers, undertook referrals to financial services etc. — and at the same time provides a means of identifying costs, whether these are actual disbursements, in advertising, for example, or costs in staff and other organisational time and resources. Paper flow is hence the vital conduit for information about costs at branch level, and about the achievement of targets at individual and branch level. Because these too are standardised through paper flow, performance can be constantly evaluated not only against targets, which are accepted as hard to rely on absolutely, but by comparison of individuals within a branch, and of one branch in a locality against another. This gives management the effective powers of intervention referred to above and puts the large, established and successful traditional office described earlier as an example of surviving professionalism in a new light. In comparison to the other, smaller office we observed, this was much less exposed and much more successful over the long term and would hence naturally benefit from non-intervention by regional management, including a tolerance of some traditional habits that might come under hostile scrutiny if that performance weakened.

If the paper flow system is seen as the skeleton, and pay and targets the muscles of corporate estate agency, the ligaments binding the two are training and career development. It was only with the success of training schemes that corporate procedures could be understood, accepted and practised competently, and estate agents in branches act also as part of the corporate whole. Significantly this was something which Davies, still very much the independent professional at heart, fully appreciated:

You would go to the office and they would be doing it this way, you go into another down the road and they would be doing it another way. So we had to change that straightaway and it was one of the first things we did.... We are lucky enough to have the foresight of a company at the top saying train the staff, we will do it properly. And that's what we have done over the last 18 months. We have spent a lot of time, a lot of money and a lot of effort in training people.

Training courses were continually being further developed for all levels of staff, he added. This had been effective in bringing down turnover to 35 per cent.

In addition there was support for the NVQ training schemes which were becoming available, and an aspiration to identify and require clear attainment standards of all staff even though this was likely to be a complex process. Appraisal was being introduced with an explicit personal and career development aspect and a less explicit individual evaluation and implied sanctioning aspect. Training programmes were at times overtly used as sanctions with, for example, the 30 worst managers in terms of target attainment being put through a training scheme compulsorily.

On the career development side the unfinished character of the system was most evident. As a senior manager put it:

> There is no definite path anyone goes, but there are a number of success stories that will be quoted if anybody wanted to know, so there is a possibility for advancement, but it is not as clear-cut as in certain companies, where you reach a grade, you pass a test, you move on.

It was recognised that identifiable career paths were necessary, though no real ideas were evident of what they would be: the differences between the bureaucratic hierarchy of the parent company and the more anarchic world of estate agent remained to be overcome in this respect.

What then of the short-term incentives for performance — pay, bonuses and targets? Like other corporates that we observed, the Beech were aware that a heavy reliance on commission or bonuses would lead to corner-cutting and overselling that would ultimately damage the reputation of the company. On the other hand individuals were to be rewarded for achieving results, and results were essential to keep within budgets. In the last analysis it was keeping within an overall annual budget that was critical. Thus, in the words of a branch manager, even if an individual merited promotion and the office manager recommended this to his superior, 'He will listen, but if the figures are bad and I'm trying to promote someone, then he will say, let's see them bringing the money in'. In other words individual promotion is contingent on the office as a whole being on target.

Office targets were set annually on the basis of the previous year's performance and were cash sums. These were then translated into numbers of houses to be sold per week on the basis of the average commission income per sale at the branch, allowing for 30 per cent of agreed sales to fall through for one reason or another. In addition, in one office, targets were allocated to valuations, referrals, viewings, price reductions and listings, on the basis that these were all instrumental to sales and profitability, the manager maintaining, for example, that a ratio of about 50–60 per cent of valuations would convert into listings. Although the number of items targeted might therefore seem an onerous profusion, the pressure of targets was not as great as it might appear since, for the most part, they were a means to achieving the overall aim of completed sales. Monitoring of individual office and managers' performance by regional management took place annually, with a dressing-down for poor performances and the automatic threat of dismissal, but without a formal relation between target achievement and dismissal.

Pay was to a certain extent individualised, with a negotiator on £6,000–8,000, a first-appointment manager £12,000, middle range £15,000–18,000 and a top rate at branch level of £20,000. On top of this were bonuses of 10 per cent of the first £15,000 of income generated over a target and 20 per cent for anything beyond that, which could be expected to add several thousand pounds to income. Finally, front-line staff were paid £5 for arranging a valuation, for a financial services referral, for a valuation survey appointment and, for staff operating building society agencies, £1 for every account opened. Whilst this might seem petty, it was designed to keep staff eyes on the targets to achieve, whilst avoiding the creation of pressures to cut corners.

Such a system is, however, bound to some extent to identify the public as targets to be converted rather than clients to be served, and indeed there was evidence that this was the case. Pressures to overvalue were, as one branch manager said, an inevitable outcome of targeting listings and valuations:

> We all have targets, and one of the targets in any office is how many houses you put on the market ... and if your target is five and in a week you have only put one on and it's Thursday night, you think you will still take it on board. You shouldn't. ... The [problem arises] when another agent has said he's going to get £75,000, i.e., he has agreed with [the vendor] ... and you think it's £65,000.

The dangers of overvaluation were increased by the newly introduced company policy of asking clients what price they hoped to achieve before offering a valuation. Life was also made difficult by the sense, which some clients had, that agents sometimes undervalued in order to secure a quick sale, with a second agent being called in to remedy this. The market and clients' aspirations hence operated in concert with the targets to create constant pressures to overvalue, even though agents knew that overvalued properties are in no one's interest since they do not sell, and cost the agency money to continue marketing them.

Attitudes to clients were fairly pragmatic, especially in one office, where there was a view that cheap property was to be taken on with 'minimum spiel', mid-market merited 'a bit more chat and advice' and the upper market the need to spend more time talking 'preferably about anything but the house, mentioning who you know' in order to gain client confidence. Is this merely the inevitable outcome of the need to shift volume, or are such attitudes enhanced by the corporate agency performance-rating and incentive systems? It is not irrelevant that Davies, the avowed professional, concentrated on the top end of the market.

On the other hand, when it came to negotiation, several staff expressed in different ways the fact that clients were disadvantaged by lack of knowledge of the market. One pointed out that when price reductions in a chain were suggested as a means of going ahead, many clients found the importance of differential as opposed to absolute prices hard to grasp. In another case clients received an offer £25,000 below their asking price after the property had been on the market a year and were dismissive until urged to go and check prices in the area they were intending to move into. The weariness of agents that we have cited before as a result of repeated exposure to the whims, pettiness and rudeness of the public was a problem that was well-recognised, and here the corporate controls through paper flow and the control card, coupled with training, probably acted as a check. Certainly there was no evidence of a predatory or unduly equivocal attitude by staff, but we question whether clients who were not reasonably alert to recognise that their interests in achieving the right price differed from those of the agent in achieving the sale — and many were alert to this — were always fully protected.

When the area of financial services, and in particular the position of purchasers in that connection, is raised we believe there are further grounds for concern. Although our intention was to concentrate on residential estate agency, we thought it essential to consider the work of financial advisers in the corporates, given the importance of the link between estate agency and the selling of the parent company's financial products. In the case of the Beech, advisers are tied for the sale of life insurance products, but not for mortgages or other financial services products, such as pensions. We spoke to the consultants attached to both the offices we observed and made some observations of their work, though observing the content of client contact was harder than for estate agency proper. In our consumer survey we made also a limited foray into the financial services area (see chapter 9). We cannot therefore answer such interesting questions as whether clients knew that consultants were tied for insurance purposes but not for mortgages and what this implied practically. All we can suggest at the outset is that there is evidence that the public are not highly aware of the nature of financial services products, which are somewhat abstract, and that in the context of house purchase, the financial services side is largely seen as a means to achieve the end object in focus, namely the possession of the property, which is an emotionally charged, tangible object. If estate agents find that their clients often need to be led through the property transfer process by the hand (if not by the nose) this is hence even more likely in respect of financial services.

Despite the fundamental interest of the parent company in using estate agency to secure sales of its products and the length of time since the Beech had entered estate agency (five years when our fieldwork started), there remained considerable confusion about the lines of responsibility, control and accountability as between the estate agency and financial services sides. In the past it was evident that financial consultants had unquestioningly been seen as part of the Beech, but with the devolution of responsibility to estate agency through regions and then areas for which consultants were responsible, estate agency had in theory become in charge of its own patch. Nonetheless financial advisers were represented at regional level, with their own regional managers. In theory consultants were responsible also to the branch manager, but in small branches they might service more than one office. In addition their working conditions were different, since the detailed interviews they required often led to evening meetings with clients at their homes, which in turn was taken to justify late starts in the morning. As the director of training put it when answering a question on lines of responsibility: 'It's like a matrix', admitting that consultants had played off financial services management against estate agency. As one consultant put it, 'I am nothing to do with residential here, which is quite good because you can get in as late as you like'.

Such a stance naturally irritated estate agents, who were required to arrive at a fixed time, and added to confusion and resentment about referrals. Both consultants at the branches we observed felt that agents regarded financial services referrals as an irritant, an irrelevant and at times obstructive addition to their work in selling houses, a view which was confirmed by some of the agents themselves and by management. One of the changes introduced with regionalisation, according to a Beech financial services consultant, was the making of management bonuses on the estate agency side contingent in part on their offices generating referrals to financial services:

> A lot of managers were originally ignoring financial services altogether. They weren't encouraging their staff to get appointments, but now, because their income, their bonus, is related to that, they encourage their front-end staff to get appointments.

On the other hand, financial consultants' pay was calculated entirely on their own sales and not related to the output of the estate agency office with salary rates and bonus or commission scales being calculated independently.

One of the consultants who was long established in the field used his career client bank to make sales, which earned commission on top of what he earned in his day-to-day work with the Beech in their estate agency offices. The difficulties of financial consultants are captured in the following exchange between the fieldworker and the consultant for the large North West branch:

> A: The integration of financial services within residential sales is very, very difficult. I think a lot of the old estate agents look down their noses at the financial services team — you are not part of any office.... And its wrong. It should be we are working together. We are all trying to help people. Because it is better if I do the mortgage for somebody that is buying because it all goes through the same — I know exactly what is going on. The girls outside know what is going on, you don't have to chase up so much.
> Q: Yes, I notice you haven't got a door for example?
> A: This is bloody awful this! This is the worst there is honestly. I used to have my own desk on the floor, but I had a big office upstairs as well to interview people.... Asking if you have arranged with your building society, it's very difficult in a Saturday afternoon.... You have got to have somewhere to go.

Thus in a large branch office, the financial adviser had nowhere quiet and private to conduct personal interviews. The advantage of using in-house financial services advice is, as he points out, control of the purchaser. Part of the Beech standard procedure was to qualify purchasers by asking them to go for a financial services interview which would establish whether they could in fact afford the property. The same applied to vendors, since their activities as purchasers were normally essential to the sale of their own properties. If vendor and purchaser, but especially the latter, were handled in-house the problem that 'Buyers are liars' would be resolved, and the chances of the deal going through enhanced, with the additional benefit of there being 'much less to chase up'. There are, therefore, organisational as well as financial reasons for in-house advice, but the financial benefits are considerable. Where vendor and purchaser could be sold mortgages and insurance, the potential commission income for the business was £2,000–3,000 against an average £500–1,000 from the sale of a property. Why, therefore, was there such reluctance by estate agents to cooperate, for reluctance there undoubtedly was according to one financial services consultant:

> The first six weeks, yes, it's absolutely dead loss. All you have got to do is just be yourself and try to talk to them [estate agency staff].... When you start they will make coffee for themselves but they won't ask you. You have got to get out there and really try and help the girls, whether it's making viewings, valuations, and actually going on those viewings, taking people round houses, answering the phone, covering for lunches.... And it does work.

There are two sorts of reasons for this resistance, organisational and professional. Because the financial consultants were seen as outsiders with different pay, reporting systems and responsibilities, they were not identified as part of the estate agency team, and were seen as potential free riders, parasites or spies — terms which overstate the strength of the feelings but reflect their quality. Financial advisers were not organisationally in a position in which they would be readily trusted, and in addition estate agency staff knew they were expected to provide referrals. Professionally this was vexing. At the least it meant that agents had to acquire the habits and skills of introducing a reference to financial services advice in the course of dealing with clients and applicants, which diverted their attention from cultivating both parties and taking such matters on trust. Underlying the diffidence of agents about financial services referrals is, we suspect, anxiety about the implication that a referral is a test of good faith and financial ability and hence an implicit questioning of whether matters should go forward, which is of course the very reverse of the confidence the agent is trying to achieve. At its most severe, agents were well aware that some clients and applicants openly resented attempted referrals, and regarded such matters as in the first place their own business not the agency's, and in the second, that greater prudence lay in taking financial advice from an independent and perhaps already tried source. At times, then, agents might feel that financial services pressure could lose them a sale.

Not that there was any benefit to financial consultants in such pressured referrals — indeed the only benefit was to the agents who might discover an applicant was incapable of making good on his offer. 'Cold leads', as they were called, were a trap for financial advisers. Agents could claim to have done their part in asking 'as part of company procedure' if an applicant would talk to a financial adviser, but the adviser was given a lead with no chance of making a sale and hence a looming problem with achieving his target. Hot leads, where the referee was uncommitted, or had made only tentative enquiries elsewhere enables the consultant to demonstrate his skills. The consultant's objective was hence to cultivate the agency team to the point at which they delivered hot leads at the appropriate moment in the referee's decision making process. If this was done both consultants were confident of achieving targets.

Both consultants had worked as financial advisers elsewhere, one for 15 other employers over the years, and both were in no doubt that the Beech was easier to work for than some financial institutions. Its insurance products, to which the adviser was tied, were regarded as sound and competitive, and mortgage business could be placed anywhere. Targets were 60 per cent of sales to result in mortgages, hopefully with endowment insurance through the Beech, and 10 per cent of business to include in addition non-mortgage-related products, such as pensions, on which double commission was paid. Consultants were somewhat equivocal about pressures to achieve targets:

A: I get an awful lot of pressure on me.... You live from week to week, 'How many have you done this week?'
Q: But your job is not on the line surely is it?
A: Oh God no! I think if you did zero, zero, zero every week and they were selling five/six houses a week you would have problems. But no they would never.... They have a good basic and a car and the commission on top is more like a bonus really.... You want good figures, but you are not desperate, you would not give bad advice because you want that extra bit of commission.... They treat you like a direct sales person ... you have got to get results, you have got to do this, you have got to sell....

As with targets in property sales, the pressures are clearly there constantly, but the size of the carrots and sticks used is relatively modest. It should be added that the consultant quoted above was plainly successful and had recently been promoted.

Contrasts were vividly drawn with other corporates. The other consultant had recently worked for one, at which he said leads were required to purchaser and vendor in every sale, and the financial consultant had to produce at least one mortgage:

Q: What happened if you didn't?
A: If you didn't the first time, it doesn't matter. The second time it doesn't matter, the third time a verbal warning. The fourth time it is written, fifth time, thank you very much [i.e., dismissal].

In addition 70 per cent of mortgage business had to go to the parent company, which was not easy to achieve when other leading lenders were offering better terms.

The consequence of working in a world in which some financial consultants were under enormous sales pressure was that familiarity with abuses was considerable. Holding back on a cold-lead offer on a property until an offer with a hot financial services lead came along was recognised as a problem in the boom, but killed off by the slump and by regulatory pressure. Poaching was not. Direct sales forces working on commission only were cited as likely to attempt to poach clients already signed up through the Beech by claiming, often misleadingly, to offer better terms. Whilst competition in offering quotations for a variety of products was relished, the rules forbid attempting to get clients to back off products they have signed up for, and of course misrepresentation is illegal. It was also said that some consultants were unscrupulous in what they sold. 'Selling a first-time buyer a deferred mortgage or a low-start mortgage.... They haven't got the equity in the house to support that — once that two years are up they have got a great big bill.' The practice of mortgage lenders providing survey business in explicit exchange for mortgage business placed with them was mentioned as rife and accepted, but was not seen to constitute an undue constraint, because there was no management insistence by the Beech to place business with certain lenders in order to obtain survey business.

The scope for abuses in financial services sales is clearly considerable and the limited investigation we were able to make in and around the Beech plainly suggests that the way to control it lies in the terms of work of advisers and the sales policies of the parent companies. An aggressive sales policy accompanied by a heavy commission system, as is characteristic of direct sales forces, is almost bound to lead to trouble. As one of our consultants put it, if your figures are down and it is the last week of the month, the question is how you feed your family.

The question that concerns us more in respect of the Beech, however, is its position in relation to vendor and purchaser in the course of the sale when it has — or hopes to have — a financial interest in both parties. Under recent regulation, conditional selling is outlawed, vendors must be advised of the agent's desire to offer financial services to prospective purchasers, and must approve this. Although, as we have pointed out, the advantage in this is that the qualification of the purchaser is clearer earlier, there are also dangers. If the agent has a financial interest in the purchaser — perhaps larger than in the vendor — is the contract between the agent and the vendor compromised? The NAEA's ruling is worth quoting in this connection: 'An estate agent acting on behalf of a seller only assists the purchaser where it is in the vendor's interest to do so. The agent is not a broker. He acts only for the party who pays the bill.' Such a view is consistent with Davies's cultivation of purchasers as a means to ensuring the deal is struck to the genuine satisfaction of all parties. Is it consistent with linked financial services sales? In the Beech, as elsewhere, there was ample evidence that puchasers are at times unaware that the agent acts for the vendor. Where the purchaser's financial circumstances were disclosed in detail to financial advisers, that information was often passed informally to agents and could be used to assess whether to press for an increased offer. At the same time the agent's interest in achieving a deal where he stands to gain from both parties, about whom he has, in this situation, extensive information makes him not so much a broker as a *tertius gaudens*, a third party benefiting from the struggles of the other two.

This concern was a matter that was identified only towards the end of our fieldwork with the Beech — we do not have definitive information to suggest that it was a conflict of interest that was grossly abused. There is evidence, however, that there are no reliable safeguards to prevent effective abuse — by which we mean agents persuading themselves that by pushing a deal through they are doing the other parties a favour, when in fact the favour is mainly to the corporate estate agency. Further, we regard such significant entrenched conflicts of interest as recipes for trouble at some future stage, when markets, company policies and other factors alter, even if they are not pressing at any given time. At the very least, to return to the general analysis which preceded this first of the three reviews of corporate agents, the model of corporate estate agency which is plainly being pursued by the Beech, of service and procedure, is even less likely to achieve a satisfactory solution to the inherent complexities of estate agency, given an additional pressure towards getting the deal done in the interest of the agent. What this example suggests therefore is that it is ensuring that the agent is genuinely capable of offering disinterested advice to the client by training, experience and structural position that is critical to identifying a sound basis for good practice. Additional conflicts of interest cannot be conducive to this.

ASH PROPERTY AGENCY

Like the Beech, the Ash is a leading financial institution, this time a building society. The Ash has created a major national network of estate agencies, mainly by acquisitions in the latter 1980s, having entered the market a couple of years after the Beech. The Ash saw itself as a long-term participant in estate agency and was forced to face the problems of acquiring a large and disparate set of agencies spread throughout the country, a problem exacerbated by the onset of recession in 1988–9. Despite a loss of tens of millions of pounds in 1989, new branches were acquired and only 100 jobs shed. By the following year, however, the pressures to contain costs became imperative. The present operations director conceded that at this point, 'The business was going like a juggernaut out of direction'. At the same time the peculiarities of estate agency and its intractability to incorporation into a large financial institution were recognised, and the same conclusion drawn as the Beech, that the simultaneous objectives of financial control and some operational autonomy needed to be achieved. Management consultants were brought in and worked with an internal team of representatives from each of the 12 regions to work out a new structure and strategy for corporate estate agency in winter 1990–1.

This resulted in a corporate plan, the detailed phases of which were confidential, but which was unequivocally geared to cost curtailment and profit maximisation, envisaging a break-even in 1991–2, and full implementation within five years. The structural side of this is simple enough. The regions were reduced from 12 to seven and a new tier of budget centres were erected within these, grouping branches together and encompassing residential sales and financial services. Each budget centre is run by an executive, supported by area managers representing residential and financial services. Professional services, such as surveying and valuing, have been hived off from their original bases in the acquired multi-disciplinary estate agencies and operate under a separate name. They have their own management representative at budget-centre level. The budget-centre executives work with a managing director, financial controller and operations support executive at regional level. The outcome is that the regional management tier is relatively weak, acting mainly as a conduit to the centre, and the budget centres are the focus of decision-making and responsibility. The company newspaper emphasised to staff the devolution of decision-making which restructuring would involve and linked it to training initiatives, cost controls and local and individual autonomy, and with it financial reward and job satisfaction.

It should be added in this connection that branding is comprehensive, with all branches going under the corporate name only and uniforms for women (men wear the usual business suits). In a powerful respect therefore, the ground was prepared for uniformity of practice, with standardised offices concentrating on residential sales and allied financial services sales. As a leading building society with an established national high street presence this was seen as a marketing advantage. The tightness of corporate control was enhanced when, not long before our research, the decision was taken to tie with a leading life insurance company. Like many other corporates, the target property market was middle and lower, though naturally with some local variations. How then could room be found for a significant degree of local autonomy? Creating a partially devolved structure was clearly oxymoronic: budget centres were to be given discretion only within strict account limits.

The solution — the strategy to accompany the structure — was another oxymoron, the managed entrepreneur. This term was explicitly devised to accompany the devolution of responsibility to budget centres and to revive sentiment about the independent estate agents that many staff had formerly been. It constitutes an apparent acceptance that good estate agency revolves round a sense of independence, and there was explicit reference in company literature about getting back to the spirit of the old partnership days. In particular, the dangers were recognised of over-long decision-making chains and wide spans of control, and their potential for leaving front-line branch office staff feeling exposed, powerless and misunderstood, whilst also being expected to produce sales. We shall have to look quite carefully, however, to discover what is the real practice behind the managed entrepreneur. Some of the benefits were evident. One budget centre manager, formerly a regional manager, found himself responsible for 20 branches not 70. 'Obviously I am closer to the ground, communications are better, at least I hope they are. I actually get around all the branches and see what's going on and I feel a lot more comfortable with that role.'

This budget centre executive was in no doubt that corporate estate agency was the future, and it only remained to get it working right. 'The sort of cottage industry approach, like with nine branches, I know some of them were little tiddly things, but it was total, an anachronism, it was under-funded, and it hadn't got much future'. In contrast the corporation had supplied massive funding for branding, staffing, office refurbishment, and training, with marketing and personnel administration support currently being lobbied for with every expectation of success. Further, the parent company 'tend to say to us, "Look we have got a good idea, what do you think of it?"', rather than imposing it by managerial fiat. Regions were not required to do things in the same way, as dictated by head office:

> They have a reporting system from the region to the centre, they obviously had to have it all basically the same, but the reporting from the branch to the region was done in 12 different ways. It still is done in different ways but we are just about to put in force a management business information system which they have been working out for about six months and involved everybody in it, everybody has had their say. Tantrums have been thrown and it has been a very patient approach so that we are ending up with a system that everyone feels comfortable with.

This system has the same functions as paper flow at the Beech, and has been introduced in roughly the same manner in the same phase of organisational development. The executive quoted above, Tim, went on to re-emphasise the change in style which it ushered in. In the context not of paper flow as an explicit tool of corporate control but of the managed entrepreneur embodying controlled freedom of action it brings to mind another oxymoron: repressive tolerance.

Nor is the emphasis on control lacking:

> It's budget time at the moment and people are saying things like, you have got to increase your turnover by 15 per cent, and I am saying what planet do you come from? ... We have found with the Ash that they are prepared to listen, accept the fact that we are experts in our field and that's led to a pretty good relationship.

But the quid pro quo for corporate commitment, financial support and restructuring is that costs are to be controlled. As another budget centre executive put it: 'There's a conflict between cost-cutting and revenue generation'. He went on to say, 'What hasn't yet been resolved are the various issues around best practice, which are being looked at. And that's not best practice necessarily from the public's point of view, but best practice from an efficiency point of view.' There is no necessary incompatibility there, but the corporate emphasis has clearly been put across. It is again evident in management style. As the budget centre executive first referred to put it: 'We have an MD who is an estate agent.... His style is such that he has the accountant who used to be a financial director. He doesn't do anything without his input. So it feels as if I am dealing with a corporate administrator', though he went on to say that in a neighbouring region the estate agent's MD marginalised the accountant.

The question arises then, as to what the local-level entrepreneur, the branch manager, is free to exercise his or her initiative on. When this point was put directly, this avowed enthusiast for the new way came up with some interesting examples:

> The way you actually generate the cash for the business, that is still very much down to the individual. I am trying to think of some examples, e.g., how you spend your advertising budget. You might decide to go like fury in the spring, and the idea is that you won't advertise in the back end of the year.... There will be opportunities to get instructions to sell bits of land and other items to do with residential estate agency business. Those decisions to seek more business, that is down to the individual.

These examples are interesting in that they do not go into the central area of traditional estate agency business, which is activating relations with clients and facing the dilemma constantly of what is in the agent's interest and what is in the client's.

The solution to this, as with the Beech, is a notion of service, derived explicitly from retailing. In the words of an area manager:

> I used to get jobs [as an independent] ... because there was somebody else at the rugby club or in the Round Table or whatever it was.... Now I am no longer in that connection.... You have got to make up for that.... You have got to be able to deliver the service. And if you are going to deliver the service you must be able to measure it. You have got, then, when you have decided what you want to deliver, you have got to train people. Now that is where the advantages come from in having a great corporate backer.... OK, you might not know the face when you go into the estate agency, you might look for the guy who sold you the house five years ago, but the fact that his office offers tremendous service and has got a reputation for sevice, that will be enough to get you to go there.... I think it's a bit overdone with Marks and Spencer's, but you do get this expression that their standard of service is a standard to be judged by.

Two important points arise out of this. First, this proceduralised view plainly eliminates the individual and identifiable estate agent as a person at the heart of a successful business, which is, Tim accepts, repeat business. The service offered here is a measured, proceduralised, impersonal one, albeit friendly, polite and efficient. Secondly, the emphasis on procedure and measurement largely evacuates any space for initiative or entrepreneurship.

Tim remarked earlier: 'The way you run the file, OK try and do it the M & S way and making sure that you have enough checks to make sure that you do deliver the service to them. But the way you actually generate the cash for the business that is still very much down to the individual.' One can now see why he continued, 'I am trying to think of some examples'.

When it comes to protecting the interests of the public the approach is, not surprisingly, sustained by its emphasis on procedure rather than content. Service is always the keynote but the qualitative problems of relations with clients that we have noted so persistently are entirely omitted:

> The Ash throughout all their operations like to appear absolutely squeaky clean. And, for example, there are new orders under the Estate Agents Act which come into force at the end of this month. And a great deal of time and effort has been put into making sure that our agency teams reflect these orders. There's also the Property Misdescription Bill which is on its way and due later this month to be enacted, and we have rolled down to our staff training sessions to reflect [company] policy but also policy on the ground. The practice on the ground is what they must do to supply and develop new forms to make their job easier and so forth.

Compliance is proceduralised, with due efficiency, so that the public can be told that they are protected.

Like the Beech, the Ash had targets set on an annual basis in a cash budget form. This was then translated into quarterly targets, with front-line staff targeted on listings, gross sales, net sales, the budget itself, and additional income from financial services and building society agency. It was accepted that the pressure of targets was significant, and in contrast to the independents, where the majority were believed not to have targets and those that did to apply them less formally. It was also accepted that setting targets was a hit-and-miss process. We looked at two regions of the Ash, both mixed areas of middle and working-class housing on the edge of conurbations, one in the North and one in the South, the latter being the more prosperous, though also affected by redundancies at a major local employer. Two branches in the South and four in the North, though less intensively, were observed, and staff interviewed. The similarities between the two sites were on the whole much more striking than the differences, reflecting the impact of corporate ownership.

In respect of targets, however, the full force of the recession had only been felt in the previous year (1990) in the North, which had meant that targets set in the light of the previous year's performance had been achieved in the early months of the year, but had been seriously missed in the latter months. Since there was considerable local management input into the negotiation and evaluation of targets, and since the impact of the recession was uniform within regions, targets were not used to put additional pressure on staff and we did not, on the whole, find staff complaining about target pressure. Attitudes of staff at budget centre executive and office manager level to targets varied significantly, however. Here is a view which sees them benignly:

I am not a person who is set a target and you go for it. I am a believer that the targets will be achieved if your team works as a team and the rewards will come at the end of the day anyway, not to ape up the figures, but if you do what you consider is your best work, and your best work is taking on houses, marketing and selling them, at the end of the day the rewards will come. Once again you come back down to service, because if people don't get that kind of service they won't come back to you.…
Q: That's no different presumably to what it was as an independent?
A: No, no, it's very similar. That's not a great pressure. The pressure you will create yourself.

In this office manager's view targeting is part of the new regime and he is happy to be managed through it, yet retain a feeling that he is an entrepreneur, at least in the sense of being able to get on with his job. A budget centre executive used targets more aggressively: 'At our quarterly meeting I do some league tables as percentage performance against budget. We don't want it too complicated, but I want people to be able to see who is top of the league and who is bottom of the league — it is important.'

Front-line staff are not, then, to be allowed to forget their obligations to the overall budget, and are to be made to compete with each other. This view and its implications are brought out by an area manager:

We are all run by accountancies, which isn't a criticism of accountancy, but it does mean that the entrepreneurial spirit and the decision-making that we previously enjoyed for a number of years is in fact slightly diminished, because when we make a commercial decision these days we don't make it with the customer in mind or the client in mind, we obviously make it with profitability at the end of the day in mind and our accountability to somebody else within the organisation who may well be asking questions.

Here management is plainly seen as stifling entrepreneurship to the detriment of the public.

It was not, however, targets that front-line staff experienced as a major irritant, but pay. This, as we shall see, tended to spread into a criticism of the parent company as a low-wage employer, whose policy had the consequence of failing to provide effective staff. It is fair to say that complaints about pay were concentrated in the southern research site, where living costs were higher, but it was admitted by senior management in both regions that the Ash had a low-wage and high-turnover problem. This is quite distinct from the case of bonuses and incentives where, like the Beech, its position was moderate. A staff member indeed made it part of a complaint about pay that a bonus scheme for financial services had been cut as part of cost-cutting. A northern budget centre executive was at pains to explain that there was an 80/20 split in favour of basic salary because of the recession, but with the objective of increasing bonus incentives as soon as the market improved. 'I don't want people being wooed away to the independents because I can't pay them enough.' This, however, was not the point made by staff.

I just lost a ... very very good secretary ... because she could not afford to stay here, because they were living together and the mortgage rate had gone up, and they couldn't afford it, pure and simple. And the [manager] said to me, 'We don't want staff coming in who do it for the money'. I only came here because it's convenient, because I live just up the hill. But the salaries are ... :
Q: Not top drawer?
A: Definitely not. I daren't tell you what I get.... I do the agency here the same as the building society, but I get paid through [the estate agency] and you are talking about probably £2,000 [less].

The complaint that building society staff in the parent body had better pay, perks and careers was a persistent one, the biggest grudge being their subsidised mortgages. The problem was exacerbated because, like the Beech, the Ash had failed as yet to develop a proper career structure for its estate agents. In the context of low pay this gave rise to a level of resentment and insecurity that was absent at the Beech, even though, as we have seen, it was admitted by both managements as a problem that needed settling if corporate estate agency was to succeed. At the Ash the solution was the traditional one in independent estate agency: when frustrated about low pay or anything else, move:

It has taken me to leave and come back before they have paid me more salary. You are offered it on the day you leave to stay, but there again they should have offered it before you left.

This quite successful assistant office manager also translated frustrations about pay into frustrations about budgetary costs:

It's very frustrating to know that perhaps somebody in another office is probably, maybe £3,000 more better off than you on a basic salary, you are doing exactly the same job, but because they budget back on perhaps cars, or they haven't got another member of staff through no fault of your own, you are on a lesser amount.

Low pay also translates into staff turnover, which frustrates the effects of training, and in turn leads to poor performance:

At the moment I feel they tend to employ a lot of young people, pay them next to nothing, they don't have the experience and therefore they don't sell the houses.... A guy that starts out is perhaps provided with a very low budget car, which is fair enough, but would probably be on something like £5,000 plus a few per cent commission just as an incentive. And it's fine for when he starts, but when he gets a taste and starts to get the training ... and very well trained I would say ... fine, then there will be another estate agent down the road who is paying an awful lot more and are only too willing to take them on with the experience at our expense.... And, OK, we will have to replace him as cheaply as possible, because we have got to keep the budgets down.... The last three people that have been here, young guys, have done that.

Sometimes the consequences of this can be dramatic:

At one time they had a bit of a crisis where they lost all their staff at the same time, and I was one man and a trainee negotiator running an office that should have had five salesmen.... I benefited from that [experience] in these later years, but I find there was no 'Well done, you really ought to be promoted', it was a case of me having to go and see them. Eventually to the managing director, I said 'I am not happy' ... and admittedly ... they provided three salesmen by the end of the month. But until that time I had gone three months after complaining to an area manager and nothing had been done. Even that area manager had not once come into the office to help out, to answer phones or things like that. And that's what they are there for.

Perhaps not surprisingly, a contradiction was seen between training for good practice and pressures to meet targets and budgets:

On the one hand you have got a training department that are telling you in ethics what you should be doing, and on the other hand you are getting the guys at the top who are from a totally different body ... and you are stuck in the middle.

As at the Beech, market pressures in a corporate estate agency produced a chronic and recognised tendency to overvalue properties. Despite publicity material for clients emphasising that: 'getting the valuation right is of paramount importance. If it's too high the consequences could be wasted time, money and considerable inconvenience. The longer that a property stays on the market, the less the likelihood of there being a successful sale at an acceptable price', there was abundant evidence that overpricing was a constant concern at all levels of management. Initiatives were taken to obtain staff compliance and there was frustration at the refusal of some to listen and of a general tendency to accept instructions at higher values than were generally justified. Some staff dealt with this problem directly:

There's no point in being the sort of agent who always says, all right, I will have a go at £72,500 and then apart from doing the details, doing absolutely nothing about it. I genuinely would go to my ultimate in order, in a way, to prove that by pushing it at £72,000 there was not a buyer there at £72,000 and you have got to come down to the £69,950 to get a buyer.

This office manager was unusually tough and determined, however. Like the Beech, valuers were ready to listen to the views of vendors and to be persuaded in many cases to take their properties on at prices specified by them, albeit with warnings that the price was unlikely to be obtained. Pressure to meet targets and competition from other agents were the main reasons cited for overvaluation, as well as the more professional reasons of the desirability of the property, a changing market which might rise, or the property's location in a spot where the board would be good advertising. Mispricing properties constitutes a potential loss to vendors in missed opportunities for a sale and in possibly blighting a property as unsellable — purchasers note that it has been on the market for months and assume it must have some defect. Management of course were more concerned at the costs of running a list which was bringing in too few sales.

It was, then, in the area of price reductions that the greatest dangers lay. As a budget centre executive admitted, 'I can see that people are concerned that undue pressures might be brought to bear to get prices down for the survival of the estate agency'. With staff being told at times that unless costs were cut and budgets achieved branches would close, this is not an unrealistic anxiety. A number of front-line staff openly admitted that they would urge vendors to accept almost any offer in the weak market that prevailed, and we saw evidence of pressure being brought to bear on vendors to this end at times. The difficulty, however, is to some extent that of the market, in which a realistic selling price may be hard to judge — we have cited examples of this in an earlier chapter. What perhaps is significant in this connection is that the training and philosophy surrounding the managed entrepreneur gave no guidance that we were able to discover on how to manage this dilemma correctly: the detail of negotiation is an evident lacuna, both here, and indeed in the OCEA code of conduct for all corporate estate agents. Although it was suggested by the executive above that one solution was to suggest taking a property off the market if it did not sell at the vendor's price, this does not answer the criticism fully, since the vendor who does need to sell may very well be in a position of needing every penny he can extract from the market. We did not see examples of agents appearing to push their clients' interests boldly, even aggressively, but openly, as their agents, to achieve this. The estate agency culture prevailed, in which relations with the purchaser are cultivated and the selling technique is slow and gentle rather than up-front and direct. As in the case of the Beech, then, we cannot say how far clients were disadvantaged by overpricing or by pressure to reduce prices and generate commission income. We can say that both tendencies were evident and were enhanced by corporate estate agency, with its emphasis on cash control and individual targets and its client orientation in terms of a retail style of service rather than a professional commitment. Once again the requirement of the corporate to maintain control, and above all financial control, militated against any sense of dealing with clients in a way that parenthesised, for the time being, business considerations of financial gain: service was proceduralised not professionalised.

How did financial services impinge upon this? Many of the same problems of lines of responsibility as between estate agency and financial services existed as in the Beech and will not be repeated here. Relations between the two had been regularly changed over the preceding few years and, as a result

of the restructuring and budget centre system with the managed entrepreneurship strategy, things were clearly moving in the direction of managing
both sides of the business in an integrated way. As it was, financial services
was answerable to a manager at regional and budget centre levels who was
usually an estate agent and financial services contributed to the overall
profitability of each centre. On the other hand, financial services consultants
were not answerable to branch or even agency managers, even though the
latter were targeted on financial services referrals and their finances
calculated on a threshold of 65 per cent of sales being converted into financial
services sales. There was middle-management pressure for more complete
integration and control and it seemed likely that this might come in due
course.

The relationship between financial services and estate agency had also
been made simpler by a recent move to tie with an insurer. This meant that
mortgages were expected to go predominantly to the parent building society,
though with freedom recently established to shop around, given that this
generated commission and hence contributed to budget centre profitability.
Endowment and other life insurance was now tied to a leading life office
which, whilst restricting for consultants, was fairly easy to defend, since the
insurer's market position was strong and it was agreed that clients would do
no better elsewhere. From the corporation's point of view this had other
advantages:

> We went down the route of FIMBRA, which is independent best advice, so
> we had to tell all our residential people that you are not qualified to give
> this advice, therefore you must refer everything. Now we have gone down
> another route which is LAUTRO, tied to one supplier [of insurance]. It
> means we can involve ourselves once more in the real job, and that is you
> are acting for your client. If you send an offer forward to your client, you
> must know whether that offer can be substantiated. Therefore you need to
> know whether that person can raise the mortgage they say they are going
> for, whether they have the equity to make up the difference, whether they
> have sold their own property, what stage their own sale is and so on and
> so forth. And from the client's point of view we try to provide that
> information with a recommendation. We have an offer of £x. Do you think
> he will go any more? Yes because we know he is not mortgaged to his
> limit.... If you are dealing with somebody, a purchaser who has gone
> through the same experience and expected his agent to provide that
> information then they don't mind passing it on, providing you explain
> what it has been used for.

We see here the entire structure of financial services provision being
presented as geared to the vendors' interests and to those of the agent, at the
evident expense of the purchaser. As this budget centre executive later said,
a purchaser who refuses to divulge such information is likely to be adversely
commented on to the vendor, since he cannot be properly qualified and his
claim to make the offer substantiated. When the implications for the

exploitation of the purchaser were put persistently to him, he eventually said, 'You are making us sound all-powerful. I don't think we are. The client inevitably has a price in mind that they wish to achieve.' Inevitably? A definite price in the thin market which prevailed at that time? He accepted that purchasers might well obtain a mortgage elsewhere. 'But we would still do a mortgage interview, because we would want to know, given that most financial people work on the same sort of multiples and lending criteria, within a broad framework, you would know whether they are heavily in debt to do this.' We submit that this is oppressive and exploitative of the purchaser.

A financial services consultant was equally unequivocal that his job was to qualify the purchaser as much as sell financial services, though of course it was the latter that enabled him to reach his targets:

> I try to get as much information to give to property services to say, right this chap is fine, no problems with his mortgage, he's qualified for looking for a house of £50,000. But you find people looking at £50,000 and they can only go to £45,000 and then you have to find if they have got a deposit.

As it happens this consultant went out of his way to protect purchasers, particularly the young and naïve. He explained at length the dangers of the 100 per cent mortgage and said he would refuse to do one, even though they were available and it might cost him the business, where he felt that his client was overexposed by it. He would even recommend borrowing a 5 per cent deposit from the bank in preference to a 100 per cent mortgage. 'It would be a personal thing, a very personal thing. Because I wouldn't want my son or daughter to go into a 100 per cent mortgage, because, number one, the minute you blink on your mortgage they are on you like a ton of bricks'. Similarly, he explained at length the pitfalls and variations of mortgage indemnity guarantee insurance, which is required for borrowing over 75–80 per cent of value, and the ways for purchasers to avoid paying unnecessarily high premiums. He was also ready to discuss the sensitive topic of endowment mortgages and to accept that, whilst he believed in their benefits as a lifetime strategy he had himself employed, he would not necessarily recommend it to all purchasers. Since endowment insurance is the source of most consultants' commission, and this interview took place before recent public debate on the overselling of such insurance had much developed, this is laudable but, of course, a matter of individual integrity and pride in the quality of advice given rather than structural protection of clients. This consultant provided examples of clients he had prevented from overextending themselves and from committing themselves to poor financial packages, but the protection against abuses and financial services misselling was, he was clear, effectively the integrity of the consultant and the streetwiseness of the purchaser. The only additional protection of the purchaser against the abuse of financial information about him or her to the benefit of the vendor and the agent was the mortgage survey. With such surveys being taken in-house, and from our observations being conducted by the in-house valuers and professional services business on a basis as limited as a drive-past and a perfunctory examination only a little more substantial than a lister's valuation, and based in the same way on comparability, that is a slim safeguard.

There are considerable similarities, then, in the experience, responses and weaknesses of the structure of the corporates that we have examined. The Ash has been more explicit in confronting the cultural challenge of estate agency for a financial institution, and probably more thoroughgoing in its devolution of responsibility to budget centres. In doing so, however, it has weakened itself by the combination of emphasis on cost control and accountability, and low pay and consequential high staff turnover. It did not seem to us that the concept of the managed entrepreneur had really either set its estate agency staff alight with enthusiasm or reassured those who were nostalgic about working for independents. Problems of career structures for estate agents in a corporate had not been resolved. Similar problems of the subordination of clients and purchasers to the interests of the business were evident, and if anything more explicit and pervasive than at the Beech. This judgment is, however, much less important than the fact that, in both corporates, the interests of vendors and purchasers were structurally more exposed than in independent estate agency, with that exposure covered by a commitment to service and the reputation of a great institution. The last word should perhaps be left to a member of front-line staff:

> He won't get the same service from the independent, no, but at the end of the day, if the guy is going to have his house sold and he was made all the promises under the sun from the independent, he won't mind if the guy turns up in jeans and a ripped T-shirt.

The final corporate by contrast makes the claim to take all this on and to transform and transcend it. So, in the familiar phrase, now for something completely different.

SYCAMORE AND ELM

In contrast with the other two corporates we investigated, the Sycamore and Elm (S & E) is a regional rather than a national business, with a strong presence in its home territory in the South of England. It is a substantial building society which has spread its lending and savings services well beyond its home base. It entered estate agency in the mid 1980s, acquiring businesses in its home area. In comparison with the other corporates reviewed it had a relatively small network of less than 100 offices divided into four regions with an overall head of estate agency who came from the building society. The network as a whole was thus less than or about the same as the size of the regions of the national corporates, and the regions about the size of the Ash's budget centres. The S & E was unequivocal that it had entered estate agency as the 'doorway to financial services' and said that the point of sale for mortgages and other financial services was shifting to the intermediary. Its estate agents traded under corporate colours, though perhaps less visually than the Ash, apart from a quite large upper-middle-market agency, recently acquired, which continued to trade under its old name. The head of estate agency said that this was at the suggestion of the Building Societies Commission, the only example we have come across of the regulatory side of this supervisory body in the estate agency field, though it has traditionally played a low-key role. In any case this arm's length relationship suited the S & E, since it wished to concentrate on getting its strategy and structure right for its mainstream estate agents which, as with other corporates, were further down-market. Because of the different market location of this agency it was not anticipated that it would ever be brought to trade under the corporate logo and was expected to maintain its own management structure for its chain of branches (suitably rationalised with the weaker ones weeded out). In other aspects it was expected to be integrated into S & E management styles, culture and systems in due course.

We observed two contrasting offices at S & E. The first of these was the town centre office in a prosperous city, itself a market town and administrative centre. The office liked to think it was rather up-market in comparison with some of the suburban branches, but in reality it dealt with all types of property in its 200 + list. There were seven staff including a financial services consultant, and the office was busy throughout the observation period. Staff worked through lunches, were under time pressure to keep up with appointments and worked late on paperwork. The office manager had had a successful career as an estate agent and obviously enjoyed his work. He had taken over the office in mid 1990 at the age of 26 'when it needed a pep pill'. With the agreement of the regional manager he disposed of the existing staff, who were redeployed, and built up a team of keen young staff whose integration as a team and willingness to work hard and get results he regarded as paramount. 'If I took on somebody tomorrow and after a fair period of three months I saw they weren't working with the rest of the team they would have to go'. This led on the one hand to a working camaraderie and out-of-hours socialising and to a deliberately maintained buzz of activity in the office, spurred on by references to 'keeping up the good work' and 'going for it', to the other hand 'Mike feels under a lot of pressure and some of it rubs off on us'. Lack of effort resulted in a disciplinary response. The branch was well thought of by management, both for its estate agency success and for its acceptance of corporate culture, on which more presently.

The other observation site was a rural office 'run by two women doing residential work and a recent school leaver acting as clerk receptionist'. Originally this office had been part of a small chain with some specialisation in the substantial properties in the surrounding countryside, but it now dealt with the full range and indeed its competitive relations were friendly with the local branch of a corporate which elsewhere we had found cited as one of the more aggressive. Less amicable were relations with an independent formed by a former S & E manager who was alleged to deliberately overprice, to underprice by buying property through a subsidiary property company, and to buy at auction without disclosing his status as an estate agent. There was none of the pressure associated with the city centre office, located in the estate agents' strip. Lunches were taken at home, viewings less rushed; nor was there any of the hype associated with the city centre office. The market was quieter and both the senior staff were well aware that its recovery or lack of it would determine the fate of their office. To say that they aspired to the professional side of estate agency would be perhaps to overstate the position: genteel at any rate. Certainly they were unimpressed by the corporate owners' culture. Paperwork was studiously prepared and equally studiously ignored, weekly training sessions dismissed as a 'pain in the neck', concern with cost control and targets as beyond their capacities, whilst at the same time recognising that 'In my time with S & E managers have gone because they didn't reach targets consistently'. In consequence the office was not seen favourably by management, and as the fieldworker remarked, always seemed to be mentioned with raised eyebrows.

The smaller size of the S & E made it easier to get a rapid sense of the overall direction in which the corporation was going, the place of estate agency in it, and of management reaction to this. In addition, however, the response at the S & E to the challenges of estate agency which we have identified in our previous two comparative reviews was more vigorous, radical and well thought out. The essence of the corporate strategy was to integrate estate agency entirely into, not the building society, but a new tripartite enterprise comprised of a marketing amalgamation of saving and lending, estate agency, and investment services (insurance, pensions, unit trusts etc.). The building society was hence attempting to shift its overall business profile in the direction of a diversified financial services operation and to integrate estate agency into that. In doing so it recognised that some of the more pedestrian and traditional features of building society business would be as inappropriate to financial services high street retailing as to estate agency. At the same time, of course, it faced all the problems of integration, socialisation and control, especially cost control, that the other corporates did.

Given this strategy, branding estate agents strongly with the corporate identity was essential. In any case it was believed that the building society had an excellent regional reputation and had strong customer loyalty for repeat business which was just what estate agency needed, and which was also a vital basis for the success of the wider financial services retail operations. The idea is to use the financial services and building society work to lead to house sales as much as vice versa. Nonetheless, like the Ash, the decision had recently been taken to tie with a major insurer, a composite rather than a specialist life insurer, and all mortgage business was expected to be with the S & E. Integrated branches incorporating the three streams of business in equal standing were due to be launched in 1991–2 and were therefore not up and running at the time of our observation. The decision on strategy and structure had by this time been taken, however, and had provoked clear and sometimes vehement responses from estate agency staff, as we shall see. The principal structural change was the creation of two separate investment services and estate agency management structures, both under the control of a retail manager. Thus, on the one hand, financial services consultants were required to apply for new jobs, and no longer expected merely to service estate agency but to sell financial services to the general public, and on the other, estate agency came under the control of a new non-estate-agency management, but, nominally at least, also a non-building-society management: retail management applied equally to all three streams of business, with each expected to serve the other, but also to serve its own independent market. In time the major three-stream centres would be paralleled with smaller offices with elements of the overall concept, but closer to the traditional estate agency branch.

The key question which this strategy raises in the light of other corporate experience reviewed above is whether the new concept and business arrangements form a bridge between the financial services corporation and estate agency, or whether, albeit they shift the emphasis away from traditional building society activities, they do not engage constructively with estate agency. The critical element here is the retail variation of the new ideology. Management staff from major retailers had been hired to make a major contribution to implementing the new strategy, and the central marketing idea of the new high street centres was to use high-grade retailing techniques to reduce public anxiety about approaching either financial services or property sales. The ultimate objective and the strategy is put by a regional manager:

> What we are trying to do is develop a relationship with a client so that that client will bond, if you like, with the S & E as being the vehicle the client will use in terms of his investments, his banking, his property advice and his personal advice, his tax relief.... I think the term retailer, I am using [as] how it is perceived, not as a definition of what we are. We want people to feel as comfortable as they would be going in to buy a bag of sweets.

The new integrated branches are hence designed to be large, well-appointed and fronted by a hotel-style receptionist, who will direct customers to a specific area providing the services they are interested in. The overriding principle is that there will be no sales pressure, and customers will be encouraged to shop around and feel free to window-shop without an obligation to buy. 'Some people really don't want to speak to people unless they are pretty sure they like something [a property]'. Customers will be encouraged to use the large browsing areas for properties and financial services, to pick up literature, and to ask questions:

> It will be a far more laid-back, less aggressive approach to estate agency.... You will have around the office various large screens which will be continually throwing up houses on the screen, because people like to see different things.... The estate agents' people will be there, but there will be access ... you having gone through a series of VDUs that you work yourself. You touch which areas you are interested in. It then gives a range of prices ... and it narrows it down as you would in an estate agent's.... Do you want it with a garden or without?

Modern technology is thus brought to bear to keep sales staff at a distance until their skills are needed, and to take the pressure off customers and make them see that they are in control. This has consequences also for the financial services side:

S & E are currently going through a major decentralisation programme, where we are actually reviewing the ability of building society staff to provide investment advice ... simply because we are not happy with the standard of advice that they can give, because they are narrow-minded. They don't sit down and react to what the client needs.

Staff are to be trained not to see customers as adjuncts of property transactions and their job as selling mortgage and linked life insurance, but as financial services customers in general. How does this square with being tied to a single insurer, which surely cannot lead to the provision of best advice?

It is not necessarily something which in the strictest terms I would say is best advice. The distinction you have is that you look at the UK, the average sum assured of the average person in the UK is £11,000 which is really shocking. ... I would say the initial objective when we have such low amounts of life insurance in this country is to get in a position to provide financial advice. ... Now that is not in my view the best way of doing it, but we are restricted by government. As I say, you either do all or you deal with one. ... For the S & E to run an independent financial advice system it would be absolutely horrendous in terms of administration, paperwork, not to mention the cost of compliance and also of actually getting sufficient people who are capable of actually handling that wide an information base. ... Our objective is not one of becoming the world's best financial advisers. ... Let's create an environment whereby somebody can actually feel they can ask whether they have got enough life assurance, because at the moment people don't like asking, because they think that people are going to try and sell them something.

Toning down the active selling element in estate agency by this strategy and increasing the prominence of financial services advice under the new concepts may be anticipated to disconcert many estate agents, but bearing in mind the interactive effect of other matters as such as pay and targeting, administrative controls and turnover, let us consider these issues before returning later to this central problem. Initial reactions were certainly not all favourable:

If you want to create an office to look not like a building society and not like an estate agent then go and look at X. ... They should have moved the ATM machine and made a bigger window and stuck houses in the window if they wanted it to look like an estate agent. We are not perceived to be a first-division estate agent in X. The trouble is we have got first-division players in there, first-division costs but we are living off third-division receipts.

As this regional estate agency manager concedes here, however, S & E did not make the mistake of the Ash in undermining the acceptability of their innovative strategy by underpaying their staff. Pay was widely accepted as good, and indeed at least as good as the opposition, which made the recruitment and retention of staff realistic. Former estate agency partners had been brought into the new management structure on a wide scale, even though staff costs were kept down and, in the view of senior management, morale and enthusiasm kept up by an estate agency staff structure that was generally biased towards the young. It stands to reason that, with as radical a break as was envisaged, older staff with more established views and habits would find it harder to adapt, and that adaptation, enthusiasm and commitment was going to be necessary to make the new system work properly. Perhaps as a result of this there was rather less resentment about lack of clear career structures than in the other corporates. Although it was true that grading and salary systems had been integrated with those of the building society, the larger problem of careers in an estate agency now part of a corporate had not been resolved; perhaps this was effectively parenthesised by the integrated retail trading strategy, however. How opportunities would finally turn out in a new order that had not yet been implemented, let alone had time to settle down and impact upon careers, was necessarily an unknown factor at the time of our fieldwork. It was also evident from the amount of corporate effort going into the new strategy that its commitment to estate agency was a long-term one, and hence that, although rationalisation and the closure of branches would take place in response to market pressures and as part of the restructuring and introduction of the new retailing centres, cutbacks and redundancies were liable to be kept to a limited level, a likelihood in any case given the smaller regional structure of S & E's estate agency operation as a whole.

Pressure to achieve sales targets did not appear to be as strong as in the other two corporates, although pressure to achieve overall profitability was certainly powerful. Although there was a pay points system for financial services referrals, there was not the same emphasis on multiple targeting. At the same time the manager at the rural office remarked that every sale had to be passed through to head office immediately for inclusion in their statistics and to trigger the centralised billing system. Targets, she said, were a source of pressure and consistent failure to achieve them would result in dismissal, but management tended to take a positive view where possible. Equally, the manager in the busy city-centre office felt under pressure to achieve sales and keep within budget, but his budget was reasonable and his targets not unreasonable and he was allowed substantial discretion in achieving profitability within his budget, which involved the lease on his premises as well as standard items such as advertising and staff costs. This manager added to his description of costs and his budget:

Although we contain costs as best we can, we don't let that affect the service we give. If at the end of the day the service we are giving is being diluted, then we basically make sure that we ... don't take on as many properties.... Whereas when I think you have got a lower register and you have got time to try and get more properties on and spend time gradually convincing the vendors to bring their price down over a number of months, then you take on properties which are a higher price even though you know they won't sell.

As we see in the latter part of this quotation the level of pressure to maintain a stock of houses was sufficiently strong to produce the same tendency to overvalue that we have seen in the other corporates. This point was confirmed by the manager of the rural office who complained at the rigidity with which S & E insisted on its fee system, and suggested that pressures to overvalue could be located in head office:

We are told that instructions are going to become more and more difficult to get and therefore the more you get now the better. I still don't think that's a very good way of getting instructions. I prefer to tell people the truth.

At the same time observation of actual transactions in this office revealed that the rules were often bent in the client's favour to get business — perhaps because the manager would sooner do this than overprice. Only seven out of 17 properties going to exchange or sale agreed in a month that we checked were charged full fee for one reason or another. It was usual, however, to ask the client's view on price, and this seemed to be a powerful guideline in the city centre office, with a clear articulation of the probable need for a reduction where appropriate. Staff here saw it as very much their job to test the market for what it would provide and, as a negotiator put it: 'If it is the case that we are a little high, we advise on when and how to come down in price'. As elsewhere, valuers had clear expectations put upon them as to the rate at which they were expected to convert viewings into instructions to sell, but staff were very aware of the dangers of an overpriced property going stale on the shelf. As a manager put it: 'The last house that you took on is the most saleable house you have got, because every day a house is on the market it becomes less saleable'. The implicit reasoning here is that once a property is exposed and marketed it is either sold or not and if not, effectively rejected by the buying public. Nonetheless section iii of the OCEA code of practice states 'In no circumstance shall a member deliberately misrepresent the potential sale price of a property for the purposes of gaining instructions'. No doubt staff would claim in their defence that the warnings accompanying the take-on price were a sufficient safeguard, but our impression once again is that clients were permitted to deceive themselves in some cases.

In several respects, then, the S & E seems to indicate a lesser propensity to fall into the errors that we have seen other corporates make, which cut the ground from under the feet of those who are attempting to create corporate estate agency. Before considering staff attitudes and experience of the corporation and their views on the transformative strategy, the place of financial services and its relation to estate agency need to be evaluated. First, however, we must note two areas which give grounds for anxiety about the implementation of so ambitious a strategy: the introduction of administrative reporting and control systems and the role of training and development.

The first of these is an issue familiar from the other corporates, and was faced at the S & E through an O & M study which was undertaken shortly before our observation period. The rationale was a familiar one, articulated here by the head of estate agency: 'We will be wanting to look ... more closely at what [estate agents] are doing and how they are doing it in order to improve service quality'. This does not mean rigid proceduralisation. The sales process differs 'depending on the type of market-place the branch operates in. If you have got a branch where you have got high volumes of low-cost properties it does operate very differently from the branch where ... most of your market is [more expensive]'. However, 'there is an enormous amount of abortive work that comes over in estate agency, which does not result in a sale at all, and it's all of that which causes slight problems'. Whether front-line staff would see such efforts as wasted and whether they would accept the greater proceduralisation is inevitably a moot point. The way in which the O & M study was carried out caused real antagonism however.

The estate agency exercise followed a similar more successful one for building society work designed to evaluate staffing levels and produce a role and capacity analysis. What O & M staff saw as a rational management tool, however, was seen by estate agency staff as a cost-cutting exercise, particularly since it involved calculating staff requirements with full-time equivalents based on a recently introduced annual hours contract. Five branches were observed and the data extrapolated to a reference period of three months, using additional head office information to produce a series of valuations by branch, retail group and region. The actual staffing figures resulting were then compared, with two models, one assuming one staff member per branch to be available at all times and the other two — 1.9 and 3.8 FTEs. Not surprisingly the outcome was a calculation that estate agency was overstaffed. The reaction to O & M's recommendation that its report be adopted as a basis for staffing branches was hostile, with claims that observation in some branches was less than two hours and a questioning of the estimation techniques. What was seen by senior building society management as just a part of the development process, which had already been applied to the building society and was necessary to ensure efficient working and cost control, was identified by estate agents as management's failure to recognise the fact that estate agency work is different from that of the building society bureaucracy. It would probably be fair to say that it is hard to identify the variety of work an agent does in less than a working week — even then some work may be missed, because it is dependent on seasonal variations.

It could be argued, however, that O & M research is a narrow technical specialism and unsuited to the investigation of other than routine tasks, and that it was bound to produce perverse results when applied to estate agency. This does not explain the error of central management's decision to apply it willy-nilly but as we have seen, corporates can learn from this kind of mistake. What it does suggest, however, is that the corporate vision of the new integrated retail financial services centres generated a top-down view of change which might block the negotiated bottom-up process of development that was eventually seen to be essential to the creation of corporate estate agency at the Beech and the Ash. Further insight is provided on this issue by the role which training and staff development were envisaged as having in achieving the transformation of S & E. Not surprisingly, we were not given access to the entire S & E corporate plan, but it was explained by the head of training that it was a highly systematic and comprehensive document designed to produce detailed measurable targets for every region, and thence every branch, every quarter. He likened it to a Christmas tree, with a corporate vision at the top translated immediately below into overall targets, including a 20 per cent return on capital invested. This was then broken down progressively into practical local targets. As we go down the hierarchy the identification of such targets is a reciprocal process, with subordinates negotiating with superiors, but in each case the target is only acceptable if it can be tracked back and justified in terms of a superior-level objective. This system was introduced by outside consultants who remained as advisers:

> We have a guy ... who is our business planning chappie, who coaches and counsels all the heads of department on how to do their business planning, so they are receiving training. We constantly submit to [him] our effort into the business plan at whichever level we are operating. If he can't find a track or is unhappy with the specificity of it he says no and sends it back. Similarly, if my staff brings me a quarterly objective that is not specific, measurable, achievable, recordable and trackable it goes back.

In addition to this, senior management were subject to mentoring, whereby frank personal advisers would counsel the manager and discuss his or her personal strengths and weaknesses. The results of these sessions were then reported back to the line manager. The mentoring was a long-term process rather like psychotherapy, again recently imported from outside consultants and designed to improve management effectiveness. Together the new arrangements must have constituted a large increase in corporate control over senior management and went along with an explicit expectation of large increases in productivity.

The counterpart for lower-level staff were regular training sessions one evening a week which, apart from getting across the new targets and the changes in structure and culture, were useful to management in picking up the groundswell of staff feelings. At the time of observation these feelings evidently included some anxiety. Training programmes of all kinds were subject to the same criteria of measurability and improved performance, though the head of training admitted that neither he nor anyone he had met had really been able to show clearly what the benefits of training were. The objective was a 40 per cent improvement in efficiency as a result of training, but, as he pointed out, if training was implemented and efficiency improved, it was impossible to say how much this was the result of the training and how much the result of other changes which were also taking place.

Overall however, the objectives of training were ambitious and ruthless:

> You will either develop people with the work ethic, the motivation in the culture and the understanding ... or you will get a fallout because people can't adapt.... You will only get a small corps of people that do really see the vision and run with it, because that is not the culture that they joined. So you arguably will get ... at least a 70 per cent fallout of experienced staff, that kind of haemorrhage, so you're getting close to your 50 people 100 per cent effective, [which was earlier cited as preferable to 100 people 50 per cent effective.]

The costs of this were recognised, but like a religious convert, the sectarian qualities and the implications of alienating the majority seemed not to be. He talked later about providing 'a generation of superhuman workers', a 'vision' likely to increase unionisation which was already on the rise still further.

This outlook went along with a view of estate agency that referred to it as 'just another product', though the risk of doing so was recognised. 'All the corporates run the risk when they are trying to corporatise the estate agency wing, or the ice-cream wing, of imposing their vision, their mission, on to a business, which essentially won't take it. So there is a big risk'. That this might be a foolish risk to take was, interestingly, beginning to be suspected following the takeover of the large up-market estate agency. Because of its size and status, its directors — now managers — had been able to resist immediate integration and to insist that estate agency is different. S & E had countered by pointing out that some of its supposedly up-market business was decidedly ordinary, and requiring the closure of some branches, but the central issue of the distinctive requirements of estate agency seemed to be on the way to some recognition. Up to that point there seems little doubt that the recognition process that we have seen developing out of other corporate experience was prevented by the takeover of management culture by outside consultants, and the introduction of the business plan, which envisioned dramatic changes in everyone's lives, starting at the top. At S & E then, the issue of integrating estate agency into an existing corporate culture and structure was effectively obscured by the need to spread the word about the new corporate vision.

We have seen in other corporates that financial services had uneasy relations with estate agency. At the S & E, however, we have seen that they too were subject to changes, with consultants being made to apply for new jobs. One parallel with other corporates was that they continued to be employed by the parent building society, not by the estate agency arm. At the time of our observation of branches this was associated with accounting and targeting arrangements which gave no credit to estate agency branches for mortgage or financial services business generated in them. As a result of the overall review of the profitability of branches that was going on at the time, it was recognised that some would be due for closure on the basis of property sales, but nonetheless produced good income from mortgages and financial services. Given that the corporate's vision included tripartite branches, with each stream having equal status, this led to a change of policy, and branches became credited and targeted for mortgages, financial services and building society savings income, as well as property sales.

As elsewhere estate agents did not tend to see financial services sales as part of their job. One typical comment from the city-centre office ran:

> If I feel the time is right, and if I remember, if I am honest, then I will remember financial services, mention [the consultant] and get him to give them a call. . . . I enjoy estate agency. I don't enjoy talking about finance to that degree, not that I am qualified to do so. But it disinterests me, and I think once again it stems back to the fact that people have actually asked you to talk about their house, not to talk about a side sale if you like.

He went on to pay tribute to the hard work of the financial services consultant, but also to cite an example in which he obtained instructions rather than another agent because the other agent had put off the client by overemphasising financial services in his spiel. The rural office referred to constant pressure to produce referrals for financial and professional services, but all in all didn't experience this as unacceptable:

> I suppose after a period of time it becomes second nature really. You get used to spotting a big garden and wondering if there is a building plot there. . . . So this all then becomes part of your spiel really.

On the other hand she believed:

> There will still be a certain type of person, I think, that would not, unless they approached me — I wouldn't approach them about the financial side of things. . . . You just know you are overstepping certain boundaries.

The regional manager, at any rate, was very pleased with the financial services referrals figures coming through: 'Our performance is absolutely first rate'.

Financial consultants were encouraged by management to keep up the pressure by calling estate agents daily to check on all the potential contacts they had had, and to try to extract leads, a practice that was confirmed to take place at least at the city centre office, and apparently without causing too much resentment. Although referrals earned pay points worth about £3.50 this, as elsewhere, was little more than symbolic incentive. There was evidence that, for their part, financial consultants were aware of the dangers that their enlarged role could pose for property sales:

> There are 13 estate agents in this road, all with people like me sitting in them, so it is a very very competitive market. . . . I still think my job is to

help them to sell houses, and to get mortgage lending arranged through S & E, and I wouldn't want to push someone to the extent that they were going to back out.... In theory I suppose one does the mortgage and then one goes back in three, four, five weeks or a few month's time, when they have settled in, and then talk to them about other aspects of the job.

At the same time this consultant's targets were three times those of the preceding year, and he claimed he had had no part in setting them. A good deal of mortgage work came from people shopping around for mortgages, in addition to those related to sales effected by S & E estate agents, and at the time the consultant was resentful that no credit was given for this — as we saw above this was changed after our fieldwork. Going tied had been a source of considerable apprehension since 'You know that Standard Life are perhaps best for endowments and National Provident are perhaps best for pensions', but in the event the insurer was in the top five to 10 on performance, with very good premium rates, and business did not suffer, nor did he feel uneasy selling the policies.

On the question of conflicts of interest arising out of financial services sales, where the information gained about the purchaser could be used by the agent and the vendor to put pressure on for an increased offer he was philosophical:

Potentially there would easily be conflict.... But my first loyalty is to my client not their client. I have told people before now not to buy houses.... I have actually talked people out of buying before now. Not very often to be honest, because they can employ a lawyer.... You are talking about a difference in offer of £2,000, my reply to the buyer then is how badly do you want this house, is it worth an extra £24 a month? ... It's a very emotional thing buying a house.

At the same time this consultant appeared quite unmoved by the beginnings of criticism about the overselling of endowment mortgages:

I firmly and honestly believe that it is the best thing since sliced bread for mortgages.... The person I enjoy most ... is the person who comes in wanting a repayment mortgage, because it is a challenge.... I think I have done two repayment mortgages in five years.

This puts in a different light his undoubted integrity when faced with conflicts of interest:

I am of an age now where I have actually got children who are older than some of the kids who come here to buy a house, and I tend to look on them as I would my own children.

[Customers] all think we are trying to use them. It's really quite interesting. I suppose some people are.

The response of the financial consultant's senior at regional manager level to the conflict of interest question laid central emphasis on the position of the building society and its reputation and regulation, in contrast to independent estate agents and brokers whose relations with each other were lucrative but not explicit — a case of a window-cleaner recently sold an endowment mortgage by a broker which would not be paid off until he was 78 was cited as an example of this kind of abuse:

> The large corporations are such that they cannot afford to do what one would suggest that they would do, because they just couldn't handle the exposure. They are legally not allowed to do it, they are accountable. The big companies, they publish their results, you know exactly how much money they are charging in terms of commission on sale, and the access to find out exactly how much commission that they can earn from the mortgage arrangement.... I think we are heading for an environment where, yes, the nature of the industry, there are going to be conflicts of interest.... I think that providing the consumer understands that, there's nothing wrong with that.

To put this more positively:

> What's obviously best for the vendor is that he gets the most money he can. What's obviously best for the purchaser is that he knows his offer has gone through, he has access to good financial advice in terms of his mortgage and also in terms of an education, in terms that he can feel comfortable with in identifying other areas.
>   The type of advice and relationship we want to develop with the client is exactly one where we don't have a direct sales force dependent on commission income and unscrupulous in pushing their tied products.

According to the consultant quoted above, a recruitment drive was currently underway to take on up to 500 financial services staff — most were being recruited from direct sales organisations. It seemed that a conversion of them to the new S & E corporate vision would probably be required.

As with other corporates, therefore, the only structural safeguard, leaving aside the integrity of the financial consultants, consumer choice and the common sense of the purchaser, to undue pressure to raise an offer remained the mortgage survey. The S & E valuer for the city centre office admitted pressure not to downvalue properties sold through S & E, though these pressures would be resisted by making it clear that the valuer was prepared to stick to his own judgment. 'Once you have done this, then they leave you alone.' Relations between mortgage valuers and estate agents were nonetheless quite close, and cases were often observed to be discussed with estate agency staff; mortgage valuation was thus scarcely an arm's-length process.

What, finally, of the responses of estate agents to their situation at the S & E? Were they motivated by the corporate vision? Did the same problems of corporate estate agency arise? We have seen some indication that they did, but were they perceived to be being dealt with more effectively at S & E than elsewhere, or less? In brief did S & E's grand plan for incorporating estate agency into retail financial services centres resolve the problems evident in other corporates, or did it rather pass them by?

Certainly working for a big corporation was regarded as a burden in the rural office. Training was viewed with some disdain, and the administrative load and pressure to report everything was experienced as onerous:

> You have got to get the sales, you have got to get the figures, there's more paperwork to do. This paperwork contradicts that paperwork.... When we were Headingtans, when we got a sale it was great. We got a sale, fine. But they understood that, because they were a family firm and were involved in it personally, they understood that there were lean times throughout the years and good times throughout the years. Whereas our chairman ... I don't suppose he has ever sold a property in his life, so he is looking at figures, figures and statistics all the time.

Her colleague, the manager agreed:

> I can compare being an independent. Although we were busy, we would be frantically busy, we seemed able to concentrate all our thoughts and time on the job that we thought we were here to do, i.e., to get houses on the register and to sell them. And to run around endlessly with people if that's what they wanted. Today I feel that I want to do that, but at the back of my mind I am thinking 'How am I going to do it, I've got so much paperwork to do?'.... And it's not just a two-minute job. It's probably sitting down for an hour.

The pressures of work were destructive of the habits of professional estate agency:

> We now, within our own company, are in a very competitive environment where we are placed, I feel, one against the other. We have our meeting every month and we all have to stand up and give a report of our month's successes and failures and what have you. And then there's a league table for boards and office effort and all the rest of it.

Being part of a hierarchical organisation could at times also be positively detrimental to delivering a good service:

> I still feel a loyalty that I have got to not let on that it's really our own company's fault that there is a delay.... We had a lot of hassle up to this latest auction trying to reach deadlines. And it was almost as though — I felt like a voice in the wilderness sometimes. I thought, 'Who is listening to me? Nobody is!' ... In the end I sat down so incensed one day, and I thought this is ridiculous, and I wrote a memo to my regional manager, which he would have had to have shown to the head of estate agency, and

lo and behold help was on its way. More or less saved the day on that one, but not on the other.

One might suppose that the city centre office would be less unhappy, given that it was run by a young and successful team of staff. The manager complained along similar lines however, that 'We get loads of [administration] thrown at us from head office, it seems to increase by the day the amount of stuff we get from head office'. He contrasted this with the enjoyment he gained from doing his job as an estate agent — selling houses. More ominously for S & E, his views of the changes in prospect were negative:

It's the by-products you can sell at the same time. And that's what they want estate agency for.... It is very much a downgrading of estate agency.

Estate agency is a different ball game altogether. It's a totally different animal to building society.... But I don't think the higher management of the corporate side fully understand how estate agency works.

This view was vehemently echoed by the regional manager, who was thoroughly alarmed by the new retail financial services centres, not only because they would not look like estate agencies and hence attract custom, but because:

I don't think you can integrate the cultures of the two businesses, because the building society makes money by opening its front door ... every £100 that is put across the table there's £2 profit in it.... The minute you open an estate agency door in the morning you are going to lose money until you make a sale. The cultures are just so wildly different ... your average building society cashier, I am afraid, is a bored housewife and always ever will be.

The institutions are saying 'Oh we'll proceduralise estate agency'.... Somewhere I have got a procedures manual for estate agency ... but how do you proceduralise it? ... It's a real seat of the pants business and the entrepreneurial flair of your [city centre office managers] of this world make it or break it.... One thing that our people don't have to do is fill in reams of paper, because that's where the regional people like myself have really stepped in and said 'No, these guys have got to be selling houses, I do not want them filling in bits of paper.

Obviously he overestimated the effectiveness of his 'stepping in'. The retailing concept led in this manager's view to fundamental misperceptions:

We have got somebody on board in a very senior position who realises we have got too much stock. And he said, don't take anymore houses on the market. And I said no, I am not doing that.... The last house that you took on is the most saleable house you have got.... What this guy is saying is that we have got 2,773 properties for sale at the moment and we sell 132 a month, that means we have got 21 years' stock. This guy is a retailer, somebody who used to be selling televisions.

Unlike televisions, of course, the properties are not stock which is owned by the estate agent: properties which are hard to shift either get sold through a price reduction or are more or less abandoned:

Institutions need people like me who actually have a hands-on knowledge of what is going on in Kingsbridge and Belton, and playing those two businesses differently, because of the markets they are in. And playing it sympathetically and getting the desired results out of them. Because if you plant a corporate plan over the top of it ... it will be the old percentage game.... Try sticking your head in the gas oven and your feet in the freezer and taking an average, you just can't do it, it just doesn't work.

I reckon that if S & E really want to get it right, what they ought to do is franchise back to the likes of me, and then I would run it much cheaper than they can run it. I would get them what they want — their mortgages and their financial services, so there would be no sweat to them. They wouldn't have to administer it.

This is a solution, that none of the corporates seem to relish because it implies a reduction of control. Least of all is it acceptable at S & E.

Not that the organisation was unaware of these problems. The head of estate agency outlined very clearly the litany of stages involved in marketing and selling a property and taking the sale through to completion, and accepted that this was very different from building society business. He also readily accepted the localism of estate agency:

What we have got to get across to these people is what they are working for is an organisation which is dedicated to estate agency. There is no question about it, estate agency remains a very important part of our sales platform.... If we had not had total corporate commitment to all those estate agents then we would not be doing what we are doing.

This is not a case, as it might appear to some of his disaffected staff, of protesting too much. There was no doubt that S & E was committed to estate agency, but as part of the corporate plan, which, as we have seen, can contemplate the loss of more than half its experienced staff as the price of producing a dedicated group of corporate visionaries. It remains to be seen what the outcome of this process will be, but the evidence so far is that the obstacles to successful corporate estate agency have not been overcome. The recipe in the corporate plan calls for the same mixture of procedures, measurable itemised service and targetable results that we have seen elsewhere, the main practical difference being the restraints imposed on agents by being located in retail centres, where they are not the centre of attention, and are in any case required to keep a low profile until their services are called upon by a member of the browsing public. It may be that a new form of estate agency will emerge from this, but it is incompatible with estate agency as it has been practised up to now, and seems likely to alienate those established in the occupation. S & E's short and medium-term prospects for property sales hence do not look good.

In the meantime the tendency of agents to allow their interests in securing a sale to override both those of the purchaser and their client, the vendor, were quite evident at S & E. Agents, as we have seen, often valued properties flexibly in order to obtain the instruction, telling the vendor that their judgment was that the asking price probably would not be achieved. Like other corporates, they then recorded a match range for the property which could lead to applicants in a lower price range being given details of the property. This is then followed by a check to see if the applicant is interested. If there is interest, it is frequently accompanied by a request for information on what might be an acceptable price, and in response the agent suggests that an offer less than the asking price might well be acceptable. The agent then uses this offer to prove the point that the vendor's asking price was too high and gets the vendor to accept the lower offer.

This is not necessarily an easy set of judgments for the agent to make — in one instance a vendor refused an offer that was higher than the price a similar but better property had been sold at recently, against the agent's advice, and the purchaser nonetheless increased the offer and the sale went through very close to the vendor's asking price. In this case, however, it was notable that the vendor had agreed to accept offers £1,000 less than the asking price, but baulked at an offer £500 less than that, given that the house had been bought during the property boom. Secondly, the relationship with the purchaser was throughout friendly and relaxed and the offer was treated by the agent, in contacts with both vendor and purchaser, as very much a reasonable one — as indeed the agent believed. The question here, however, is what the vendor's interests were. The vendor had had the property on the market five months and was in no state of panic to sell. In this and other instances, it seemed that the agent's concern to bring off a deal was effectively the overriding consideration and that management of both vendor and pur-chaser could be subject to practical rationalisation whereby the achievement of this objective did not appear to compromise their interests.

Where estate agency is submerged in a grandiose corporate plan, in which targets, budgets, reporting procedures and the new vision are required to preoccupy the estate agent on pain of eventually being squeezed out, what safeguards are there against such abuses? There was evidence at S & E that agents were concerned to maintain the kind of client-oriented service they had been used to in independent agency, but found that they could not sustain, and were not rewarded for sustaining, in a corporate environment.

NINE

The Public's Experiences of Estate Agency

INTRODUCTION

In the course of our research, the interaction between estate agents and the public was closely observed affording valuable insights into the services provided to the public, and the risks to which the public are exposed. Estate agents, and our own observation, have conveyed a number of consistent views about the public, notably that they are largely unaware of the nature of estate agency whilst, at the same time, holding to an image of estate agents as untrustworthy and at times incompetent and greedy — the popular negative stereotype. The public are held by agents to be often naïve about buying and selling property. As we have seen, estate agents believe that they often suffer from the prejudices of the public, but they have mounted no sustained or collective effort to inform the public better about what they do. Rather their remedy is individualistic: an attempt to persuade the individual client of their integrity and competence, with the outcome that their role as the vendor's agent is, often deliberately, made ambiguous, especially in contacts with potential purchasers. These conflicts of interest between obligations to buyer and seller, and the agent's own interest in his or her commission, can be heightened in certain circumstances, for example, where an agent is engaged by the vendor of a property who is also likely to buy another on the agent's list. A further level of conflicts of interest is introduced by the provision of financial services products alongside estate agency by the corporate agents.

Our aim throughout has been to identify the circumstances in which estate agents work and their responses to difficulties of these kinds. This provided only limited direct information on the way in which estate agency is experienced by the public. Accordingly, alternative sources of information were sought. Time pressures ruled out the most effective way of achieving this, which would be to follow through with vendors and purchasers the whole process of sale and purchase: even if we had been able to spend the time on this, it is likely that our presence, even if discreet, would have put agents on their mettle to behave well. In order to tap public experience we decided to cast our net as widely as possible to solicit a response, and to give the public a chance to relate their views and experiences. Again, time considerations prevented the application of a large interview programme and dictated the use of a postal questionnaire.

Since we wanted to reach a good sample of those members of the public who were actively involved in property sale and purchase, and avoid relying on distant events, we collected property details in all the areas of the country in which we undertook observation: the North-West, the Midlands, the South-East (including London) and the South-West. This gave us a sample of 2,000 properties, which we stratified to be roughly balanced as between the regions, and as between corporate and independent agents, as shown in table 9.1.

Table 9.1 Distribution of Consumer Survey Sample

	Independent	Corporate	Total
Midlands	277	233	500
North-West	299	236	535
South-West	231	269	500
South-East	221	244	465
Totals	1,028	982	2,000

When collecting details from estate agents, we attempted to ensure that a reasonably full range of properties of different types and price bands were included, but it was not practical to stratify the sample formally by property types and price bands. We were also not able to undertake formal random sampling of estate agents, but we did spread our net fairly wide, tapping both large and small agencies in a variety of locations in each region. London is probably somewhat under-represented in relation to its position in the total national housing stock, and of course we did not sample Wales, the North-East or East Anglia. Nonetheless, we are satisfied that our sample, like our sampling of working estate agencies, is representative of the mainstream of English property and estate agency.

Constructing a questionnaire which stands any chance of a reasonably good rate of return is a delicate business. People are reluctant to apply themselves to completing a questionnaire that is too long, complex, or personally intrusive, yet a brief questionnaire on a subject like this will yield little useful information. Above all we wanted, if we could, to tap people's experiences rather than their attitudes and prejudices. We therefore opted for a largely structured questionnaire on which respondents were also encouraged to add their own comments and accounts in reply to two final questions.

As elsewhere in this research, respondents were guaranteed anonymity and questionnaires were not coded to enable us to trace the response back to the property details that had been used to construct the sample. This would have had benefits for us as researchers, but we believe that the importance of the guarantee of anonymity overrides them. With a good deal of juggling by our research secretary, we managed to get the questions into a four-page formula, still leaving room for written comments on the last page. This we judged to be about the limit of the tolerance of respondents. (A copy of the questionnaire is at the end of this chapter.) The questionnaire was piloted for response rate and intelligibility in Spring 1992, and, since no evident problems arose, was mailed to the full sample a few weeks later. The final response rate was 524, just over a quarter, which, apart from generating a useful sample of replies to analyse, is well up to expectation for a postal questionnaire.

The other obvious source of bias was that the questionnaire would act as a channel for ventilating complaints and that we would end up with a pile of horror stories. Perhaps in part because of the depressed state of the market we did not — it was evident that most respondents' concerns were to sell their property in a difficult market. There was widespread recognition that this made it difficult for estate agents to act quickly and effectively in achieving a sale. In addition, when we asked for a simple expression of satisfaction or dissatisfaction with the agent most recently involved, there was, as we will detail below, by no means a generally hostile response. Further, the detail of the responses when analysed suggests a restrained appraisal by the consumers of estate agents and their services on the whole, given the grounds for complaint that many of them had. The overall impression conveyed, especially by reading the written comments which were added at greater or lesser length — not more in almost all cases than two thirds of a page — is one of a phlegmatic realism as to the nature of the market and the limitations of estate agents, and hence the expectations it was reasonable to have of them. This could and did lead to cynicism at times, but complaints were presented with irritation rather than rage, and compliments were by no means absent.

The results of the structured part of the questionnaire will be presented first, followed by an analysis of the qualitative comments. The reader unfamiliar with questionnaire responses should bear in mind that respondents vary enormously in their diligence and competence. Some will meticulously and clearly complete every question where others will leave some out, change their minds and alter their replies more or less intelligibly, add comments more or less relevantly and legibly, and misunderstand the questions. The art of questionnaire design is to minimise these problematic habits and maximise the usable information returned, and our pilot study suggested that we had done reasonably well. Nonetheless, in the full sample there are bound to be replies that are difficult or impossible to interpret. For this reason we will present the results in terms of the usable responses to each question, rather than in terms of the total sample of replies (524). In cases where multiple rather than forced choices were asked for, the number of responses may hence greatly exceed 524.

Another matter to bear in mind throughout and to which we shall return later is that the property buying and selling public is extremely varied. It includes those who have bought and sold a dozen times in as many years, as well as those who have not done so for over 30 years, and first-time buyers; they include the educated and sophisticated, and the uneducated and ignorant; the assertive and the passive; the lucky and the unfortunate; and of course the full gamut of domestic circumstances. People's experience of estate agents varied here not only in quality but in extent. At times this posed a problem in analysing the results, especially since the adverse market had led people to change agents in order to try to sell their properties. Most respondents did, however, make their answers clear and, where they wished to relate what happened in the past, did so in a way that did not compromise their account of their recent experience of estate agency. As table 9.2 suggests, the sample was reasonably successful in tapping the recent or current experiences of users of estate agents, although this process was greatly extended by the depressed market, and written comments indicated that some had been trying to sell for up to three years.

Table 9.2   Date agency instructed

Before January 1989	22
January–June 1989	12
July–December 1989	20
January–June 1990	58
July–December 1990	58
January–June 1991	154
July–December 1991	177
January-June 1992	241
	742

Of the 456 replying to this question (Q11) three quarters (345) had not sold their property at the time of completing the questionnaire (the remainder were first-time buyers who were therefore not selling a property). In response to a direct question (Q1) 454 said they were selling a property and 54 that they were not — first-time buyers. Sixteen respondents failed to reply to this question.

The questionnaire was posted in May 1992 and returned during May–August 1992. Figures exceed the number of respondents because some respondents noted changes of agents.

We attempted to discriminate between users of corporate and independent estate agents by stratifying the sample as we have described. We also enabled ourselves to discriminate the replies by either numbering or not-numbering the pages of the questionnaire, with the object of comparing the responses in respect of corporate and independent agents, but this, of course, only worked if the property was unsold and the agent unchanged. Where the property was sold and the move had taken place, our questionnaire will have been completed by the purchaser, who would probably have used a different agent to sell his or her property. We took steps to deal with these difficulties as follows. The coding of the reply was checked against the most recent estate agent cited as instructed, to cover any changes between the time we collected details and the date the questionnaire was completed for the three in four respondents who had not yet sold their properties. These numbers were enhanced by a further group where there was internal evidence that the sale had not been completed. For those who had completed and where the questionnaire was answered by the purchasers, we amended the corporate/ independent status according to the information given as to the agent most recently instructed. This gave us reasonably accurate data on this issue as regards the sale, but we were not able to discriminate as regards purchasers and hence not in the final two questions, which allowed respondents to comment either as buyers or sellers. We will present the results of the survey in terms of the total sample first and return to the corporate/independent differences later.

STRUCTURED REPLIES: SELLING EXPERIENCES

When asked why they chose to instruct an agent rather than sell the property themselves (Q2) by far the leading response was because of the marketing and advertising services of an agent (306 or 30.9 per cent). As we shall see later, this perception of the advantages of using an agent was associated with criticism when it was felt that agents were not marketing the property actively enough. Of the few respondents who took up the issue of private marketing of properties by comments in the miscellaneous 'other' response to this question (36 or 3.6 per cent of responses, including various other comments), several suggested that there was public prejudice against private sales and that such sellers were seen as having something to hide, or alternatively that agents were some kind of guarantee against things going wrong. Against this, however, there were a few respondents who commented that estate agents were unnecessary in the normal market, though only in one case was there clear evidence of repeated success in marketing properties privately on the open market. Another respondent described the experience of selling successfully through an agent in a good market, whilst a neighbour with a similar property who advertised privately failed to get any response at all. One respondent shrewdly remarked that in a poor market a benefit of agents was that they would fund up-front costs of advertising and marketing, which might need to run for some time before being recouped at the sale.

The other reasons suggested by the questionnaire as a basis for instructing an agent were cited with almost equal frequency: that this is the normal way of selling property (168 or 16.9 per cent); lack of time to do the job personally (173 or 17.5 per cent); because agents are thought to do a better job (166 or 16.7

per cent); and because the agent can act as a buffer between the seller and potential buyers (142 or 14 per cent). As we shall see, there is reason to believe that this last reason was particularly important to some categories of sellers, who felt themselves to be vulnerable in the property market-place.

When asked why they had instructed a particular agent, the reasons suggested in the questionnaire were cited by all but 75 (7.1 per cent) of 1,051 responses. Again, there was a clear leading response: that the agent was well-known in the area (256 or 24.4 per cent), confirming estate agents' conventional wisdom about the importance of a strong presence in the locality through sale boards and well-placed shop fronts. This reason was well ahead of the next, that a reasonable fee was charged (172 or 16.4 per cent) suggesting, as other evidence here and in earlier chapters confirms, that sellers' prime concern is achieving a sale, an obviously vital consideration given the state of the market.

Agents' cynicism about valuation is supported by the order of the next two most popular responses. Some 124, or 11.8 per cent, said that their agreement with the agent's valuation led them to instruct, as against 99 or 9.4 per cent, who said that they liked or trusted the valuer. A similar number, 98 or 9.3 per cent, were influenced by the fact that the agent was part of a large chain, which in most, if not all, cases will nowadays mean being a corporate. No specific mention was made of the status 'corporate', but the respondents were offered the attractions of an independent; only 62 or 5.9 per cent accepted this as an influence, suggesting that corporate and independent status is not very influential.

There is evidence elsewhere to suggest that respondents were not necessarily aware of this, and indeed in cases where corporately owned agents were trading under their independent name, corporate status is far from obvious. It is evident, however, that the public are not greatly attracted by the well-publicised status of those who make their ownership by large financial institutions evident; rather, it seems to be the perceived market position of the agency that attracts. This impression is confirmed by the lowly position of the other responses, all of them well below double figures, and including factors which estate agents hold dear; only 69 (6.6 per cent) instructed on the recommendation of family or friends, and only 40 (3.8 per cent) on the basis of the agents having sold a previous property of theirs. Only 56 (5.3 per cent) chose the agent because they were purchasing a property through him and there is some evidence in the written comments that reduced fees were offered in these circumstances, and there would, of course, have been a reasonable expectation that the agent would work hard to achieve the double sale.

The next three questions shed light on the degree of sophistication of sellers, since they all concern action taken around the time of instructing an agent. As we have seen, the valuation interview is regarded by agents as critical to obtaining instructions. This is confirmed by the answers to Q7, whether the agent was instructed at valuation or later. Of those replying, 321 or 69.8 per cent instructed on the spot, and only 140 or 30.4 per cent later. Further, 171 or 37 per cent did not invite other agents to value. Although some of this group may have had strong reasons for so limiting themselves, we have seen that established links with agents are not strong. Hence, although nearly two thirds (291 or 63 per cent) obtained more than one valuation, a significant minority failed to take this elementary precaution. The impression thus created, that for a substantial number of vendors selecting an agent is a rather haphazard, even casual, matter is confirmed by responses to Q5, which identified other matters that might, or should, be discussed before instructing. Our observations identified these as topics anticipated at valuation by agents, though they are happy to be instructed without having to negotiate them in a good many cases.

As we have seen, the reasonable level of the fee was identified as the second most important reason for selecting an agent, 402 respondents out of 462 did so (87 per cent). On the other hand, only 93 (23.3 per cent) discussed a withdrawal charge, 139 (30 per cent) advertising expenses which, of course, may or may not be included in the fee, 282 (65.3 per cent) sole or multiple agency and 53 (13.3 per cent) mortgage advice to seller or purchasers. Thirty-two (6.9 per cent) admitted discussing none of these things. It may be, of course, that memories are less than perfect and it is likely that at least some of these matters will have been discussed later, but we have seen instances of agents, for example, prudently failing to mention withdrawal fees; and frequent examples of instructions being taken on an informal basis at the valuation interview, with the expectation of both parties that the property would be advertised within the next day or two. Although it seems likely then that a majority of sellers are reasonably circumspect in selecting an agent and negotiating terms, it is also probable that a significant minority are not, and are not fully aware that they may be tying themselves to an agent for a substantial period, and incurring significant costs.

We saw in previous chapters that the position of the agent during negotiations is a particularly delicate one in which his interest in bringing off a deal, and for earning his commission, is at risk of compromising his obligation to secure the best price for his client. In the absence of a face-to-face interview with respondents, this was a difficult matter to get at clearly, but we attempted to shed some light on whether the agent played an active role by asking whether advice was given to accept or refuse offers (Q8). Of the 461 responses to this question, 191 had had no offers. Of those that had received offers, 133 had been advised to accept or reject them by the agent and 137 had not.

Thus, about half of offers involved, in the recollection of respondents, the active intervention of agents. We cannot tell how many of those that did not involve advice did not do so because they were immediately recognised by both parties as acceptable, but a proportion must have been of this sort. Conversely, a number of comments included remarks to the effect that estate agents were putting undue pressure on clients to reduce asking price and to accept undesirable offers. It is hard to quantify what were not always clear comments, but this did constitute an element in the sources of dissatisfaction with agents, and one reason for changing agents. In a difficult market such as prevailed at the time, when offers were few and far between, both vendors and agents were obviously in some difficulties at times in accepting offers. The evidence of the survey does not — to anticipate our review below of the written comments — suggest that agents were generally overbearing and insistent on acceptance of offers to push sales through, but the figures here clearly indicate an active role. This, in turn, suggests to us that this critical point in the sale of a property needs careful evaluation if the interests of clients and purchasers are to be adequately secured.

The final two questions on the selling process concerned levels of satisfaction with the estate agent. Here we made a distinction between administrative efficiency — answering letters, taking messages, fixing appointments and avoiding confusion — and professional services. In the latter case our question cited advice on asking price, assistance in negotiation, support in seeing the sale through to completion, and an active search for a buyer. We made this distinction for a variety of reasons: it is intuitively an obvious one; it enables a specific focus upon the professional side of estate agency which can, of course, be compromised by the failure of support staff to provide administrative effectiveness; and we suspected (rightly as it turns out in the analysis of written comments) that administrative shortcomings were a significant cause of frustration. We asked respondents to choose between five levels for the administrative question since we felt that even persistent incompetence here may not lead to real disadvantage; hence we added to the 'very dissatisfied' category a further one 'disastrous', in which administrative failings had serious consequences. In the case of professional services it was logical to suppose that serious failings occasioning great dissatisfaction would have serious consequences, and we hence confined ourselves to four categories.

Although this picture will be qualified by the evidence of the qualitative comments below, the overall statistical picture is reasonably favourable to estate agents. On the question of administrative services (Q9) 351 (73.4 per cent) were very or generally satisfied, with 120 of those (25.1 per cent) very satisfied, leaving only 127 dissatisfied, with 75 (15.7 per cent) of those only dissatisfied, 39 (8.2 per cent) very dissatisfied, and 13 (2.7 per cent) suffering disasters. Roughly speaking then, three quarters of clients were happy with the administrative side of their agents' services.

Levels of satisfaction with professional services were less good. Of 421 respondents (as opposed to 478 answering the previous question), 93 (22.1 per cent) were very satisfied and 147 (34.9 per cent) generally satisfied (57 per cent combined), as against 135 (32.1 per cent) dissatisfied and 46 (10.9 per cent) very dissatisfied (43 per cent combined). How are these figures to be interpreted? They are roughly confirmed by replies to our final question (Q20) which forced a choice between an overall response of satisfied or dissatisfied, counting experiences as both buyer and seller. Almost exactly two thirds of the 501 replies (331) indicated satisfaction, and one third (170) dissatisfaction. This overall satisfaction was confirmed when answers to Q10 on satisfaction with professional services, and Q20, overall satisfaction, were cross-tabulated with answers to Q11, whether the property had been sold — see table 9.3.

Three things are noteworthy about these figures. First, the pattern of satisfaction is the same in the two separate cases. Secondly, the sale of a property appears to be a good reason for clients being satisfied — relatively few are dissatisfied when their properties are sold. However, failing to sell a property is not in itself an overwhelming source of dissatisfaction. More respondents who had not sold their properties were satisfied than dissatisfied. Evidently the difficulties the market posed for estate agents were widely recognised. The question which arises is hence, were the dissatisfied customers blaming the estate agents for the limitations of the market or for other failings?

Table 9.3   Satisfaction with estate agency professional services (i)

		Property Sold	
		Yes	No
Q10	Very/generally satisfied	83	151
	Dissatisfied/very dissatisfied	30	149
		Yes	No
Q20	Broadly satisfied	82	201
	Broadly dissatisfied	26	127

Our question about sale was strictly specified as meaning either completed or exchanged contracts. For the purposes of this evaluation it is likely that having the property under offer, or sold subject to contract (STC), would be also likely to influence the overall satisfaction with estate agents' performance. In the prevailing market it might also be maintained that having a reasonable flow of viewers would influence satisfaction levels, given that lack of viewers was an often cited cause of dissatisfaction and reason for changing agents (see below). Information on both these matters was dependent upon respondents writing this information in either at Q11 or

Table 9.4   Satisfaction with estate agency professional services (ii)

Property sold/STC			Property sold/STC/viewers adequate		
Q10	Yes	No	Q10	Yes	No
Satisfied	98	136	Satisfied	111	123
Dissatisfied	33	146	Dissatisfied	34	145
Q20	Yes	No	Q20	Yes	No
Satisfied	97	186	Satisfied	110	173
Dissatisfied	29	124	Dissatisfied	30	123

Q20. In the event we identified 19 who indicated that their property was under offer, of which 15 were satisfied, 3 dissatisfied, and one unclear, and 15 cases in which a reasonable flow of viewers was remarked, of which 13 were satisfied, one dissatisfied, and one unclear. The outcome modifies the above tables as shown in table 9.4.

As can be seen, the explanatory impact upon satisfaction of the sale or prospects of sale of the property increases, but still leaves a preponderance of properties unsold with a substantial proportion of clients nonetheless satisfied with the services being received.

One might interpret this as not at all bad given a very difficult market for estate agents and plenty of evidence of clients switching agents to attempt to get sales, as well as the generally poor image of estate agents. Alternatively, one might say that any occupation in a service industry failing to satisfy one in three of its customers should be seriously worried and embarrassed. This view should be qualified by the point that became clearer in the qualitative comments, that experiences of estate agency vary, and that some agents are plainly much more efficient and effective than others. It might also be added that property sales and purchases are at the best of times fraught and complex, and may be attendant upon divorce, bereavement, job loss and other personal tragedies. Nonetheless, if the evidence thus far is interpreted as meaning that up to a third of agents are not giving their clients satisfaction, it seems that something needs to be done to remedy the situation. It seems unlikely that that remedy will come from the market — clients are too naïve and inexperienced, and too many of them are too infrequent players for the market to function to put much pressure on an ineffective minority; but this is to anticipate the discussion of our concluding chapter.

STRUCTURED REPLIES: BUYING EXPERIENCES

The second part of the questionnaire asked for reactions to the experience of buying a property. Some 159 (30.7 per cent) of those replying (515) said that they had only bought once, though, as we have seen above, only about a third of these were first-time buyers at the time of completing the questionnaire, the rest being then involved in selling that first purchase. This leaves more than two thirds of respondents (356 or 69.3 per cent) as relatively experienced repeat buyers, though, of course, over very varying timescales. Since our judgment is that it is the purchaser who is most vulnerable in property sales because he or she has usually no independent professional advice until a lawyer is retained, which is usually after an offer has been agreed, we asked a number of questions about buyers' relations with estate agents.

The first of these asked for a general appraisal of the agent from the buyer's experience in terms of negative and positive characteristics — helpful/unhelpful, reliable/unreliable, available/hard to contact, honest/untrustworthy. It is noteworthy that 100 respondents said that they did not buy through an agent, about a fifth of the total sample of respondents, and a rather higher proportion if one deletes current first-time buyers (100 out of 462 or 23.8 per cent). The question was put as an open multiple choice rather than multiple forced choice, i.e., respondents were not required to choose either helpful or unhelpful etc., but could choose as many of the eight characteristics as they wished. In practice, most chose two or three.

The outcome is generally flattering to estate agents. Of the 842 choices, the leading ones were helpful (275 or 63.3 per cent of the 421 respondents who said they used an agent), usually available (202 or 48.0 per cent), and reliable (133 or 31.6 per cent), followed by honest (86 or 20.4 per cent). Positive appraisals then outranked all negative appraisals which were: unhelpful (48 or 11.4 per cent), unreliable (36 or 7.8 per cent), untrustworthy (35 or 8.3 per cent), and hard to contact (27 or 6.4 per cent). Overall positive views predominated by 696 (73.9 per cent) of all choices, against 146 (26.1 per cent). One might carp at agents being seen as helpful and available consistently more than being honest, and suggest that some of the image of slipperiness persists, but at any rate these responses suggest that agents were experienced by buyers in a generally positive way. Were they, however, manipulated or taken advantage of unbeknown to themselves?

The answers to the next question indicate the confusions that exist in the minds of buyers. This question asked whose side the agent seemed to be on: buyers, sellers or neutral. Of those responding as buyers, 201 or 46.6 per cent perceived the agent as neutral, 166 or 38.4 per cent as on the seller's side, and 80 or 16.2 per cent as on their own, the buyer's side. These figures seem to reflect precisely the position we discovered in field research. Agents are, and are supposed to make it clear that they are paid agents of the vendor; yet because they mediate between vendor and purchaser, and because purchasers are especially important in the current market, agents often deliberately put themselves across as at least neutral. Without supplementary questioning as to how the purchaser actually understood their relationship with the agent during the process of buying, it is impossible to say how far purchasers were misled, still less with what consequences. These figures do suggest, however, that the well nigh universal declarations from professional and regulatory bodies that agents are sellers' agents and should make it clear at all times that this is the case, need careful reconsideration. Our observation has indicated that many agents do not behave in that way because they believe they cannot do their job properly if they do, and the perception of purchasers here is plainly that they do not. At the very least the erroneous perception of 16 per cent of buyers should be a cause for concern.

FINANCIAL SERVICES

The next four questions concerned financial services. The first (Q15) asked whether, as either buyer or seller, financial services of various sorts had been offered. A surprisingly large number of respondents (212, 41.5 per cent of those answering this question) said that none had been offered. Even though we asked them to consider a single recent relationship with an estate agent and some may have referred to contacts which were in their early stages, this is a low figure and we suspect it reflects the concern of agents to sell properties as a priority and to allow financial services sales to be brought in at a later stage. Of those citing financial services offered, mortgage arrangement was by far the most common (264, 51.4 per cent), followed by property surveys (123, 24.0 per cent), insurance policies, including endowments (107, 20.9 per cent), conveyancing (48, 9.6 per cent), and pension planning (13, 2.5 per cent). The marginal position of financial products not directly related to property sales — we cited pension planning as an example of this — is confirmed by other data discussed below. Overall it appears that the pushing of financial services is much less of a feature of estate agency than might have been expected.

This picture is confirmed by responses to the next question which asked whether an estate agent had ever been used for financial and property services of different kinds. A remarkable 358 (71.2 per cent of those answering the question) replied 'None', and figures for those services used were very low: mortgage arrangement 91 (18.1 per cent), property survey 86 (17.1 per cent), insurance 64 (12.7 per cent), conveyancing 25 (5.0 per cent), and pension planning 3 (0.69 per cent). Why was this? It does not at any rate seem to derive from overwhelming objections to the offering of these services. The next question (Q17) asked whether it is desirable for agents to offer mortgage and other financial services, and produced a fairly evenly divided response among the 512 replying. Some 235 (45.9 per cent) were in favour as against 156 (30.5 per cent) opposed, and 121 (23.6 per cent) not sure. On the other hand, these figures do not suggest enthusiasm for financial services in estate agency, and it may be that in practice customers displayed caution. This view is confirmed by the final question on financial services which asked whether respondents realised that commission income from financial services products could equal or exceed commission from the sale of the property. Almost exactly two thirds (340 of 517) said that they did, as against 113 (177) who did not. Although some respondents may have been reluctant to admit to their ignorance, even anonymously and without having to face an interviewer, these figures indicate a greater level of awareness of the advantages to agents of financial services sales, and hence of conflicts of interest, than we had anticipated. This may in turn explain the practical reluctance of respondents to use agents for the provision of financial services.

UNSTRUCTURED RESPONSES

The final two questions invited written comments as well as prestructured answers. The first (Q19) asked if any action was taken if the respondent's most recent experience with an estate agent, as buyer or seller, caused dissatisfaction. Of the 384 replies, 113 said that they had taken action and 121 offered a written comment. The number exceeds those taking action because cases of dissatisfaction obviously exceeded those where the respondent took action to complain. We wished to concentrate on those where customers had felt the case to be serious enough to warrant a complaint. Coding the written accounts of complainants was not possible in detail but some matters could be specified. By far the commonest place of complaint, 67, was the estate agency itself, with only five instances of other bodies, such as the Law

Society, being cited. The commonest remedy was to change agents (26 cases) with successful outcomes in a broad sense being achieved in a further 22 cases, and unsuccessful ones in 27 cases, leaving 46 cases difficult to evaluate. It is relevant to add here that respondents varied greatly in their clarity and articulateness in explaining their problems, and in the degree of explicitness used to get them across. At times this might involve up to a page of close writing detailing several problems, at others little more than a shorthand account which in some instances left a good deal to the presumption of the reader. In addition, written comments in reply to this question overlapped with those in reply to the final question, which, as we have seen earlier, asked for a general expression of satisfaction or dissatisfaction, which split 2:1 in estate agents' favour, and a written comment on the reasons for this. Where respondents were dissatisfied, the cause of this was often to be found in their answer to the previous question. Respondents often explicitly linked them with each other.

Analysis of the complaints identified a total of 148. Some respondents had more than one complaint, of which the leading one, 24 cases, was administrative failures, closely followed by communication failures, 22 cases. Both of these causes of complaint fall into our administrative rather than professional services category earlier in the questionnaire, where, it will be recalled, estate agents came out quite well overall. Administrative efficiency, and keeping in touch with customers and responding promptly and effectively to them, are clearly essential to successful estate agency and only too easily lost when staff are poorly trained and disciplined, immature, and subject to high turnover, all problems that the industry has faced in the recent past. Professional services in one form or another account for the next three most common causes of complaint, that the property was unsold or insufficient efforts were made to sell it (16 cases), that staff were incompetent at dealing with clients and others (15 cases), and that advertising and marketing were inadequate (14 cases). Together these make up 45 cases of complaint as against 46 on the administrative side, though here the caveat should be added that the pressures of the market are plainly entering in. As we shall see when considering general sources of dissatisfaction, respondents sometimes failed to recognise the limitations upon effectiveness that a declining market imposed, and blamed the agent. There is probably some element of this in specific complaints about unsold properties and lack of marketing.

The remaining causes of complaint involve few cases: staff attitudes, mainly rudeness and apparent lack of interest, 11 cases; fees regarded as too high or the subject of dispute, 8 cases; general lack of interest in the client, 6 cases; and financial services, 2 cases. In 30 cases, the cause of the complaint was unspecified or unclear. Again it is striking that financial services are responsible for so few complaints, and this is consistent with the low take-up found in answer to earlier questions. Overall it is notable that complaints are in the great majority those deriving from a working relationship with estate agents, rather than those deriving from clear exploitation. There were no complaints of fraud or outright dishonest dealing, or gross misrepresentation, which no doubt accounts for the general tendency for them to be dealt with by recourse to the agent rather than taking them further — there were few references to court action, professional bodies or the OCEA scheme. It was also noticeable that complaints referred (often implicitly) overwhelmingly to experiences as a seller rather than buyer. This raises the question whether this would have been the case had our survey been conducted during the property boom.

Comments on general reasons for satisfaction or dissatisfaction were the richest source of qualitative material and shed further light on customer expectations of and attitudes to estate agents, as well as on sources of frustration. Of the 501 respondents to this final question, 394 offered a comment, of which 104 (26.4 per cent) could be classified as mainly satisfied, 219 (55.6 per cent) as mainly dissatisfied, and 70 (17.8 per cent) as expressing mixed experiences. We then coded the comments in detail and identified 146 satisfied comments and 294 dissatisfied comments. The satisfied ones are easiest to deal with in the sense that most are general, whereas expressions of dissatisfaction tend to refer to specific events and experiences. Here is an articulate and quite fulsome expression of satisfaction:

> The agents instructed were very reliable, worked hard to match my property to suitable persons on their mailing list, saw viewings through, i.e., made follow-up telephone calls, so if somebody did not wish to purchase they found out the reason why, were very sympathetic when problems arose with the sale etc. They did offer additional services but were not 'pushy' with these. (Case 331, house sold.)

Similar views were at times put more succinctly: 'Gave advice. Advertised in local paper. Made appointments. Phoned to discuss lack of buyers' (case 251, house unsold).

Sometimes, of course, the plaudits reflected a success story. The following will be music to any estate agent's ears:

> Valuation given promptly. Details produced efficiently and promptly. Advertising took place as expected. Three couples viewed the property within two weeks. House sold in 16 days. (Case 308.)

Satisfaction did not, however, always depend on success in achieving a sale, and the problems of the market were widely but by no means universally recognised: 'Good service but let down by the difficulty of selling at today's glut market' (case 022).

By no means all satisfied customers were as unequivocal in their satisfaction. A significant minority expressed elements of reservation not only about the service provided but about their own expectations. Here is one customer who indicated overall satisfaction: 'They helped to settle some points of negotiation. Though they also got several messages totally wrong and upset both parties at times' (case 002). Compare the above with the following also 'satisfied' customer:

I make the above assessment on the basis that I approached the estate agent I used with many reservations about the usefulness of estate agents, so that the estate agents in the end did not need to do much to please me. There is certainly some value in a good local agency which knows the value of local market for homes in their area. (Case 328.)

This theme of low expectations of estate agents is a persistent one, though because it is not always explicit it is hard to quantify. Here are a couple of fairly clear examples which indicate why expectations are limited: 'Did the job required, i.e., be available to prospective buyers to arrange viewing with themselves and pass on any offers, i.e., estate agents just a "clearing house" for properties' (case 480, property sold). 'Service is what I would expect, but I don't think it is worth the fee charged' (case 488, unsold).

At times such low expectations can turn 'satisfaction' into a distinctly backhanded compliment:

Although they are glib, self-interested and obsequious, they perform a necessary service. (Case 284, unsold.)

At the end of the day the estate agent's only real interest is getting his commission. He will say whatever he needs to, to whoever, to keep things moving. If one appreciates this one can get satisfaction from the right agent. (Case 024, sold.)

These comments also raise a number of points made, positively and negatively, by a number of respondents. The notion that the agent's interest in the commission predominates was quite widely expressed and we will return to it below. The understanding of agency as a 'clearing house' was, not surprisingly, given the market, a minority one and a number of respondents complained, as we shall see, at lack of marketing. This in turn relates to the issue of respondents' understanding of the capacities of the agent in a weak market. As we have seen above (case 022) some appreciated the agent's efforts despite lack of success; others were either incapable of doing so or unwilling to do so. The undertone of cynicism running through many of the replies does, however, take the gilt off the gingerbread. This is a matter we shall deal with more fully when considering dissatisfaction.

Despite the difficulties of doing so, we classified the satisfied responses in 10 different ways which give some indication of the source of satisfaction. The leading one is clearly staff attitudes, 52 cases — staff were cited as being helpful, available, friendly etc. This confirms the emphasis which agents put on forming good positive relations with clients and purchasers. The second most frequently mentioned cause for satisfaction is, not surprisingly, the sale of the property, or at least the introduction of a number of viewers (17 cases). Staff competence in handling the transaction was mentioned in 16 cases, and good communication in one form or another in 15 cases. Prompt and accurate advertising was cited in 12 cases, and general expressions of trust in estate agents in 11 cases. Administrative soundness earned 5 plaudits, and good-value fees and financial services 4 each, leaving a group of 10 cases unclassified.

Before dealing with the sources of dissatisfaction in detail, it is important to note that a good many respondents clearly had quite different experiences with different agents. Here are two examples, articulate in quite different ways, and with different outcomes. Both expressed themselves broadly dissatisfied but both also describe satisfactory relations with agents:

With first agents inaccurate information, no interior photos (as promised), promised accompanied viewings (never happened), apparently lost key (borrowed one from neighbour without our permission and took two weeks and numerous phone calls to return it), and denied losing the key in the first place. When I went to complain no information available at branch on our house, master copy still did not have alterations which had been pointed out several months previously. Only a handful of viewers in approximately nine months. Withdrew from agreement. Threatened with legal action for recovery of withdrawal fee (£100 + VAT) — no time-limit on withdrawal. It seems they would have still felt entitled to it had the house been on the market for 20 years — still unpaid following numerous letters between my solicitor and company. I feel so strongly that I would go to jail rather than pay them.

Please note: My answers relate to Global Properties solely. I was continually 'fobbed off' with excuses about the state of the market, that my home was in a low-demand area etc.

When I changed to Dazzlers (with whom I was completely satisfied) I was told that my house was in a *high*-demand area (as I had felt) and that they could sell the house within a month, which is exactly what they did.

I feel embittered at the service we received from Global and had it not been for Dazzlers tempering the bitterness and cynicism which I felt (and still feel) I would probably not have dealt with *any* in future. May I also say that [named] estate agents could not have been more accommodating when buying my present house. On an informal level they acted as very useful mediators between myself and the vendors. (Case 074.)

1   They expect sellers to show viewers round.
2   Short notice of appointments.
3   [Only] one [named agent] even bothered to follow up afterwards and let us know the results of the viewing.
4   Lousy salesmanship.
5   Total inability to value property correctly.
6   Generally poor management of their business.
7   Expect a child to show client round never having visited the property before, usually wearing white socks, gold bracelets, smelling like a Chinese whore.
8   Generally an unprofessional approach with little ability to assess advantages and disadvantages of a property or situation.

9   I have taken this property off the market and shall probably sell it privately in due course.
10   Except [named agent] who performed well. (Case 061.)

It is evident from these examples that categorising sources of dissatisfaction is not easy, even if in some form it is essential to conveying the views of 294 respondents in a reasonable compass. We eventually came up with nine categories with which we were reasonably content, leaving 14 cases unclassifiable. The least cited cause of complaint, which fits its profile so far, was financial services, with 10 cases, most of them citing bad advice or over-pushed products. Only one case of blatant churning was cited, itself the cause of a complaint to LAUTRO.

Next most important was advertising and marketing, 22 cases. What was interesting to us here was less that this was an issue, given the problems of selling property, than that it should have been explicitly referred to by such a number of respondents, many of them clearly having some training in marketing themselves. Most of the comments were of the 'marketing quite inadequate' general type, but one mentioned preparing and forwarding explicit marketing plans to his agent, which were later returned without comment, save for coffee stains. What this suggests to us is that, especially in difficult times, clients who are capable and willing to work with agents in selling a property should be encouraged to cooperate much more as equals than is normally the case. Of course, there will be many, no doubt the majority, who want to hand the whole business of selling their property over to the agent and have a minimum of further involvement. As we shall see in a moment, there are other critical comments suggesting that agents do not at times go far enough in this direction and leave too much, especially in respect of dealing with prospective purchasers, to clients. Others, however, are clearly keen to be involved and capable of making an informed effort. Given the tone of some comments to the effect that agents were in the end ineffective in selling the property and clients did it themselves, which is not insignificant in one form or another, it is surely important that the efforts of both parties be coordinated. In some cases those comments were to the effect that clients found buyers where agents could not or did not; in others the complaint was more general: that they were ineffective in their marketing efforts. One case recognised this problem clearly and came to an amicable arrangement with the agent (187):

The agent offered a broad overview and perception of the housing market, which was helpful in our decision-making process. The agent also allowed us to advertise privately, with no fee payable in this respect.
    We make more on the sale if sold privately — but they have earned their fee, through advice, publicity etc. if they sell — a mutually supportive arrangement. (Corporate agent, satisfied client, property unsold.)

The issue of marketing is closely tied to the next most important source of dissatisfaction with 23 respondents citing it, the failure of the agent to sell the property or produce a reasonable number of viewers over time, a matter which clearly led to changes of agency in a good many cases. It obviously relates to clients' perceptions of the market, as well as of agents, and we shall have more to say on this in a moment.

The next most important category of dissatisfaction, 25 cases, is complaints of poor or unreliable service producing a general lack of trust by the client. The following gives an indication of this kind of problem:

> Very poor service provided by estate agent selling my property. Don't think that people employed in the office are trained to a standard that is required for this type of business. Our sale was to someone whom we knew, not to someone sent by estate agent. (Case 031.)

The next most common problem was the opposite side of the satisfaction noted earlier with administration. In some cases this was plainly inadequate or had broken down, and failure to record details of the property accurately and amend mistakes promptly was a particular source of irritation and dismay. In all 33 respondents cited this as a cause of dissatisfaction.

This was exceeded slightly by the number citing the level of fees as a cause of dissatisfaction, 35 cases. Quite often the objection was not specific to the property sale in question, but general to estate agency, questioning why agents are paid so much for so little work, why they should ask for the same level of commission on a property worth £80,000 as on one half that price, when the selling task was the same, and so on. Many commentators of this sort either did not understand or did not accept that the sales of the few financed the fruitless enquiries and lack of sales of the many. Again this is a topic to which we shall return shortly.

The three leading sources of dissatisfaction we categorised as communication failures — failure to keep the client informed and to respond to calls (37 cases); quality of advice and staff negligent, incompetent or unprofessional (47 cases); and a poor attitude or effort by staff, who were generally unhelpful or unenthusiastic (48 cases). The first two of these — communication failures, and professional incompetence, are again the opposite side of the expressions of appreciation noted by satisfied respondents, though the figures are two or three times as great. The following are typical examples, first of communication failings:

> Viewings not accompanied. After receiving an offer not enough information given and found that we were always having to telephone the office to ask questions. Never returned telephone calls and had to keep bullying them to get them to move on certain issues. (Case 361.)

This case also raises a specific point mentioned by 18 respondents, the failure of agents to accompany viewings when the client was at home. A number of satisfied respondents referred to agents holding a key and taking viewers round their properties while they were at work or on holiday, as well as others who complained of lost keys, failure to lock up properly and other matters. The complaint here was specifically that the agent should accompany the applicant and not leave the vendor to conduct the viewing, sometimes because the vendor felt that he or she had not the necessary selling skills but frequently because the vendor felt vulnerable as a woman alone with children, or because elderly. If there is one specific recommendation to improve service that arises from this consumer survey it is this: some respondents were particularly aggrieved because accompanied viewings were promised but not delivered.

The client clearly believed the agent's professional advice was poor in the following cases:

> We had bad advice on the buyers of our property. While all this was going on we had other people interested whom we lost as potential buyers due to time wasters. (Case 174.)

> The agent did not value the house in accordance with the market. They were not quick enough to reduce to more realistic levels. Advertisement was poor. Generally felt they were not trying.
> I had no time to keep on their backs to ensure things were carried out satisfactorily and eventually got despondent and took the house off the market.
> I feel that they duped me in the first instance being confident they could sell the house and knew the market for the specialised market I am in. They obviously did not live up to this.
> Now of course the price of the house has dropped even more. I feel aggrieved as the two houses beside me sold last year and mine didn't. Now I have to sell for even less. (Case 023.)

This last is an interesting set of comments because it raises the issue of whether it was the market or the agent who was responsible for the lack of a sale. In this, as in many other cases, it is impossible, without fuller evidence, to be confident which is the more important. This issue is further identifiable in the leading source of dissatisfaction, cited by 48 respondents: unhelpful and unenthusiastic estate agents who made inadequate efforts. Here are some examples:

> They were keen to help until a formal offer had been accepted, then couldn't be bothered to help arrange visits for me to measure for curtains etc. (the sellers were away on honeymoon).
> It took me two weeks and several phone calls to get the 'for sale' sign taken away. Their whole attitude was most unprofessional. (Case 033.)

> Found out that a few people enquired about viewing but were discouraged by agent's staff not being available.
> No viewings in last 12 months!!. (Case 036.)

There just doesn't seem to be any personal service. Every time one visits or phones you get a different person and they only seem interested in the properties, neither the vendor nor the buyer really. (Case 482.)

Our bungalow has been on the market for two years. Our latest estate agent has sent three couples in that time and none of them were in a position to buy, not having sold their own property. We keep changing the agent hoping for a better service but they are all with the 'couldn't care less' attitude. (Case 495.)

Not all estate agents that we used were helpful but [named agents] were. Unfortunately our sale fell through at the last moment. After being on the market for two years we gave up.
　　We felt that most agents are enthusiastic for a short time and when it is not sold quickly they forget you. (Case 026.)

This last quotation from a broadly satisfied respondent has been added here because it puts concisely a view expressed by many dissatisfied respondents, that agents not only failed to achieve results, but lost interest and failed to put in any real effort. There was a clear appreciation by a good many respondents of the way in which the commission system and the market interact to produce a cycle of enthusiasm and effort on obtaining instructions, followed by a fall-off of effort and gradual loss of interest in the property and contact with clients. Our reading of the questionnaires, and especially the qualitative comments, suggests that in the event of a lack of sale or at least the production of regular viewings and a few offers, the relationship between vendor and agent deteriorates over a period of three to six months and leads regularly to vendors changing agents to restart the cycle. When seen in conjunction with the willingness of some vendors to take an active part in marketing, and the experience of others in being able to sell their properties privately, nearly always it seems through informal networks rather than private advertising, which, as we have noted earlier, seems to carry some kind of stigma, the nature of the relationship between vendor and agent seems to be called into question. As we have noted, there is an undercurrent of hostility to the commission system and the size of the fees it results in, which may bear no relationship, from the vendor's vantage point, to the amount of work put in on his or her behalf by the agent. The vendor is really uninterested in the agent's claim that this must go to subsidise greater efforts elsewhere. Sometimes, it is true, the evidence seems to suggest that frustration with the market is being projected on to the agent:

They never get in touch, unless it is to ask you to drop the price. When they first call to see you, oh, they would have no problem selling it, it was their job to get clients in to view. You have to check up on their advertising, they never find out if you have done any alterations to the house in the time it has been on the market. The picture on the write-up is the same as it was in 1990. (Case 002.)

Estate agents should sell houses for the vendor. They seem unable to do so citing 'market forces'. Price too high — their valuation, price too low, needs to be seen — their job surely to show people. Not once did they blame incompetence or lack of interest. (Case 276.)

1 The agents are quick to press you to accept a lower, *much lower* offer but reject any suggestions that they should cut their fee.
2 They fail to note (record information given to the office, then suggest they have not been told).
3 Close offices (move locations and fail to advise those on their books).
4 Change/dismiss/lose staff with the new staff unaware of the client register unless you ring them. (Case 263.)

This last case gives an indication of just how disruptive the market has been in relations between agents and clients, and reinforces the suggestion adumbrated above that maintaining a close and cooperative relationship with clients is vital, and that engaging their full participation may mean, in at least some cases, a willingness to think much more openly about the commission system. As has been explained in earlier chapters, this system is effectively premised upon the agent undertaking to sell the property within a period of about six to eight weeks, accepting that there will be some properties that are hard to shift. The present market has in most cases destroyed that expectation and the agent–client relationship has clearly come under pressure.

In 140 cases there was evidence that respondents had changed agents frequently, also moving from sole to multiple agency. In an additional nine cases properties had been withdrawn from the market. When it is considered that not all respondents were selling a property, that some who were had sold and that others had not been on the market for long, it is evident that market pressures have been putting great strain on estate agents' relations with clients. It would seem that at least some clients are interested in a fee-based package that offers tightly specified marketing and advertising for a fixed period on the model often adopted for advertising costs, and in recent times also for the provision of sale boards and specialist photography. The input of some clients in marketing the property themselves could also be taken into account in agreeing a fee which would then be sure rather than contingent income from the client. If such a system were adopted for the minority who wanted it, it should in time act to promote a more robust view by agents as to the saleability and value of all properties. Certainly it seems that clients have been induced by the housing slump to ask in increasing numbers what they are getting from agents. Agents should be willing and able to specify precisely what that is when asked, albeit in other cases the client will continue to want the traditional relationship in which the agent carries the burden and is judged by the end result.

These suggestions are the more pertinent given that they confront what we believe to be one of the most damning criticisms of estate agents to emerge from the survey, namely that they allow their own interests in earning commission from a sale to predominate over their duty to their client to obtain the best price, and to treat the buyer fairly. In 27 instances we identified remarks that clearly indicate this, besides one additional case in which the agent was strongly suspected of acting for a third party, by implication not himself alone. In some instances, answers to Q14, which asked whose side the agent appeared to be on in the buyer's experience, were accompanied by comments stating that the agent acted in his or her own interest. In other instances similar comments were made in answer to the final request for a judgment of satisfaction of dissatisfaction. Although this could have been an expression of general prejudice against agents there was only one obvious example of this. The rest came over as often rather reluctant judgments based on experience, with phrases such as 'out for themselves' and 'self-interested' being used. It could be maintained, of course, that this reflects an entirely healthy appreciation on the part of the public that agents do have an interest in earning their commission, and that a commission rather than fee-based system means an inevitable difference of interest from that of their clients at certain points, as we have remarked in earlier chapters. Equally it could be pointed out that a difficult market makes it hard for agents to earn their commission in the normal way and to an acceptable timescale. The introduction of withdrawal fees and deposits, which was noted in fieldwork on Langfords and Malcolm Devon, as a means of avoiding losses from outgoings when properties do not sell, is an indication that the commission system is under strain. The critical point, however, is that allegations that the agent will subordinate the client's interest to his or her own put agents firmly in the market-based rather than the professional camp. It may be that all professions are a conspiracy against the laity, but one essential trick of professionalism is that clients are not led to believe this. It may well be questioned by agents whether clients would accept an itemised fee, given that such a service could not guarantee a sale, but it would lead to much greater circumspection by clients before committing themselves to an agent and much closer scrutiny of their performance.

If there is one conclusion to be drawn from this expression of public attitudes and experiences, it is that there is relatively little knowledge, in many cases, of the qualities and capacities of different agencies, and considerable variation in the quality of service delivered in terms of both administrative and professional competence, and of what can be termed, if not dishonesty, then at least deviousness. Some, probably a reasonable majority of agents, emerge from the survey as competent and reliable, but a minority are less competent, unreliable and untrustworthy. The customer with the misfortune to instruct an agent who cannot or will not deliver a consistently high-quality service can be, as we have seen in some of the respondents' comments quoted above, severely antagonised and become cynical: the damage done by the minority has a disproportionate effect on the majority and contributes to the theme of low expectations of agents which we noted earlier. At present the public have, with limited exceptions, no real basis for identifying the good agents. True, the worst, who alienate their clients, are often small and usually go out of business, but there are evidently a number of established firms who survive. As we have seen, many vendors call on several agents to value and many discuss fees, but few have any inclination to check the agent's track record. One wonders what the reaction of the average agent would be if asked to produce the telephone numbers of his or her last 20 clients for the purposes of a quick quality check. Or to the possibility of anonymous inspectors making random checks on client satisfaction and publishing the results, as is the experience of pubs and restaurants. The idea of a good estate agency guide seems to be beyond the limits of the imagination of the consumer movement at present.

RELATIVE PERFORMANCE OF CORPORATE AND INDEPENDENT ESTATE AGENTS

Given the distinctiveness of corporate estate agency both in its aspirations and, as we have seen, in its attitudes and practices, we were naturally concerned to identify whether the public experience of the two types of estate agencies differs. Because we asked respondents to identify their selling agents at the beginning of the questionnaire, it was possible in some cases to be sure that either a corporate or an independent agent was used, though of course some respondents did not identify their agents, and in other cases there had been changes of agents or the use of multiple agency. Where more than one agent was identified we coded the respondent 'independent' or 'corporate' only if all the agents were of the same kind. By this means we were able to code a subsample of 312 questionnaires, 172 corporate and 140 independent. This sample was likely to be biased away from respondents experiencing serious problems with agents, since this is likely to lead them to change agents, but the subsample is a sufficiently large proportion of the total sample of 524 to be likely to reveal significant differences.

Of course the fact that we, and the estate agents themselves, were conscious of differences of style and habits in the two kinds of estate agency, does not entail that the public were necessarily aware of differences, and indeed this generally appears to be the case. The rerun of the data could only provide meaningful results for the first part of the questionnaire, which was concerned with selling, since the agent concerned in the purchase would usually be different and quite likely not in the same category as the selling agent. Although there was information on some of the questionnaires which would have made it possible to identify the purchasing agent as corporate or independent, this was not common enough to make it possible to construct a second subsample. The other question on which it made sense to discriminate the experiences of respondents using independent or corporate agents for their sale was the final question on overall levels of satisfaction. Although answers here were at times influenced by experiences with the agent used for the purchase, the norm reflected an appraisal of the selling agent. The responses here need to be treated with caution.

In general, what is striking about respondents' experiences of estate agents is the lack of difference between corporates and independents. Thus on matters such as reasons for choosing an agent and for instructing the selling agent, and matters discussed on instruction (Q2, 4, 5) the profile of responses is sufficiently similar to make it unworthy of citation in full. This pattern was repeated for Q8, whether the agent advised acceptance or rejection of an offer — see table 9.5.

Table 9.5   Advice on offers

Accept/Reject offer	Corporate	Independent
Yes	39	48
No	57	39
No offers	71	52
	167	139

When we come to Q9 and 10, however, on levels of satisfaction with administrative and other services, there are some real differences — see table 9.6.

Table 9.6   Satisfaction with administrative services

	Corporate	%	Independent	%
Very satisfied	44	25.6	47	33.6
Generally satisfied	80	46.5	69	49.3
Dissatisfied	26	15.1	15	10.7
Very dissatisfied	17	9.9	8	5.7
Disastrous	5	2.9	1	0.7
	172	100.0	140	100.0

Independents clearly came out better here, whether one looks at the distribution of extreme responses or categorises responses into satisfied/dissatisfied — corporates have a 27.9 per cent dissatisfaction rate as against the independents' 17.1 per cent. Given the expressed concern of the corporates with a tightly administered delivery of service as the hallmark of their quality, this must be particularly disturbing, even though, of course, many senior staff in the corporates to whom we spoke were quite candid in saying that 'We haven't got it right yet'. After five years in estate agency in most cases, however, one may be forgiven for wondering how long it will take for the corporates to get it right.

A similar pattern is evident in answers to Q10 on other services, that is, effectively professional ones — see table 9.7.

Table 9.7   Satisfaction with other (professional) services

	Corporate	%	Independent	%
Very satisfied	28	18.2	41	33.1
Generally satisfied	52	33.8	46	37.1
Dissatisfied	59	38.3	27	21.8
Very dissatisfied	15	9.7	10	8.1
	154	100.0	124	100.1

Once again the independents manage to obtain a much greater 'very satisfied' proportion of the subsample, though on this occasion their proportion of very dissatisfied is close to that of the corporates. In terms of a satisfied/dissatisfied split the independents clearly came out ahead with 70.2 per cent satisfied as against the corporates, 52 per cent.

When these results are compared to responses to Q20 on overall evaluation of estate agents the same tendency is apparent — see table 9.8.

Table 9.8   Overall satisfaction

	Corporate	%	Independent	%
Mainly satisfied	33	26.6	35	32.7
Mainly dissatisfied	73	58.9	51	47.6
Varied experience	18	14.5	21	19.6
	124	100.0	107	99.9

Because this is an analysis of comments on which respondents were given the opportunity to air their grievances, the dissatisfaction rate has gone up but independents still come out ahead of corporates. It would be nice to hope that the detailed coding of these responses would enable a discrimination of just what it is that corporates and independents are failing to do for customers. In practice, the profiles of each kind of estate agent are similar, whether analysed by positive categories of comment or negativeness. In addition, numbers in the cells fall too low to make a meaningful analysis. Thus to take the example of the greatest difference between corporates and independents, the corporates were castigated by double the proportion (13.5

per cent as against 6.4 per cent) and three times the numbers (12 against 4) of cases for failing to sell the property, or making insufficient efforts to do so. In a sample of over 300, however, these figures cannot be regarded as meaningful. Overall the evidence seems plain enough that the public's experience of independent estate agents is better than that of corporates, though it should of course be remembered, first, that experiences varied very widely, and, secondly, that overall levels of satisfaction are a good deal better than might have been expected, if the conventional wisdom, which counts agents as a lower form of life, along with politicians and journalists, is to be believed.

NATIONAL CONSUMER COUNCIL ESTATE AGENCY SURVEY

As part of its response to the OFT's consultative document on estate agency in 1989, the National Consumer Council (NCC) commissioned a survey of 300 house buyers who had moved since 1988. This is to our knowledge one of the few examples of reasonably substantial and serious research on public attitudes to estate agents, most of the frequently aired polls being similar to that conducted by the Law Society, and cited by the NCC, which ask respondents to evaluate different occupations. The NCC research is important because it asked respondents to focus on their own recent experience, as our survey did. The comparative interest of the survey is that it was undertaken at the peak of the housing boom rather than in a slump as ours was. The results are set out in tables 9.9, 9.10 and 9.11. The NCC asked, apparently by an unstructured question, why the selling agent was instructed. The results shown in table 9.9 are quite close to our own.

Table 9.9   Reason for choosing the estate agent(s) concerned

	%
A familiar/well-known name	33
Well-known in the area	32
Reliable	25
Rate charged/cost	15
They were part of a large chain/part of a group/large group	17
Sold my previous home	12
Advertise a lot/well	11
They sell houses quickly	9
Have bought from them previously	8
Friend/acquaintance	6
Good service/attitude	3
Other answers	11

Base: 146 buyers who used an estate agent to sell their home.
Source: National Consumer Council survey July–August 1989.

Table 9.10   People's opinion of the estate agent selling their old home

	Agree %	Disagree %	No opinion %
'They kept me well informed'	63	16	21
'I understood what they were telling me'	76	4	20
'I was satisfied with the time that they took'	62	14	24
'I felt they were on my side'	58	11	31
'They provided good information about their charges/rates'	66	8	26
'Their charges/rates were reasonable'	50	20	30
'Overall they provided a good service'	59	13	28

Base: 146 buyers who used an estate agent to sell their home.
Source: National Consumer Council survey July–August 1989.
'No opinion' column added by deduction.

Table 9.11   People's opinion of the estate agent from whom they bought

	Agree %	Disagree %	No opinion %
'They kept me well-informed'	52	17	31
'I understood what they were telling me'	54	5	41 .
'I was satisfied with the time they took'	57	13	30
'I felt they were on my side'	41	14	45
'Overall they provided a good service'	52	11	37

Base: All buyers answering — 260.
Source: National Consumer Council survey July–August 1989.
'No opinion' column added by deduction.

Perhaps of more interest are the two tables on opinions of agents as buyers and sellers (tables 9.10 and 9.11). As in our own survey, estate agents come out quite well, with majorities of positive assessments, except for buyers of whom 'only' 41 per cent felt they were on their side! The disagreement rates are relatively low, and what is striking is the size of the no opinion category, which we have added. Whether this is because interviews were conducted in constrained circumstances and respondents did not have time to reflect and form an opinion, or whether in the boom market properties were moving so fast that customers at times did not actually have much of an experience of estate agents, we cannot say. What is of interest is that, like our survey, the overall balance is strongly positive, based on recent experiences, and that this survey was conducted in quite different market conditions and at a time when, as a good many informants in our research have been glad to regale us, all kinds of abuses from gazumping to forced tie-in sales of life insurance were taking place. Nor did agents take the blame for delays in property transactions: only 19 per cent blamed the buying agent and 16 per cent the selling, but 34 per cent blamed their buyer, 24 per cent the people they were buying from, and 23 per cent their solicitor. This is unsurprising given the agent's interest in completion in order to earn commission.

APPENDIX   CONSUMER SURVEY QUESTIONNAIRE

This survey is <u>anonymous</u> and <u>confidential</u> and no person or organisation
will be identified or identifiable in any report arising from it

SELLING OR BUYING A PROPERTY THROUGH
AN ESTATE AGENT

1.   **HAVE YOU SOLD OR TRIED TO SELL A PROPERTY RECENTLY?**

Yes ☐   No ☐

If yes please answer ALL questions
If no please answer questions 12 to 20

2.   **THINKING OF THE LAST TIME YOU SOLD OR TRIED TO SELL
A PROPERTY, WHICH OF THE FOLLOWING REASONS EXPLAIN
WHY YOU USED THE SERVICES OF AN AGENT RATHER THAN
DO-IT-YOURSELF?**   [You may tick more than one box]

Because this is the normal way of doing it   ☐

Because of the marketing and advertising services
of an agent   ☐

Because of lack of time to do it yourself   ☐

Because you thought they would do a better job
than you   ☐

Because the agent could act as a buffer between you
and potential buyers   ☐

Other (please specify)   ☐

3.   **THINKING OF THE LAST TIME YOU SOLD OR TRIED TO SELL
A PROPERTY PLEASE INDICATE THE ESTATE AGENT/S
INSTRUCTED, WHETHER THE AGREEMENT WAS FOR SOLE
AGENCY, JOINT AGENCY OR MULTIPLE AGENCY, AND THE
DATE EACH AGENT WAS INSTRUCTED.**

Name of Estate Agent/s instructed [Write in each name]	**Type of Agency Agreement** [Please tick]				**Date instructed** [Write in]	
	Sole	Joint	Multiple	Not known	Month	Year
....						
....						
....						
....						
....						
....						
....						

4.   **WHICH OF THE FOLLOWING LED YOU TO INSTRUCT YOUR SELLING AGENT/S?**   [You may tick more than one box]

   Sold my previous property   □

   Well known in this area   □

   Agent was an independent   □

   Agent was part of a large chain   □

   Reasonable fee charged   □

   Wished to buy one of the agent's properties   □

   Liked/trusted the valuer   □

   Agreed with agent's estimate of value   □

   Recommended by family/friends   □

   Other (please specify)   □

5.   **WHEN THE VALUER/S OF YOUR AGENT/S VISITED YOUR HOME, WHICH OF THE FOLLOWING WERE DISCUSSED?**
[You may tick more than one box]

   The fee or commission   □

   Withdrawal charge   □

   Advertising expenses   □

   Type of agency agreement e.g. sole or multiple   □

   Mortgage advice to yourself or purchasers   □

   None of these   □

6. **BEFORE CHOOSING YOUR AGENT/S DID YOU INVITE ANY OTHER AGENTS TO VALUE YOUR PROPERTY?**

     Yes □   No □

7. **DID YOU AGREE TO PUT YOUR PROPERTY ON THE MARKET AT THE TIME OF THE VALUATION OR LATER?**

     At the time □   Later □

8. **WHEN OFFERS WERE RECEIVED ON YOUR PROPERTY DID YOUR AGENT ADVISE WHETHER TO ACCEPT OR REFUSE THE OFFER?**

     Yes □   No □   No offers received □

9. **LOOKING AT THE ADMINISTRATIVE SIDE OF THE ESTATE AGENT'S WORK FOR YOU — ANSWERING LETTERS, TAKING MESSAGES, FIXING APPOINTMENTS FOR YOU, AVOIDING CONFUSION — HOW SATISFIED WERE YOU WITH THE SERVICE PROVIDED?** [Tick one box]

     Very satisfied; the agent was completely reliable at
     all times   □

     Satisfied; the agent was generally reliable but
     there were minor lapses   □

     Dissatisfied; there were occasional failings that
     required sorting out   □

     Very dissatisfied; there was a pattern of unreliability
     such that there was a continuous need to sort out
     and verify arrangements   □

     Disastrous; the unreliability of the agent had serious
     consequences for the sale of the property or other
     aspects of moving house   □

10. **QUITE APART FROM THESE ADMINISTRATIVE FEATURES OF THE ESTATE AGENT'S SERVICE, YOU SHOULD HAVE HAD PROFESSIONAL SERVICES SUCH AS ADVICE ON ASKING PRICE, ASSISTANCE IN NEGOTIATION WITH A BUYER, SUPPORT IN SEEING THE SALE THROUGH TO COMPLETION AND AN ACTIVE SEARCH FOR A BUYER. HOW SATISFIED WERE YOU WITH THESE SERVICES?** [Tick one box]

Very satisfied; the agent provided sound advice
and support and worked hard on our behalf ☐

Satisfied; the agent achieved results but without any
evident effort on our behalf ☐

Dissatisfied; the agent failed in certain respects to
deliver an adequate service but the consequences of
this were not seriously disadvantageous ☐

Very dissatisfied; the agent failed in an important
respect to deliver an adequate service with serious
consequences for me/us ☐

11. **HAVE YOU SOLD YOUR PROPERTY (EITHER EXCHANGED CONTRACTS WITH A BUYER OR ACTUALLY COMPLETED)?**

Yes ☐   No ☐

12. **CONCENTRATING ON YOUR EXPERIENCE OF BUYING THE PROPERTY YOU ARE NOW LIVING IN, WAS THIS THE FIRST TIME YOU BOUGHT A PROPERTY?**

Yes ☐   No ☐

13. **THINKING OF YOUR EXPERIENCE OF BUYING THE HOUSE YOU ARE NOW LIVING IN, WHICH OF THE FOLLOWING MOST ADEQUATELY DESCRIBE THE ESTATE AGENT FROM WHOM YOU BOUGHT?** [You may tick more than one box]

Helpful   ☐   Usually available   ☐

Unhelpful   ☐   Hard to contact   ☐

Reliable   ☐   Honest   ☐

Unreliable   ☐   Untrustworthy   ☐

Did not buy through an agent   ☐

14. **THINKING OF YOUR EXPERIENCE AS A BUYER OF PROPERTY, ON WHOSE SIDE DO YOU THINK THE ESTATE AGENT SEEMED TO BE?**

On the side of the seller   ☐   Neutral   ☐

On your side   ☐   Did not buy
through an agent   ☐

15. **HAS AN ESTATE AGENT WITH WHOM YOU HAVE HAD RECENT CONTACT AS EITHER A SELLER OR A BUYER OF PROPERTY OFFERED YOU ANY OF THE FOLLOWING SERVICES?** [You may tick more than one box]

Mortgage arrangement   ☐   Pension Planning   ☐

Property survey   ☐   Conveyancing   ☐

Insurance policies   ☐   None   ☐
(including endowment
policies)

16. **HAVE YOU USED AN ESTATE AGENT FOR ANY OF THE FOLLOWING SERVICES?** [You may tick more than one box]

Mortgage arrangement   ☐

Insurance policies (including endowment policies)   ☐

Pension planning   ☐

Property survey   ☐

Conveyancing   ☐

None   ☐

17. **DO YOU THINK THAT IT IS DESIRABLE FOR AN ESTATE AGENT TO BE ABLE TO OFFER MORTGAGE AND OTHER FINANCIAL SERVICES TO BUYERS AND SELLERS?**

Yes ☐   No ☐   Not sure ☐

18. **DID YOU KNOW THAT AN AGENT CAN EARN COMMISSION FOR PROVIDING A MORTGAGE AND RELATED FINANCIAL PRODUCTS WHICH MAY EQUAL OR EXCEED THE FEE PAID BY THE CLIENT TO SELL THE PROPERTY?**

Yes ☐   No ☐

19. **IF YOU WERE DISSATISFIED BY YOUR MOST RECENT EXPERIENCE OF ESTATE AGENTS (EITHER AS A SELLER OR BUYER) DID YOU TAKE ANY ACTION TO COMPLAIN?**

Yes ☐   No ☐

If YES, please explain the causes of the complaint, who you complained to, and the outcome of the complaint, if any.

20. **CONCENTRATING ON YOUR MOST RECENT EXPERIENCE AS EITHER A BUYER OR SELLER, PLEASE INDICATE YOUR OVER-ALL ASSESSMENT OF THE SERVICE PROVIDED BY ESTATE AGENTS.**

Broadly satisfied   ☐   Broadly dissatisfied   ☐

Please comment briefly on your reasons for this judgment. If you wish to explain your reasons at greater length please do so on a separate sheet.

TEN

Estate Agency in Other Countries

INTRODUCTION: ESTATE AGENCY REGULATION PRACTICE AND REMEDY

Previous chapters have presented evidence from a variety of sources bearing on our central concern: what is the nature of estate agency and how can it be best regulated? In the opening chapters we described how attempts to pursue conventional professionalisation of estate agency were frustrated (a) by the fact that estate agency was the last of the professions of the land to emerge, and (b) by the ambiguity between its market-based selling side and the need to provide a specialised service to clients in the process. The latter can only be fully successful if delivered with a degree of dispassionate sympathy and competence. Professional aspirations finally foundered on the growing consumerist scepticism of professions and on the strong market orientation of governments from 1979. The arrival of the corporates further complicated this vision of regulatory success.

Our exploration of the practice of both independent and corporate estate agents led us to emphasise further the ambiguities and conflicts of interest inherent in their work. It also reinforced recognition of the differences in orientation between those agents emphasising estate agency as selling, and those emphasising the delicacy and detachment of it as a professional service, though very much as tendencies rather than as a dichotomy. Despite the aspiration of corporate estate agency to uniformity of service, the attempt to achieve this by proceduralisation and the integration of estate agency into the corporate bureaucracy, which is powerfully hierarchical and centralised, is incompatible not only with the individualism and localism of estate agency, but also with the client-orientated autonomy in the provision of an individualised service essential to professionalism. In addition, the desire to control costs and achieve targets and to sell financial services products generates further conflicts of interest that the corporates have been unable to resolve fully, and which are also incompatible with the professional model.

Corporate estate agency has hence not yet produced, in our judgment, a viable alternative model of estate agency that can inspire public confidence in its regulatory soundness. The professional model remains as an unfulfilled, and for the reasons we have cited, unfulfillable aspiration, but one that offers the best prospects of any degree of success so far identified.

Our survey of consumer opinions and experience, whilst it produced some interesting outcomes, only reinforces this somewhat confused picture. Expectations of estate agency are often low, experience varies very widely and so does consumer sophistication. Whilst some indications of ways in which estate agency might be better managed, and the public's interest better served, are provided in our survey no overall clear agenda for change is evident.

The model currently espoused by the State for the regulation of estate agency, outlined in chapter 3, must be set against this background. The approach is minimalist: intervene as little and specifically as possible, outlawing abuses only where they clearly exist and constitute a genuine problem. By implication matters such as competence, conflicts of interest, and confusion and ignorance on the part of the public are matters to be ignored unless and until they continue to produce specific abuses. It should be evident that we do not regard this as a satisfactory response. We shall discuss in more detail the existing professional, corporate and State-based machinery for regulation in chapter 11 before reaching our conclusions. Before doing so, however, it is worth stepping outside the confines of the English property market and legal system and considering how estate agency is managed elsewhere in the world. If no obvious solution arises out of our investigations at home, maybe there are lessons to be learned abroad.

One of the starting-points of our research was that estate agency in Britain is, by comparison with most other countries, relatively little regulated. In particular some form of registration is very widely required elsewhere, acceptance into the register depending on a varying combination of educational, professional (experience as a practising agent before becoming a principal) and fit and proper person (lack of criminal record, financial guarantees) qualifications. In addition, the legal system for the transfer of real property varies considerably, most obviously as between the Anglo-Saxon world with legal systems based on English law, and the European Continent with systems derived from Roman law. The law itself is, however, of less importance than the way in which it is administered, with such matters as the extent to which title is formally registered in an easily accessible way, as well as convention, influencing the extent to which lawyers' part in property transfer includes estate agency. The problem that we encountered is that almost all the published information on property transfer appears to have a strong legal bias and it was difficult to locate adequate sources identifying how the function of estate agency is performed in other countries, even those, such as the USA, where each occupation tends to generate its own literature.[1] Because this was necessarily a limited feature

---

[1] A useful summary of property law in the EC can be found in the *Estates Gazette*, 16 November 1991, pp. 76–79.

of our research, we were not able to make exhaustive enquiries abroad. We do conclude, however, that there is scope for further enquiry as to how estate agency is undertaken in various countries, with what hazards to the public, and with what degree of regulatory effectiveness. As a result of our enquiries, we are able to make modest remarks, which are nonetheless of relevance to the English system, in respect of France, the USA and Australia, and rather more extensive comments, as a result of a field trip by one of us, on Scotland.

Table 10.1   Real estate profession in the EC, 1988

Country	Number of real estate professionals	Number of members of professional bodies	Percentage of transactions dealt with by agents	Number of main professional or regulatory bodies
Belgium	n/a	2,400	60	1
Denmark	3,100	2,860	70	1
France	12,000	9,000	50	2
West Germany	10,000	4,600	60	0.75
Greece	4,000	3,000	25	–
Ireland	2,000	1,200	80	2
Italy	15,000	8,000	35	1
Luxembourg	80	55	90	1
Netherlands	3,000	2,100	70	2
Portugal	n/a	680	20	1
Spain	n/a	19,000	20	1
UK	70,000	65,000	90	3

Source: M. Treays, *1992 General Practice Guide to the Single European Market* (RICS, 1989), app. 3.6, 3.7.

Tables 10.1 and 10.2 summarise information collated by the RICS in order to prepare its members for the advent of the single European market. As is evident from the gaps, it was by no means easy to obtain adequate information on all countries and in some estate agency functions in a rudimentary way. Although, as table 10.2 indicates, licensing is common, it is evidently by no means always stringent, and not often backed up by financial guarantees. By comparison with other countries, English estate agents offer a larger range of services and, as table 10.1 shows, the number of estate agents is much larger in the UK than elsewhere. The principal reasons for this are, first, the involvement of lawyers in estate agency, second, the level of property ownership, and third, the frequency of property transfers. Systematic figures could not be identified for all these factors but a recent

Table 10.2 Right to practise as an estate agent

Country	Normal range of services	Fees regulated	Is a licence required?	Who issues the licence?	Financial guarantee	Legislation
Belgium	A, V, M	No	No	-	No	Law 8/6/66 Notice 8/12/86
Denmark	-	No	No (Yes to become a 'Stats-Ejendomsmaegler')	Government		
France	A and some move now into V, M and D	No	Yes.	Government	Yes	Loi Hoguet 2/1/70 Carte professionelle
W. Germany	A, M	No, scale fees banned	Yes. Licensing is a formality	Government	No	Gesetz zur Änderung der Gewerbordnung vom 16/8/72
Greece	-	No	Yes. Licensing is a formality	Ministry of Commerce	No	
Ireland	A, V, M	Yes	Yes	Commerce Court	Yes	Auctioneers and Estate Agents Act 1947/73
Italy	-	No	Yes	Chamber of Commerce	No	-
Luxembourg	-	Yes	Yes	Ministry of Economic Affairs	No	
Netherlands	A, V, M	Yes	No		No	The title 'makelaar' is protected
Portugal	A, V (M is a separate profession)	-	No	-	No	-
Spain		Yes	Yes	Provincial Collegio	No	Law 31/7/81 Real Decreto 19/6/91
UK	A, V, M, D and at times others — auctioneering financial services	No. Scale fees banned	No	-	No	Estate Agents Act 1979

A = agency; V = valuation; M = management; D = development advice.

Source: M. Treays, 1992 *General Practice Guide to the Single European Market* (RICS, 1989), app. 3.7, 3.8.

survey by the European Confederation of Estate Agents (cited in *The Scotsman* property supplement, 9 August 1990, p. 1) estimated that, whereas 75 per cent of Britain's property purchases take place through an agent, in France, Germany and Spain, the figure is around 50 per cent , a figure which is characteristic of Scotland, where solicitors have a large share of the market. In much of Europe, then, properties are sold by the lawyers, who manage the legal transfer, and estate agents are forced to compete with them, often specialising in selling new properties in conjunction with a developer, or taking on properties from lawyers when they find it difficult or inconvenient to sell them. The extent to which properties are sold privately could not be discovered, but it is certainly a feature of property sales in France, and also exists in other Continental countries, probably in some cases to a significantly greater extent than in Britain. In most countries where lawyers have a significant share of the market we suggest that they are not likely to offer the strong marketing characteristic of the English estate agent, and we conjecture that in this context estate agency itself may be less assertive and well organised.

Home ownership is higher in Britain, at around 67 per cent, than in other European countries. The survey quoted above cites Spain and Germany at 45–50 per cent and France at 53 per cent. Property may also be viewed in a quite different way in different countries, with not only an expectation of renting a flat rather than owning a house, but with home ownership seen as a long-term, perhaps retirement goal, and the home favoured being hence in a rural location and new. This may also indicate a much lower rate of house moving than in Britain, where the average mortgage lasts about seven years. This reflects not simply the tendency of the British to prefer home ownership and to attempt to trade up-market over time, as well as a willingness to move in search of work, but the availability of tax relief on mortgages, and more critically the availability of long-term high-percentage mortgages. In a number of European countries mortgage finance is restricted — to 80 per cent in France and 60 per cent in Spain and Germany — and repayment periods are much shorter — no more than 15 years in France and Spain normally. Although we were not able to obtain figures demonstrating this in terms of property transactions per 1,000 population per annum, this indirect informa- tion clearly suggests a property market that is much livelier in Britain, and especially England and Wales, than elsewhere in Europe, and in which consequently estate agency has come to play a much more prominent service role. It is an open question, therefore, whether the kinds of regulatory problems that have arisen in England and Wales have yet to surface elsewhere, at any rate as pressing problems. As we noted above this is a subject which merits further investigation.

SCOTLAND

A number of respondents to our consumer questionnaire spontaneously cited the Scottish way of dealing with property transfer as superior to the English, and it has been raised at official level in the past. In 1988 the Lord

Chancellor, himself a Scotsman, was reported (*Financial Times*, 18 July 1988) as being about to investigate whether the extension of Scottish procedures to England and Wales might not put an end to gazumping which was causing some concern in the boom market. It seems these enquiries came to little, in the wake of the government reshuffle later that month. The Interprofessional Working Party on the Transfer of Residential Property, led by the RICS (report published June 1989) also considered the Scottish system, but recommended that on balance the disadvantages of it did not warrant its transfer to England and Wales and that its benefits could be obtained by widening the availability of bridging finance and giving tax relief on the interest (Report 8.18–8.21).

What is the Scottish system? Although this involves essentially matters of legal procedure and administration in the transfer of title to properties, the way the system works cannot be appreciated in the absence of an account of estate agency and its development in Scotland. As was remarked above, differences in the law on property transfer are usually less significant than differences in the procedures for administering it. Though, as we shall see, there are some advantages to the Scottish system, there are also considerable drawbacks. To reach an overall evaluation we look first at the legal situation, then at the development of estate agency in Scotland, and finally at the problems and abuses the system has produced.

The legal situation

In a number of respects the law and its administration gives an enhanced position to solicitors in Scotland, in comparison to England and Wales. Registration of title to real property is much less far advanced than in England, although it is in progress, and hence detailed searches of the history of the title are usually required. In addition, ownership of title in Scotland is still feudally based, with all land formally being owned by the Crown and devolved to a hierarchy of feudal vassals. The system has, of course, decayed in substance so that the rights of the immediate owner are all but absolute, but a question always remains in respect of the 'all but'. Feudal superiors may be protected by rights and covenants over land which may affect, for example, change of use, and development or alteration of property, in addition to any restrictions which are subject to local authority or Department of Environment planning or heritage regulations. Feudal rights have hence to be identified by lawyers and negotiated satisfactorily for the new owner.

The more obvious respect in which a lawyer is called into the property transfer process, however, is to advise on bidding. This is a matter of conventional legal procedure which, as we shall see below, is often varied in practice but a stereotypical example is as follows. The property is advertised at an 'upset price', similar to a disclosed reserve price at auction, or the English equivalent of 'offers over'. Interested parties then view the property and if they want to take the matter further send a 'note of interest' to the vendor's solicitors, which puts them on notice that a formal bid may be forthcoming. Such a bid is written and legally binding, which means that the bidder has to be certain that he or she wants the property and that it is worth the money bid. This in turn means that mortgage finance must be arranged in advance and the legal status of the property ascertained by the appropriate searches. A solicitor will hence be called in to undertake this work in preparation for the bid.

When the vendor's agent or solicitor has tested the market and is satisfied that all interested parties have been alerted, a closing date for bids is set. This action will normally be taken after the receipt of a number of notes of interest, followed up by surveys, indicating that bids are likely to be forthcoming. At the closing date the bids are submitted and reviewed by the vendor and his agent and/or solicitor and the best one informed of his or her success. In almost all cases this will be the highest bid, since bids are legally binding and it is almost unheard of for bidders to have failed to ensure that they can produce the money. As is evident, this procedure puts the seller in a dominant position by turning up ready, willing, able and committed buyers, where the English system puts the buyer in a dominant position. The practice of submitting bids on a number of properties to see what response is forthcoming is impossible in Scotland. Even if disaster strikes and the bidder becomes unemployed, or the spouse dies, the legal commitment remains and the bidder is required to produce the bid price, usually on the basis of a bridging loan. Scottish banks are much more willing to provide bridging loans than English ones.

A completion date will have also been put with the bid, often with the agreement of the vendor, and is frequently a month or two later than the closure date, so allowing the arrangement of the other property transaction, the sale of the bidder's property, to be coordinated. It is much more common in Scotland, however, for property transfers to involve a period in rented accommodation, with the concomitant advantage that there are no chains to extend artificially the transfer process, which is rather broken down into its discrete transactions.

Conditions are usually injected into the bid, which may be more or less onerous. It is up to the vendor and his or her solicitor to judge what these really amount to. Standard conditions refer to any alteration having had local authority planning permission and work being completed to local authority standards, but warranties may also be asked for, as to, for example, the wiring or the state of the woodwork. These are matters subject to negotiation in an English sale and if included as conditions of the Scottish bid take on a much more momentous significance, since they stand to void the bid and allow the bidder to back off if not met. When the bids are reviewed there hence follows a period of 'exchange of missives' concerned to 'purify' the conditions of the bid accepted, that is, to establish a common understanding of the effective conditions. It is open to the vendor to dismiss a bid which has too many conditions, in favour of one that has few, or to suggest that some conditions are dropped as unrealistic and to put the onus upon the buyer to make appropriate enquiries. What does not, at least in theory, take place, is a period of haggling over the agreed price in the light of discoveries about damp, access, easements and so on. In Scotland this exchange of missives can last a week or so, but is often completed in a few days and contracts are thereby exchanged.

The advantages of the system are several. As pointed out above, it eliminates chains and avoids delays. It eliminates gazumping and gazundering, because bids are binding and cut off by the closing date. It also means that the purchaser is legally advised at a much earlier stage than is common in England, where, as we have seen, a purchaser is often vulnerable during the negotiation process.

There are, however, disadvantages. Many people used to the English system will be averse to the use of bridging loans and to the prospect of moving twice as an alternative, once into rented accommodation following the sale, and then into the purchased property. But perhaps these are disadvantages worth bearing with for the sake of the certainty offered by the Scottish system and the elimination of chains, which can be a source of great frustrations.

A second disadvantage is less easily countered, though it may not amount to a very great burden. This derives from the fact that a bidder cannot negotiate and is allowed only one bid, and hence may fail to get a property even after having it surveyed and taking legal advice. If this happens several times, as is not uncommon, the additional expenses incurred may be significant. Of course, the same problem may arise in England where a fresh purchaser arrives and bids up the price, a process referred to as gazumping where a clear informal agreement has been reached, but contracts not yet exchanged. It is more common and accepted for negotiation on a reduction in price to occur as a result of a survey conducted after the informal agreement of the price. Here the reversal of the dominance of vendor and purchaser in the two systems is plain.

The most significant disadvantage in the Scottish system, it seems to us, derives also from the closed bidding system. The bidder does not know how much the other parties are prepared to bid or even if in the end they will bid. The object is obviously to bid just a little better than the next highest bid. Experience of failure and consequent expense in order to be able to bid on a fresh property must influence judgment in these matters, even if, as is the case, solicitors can assist in advising what a winning bid should be. Even when the bid succeeds, it is not disclosed by how much, but there are certainly times when the margin is considerable. Here again the problem is a direct result of eliminating the open negotiation of the English system, where any bid is automatically referred to other interested parties until only one remains. Scottish buyers hence do not know whether they have spent £500 to beat the opposition or £5,000. The latter may be a modest proportion of the purchase price and well within a reasonable range of judgment, but as a capital sum to be paid off over 25 years it is a significant consideration. Despite putting this point to a number of Scots sources in estate agency and the law, none could respond to it as a serious problem and all were inclined to say that the value of a property was measured by how much people were prepared to pay and that in turn was governed by what they could afford, and how much they wanted it. It was widely asserted, however, that big overbids were not experienced as a problem in Scotland, largely because buyers never get to know how big a margin there was between theirs and the next bid.

The above account applies to a standard market in which there are several bids for a property. The situation can be worse where bids fail to materialise and one bidder is left in, believing that there is competition and not disabused of this by the vendor or his representatives. Here a bid much greater than necessary may be made. On the other hand, where there is only one interested party in a weaker market or where the vendor decides it is best, for whatever reason, to deal with one party, terms can be and are negotiated in much the same way as they are in England. In general, sources suggested that a move to more extensive negotiation seems to be taking place in Scotland, though the recourse to a closing date for formal bids shows no sign of declining into abeyance. It would seem that, with the development of the property market in Scotland to levels closer to those in England, English habits are beginning to emerge and that the conservatism, reticence and trust of the Scots is beginning to decline.

The development of estate agency in Scotland

Up to the 1960s estate agency in Scotland was undertaken almost entirely by solicitors. The principal exception was the upper end of the market, where English estate agents were established, mainly through their work as land agents serving the great estates. They were also able to take advantage of relationships developed with major property owners in England whose families also had properties in Scotland. Thus the upper end of the Scottish property market was and is dominated by the same group of up-market agents as the English market. There the similarity ended. Solicitors practised as estate agents as part of a multifaceted role as 'men of business' in Scotland, in which they would act as financial as well as legal advisers. The position of respect in which Scots solicitors have been held, a position which has led to them being used for many kinds of practical advice, has its foundations in the position of solicitors, for long an all-graduate profession in Scotland, as practitioners of the law, one of the three excepted institutions under the Act of Union, the others being education and religion. In a sense this made them, along with ministers and educators, custodians of Scotland's recognised distinctiveness.

The idea of the solicitor as a man of business survives to the present and solicitors continue to have about half the Scots estate agency market. The situation today is, however, very different from what it was in 1960. Then home ownership was only about 25 per cent. Today it has risen above 50 per cent, still well below English levels, though in the middle-class city of Edinburgh it is 62 per cent. The market in the past was small and the activities of solicitors as estate agents limited, even dilatory. Estate agency consisted, by all accounts, of the preparation of brief details and the insertion of an advertisement in the local paper on the appropriate day of the week.

Solicitors felt secure in their dominance of estate agency, not only because of their respected and established position, but also because of the commercial conservatism of the Scots. In addition, because the system of property transfer gives solicitors a more prominent and early role in the transaction than in England, they are naturally consulted by buyers as well as sellers. For solicitors, estate agency had and has an additional advantage in being a form of permitted advertising in a profession where advertising was banned and personal recommendation was supposed to be the only acceptable means of obtaining clients. Indeed it was not until the latter 1970s that solicitors were allowed to refer to their practice as 'solicitors and estate agents' and not until 1985 that solicitors were allowed to advertise, and then only with considerable restraint. Not surprisingly in these circumstances marketing of properties was non-existent and the prevailing wisdom was that properties sell themselves and need only to be exposed to the market so that people looking for a property are reasonably sure of coming across them.

In 1963 the solicitors were challenged by a lively and energetic estate agent in Glasgow, James Davidson, ARICS, who founded the Villa Estate Agency and began marketing properties in a way reminiscent of Roy Brooks in London in the same period. For example:

Pollok Fields (Aytoun Road)
Well, what a bargain for anyone who wants to make a home out of a decrepit mausoleum. The electricity bills in this 6/7 apartment semi greystone VILLA are nil, simply because there is no electricity. Yes, dignified Victorian gas lighting sets the Dickensian scene, where the grotty dull ancient decoration somehow seems in place. Massive two tractor and car garage (there presently are two tractors and what once passed for a car in it now). Regardless of your fear of 'strange' houses, surely £1850 must tempt lots of viewers.

Davidson flourished and established a chain of high street agencies with the usual paraphernalia of outgoing staff, eye-catching displays, reasonably well-presented details and attempts to market properties and service clients' needs on the English model described in earlier chapters. Taking advantage of the growth in home ownership, he was emulated by others and the stranglehold of solicitors on estate agency in Glasgow was broken. Solicitors were forced to respond by improving their services if they wanted to remain in estate agency. Some, not surprisingly, decided to forego the pleasure and thus remained as agents but also passed on properties for marketing by estate agents when they felt they might be hard to shift. As in England, reciprocal relationships developed between solicitors and estate agents, but were especially important in Scotland because of the solicitor's role as adviser to the buyer in preparing a bid.

Estate agents did not have the success throughout Scotland, however, that they did in Glasgow. In the east and north of the country, from Edinburgh through Aberdeen to Inverness solicitors hold sway. Various explanations have been suggested for this, none of them entirely satisfactory — cultural differences consequent upon the commercial character of Glasgow, for example, with its large working-class population and Irish Catholic element, as against the more conservative, Presbyterian and middle-class east of the country, this conducing to a strong resistance to the blandishments of estate agents. It is also suggested that the large private rented sector in Glasgow, which was managed by factors (agents) provided a natural base for the growth of estate agency and the provision of financial services advice. In addition, the amount and diversity of commercial work available to solicitors in Glasgow meant that there was less attachment by them to estate agency. It seems likely that the market, and solicitors' willingness to respond to it, have been the more important factors. In Glasgow that response seems to have been too weak and too late.

In other towns, notably Aberdeen and Edinburgh, solicitors organised themselves collectively to resist estate agents and founded solicitors' property centres, showcases in the centre of the city in which the properties of all subscribing solicitors are pooled and displayed. Although the centres are staffed, the staff do no more than assist the public in obtaining details of properties they are interested in and in referring them to the appropriate solicitor's estate agency arm. In some cases a qualified solicitor is present to give advice, but in no case does the centre market properties. In conformity with solicitors' traditional views, the property centres are a means of exposing the properties to the market, with active marketing being left to individual solicitors' firms. Where they are successful, however, the property centres can be a very powerful marketing tool and the focus of so many properties in the area that no serious buyer should fail to spend time checking what is available there. The first real property centre was in Aberdeen, following an experiment in collective display of solicitors' properties in the Glasgow faculty of advocates library. The Glasgow experiment failed to take off and has now been effectively replaced among some of those solicitors practising as estate agents, by the SEAL (Solicitors Estate Agents Ltd) chain of agencies run cooperatively by solicitor agents in Glasgow.

The full-blown centre in Aberdeen was founded in 1969 and has never been seriously challenged, with 50 law firms subscribing and listing 2,000 properties at the time of our research visit in 1991, and 7,000 at the peak of the Aberdeen oil-based property boom a few years earlier. The centre has over 90 per cent of the estate agency market. With commission rates at 1 to $1\frac{1}{2}$ per cent and its own property paper prepared in competition with the local paper to stem advertising costs, the Aberdeen centre has clearly established an extremely powerful position, taking advantage of the price boom and rapid rise in home ownership caused by the expansion of the oil industry, and building on the strength of professional cooperation among a relatively limited number of solicitors' practices. The centre survived the property slump of 1985–9 (oil related) and even though owners were desperate to sell, nearly all remained with solicitors and did not move to the corporates, who attempted to get into the market in 1987. In 1991 the centre's own research indicated that the corporates, of which two are represented in the area, were doing poorly, with one having only 27 properties listed and another, with three offices, having only 98 between them, whereas active solicitors' estate agencies had well up to 150 each.

Aberdeen is an interesting case of success, not least because of the influence of oil, which has brought a substantial influx of well-paid outsiders, well versed in the ways of commerce, and the oil money's effect on prices clearly made the local property market attractive to agents. Solicitors seem to have learned enough about ease of access and good presentation of properties to compensate for lack of active marketing — practices vary in the extent to which they employ specialist staff for this. The centre itself is a sufficiently powerful weapon to be able to refuse local press advertising and to charge the public for copies of property details.

The same cannot quite be said of the Edinburgh solicitors' property centre, though it had just over 80 per cent of the market in 1991, a share which was reasonably stable. The Edinburgh centre was founded in 1971 and in 1991 had 200 member firms listing 5,300 properties in prime city-centre premises adapted to display each one. Its drawing power to the public, backed by a television advertising campaign advising that 'It's never too early to call in a solicitor' is plainly formidable. It was not always so, however, and it was only in 1986 that the centre took occupation of premises large enough to display all properties. This was a period of strong competition from estate agents, whose market share grew significantly after a period of market cohabitation in which estate agents were accepted at the top end of the market, and at the middle and lower end tended to be passed properties by solicitors which were hard to sell. Whilst the establishment of the property centre in the 1970s seems to have been an effective holding operation, the suggestion was that estate agents did not make serious efforts to gain market share in Edinburgh until the 1980s.

Edinburgh solicitors proved capable of clawing back their market share by investing in the new property centre, taking advantage of the Law Society's relaxation of the prohibition on advertising in 1985, and learning the basics of marketing, accessibility and presentation. As a result, many of the Edinburgh solicitors who have stayed in estate agency have recently developed specialist estate agency offices with designated and trained staff. The property centre has recently appointed a training officer, and solicitors have widely accepted that the skills required for estate agency are not those required in the practice of ordinary solicitor's work. Properties are now actively marketed by many solicitors' firms but there is a degree of restraint and decorum uncharacteristic of the brasher estate agent. Solicitor estate agents are imbued with the service culture of the legal profession rather than the sales and marketing culture of estate agency, a feature of which is reflected in their working conditions.

Staff are not paid a commission or bonus, though of course their performance, like that of any other worker, will affect their careers. They are, however, entirely paid by basic salary with the perk of a car in some cases. They may only act for the seller or the buyer, not both, except under very restrictive circumstances such as intra-family sales. Some firms also provide financial services advice, but invariably on an independent basis and again acting for one party only. There are two organisations, one a large commercial broker and the other managed by solicitors, which provide a specialised service on financial services products for Scots solicitors who subscribe to them, enabling them to offer best advice as independent intermediaries under the terms of the Financial Services Act 1986. Clients may hence obtain more or less 'one-stop shopping' — conveyancing, property purchase and mortgage and insurance — and in this case commission from financial services sales is integrated into a package with legal fees which will reduce them.[2] Financial services advisers too are paid on salary not on commission. Many of the sales pressures and conflicts of interest that we have found in English estate agency are thereby eliminated or mitigated.

Solicitors in Scotland hence seem to have adapted and developed to produce an interesting new model of estate agency. Whether they would have survived were it not for their previous near monopoly and the slow and late development of estate agency need not detain us. The fact is that they have preserved in their estate agency some of the concern for client interests and avoidance of conflicts of interest that characterises solicitors, a matter in which they are supported by the Scots property transfer process, in which the buyer is legally represented before bidding. They have nonetheless learned important lessons from estate agents: to make themselves accessible, to provide adequately trained staff, congenial premises, well-prepared but not over-written advertising and, these days, adequate marketing provided the right firm is selected. In the property centres they have recognised the effectiveness of powerfully presented multi-listing, a weakness of most English estate agents outside London. They do not, however, go as far as the dedicated professional-style English estate agent in cultivating relations with a vendor or purchaser and working actively with them to identify a property to buy, or to sell the property. It appears that the Scots public is reasonably content with a less intensive relationship, provided reasonable attempts are made to sell the property. On questions of valuation, solicitors may either ask qualified estate agents to do it for them, or base their 'upset price' upon the considerable volume of sales data to which they have access through the property centres.

They are cautious, however, in their designation of price and repeatedly insisted that, unlike estate agents, they will not say to a vendor 'I will get you £50,000 for this house' but rather 'My judgment of it is £45,000–50,000, but you will have to see what the market will bear'. In general it is a low-key approach, which leaves a good deal to the buyer, a model not unacceptable we suspect, to many English vendors, provided that it is not accompanied by a sense, notable in our consumer survey, that not enough effort is being made

---

[2]There is some disagreement among solicitors about the extent to which commissions are rebated to clients, with some maintaining that this is an absolute requirement of the Law Society and that solicitors may not accept commissions for financial services advice, and others saying that only partial rebating involving fee reductions is involved. This no doubt reflects accounting procedures; some solicitors may have completely separate estate agency firms, which are hence not bound by Law Society rules, where others integrate estate agency in their legal practice.

to market the property. Scots solicitors claim to have learned their lesson in this respect and their retention of 50–70 per cent of the national market would support this. With the emergence of specialist estate agency staff in solicitors' firms, it seems likely that that lesson will become entrenched. It remains open to question, however, whether the Scots solicitors' model is capable of transfer elsewhere. The successful assault on solicitors' estate agency in Glasgow suggests that, once pushed into disarray they find it hard to come back, and the pressures of the difference in style between the meticulous, methodical and cautious work of the legal practitioner and the outgoing individualism of the estate agent lead most to retrench into specialist legal work.

The cross-subsidies inherent in solicitors' estate agency and their tendency to limit advertising and marketing, as well as competition both between and among estate agents and solicitors, have tended to keep commission rates in Scotland low, at 1 to $1\frac{1}{2}$ per cent in 1991, in a market which was not then greatly affected by the English slump, not having experienced the English boom — prices were moving up at 4 per cent a year or so. These pressures have probably made it difficult for estate agents who want to offer a fuller service and charge accordingly, on the basis, as we have seen in England, that 'we are not the cheapest but we are the best'. Nonetheless, the estate agency market looked sufficiently attractive in the mid 1980s for four of the corporates to buy into it (Royal, GA, TSB and Nationwide). One leading building society which has a national chain in England specifically refrained from going into Scotland, on the ground that it derived a great deal of its Scots business from solicitors and did not wish to compromise that by competing directly with them.

Although the Scots market is small by comparison with England the four corporates evidently hoped to use their financial muscle to build on the chains of agents they bought up and to make inroads into the solicitors' market there. By all accounts they have not been very successful. Although well-established in the Clyde region as a result of takeovers of estate agents, they were, as we have seen, repulsed in Aberdeen, and beaten into a corner in Edinburgh, though they have perhaps done better in the rest of eastern Scotland. A number of sources also said that corporates had failed to tie leading practitioners in the firms they bought up — at handsome prices as in England — with restrictive contracts. In consequence, when the ex-partners fell out with their corporate employers, they were free to go back into business and compete with them, which some had done with considerable success. As in England, the corporates have sought to use estate agency as an outlet for their financial services and, prior to the advent of the more restrictive regime under the Financial Services Act 1986, which took effect from 1989, it seems that there was a good deal of hard selling and some outright churning.

It is interesting in this connection that two of the chains that formed the basis of the corporates' presence in Scotland were involved in the sale of financial services products before they were taken over. In one case hard-selling practices led to a crisis, following the takeover and the introduction of the regulatory regime under the Financial Services Act 1986 in 1988, with a consequent sharp turnover of staff and substantial change in practice. In some cases there is still an aggressive view of financial services sales that emphasises the virtues of selling insurance cover as a benefit in its own right which outweighs in importance the value of best advice and independent brokerage, though it should be said that other corporately owned agents operate on the basis of independent advice. The contrast at any rate between the style of the corporates and their main competitors in Scotland, the solicitor estate agents, is more dramatic than that in England between the corporates and the independents, which are a large and diverse sector. Independent estate agents still exist in Scotland, both traditional house agents and professionally qualified agents and valuers, the latter often having good business relationships with solicitors, to the point even of co-marketing properties (a practice which requires careful circumnavigation of the Law Society's prohibition on fee sharing). The tendency evident in England for corporates to be more oriented to middle and down-market properties and to first-time buyers and the young as prospective targets for financial services sales is more obvious in Scotland, where solicitors recognise that the traditional respect for the solicitor as a man of business has not carried through to the rising generation of property owners.

The response of the corporates to their failure to make the inroads anticipated was, as in England, retrenchment — one cut its outlets by 20 per cent, another by one third. We were not able to identify how successful they have been, in relation to England, in selling financial services, but the overall picture is hardly encouraging. The Scottish market as a whole is not large and, given the stabilised position of solicitors and the advantages which the Scots property transfer procedure gives them over England, it seems unlikely that the corporates will succeed in dominating estate agency in Scotland in the way in which they anticipated, and may still succeed in doing so in England. Of course it may be that Scots solicitors will be induced to sell out to the corporates, but the spending spree has clearly ended for the present. As things stand the estate agency market appears to be difficult for any party to penetrate. The Glasgow conurbation is now dominated by six or eight agencies, including the corporates and the solicitors' estate agency, SEAL. Solicitors dominate the East, especially Edinburgh, Aberdeen and Inverness, though there is competitive space in other East Coast towns such as Perth and Dunoon, where solicitors' property centres have failed to establish themselves successfully, and where the corporates have a stronger foothold. On the whole, however, there does not seem to be much room for movement in a limited market, and the corporates were probably too late in their arrival to take effective advantage of the market growth in the 1970s and the failure of solicitors to respond to it promptly.

In addition the burden of training is considerable, especially under the more stringent conditions of the Financial Services Act 1986 and the recent Estate Agents Act 1979 regulations, essential for a large business that must be seen to be above suspicion. Training programmes have to be devised and implemented for the Scots system, but their output is in danger of being lost to solicitors' practices, most of which do not as yet train their staff, though the development of this is in hand in Edinburgh. They have, however, contributed greatly to the competitiveness of Scottish estate agency in recent years with beneficial results, as indicated above. What, however, of the problems such pressures often generate?

Problems and abuses

We have already seen that, whilst the Scottish system of submitting legally binding bids by a closing date has the merit of certainty for the vendor and a rapid decision for the purchaser, it has a number of drawbacks, which mostly derive from the closed nature of the bid: bidders may bid once and are ignorant of other bids. This means that the price of the bid is significantly determined by how much the bidder thinks a property is worth and can afford and less by the necessity to outbid the competition. As we have seen, one consequence of this is the need for repeated surveys and legal preparation — because they are binding, bids are always submitted by lawyers. Secondly, there is no way of telling the amount by which a successful bid will exceed its closest rival. Although the experience of estate agents and solicitors is valuable here, no source that we spoke to could suggest a way of avoiding the risk of a substantial overbid and all agreed that it was normal for the extent of the difference to be kept confidential. The best the bidder can hope is to achieve the same result in the sale of his own property. Because bids are legally binding it is unusual for the highest bid not to be accepted, as in England it may not be, for fear that the offerer will be unable to raise the finance.

A further difficulty arises in this connection where bids do not materialise. A closing date may be set in the reasonable expectation that bids will arise, but it does happen that only one is eventually made. In this situation a keen purchaser may be paying far more than is necessary for the property. In addition of course, there is the possibility that the estate agent may overrepresent the likelihood of there being other bids to a keenly interested party so that a high bid is submitted. It was not suggested that this practice was widespread, but it is clearly difficult to control. One means of managing it is employed in Aberdeen, but not elsewhere, it seems. This is for the bidder's solicitor's representative to attend at the estate agent solicitor's office at the deadline with two sealed bids. If other bids arrive by the deadline the higher bid is submitted; otherwise the lower bid is handed over.

Another way of avoiding the problem is for the acceptable bid to be agreed in advance. This essentially subverts the bidding process and turns it into negotiation. Where the market is weak, or where the vendor prefers negotiation, this is quite feasible and common, and the situation becomes more or less that obtaining in England. It was suggested that, in practice, negotiated bids are becoming more common, though, of course, once agreement is reached and the bid is submitted, it binds the bidder, unlike the offerer in England. At times estate agents were said to push a client's interest by offering to bid at a certain level, subject to the vendor's undertaking to accept the bid, so attempting to recover some of the disadvantage in which the Scottish system puts the bidder, but it was maintained that no good estate agent would be browbeaten by such rough tactics and would simply call a closing date.

An abuse related to the bidding system which was repeated by some sources as being persistent, though hard to pin down, is the manipulation of bids so that the one accepted is the one carrying additional benefits to the estate agent in the way of financial services sales. One source said that if bidders were anxious about the process he would allow them to be present when bids were opened to see that the highest one was accepted, but that normal practice was for bids to be opened as they arrived on the closing date. If the ground had been carefully laid by cooperation between the vendor's agent and a bidder's solicitors, it was maintained that scope for fixing the winning bid was substantial. Abuses, it was said, certainly occurred, with the collusion of solicitors, who would be repaid by the future provision of conveyancing and other work.

The possibility of this happening is made the easier by another development in the bidding system in recent years. In the past bids, whilst not unconditional, usually specified only a limited number of easily fulfilled conditions. In recent years the trend has been for conditions, notably as to warranties and guarantees on the quality of wiring, repairs, extensions and woodwork, to be included in four or five pages of provisos, or over 30 conditions. One effect of this is that the process of 'purification' — negotiating agreement on these conditions — is now longer and may last a week or two. The vendor's advisers also have to reach a judgment as to what line to take on conditions — whether to accept and hope for the best, or demand that they be dropped, or attempt to fulfil them meticulously. Extensive conditions do, however, also mean that the highest bid will not any longer necessarily be the one accepted, since it may be that some bids are being put in at a level which the accompanying conditions make plain carries a presumption that no expenses will be incurred by the new occupier for quite a long period in the future. Once again it should be noted there is a tendency for the Scottish system to be moving in the direction of the English one, that is, to a negotiated deal.

The temptations of financial services have been referred to above as a corrupting influence in the bidding process. A number of sources reported that gross abuses of financial services sales had occurred up to 1989, with conditional selling and churning common, as well as very large commissions taken by the big lenders in the sale of mortgage indemnity guarantee policies on 100 per cent or near 100 per cent mortgages, an abuse expounded on at length by one of the English financial services advisers to whom we spoke. There was agreement, however, that the new regime under the Financial Services Act 1986, and bad publicity, had largely eliminated such abuses, although evidence of churning was still unearthed from time to time by solicitors.

More significant today and in contrast to the situation in England, was the often strongly expressed opinion by independent estate agents and solicitors at the mode of operation of corporate estate agents, and especially their financial services parents and other retail financial services institutions. Considerable indignation was expressed at the overselling of credit, the constant extension of borrowing limits, competition to lend, and encouragement to borrowers to overextend themselves. This, it was said, contributed significantly to house price inflation, led borrowers into unsustainable debt and was greedy and irresponsible. Further, financial institutions were content to market their own products heavily, without consideration for matters of best advice or, often, appropriateness to the client. Sales and market share were paramount objectives, regardless of the public's interests, it was said.

This sentiment reflects, we believe, on the one hand the speed of development of the housing and retail financial services market in Scotland, which is, for historical and cultural reasons, rather more conservative in these matters than England. On the other hand, it reflects the powerful position of solicitors, who have traditionally advised their clients on financial matters, whilst also taking care of a number of other important issues in their lives, and who now, as before, are required to be clearly independent in the advice they give. In the face of the marketing muscle of the big financial institutions a number are plainly dismayed. Naturally this is linked to distaste at the zeal of corporates to use house purchase as a free pitch for financial services, but that is to be expected. What is of more interest is, first, in the light of the evident reluctance of English respondents to our consumer survey to take financial services advice from estate agents, whether there is not some degree of scepticism among the English public too as to the wisdom and acceptability of constant offers by commercial institutions to borrow and 'invest' (i.e., commit the investor to long-term payments). Secondly, it is of interest what the level of advice by English solicitors is to their clients on financial services matters. Most arrive on the scene late in the house sale and purchase process, almost none are estate agents and relatively few are registered to offer financial services advice. It may well be that such an independent source of advice is a valuable element of the Scottish system.

The final problem area is fees, which are relatively low — 1 to 1½ per cent in Scotland. It is perhaps not insignificant that the one delinquent solicitor estate agent — referred to as a cowboy by a highly placed legal colleague — that we heard mention of, was involved in fee-cutting business. For several years he offered estate agency at ¾ per cent, taking substantial press advertising space and generating a great deal of business. No one that we met suggested he was dishonest, but he did go bust because, it was said, he simply could not service the business he was generating. With estate agency dominated by solicitors, whose traditional view of it has included no marketing and only limited advertising, and with strong competition for the estate agency market, it is not surprising that fees are low. Many English estate agents would doubtless say that they are too low, at any rate for middle and low-market properties, for enough time to be allocated to the client to provide a proper service, and for purchasers and applicants to be adequately catered for. Even with an element of cross-subsidy from legal fees and some financial services commission, solicitor estate agents will find it hard to extend their service to include full marketing on the English model if, and it is a large 'if', that is what they and their customers want. This is a judgment which it is, of course, hard to make with certainty, but one piece of evidence suggests that it may be or become a significant issue.

Scottish research was cited (but not sourced) to us which showed that Scots people spend considerably less time choosing a house than choosing a car. This was supplemented by the experience of solicitor estate agents who avowed that purchasers often only view a property once before bidding, where several viewings would be the norm in England. Further, they are invariably shown round by the vendors, unless the property was vacant. Pleas for accompanied viewing, by English consumers apart (see chapter 9), leaving the vendor to do the job of selling the property would be seen as undesirable by many English agents. More importantly, however, it seems to go along with a cautious attitude to viewing, probably induced by the bidding process: too much viewing betrays enthusiasm and expectation of a high bid, where in England enthusiasm is a precondition of negotiation. Perhaps here the bidding and the low fee system interact to reduce the amount of time a purchaser spends looking at a property before committing themselves irrevocably. Certainly if that habit is indeed characteristic of Scotland it seems likely that the new occupants of properties are often disconcerted on taking up occupation, since it is notorious that only a general impression of a property is usually gained on the first visit, particularly if it is necessary also to negotiate a relationship with the vendors.

USA

The recent professional history of estate agency in America provides some interesting points of comparison with Britain. Divisions between functions are somewhat sharper, with valuation or appraisal being separately represented from estate agency or brokerage. Although many of the functions associated with estate agency in Britain, such as development advice, property management and financial services advice, are at times part of an estate agency business, the long-term trend, until the developments of the past five years or so, has been to specialisation. Like the chartered surveyor in Britain — its closest, though by no means identical, equivalent — appraisal has been subject to a more overt process of professionalisation than brokerage because of its role in providing valuations for mortgage lending and tax purposes (in the latter case appraisers are referred to as assessors). Because of its recent role in major regulatory failures, notably the savings and loan (S & L) crisis, it is worth briefly reviewing appraisal before passing on to brokerage.

As recently as 1987 an estate agent could announce with dismay to an international audience that there were nine accepted professional appraisal bodies in America generating at least 21 different membership categories and professional qualifications. Only recently, as a result of sustained government pressure, had they accepted a uniform policy on professional standards. At the same time it was estimated by lawyers that only 10 per cent of the 250,000 appraisers in America were members of any professional society which, given their current house sales of 5.9m, made a predominantly unorganised and unaccredited occupation responsible for fee income of about $1.5 billion.[3] Although later estimates put professional membership higher (e.g., 40 per cent of 150,000 appraisers[4]) it was not until the foundation of the Appraisal Institute in 1991, as a result of the amalgamation of the American Institute of Real Estate Appraisers (AIREA, founded in 1932), and the Society of Real Estate Appraisers (SREA), that a clear leading professional body emerged. The contrast with the much earlier professional success of the RICS is evident.

These developments and the accompanying improvements in training and accreditation took place as a result of government pressure referred to above, which came close in the early 1990s to outright government imposition of regulatory control. The reasons for this lie in the persistent failure of appraisers to eliminate fraud and incompetence in their valuations. The Real Estate Investment Trust débâcle in the 1970s, and the recession and its impact on property in the early 1980s, were capped by the spectacular abuses of the savings and loan crisis of the 1980s, in which America's equivalent of building societies with similar, and as deregulation progressed under the Reagan regime considerably greater, tax privileges became very widely unstable, compromised or bankrupt, the greatest series of financial failures in American history since the 1930s.

This is not the place to detail the extraordinary regulatory failings which generated the S & L crisis, save to note that they resulted from combining continued State guarantees, through Federal insurance designed to protect small savers, with total deregulation, whereby S & Ls, or 'thrifts', could be owned by one person and invest in anything they pleased, rather than in the loans on numbers of residential properties for which they had been designed. The fraud and speculation that this encouraged hinged in many instances upon the active complicity of appraisers, whose compliant valuation of properties was essential.[5] This was the easier given the lack of professional organisation and low rates of membership of appraisers, and the fact that they work both as independent fee-earning practitioners and as in-house employees of financial institutions. Further, as Marshall puts it:

> The lending industry in the USA has always tended to rely on the underwriter rather than the appraiser in making its loan decisions. As a result the appraisal is often considered to be a necessary piece of paper for

[3] J. Birnholz, 'Comparative American professional designation requirements', FIABCI Conference, 1982.

[4] V. Barrett, 'International and national demand for industrywide valuation standards', *The Valuer* (1989), p. 456.

[5] A good account is to be found in P.J. Marshall, 'The role of the appraisal industry in the US savings and loan crisis', *Journal of Property Valuation and Investment* (1992), pp. 491–503. See also, G. Newell and S. Mooney, 'The appraisal profession in the USA', *Journal of Property Valuation and Investment* (1992), pp. 1–5.

the file rather than a critical decision to take out a loan. Hence loan underwriters would have only those appraisers who would come up with the required valuation.[6]

Similar stories were detailed to us by valuers in Britain in respect of the recent property boom, though then, of course, valuers could take comfort in the fact that, if the valuation was a little generous now, it would not be in a few months' time. The importance of independence unfettered by compromising pressures by way of reciprocal or repeat business is, however, underlined.

The S & L crisis did not explode suddenly but gathered momentum through the latter 1980s as the consequences of abuse became ever more publicly evident. Congressional concern developed in earnest in 1985 with hearings by the House Subcommittee on Commerce, Consumer and Monetary Affairs at which AIREA and SREA testifed. The subcommittee called for the creation of a national licensing system supervised by the Federal government. This led to the acceptance of uniform standards of professional appraisal practice by nine professional bodies in 1986, and the formation of the Appraisal Foundation (AF) in 1987. The function of the AF is to create and fund the Appraisal Standards Board (ASB) to develop standards of practice and the Appraisal Qualifications Board (AQB) to improve accreditation criteria and the education of appraisers. The ASB then sought to require all loans involving federal funds and guarantees (which would involve most residential home loans) to be subject to State-licensed appraisers and the Office of Management and Budget duly issued a circular bringing this into effect in 1991.

At the same time Congress introduced legislation under the Financial Institutions Reform Recovery and Enforcement Act 1989, a wide-ranging measure designed to remedy some of the damage of financial deregulation, and cope with the S & L crisis. Title VI of the 1989 Act created an appraisal committee to monitor the implementation of State licensing of appraisers and created State boards to license appraisers. This system hence creates a government system of accreditation for appraisers rather than a self-regulatory system as is the case, for example, for accountants in America, who have a similar regulatory system, but with accreditation managed by the profession through the Financial Accounting Standards Board and the American Institute of Certified Public Accountants. Although accounting abuses were important in the S & L frauds and abuses, as they have persistently been in other examples of corporate financial misconduct, both spectacular and routine, the Armerican accounting profession was better organised and more unified and therefore more effective at political lobbying than appraisers by the 1980s.

State licensing has not, however, been a complete success. Appraisers are divided into three classes: licensed, requiring 75 hours' education in appraisal and 2,000 hours' experience and the AQB residential appraiser

---

[6]Op. cit. (note 5), p. 495.

exam; certified residential, requiring 105 hours' education, 2,000 hours' experience over two years and the residential exam; and certified general requiring 165 hours' education, 2,000 hours' experience over two years, at least half in large residential or non-residential business, and the AQB general appraiser exam. The problems arise with the kinds of authorisation these classes of accreditation give to the appraiser, which reflect considerable lobbying by a variety of interest groups, especially rural banks. This resulted in the three categories being restricted by the value and complexity of the transaction involved, not by the type of property being valued. Hence the lowest-grade State-licensed appraisers are entitled to handle commercial transactions to $250,000 as well as non-complex residential ones up to $1 million. Property of less than $100,000 was, under the original proposals, not required to be appraised. Under pressure from appraisal bodies, this exemption limit was reduced to $50,000, but this still exempts more than half of standard residential property transactions. The blurring of the distinction between accreditation for commercial and residential transactions which require quite different kinds of knowledge is also a weakness of the licensing system. With some loan officers still being paid commission on the loans they generate, the prospects for a fully effective and independent valuation system in America do not seem bright in the immediate future. Given that the system is now under government control, however, it will in the longer term be subject to pressure for improvement which is less easily fudged and avoided than it usually is when professional bodies have licensing authority.

Brokers

Like appraisers, brokers are also subject to state licensing but the growth of this seems to have been a gradual process since California became the first State to require it in 1917. All States now require a licence to practise, the sanction being the legal inability to collect a commission or fee unless licensed. Licensing requirements vary from State to State but have generally become more stringent with time as real estate broking (estate agency) has emerged as an independent occupation, from being an adjunct of insurance, stockbroking and legal practice, which it did by about 1950.[7] As in Britain, brokerage attracts individualists with little capital because of its low start-up costs and overheads. Most States require experience as a salesperson before a broker's licence can be granted, though sales staff are not usually employees, but independent sales associates generating their own commission as subagents of the broker, who is nonetheless liable for their actions. This relationship avoids the broker taking on employees' tax liabilities, but it also means that close monitoring of sales staff is limited by the need to keep to the Internal Revenue code. Although a minority of brokers charge fees, the majority work on sales commission, with typical incomes in the

---

[7]See G.E. Greer and M.D. Farrell, *Contemporary Real Estate: Theory and Practice* (Random House, 1982); E.F. Ficek et al., *Real Estate Principles and Practice* (Merrill, 1987).

$20,000–25,000 range, but with star performers well into six figures, and principals running multi-branch operations likewise. The structural relationship of a sales associate dependent on commission reinforces the individualistic isolation of the broker. The extent to which this leads to abuse is not clear.

The standard career progression is from residential sales, perhaps initially on a part-time basis, to residential brokerage as a principal, or sideways into commercial property, or specialisation in industrial property, agricultural land, office leasing or property management. Some high-flyers become property consultants giving advice on investment and development in the way some surveyors do in Britain. These opportunities are, however, provided by the larger towns and cities, and small-town brokers serving a local market may well have additional commercial incomes from insurance brokerage, law or construction.

In recent years, however, the American market has undergone dramatic changes, similar to those in Britain. Although considerable numbers of small brokers serving a limited residential area survive, some have grown to substantial multi-branch operations dominating a region with 35–150 offices. In these cases the skills of the principals in selling residential or commercial property have necessarily been developed and supplemented by those of managing a business of significant size. Those that have been successful have recently become the targets for takeover by large, often financial corporations. Some have resisted but others have sold out, resulting in the formation of national networks of brokers. These have taken advantage of their scale by offering employee relocation services, as the British corporates have done, as well as national listing and referral services. In addition, financial and other services are often on offer, through mortgage and insurance subsidiaries. Corporate estate agency in America is hence much the same novel reality as it is in Britain and there seems, as yet, little information on how it has fared.

An additional feature of American brokerage is franchising, with four businesses responsible for more than 1,000 franchises each, and the largest for more than 5,000. Franchising allows the benefits of national branding, promotion and support at the price of affiliation fees and annual commissions of 2.5 per cent of gross income, as well as a contribution to advertising. As a result there is a 10 per cent defection rate, with the constraints of keeping to the franchiser's terms of doing business as much an irritant as the costs of maintaining the franchises. Nonetheless, franchising is a significant and apparently permanent alternative model of estate agency and has obvious benefits for servicing an ever mobile population — Americans are reckoned to move once every five years as against seven in Britain, and long-distance moves are facilitated by the national referral systems that the big franchisers can offer.

The leading professional body is the National Association of Realtors (NAR) with over half a million members. It was founded in 1908 and in 1916 coined and registered the term Realtor, a term now widely used to refer to an estate agent in America, but technically only referring to an accredited member of the NAR. This parent body also has a number of specialist subsidiaries whose purposes are evident from their titles: the Society of Industrial Realtors, the Institute of Real Estate Management, the Farm and Land Institute, the American Institute of Real Estate Appraisers (now amalgamated with the Appraisal Institute, see above), the Real Estate Securities and Syndication Institute, and the American Society of Real Estate Counselors, for example. The NAR appears to operate as both a professional body and a trade association, with the former function necessarily mitigated by the control of licensing exercised by the States. It offers three basic categories of membership for self-employed licensed brokers, sales people and affiliate membership for those with an indirect interest in its activities.

Real estate education is provided largely through colleges and universities with bachelor's, master's and doctoral degrees on offer at some institutions. Most States require at least one college course as a licensing requirement, and additional courses for a broker's licence. Some States also require continuing education. Estate agents in America are hence at least qualified in a limited way before they are permitted to practise, and, as mentioned above, the tendency is for educational and licensing requirements to increase. Bonding indemnity insurance and audited client accounts are generally required of brokers as part of licensing.

Like British estate agency, practice in America is quite often diversified in order to generate a stable income, although overall there is a more powerful tendency to specialisation. This is assisted by an important difference between Britain and America in rates of commission. As against British rates of 1–3 per cent, those in America are 5–7 per cent. This has important consequences for practice. It allows agents to depend on commission income from residential sales more easily, at the same time as allowing brokers to concentrate on a much smaller list and number of sales than is feasible in Britain. The broker has hence more time to spend with vendors and purchasers, and to develop consciously professional practices. For example, the British habit of allowing vendors to show the property to applicants is not accepted. Not only are viewings invariably accompanied by the agent, but the vendors are asked to absent themselves to avoid the possibility of inhibiting the applicants. The agent's objective then becomes to use the viewing not just to sell the property but to identify the kind of property they really want — which may not be the kind they have initially specified — and to bring out and discuss any reservations they have about the property being viewed.

As a leading West Coast broker, D. Stone, put it:

> Buyers give you their specifications, but they buy their motivations, and specifications are not motivations, motivations are things down underneath. As a result, I've sold a lot of property in my life but I've never sold a whole house yet. I've sold bits and pieces, the rest comes free.[8]

---

[8]D. Stone, Address to National Association of Estate Agents, 1983, transcript, pp. 3–4.

The orientation is hence to the customers, be they vendor or applicant, rather than the property:

> I am not in the real estate business, I am in the business of real people.... There is no value in property. There is only value in people who buy, sell, lease and utilise property, and when I spend my energies and time trying to understand the human factors and the people involved, then I become a reasonably good estate agent.[9]

The cultivation of clients and contacts can be taken to considerable lengths, as it was in an example of an associate cited by Stone. This agent built up a list which he indexed of everyone he knew and ensured that he contacted them one way or another every three months. Purchasers would receive a card on the anniversary of their purchase. Gardeners and babysitters would be arranged for purchasers. Those applicants who failed to purchase from him would be pursued to find out what they had purchased and why, and sent a congratulations card. The outcome of such systematic and personalised service was constant referrals of business and an income four times the average. Such tactics are possible where commission rates are higher, and generate a system in which 35 per cent of purchases come from referrals, 20 per cent from 'for sale' boards, and only 15 per cent from advertising. Similarly 55 per cent of instructions come from referrals (according to NAR studies cited by Stone). Under this system the applicants are systematically worked on to identify what they are really interested in buying and their objections to properties they are shown — which are always expected by the agent — gradually resolved by discussion. This is plainly very time consuming. Many British agents would argue that it is impossible to achieve given time constraints, and we have seen evidence that cheaper properties generating less commission are subject to less attention by the agent. At the same time the model of estate agency proposed here, with people at the heart of it is very similar to the model of professional estate agency espoused by some English estate agents.

There are, however, dangers as well as differences in culture. Although Stone's account of professional practice lays considerable and sophisticated emphasis on not only qualifying purchasers in terms of their need to move and capacity to buy but also their underlying preferences, there is no question that the applicant is a sales prospect:

> We are in the job of selling, we have got to educate and motivate. People don't understand it, I think back in America 3 per cent think, 12 per cent think they think and 85 per cent are waiting for a slogan. Our objective is to help motivate people to do things....
>
> I see my prime role in this negotiator art of being between a vendor and a purchaser, and just a commission apart of being in a role of trying to bring these parties together. I have to build a bridge to agreement. Now I always start on the side of the person I am with. That's not because I am

---

[9]Ibid., p. 2.

dishonest, that's because that's the role. I have got to build perceived value high enough so that they understand what they are looking at.[10]

In the light of these remarks it is not insignificant that Stone called his address 'Selling is Selling is Selling', not 'Service is Service is Service' despite the emphasis upon 'rendering superior service'. Service is a means to an end, including the sale, and the agent's interest in his commission is quite evident here. Of course, Stone argues that the successful agent, prospering on referrals from satisfied customers, provides service to satisfy customer needs rather than to force a sale, but one wonders how great the difference is between education and leading by the nose:

> Vendors are misinformed and uninformed and purchasers are misinformed and uninformed. My role is to inform and document and be accurate. And be a professional.[11]

Without detailed evidence of the practice of American estate agents in negotiations, it is hard to be certain, but there seems to be no structural safeguard for the purchaser in America in the way the solicitor functions in Scotland. Neither does there seem to be the emphasis upon an explicit professional obligation to the vendor, who, as in Britain, pays the commission. Rather, the intermediary role as deal maker is explicit. Further, the amount of time and energy available to conclude the deal is considerably greater. Whether American purchasers feel as a result that they have been manipulated or that the value of the property they have bought, which the broker has built in their minds, dissipates on occupation we cannot tell. If the broker is honest and the information he uses on sales of comparable properties is accurate and relevant, this should not be so, but the room for abuse seems considerable. Certainly American estate agents seem to suffer from the same image problems that British ones do:

> How many of your parents said to you the number one thing we want you to be when you grow up is an estate agent? ... An estate agent — can't you do something honest for a living? We have a credibility challenge in this business and the credibility is proving to other people that we are really worth what we believe we are worth and performing. And I believe I have to document my position and I have to market myself as well.[12]

FRANCE

The Anglo-Saxon inquiring into the organisation and practice of estate agency in France is immediately confronted with significant cultural differences which are the more perplexing because they underlie easily

---

[10]Ibid., p. 19.
[11]Ibid., p. 20.
[12]Ibid., p. 11.

discoverable external facts. We begin, therefore, with a few easily digested facts and work towards an appreciation of the differences. Estate agency in France is undertaken by lawyers and by estate agents with the latter accounting for about half of property sales (see table 10.1). Lawyers account for rather less because there is a significant, although not substantial, number of private sales which do not involve an intermediary. It is not necessary to belong to a professional body to practise as an estate agent, and of the roughly 12,000 agents, 9,000 belong to a professional body, 6,500 of them to the leading one, the FNAIM (Fédération Nationale des Agents Immobiliers). The other leading body is the CNAB (Confédération Nationale des Administrateurs de Bien). This is the body which represents property managers, who are separately licensed from estate agents and who, because of the amount of rented property in France and the requirement to have a managing body to run co-owned properties such as blocks of flats, have a more prominent role in France than in Britain. A statistical breakdown of FNAIM members indicates the sorts of activities associated with estate agency. Of its 6,500 members, 5,800 are involved in property sales, 3,800 in property management (for which a different licence is required), 2,200 in commercial property, 500 in valuations, 850 in leisure property, 1,100 in property dealing, and 1,300 in legal work. The FNAIM accounts for 45 per cent of French estate agency licences and 56 per cent of property management licences.

Practice as an estate agent is governed by the Loi Hoguet introduced in 1970 after a property boom in the 1960s was associated with a number of abuses. It regulates the function of estate agency, although it specifies that there must be an actual involvement (*entremise*) in the transaction not simply the bringing of purchaser and vendor together, for example, by circulating lists of properties for sale.[13] In order to practise as an agent it is necessary to have a *carte professionelle* for the issuance of which there are four criteria:

(a) Evidence of professional competence. This may be demonstrated by either professional experience and relevant qualification or professional experience alone. In the latter case experience may be for four years as, for example, a notary's clerk or subprincipal advocate's clerk, or in the management of HLMs (Habitations à loyers Modérés, very roughly council housing), or for 10 years in lower positions in similar property related business, including estate agency and property management. Entry by diploma can be obtained with only one year's experience in property related businesses with, for example, a *baccalauréat* or legal qualifications, or with two years' business experience and specialist diplomas in law or property provided by professional and higher educational institutions.

(b) A financial guarantee minimum of FF50,000 but maintained at FF500,000 for FNAIM members.

(c) Professional indemnity insurance.

---

[13]See R.A.D. Urquart, 'Estate agency in France', *Law Society's Gazette*, 24 June 1989. F. Plimmer and S. Glasgow, 'The valuation profession in France', *Journal of Property Valuation and Investment* (1991).

(d)   A fit and proper person test — lack of criminal record, especially in financial matters, undischarged bankrupt etc.

Enforcement is by the State and penalties involve fines and disqualification. French estate agents are hence regulated in a fairly systematic, if in practice quite basic, way but the existence of registration eliminates known rogues and ensures that practitioners have at least a basic level of competence. It is plainly easy for lawyers to obtain a *carte professionelle* as estate agents, and a good many, especially in small and medium-sized towns, have estate agencies as a sideline. Relations with estate agents seem not to be hostile, perhaps because neither lawyers nor agents proper engage in the extensive marketing that is common to the Anglo-Saxon world.

The great majority of agencies are small and local with fewer than six offices. Although there are some larger chains, including four more or less national ones, these are run as franchises. The largest is now owned by an insurance company, but otherwise there appears to be no corporate estate agency. Estate agents may not obtain commission for the sale or referral of financial services products — this is seen to be against the public interest. Nonetheless, as one source put it, there is a good deal of local backscratching, and agents may have separate businesses as insurance brokers for which a separate licence is required, or have an associate or family member in that capacity.

The costs of operating as an estate agent are comparatively low. Office rentals are as little as one fifth of those in Britain and commissions are usually 6 per cent. Overheads tend to be kept low and investment in smart offices, modern office equipment and strong high street displays is not the norm for the smaller agent, although higher standards are required of franchisees. Similarly, details and photographs may be poorly prepared and presented and advertising uninformative. On the other hand, high commissions and professional accreditation encourage a quite high level of professional practice, with agents generally willing to spend considerable time with vendors and purchasers, and accompanied viewing the norm. Commissions are normally paid by purchasers, but practice varies from area to area and there is a move to shift the burden to vendors.

It is at this point that French estate agency becomes distinctive. In French property transactions it is made to appear to matter less who pays the commission than how much the final price, including extras, is. The lawyer normally acts for both parties and may of course also be the estate agent. Legal costs and taxes amount to about 10 per cent of purchase price, making an addition of 15 per cent with commission. Agents will often quote prices including commission and will involve themselves in negotiating a deal by cutting their commission to get agreement on occasions. What appears in the Anglo-Saxon world as a contested market-place deal is made to appear in France as an uncontested agreement in which all parties have an interest and negotiate. However, the principle of *caveat emptor* obtains, and although the vendor is required to disclose any known defects in the property, there is in practice little remedy by the purchaser, who is required to make his or her own inquiries as to the state of the property. Nonetheless, surveys are uncommon and usually conducted by architects where they are undertaken. They are not undertaken by mortgage lenders who lend on the security of the borrower and his or her means, as much as on the property. In part this is because dry rot and rising damp are almost unknown, for climatic reasons, except in Northern France. All this is likely to make the prudent English purchaser extremely wary. How does it work?

There are two answers to this, one more technical and concerning the law on property transaction, and the other cultural, concerning the place of property in French society. In respect of the first, as one source put it, the French attitude to business is that it is invariably exploitative and therefore requires regulation and strict procedure. The State is omnipresent in business relationships, and self-regulation, codes of conduct and similar nebulous gentlemanly notions are viewed with incredulity. What is needed is strict procedure and adherence to that will offer protection. In relation to property, this begins with the *mandat de vente*, the sale instructions, which is an exhaustive contract catering for all contingencies and giving the agent the right to sell. Vendors may or may not read or understand it, but they know that disputes will be resolved by reference to it. If a purchaser offers the asking price, the vendor must sell to him but, of course, negotiated sales are the norm. When agreement is reached on the sale price, the purchaser and vendor sign the *compromise de vente*, which is legally binding, subject to very restricted conditions. The transaction will then be completed by the *notaire*, who will act for both parties and take his or her fee and taxes out of the sale proceeds, though it is open for the purchaser to retain a lawyer to represent him. Deposits of 10 per cent are normal and are held by the *notaire* or the agent, and are forfeited if the purchaser backs off the sale. Contracts often also include clauses requiring both seller and vendor to pay commission to the estate agent in the event of the sale falling through by mutual agreement. This is because of bitter experience of the parties pretending to drop the deal and then going quietly to the *notaire* to complete it, so avoiding the agent's 6 per cent commission.

Like the Scottish system, the French more or less eliminates gazumping, and chains (see below) are not normally a problem. The principal risk in the remainder of the transaction, the completion of the conveyance, is that the *notaire* is sloppy and does not pick up information on, for example, easements and covenants or provides a poor title. The English system of separate legal representation guards against this, but the French appear, on the whole, to be content to trust the professional and legal obligations upon the *notaire* to get things right.

All this bespeaks a level of concern about property ownership and transactions which is very much lower than in Britain. Partly this is, as we have seen, because there is a predisposition to trust the State-backed system, but partly also it derives from property ownership having a much lesser significance in France. Some 54 per cent of property in France is owned, 46 per cent rented, but these figures do not fully represent more significant differences. The urban professional and managerial classes, the backbone of

French society, do not necessarily own their principal residences, though they may often own a second country home. It is more important to live in a flat in a good area in which one can entertain and have access to good restaurants, theatres and social contacts, and flats are often rented. The notion so central to the English mind of home ownership as a lifelong financial investment involving heavy expenditure and constant trading up is not part of French culture. Property ownership does not convey status in the same way and expenditure on property is less important than other aspects of lifestyle, notably food and drink.

Not only are the French less besotted with property ownership than the British, they also are less likely to move when they do own. Coupled with the impact of taxes and legal charges, amounting to 10 per cent of the purchase price of a property, the outcome is that the French move roughly once every 12 years, half as frequently as the English. Regional identities and attachments are powerful and inhibit mobility. When coupled with a willingness to rent when career moves are necessary, this leads to a focus upon home ownership as appropriate to where your roots are. Properties are often bought for retirement — these days very often new ones. In comparison to Britain, therefore, the role of retirement, job-related moves for those who do own properties where they work, and inheritance and the resale of properties are proportionately more important in France, because of the relatively limited incidence of that bugbear of the British estate agent, the entirely voluntary move, often associated with trading up.

The effect of this on the property market is to dampen considerably the tendencies to boom and slump evident in Britain. Greater restrictions on the length and percentage of mortgages also inhibit and delay house purchases until later in life and make the whole business less a matter of consumer lifestyle than it has become in Britain. In sum a brief look at France stimulates an awareness of the extent to which property transactions have been facilitated in Britain and the extent to which the British public are expected to participate on a regular basis in the property market. This is a fact, created and sustained by entrenched historical support for home ownership, but it is cultural, fiscal and hence institutional reality rather than an economic necessity for an industrialised economy.

If home ownership is less of an issue and rental an equally acceptable and available option until the time comes for a permanent settlement in one's home region, it follows that estate agency and the property market will have less salience. Estate agency has hence not quite the unsavoury image that it has in Britain, in part because of State regulation, which is at least partially effective, but in part also because it just does not affect the majority of the population as often or as vitally as in Britain. The theme that estate agents perform a necessary service but that their customers would often rather do without them, was evident in the consumer survey. In France there seems to be less anxiety on this score because there is less opportunity for exploitation of the market, particularly in the absence of feverish booms with evidently speculative elements such as the 1986–8 period in Britain. French estate agency is hence apparently less developed than in Britain but not evidently subject to the same extensive abuses that characterised British estate agency in the interwar period and the 1950s and 1960s — fraudulent deposit taking, gross misrepresentation, gross exploitation through property dealing etc.

AUSTRALIA–VICTORIA

Estate agency in Australia is subject to licensing by the eight State and Territorial governments. In each case there is primary legislation providing for registration, licensing and a board headed by a chief executive to administer the regime. Agents are normally required to have worked as agents before becoming eligible for a full agent's licence. In addition they now have to pass written exams to obtain an agent's or subagent's licence. They are also required to adhere to the terms of the fidelity and guarantee fund and pass a fit and proper person test. An annual conference of licensing authorities acts to promote the coordination of licensing and has developed such matters as reciprocal recognition, cross-border practice and a common educational curriculum. This latter has developed rapidly over the past few years to the extent that it is now all but essential to undertake at least 50 hours' specialist education before becoming a subagent, and further, more extensive, courses before obtaining a full agent's licence. The boards also investigate abuses and run disciplinary proceedings.

Although there are increasing similarities between the regimes in the different States, there are also differences; this account will concentrate on Victoria.[14] Legislation here goes back to 1922 when licensing and trust money requirements were introduced. This Act was superseded by the 1958 Act, which was more comprehensive and established an Estate Agents Committee consisting of industry and appointed members with wide powers to lay down standards of conduct, discipline and education. The committee did not, however, have much in the way of personnel. By the time of a comprehensive review of the working of estate agency licensing at the end of the 1970s there were only two full-time officers monitoring the licences of some 8,000 estate agents with responsibility not only for property sales but also for property management, including tenancy agreements in the private sector, which were usually short-term and covered a large number of individuals.

A number of abuses were evident in the review. The most notorious were the widespread practice of licence lending, which weaknesses in the existing legislation had allowed to develop to make the regime a mockery — an agent could lend his or her licence to someone unqualified and unregistered, and the law, even when invoked, seemed ineffective in controlling this abuse. Secondly, one leading firm of agents was shown to have engaged in the long-term practice of charging tenants a fictitious government tax, which the agents then pocketed. Even when denounced in Parliament, the most that happened was that the agents agreed to refund monies up to a certain date (very generous to the agents) and no prosecution either under estate agency

---

[14]We are grateful for the generous assistance of Mr N.P. Dalton, of the Estate Agents Board of Victoria.

law or for fraud was forthcoming. Those familiar with the rougher side of Australian politics and business, as became quite publicly evident in the 1980s, will not be greatly surprised at this. Indeed, perhaps what is more striking is the consumerist momentum of the reforms which led to the 1980 Estate Agents Act and its subsequent implementation.

The terms of the debate sound familiar to anyone who has looked at the English attempts to secure registration, culminating in the Estate Agents Council in the latter 1960s (see chapters 2 and 3), though the scepticism then of British MPs about the public benefits of establishing a professional monopoly were not shared in Australia, where it was taken for granted that the new board would be dominated, like the old committee it was to replace, by estate agents' representatives. The original proposal was for a seven-person board with four industry representatives, an accountant, a lawyer, one other and a legally qualified chair. When a proposal was put for an additional two members representing tenants and consumers by the opposition (Labour) party, this was met with resistance. The leader of the National Party remarked that:

> The original number was chosen with the deliberate intent of having estate agents being able to run their profession. There is nothing wrong with that. It has been the practice of other professions for many years and estate agents should have the opportunity of controlling their own destiny in the best interests not only of their profession but also of the people.[15]

This despite shortly being forced to admit that estate agents were not 'yet' professionals, that they would be entitled to set maximum scale fees for themselves, which in practice became standard fees (usually around 3½ per cent for residential sales), and that the board would have sole effective responsibility for discipline and standards in a field involving the greatest financial commitment by citizens. In addition, the largest professional body accounted for only 63 per cent of estate agents at the time, and 30 per cent of agents belonged to no professional body. In the event, the government compromised and agents lost their built-in majority when the board was increased to eight.

The key developments, however, would seem in retrospect to be the conferring on the board of the power to investigate and initiate disciplinary proceedings on its own account, rather than relying on public complaint. Secondly, the funding of the board is curious and very generous. Rather than being voted an annual grant which is inevitably the subject of argument in recession, the board is funded in part by licence and other fees, but largely by the interest paid by financial institutions in respect of monies held in client accounts for deposits etc. This is negotiated annually with the banks and naturally increases with housing market activity and house prices. It was anticipated to be well in excess of what would be needed to fund the board's activities and hence provision is made for any surplus to be directed to

---

[15]Parliament of Victoria, Assembly 23 April 1980, p. 8484, Estate Agents Bill.

supporting access to housing for the poor. The board allocated A$45 million for this latter purpose over 1985–90. The board hence acquired the powers to license, fine, reprimand and delicense, as well as to investigate, to develop educational programmes and standards and to increase consumer awareness. As a result, the chief executive can now claim that 'regulation in the State of Victoria and across Australia is substantially driven by consumer protection issues'.[16] To this end the Board has a programme of consumer education, produces literature and provides advice to the public on how to complain against an estate agent. Access to the complaints system has been made easier and less legalistic.

Like other countries, but unlike Britain, valuation is separately professionally organised and regulated in Australia, and so is the provision of financial services. Agents are quite often active in other areas, including insurance, travel agency and valuations, but the level of complaints arising from this would seem to be limited. In part this seems to be because of strong State support for the high levels of home ownership in Victoria, buttressed by government-backed home lending programmes. Adequate information was not available in this area, however.

What is plain is that licensing standards have been induced gradually to rise. Although the 1980 Act provided for the effective licensing of all practising agents through so-called 'grandfather' clauses, the route to a full licence now requires two years licensing as a subagent and completion of the three-year part-time Advanced Certificate in Real Estate. A subagent's licence in turn requires, besides employment by a fully licensed agent, completion of the 50-hour subagent's preliminary course at a technical college. These are no doubt not extensive academic requirements, but they do constitute a system whereby estate agents are gradually trained to the point of acquiring principal's licences and monitored the while. They are also subject to regular inspections by the board and to special auditing provision in respect of client accounts. Total numbers of agents have risen recently as shown in table 10.3.

Corporations are also licensed and required to have at least 50 per cent of their boards holding a full licence, and a fully licensed officer to control estate agency business. Subagents may not control more than 35 per cent of voting shares.

Claims on the Estate Agents Guarantee Fund, which protects client moneys and clients from fraud and gross incompetence by agents, have fallen from 230 in 1982–83 to 12 in 1989–90 and their value from A$191,000 to $13,000. Complaints fell from 497 in 1981 to 256 in 1987, and then rose to 427 in 1990, still giving Victoria the lowest volume of complaints per capita of state agents' licences in Australia. Seventeen objections to new licences have been made over the years 1987–90, 15 of them at the board's own initiative. Only two have resulted in costs being awarded against the objector. Over the period 1984–90 disciplinary proceedings have resulted in the cancellation of 15 licences, four surrenders, seven suspensions, 15 admonishments or

---

[16]N.P. Dalton, personal communication, 10 September 1992.

reprimands, and 19 fines ranging from A$500 to A$5,000. A summary of complaints at mid 1991 is provided in table 10.4.

Table 10.3   Numbers of estate agents in Victoria

	Estate agents	Corporations	Subagents
1986	2,636	865	5,804
1990	3,002	1,075	8,597

Source: Estate Agents Board State of Victoria.

Table 10.4 Complaints against estate agents in Victoria

| | Open | Closed since 1 July 1990 | | | Total |
		Justified	Not justified	Under investigation	
Trust moneys irregularities	36	10	5	8	59
Property mismanagement	67	36	19		122
Appointments	6	3	1		10
Fake advertising	3	8	1		12
Executive charges, commission, advertising etc.	16	7	6		29
Commission disputes	9	2	7	1	19
Sole agency restrictions	0	1			1
Professional conduct: fairness and honesty (a)	14	5	2	1	22
Professional conduct: detrimental conduct (b)	42	12	11	2	67
Professional conduct: competence (c)	11	7	7	1	26
Professional conduct: deception (d)	42	23	10	5	80
Professional conduct: duty to principal (e)	29	7	5		41
Agent purchasing property	2			9	11
Professional conduct: illicit listing (f)	9	11	7		27
Controversy between agents not above	3	1	4		8
Miscellaneous	1	2			3
Totals	290	135	85	27	537

Notes: The professional conduct code was revised in 1992. The rules referred to in the table are as follows: (a) an agent shall at all times in the conduct of his profession act fairly and honestly and to the best of his knowledge and ability; (b) an agent shall avoid conduct that is detrimental to the reputation or interests of his profession or contrary to good estate agency practice; (c) an agent shall use reasonable endeavours to ascertain all available information relevant to a service or transaction to be provided or performed by him in the conduct of his profession; (d) an agent shall not in the conduct of his profession knowingly engage in any form of exaggeration or concealment or any conduct that is misleading or deceptive or likely to mislead or deceive; (e) an agent shall not purport to act on behalf of a person as if that person were his principal without authority . . . and shall carry out his principal's instructions; (f) an agent shall not solicit a listing of any real estate or business from an owner where the agent first becomes aware that that real estate or business is for sale or to let by reason of its being advertised by another agent who has been engaged or appointed as agent by the owner.
Source: Estate Agents Board, State of Victoria.

Interesting as they are, these figures reveal nothing of the detail of cases, and time and distance regrettably precluded further inquiry. It is evident, however, that the system is working in allowing the processing of complaints about estate agents. It would seem that the majority of complaints either derive from the public or from the board's own investigations and inspections or the work of auditors, rather, as is the danger with professional bodies which regulate themselves, than being dominated by inter-professional disputes. The most fertile territory in estate agency is touting, which does appear as a separate category (professional conduct — solicit listing) but which does not account for a significant proportion of the total. It is, of course, impossible to tell whether the system is acting to permit the effective articulation of grievances by the public against agents, still less if it is acting to identify and pursue the preponderant majority of cases of abuse by estate agents.

It does seem, however, that the regime in Victoria constitutes a well-funded and staffed, reasonably consumer-oriented and vigorous system of regulating estate agents that is now well-established and making progress in the improvement of standards. It appears to command widespread acceptance and respect and to be in advance of any regulatory regime we have identified elsewhere. Like regulatory systems elsewhere that we have reviewed, with the exception of Britain, it accepts that State management of regulation is essential, coupled with registration of functions. Estate agents are well represented in the regulatory system but they do not monopolise it and their interests are balanced by a growing consumerism. Like other systems, again with the exception of Britain, a commitment to the establishment and increase in standards of competence of estate agents is accepted as essential to the improvement of overall standards of conduct, whether in terms of competence or probity. We shall return to these matters in the next chapter.

CONCLUSION

What lessons can be drawn from these brief international comparisons? The first must be caution. Estate agency is organised in somewhat differing ways in different countries and reflects differences in legal systems and in the size and level of activity in residential property markets. It is noteworthy that in a number of respects the system most different to the English of those reviewed here is that which is also the closest geographically and politically, namely Scotland, yet it is doubtful if the advantages of the Scots system can easily be transferred to England. The most important of these is the involvement of solicitors as advisers to the purchaser at a relatively early stage in the transaction, a role which Scots solicitors, if they also act as estate agents, are well placed to fulfil. It may be that English solicitors could develop a greater capacity for giving early advice to purchasers than they now do, particularly if the recent trend to specialisation among solicitors continues. They may also come to have a cautionary and advisory role in monitoring the financial services packages offered to purchasers, even where they do not actively advise on financial services themselves, though Law Society and Financial Services Act 1986 regulations do not make a limited advisory role easy. Certainly the lesson to be drawn from Scotland is the importance of early advice to purchasers; the problem for English purchasers is where it could possibly come from. Estate agencies themselves might take on a more formal role here but that would not be realistic unless it involved some form of payment and hence a revision of the commission system, something which English estate agents are reluctant to contemplate, though it appears to be less of an issue in France than in the Anglo-Saxon world.

Does France offer an alternative State-supported less contentious model of property transfer? We think probably not. The residential property market is less developed than in England and hence less subject to the stresses that an active market and a view of property as an investment as well as a home brings. Further, the cultural, political and economic entrenchment of the State in France, as pervasive as it is paternalistic, is simply unthinkable in the Anglo-Saxon world. It will take many years of Britain's further integration into the EC for a significant shift in this direction to take place, and in the process, of course, the political habits of European institutions may themselves be influenced by Anglo-Saxon attitudes.

In one matter, however, most jurisdictions, including some we have not reviewed in any detail, are agreed. State supervision and regulation of estate agency is the only satisfactory solution to its inherent preculiarities: to its conflation of professional service and sales orientation, and to its inherent conflicts of interest between vendor, purchaser and agent. In no case have the professional bodies representing estate agency become organised and powerful enough to bid successfully for self-regulation, though active cooperation with the State in regulation is evident in Australia and the USA. In failing to take on this responsibility and reserving itself to a piecemeal approach in targeting specific abuses and dishonesty, Britain is clearly anomalous.

Before saying more on these matters, the way in which estate agency is currently regulated in Britain needs to be reviewed, which is the subject of the next chapter.

ELEVEN
Regulation

The first part of this chapter reviews the machinery intended to protect the public against abuses by estate agents. Much of it has been remarked on at various points in the preceding chapters and we shall not attempt an exhaustive account of its workings here. Rather we evaluate each remedy on its own merits and in relation to others in order to reach an overall appraisal of the regulatory machinery. Existing machinery is piecemeal and limited. It comprises six elements: professional self-regulation through the complaints and disciplinary procedures of the professional bodies (NAEA, RICS etc.); the compensation scheme introduced by corporate estate agents alongside the code of conduct for its members (OCEA); the Estate Agents Act 1979 and orders made under it and the Property Misdescriptions Act 1991; the establishment of standards of competence for estate agents through the development of national vocational qualifications; the oversight and regulatory policies and practices of the state agencies responsible, that is, the OFT, the DTI and the local trading standards officers; and the efforts and policies of the consumer lobby on behalf of the public.

These elements clearly do not constitute a coherent system of regulation. The reasons lie partly in the history of regulatory policy and partly in the intractable nature of estate agency itself. These will be taken up in the latter part of this chapter, where the lines upon which relevant and effective regulation might take place are identified. At this stage, however, we consider some of the questions pertinent to this appraisal. The most obvious question to ask of regulatory arrangements is: are they effective, that is, do they achieve the ends they set out to? This, however, is very much to take such arrangements on their own terms. We believe that at least two additional questions are essential. Is the machinery accessible, that is, is it known to the relevant public and can it be made use of without undue difficulty? Secondly, is it relevant, that is, does the machinery address either the problems that the public experience as needing redress and, more fundamentally, does it deal with problems that the public may be less aware of, but which may still be detrimental to their interests?

As is evident from this latter point, we do not regard regulation as what might be called a fly-swatting matter. By that we mean that an appropriate regulatory system is not one which simply provides a mechanism to respond to the agitation of a member of the public in respect of some aspect of that individual's experience of estate agency. Rather we view effective and appropriate regulation as a regime which conduces to the recognition and maintenance of standards of conduct which protect the interests of the public, regardless of whether individual members of the public recognise that they have been compromised. We recognise, in other words, that, as in other relationships involving complex services to lay clients, the onus must lie upon the service provider to be aware at all times of the interests of the client and other members of the public, since the lack of information and expertise of the client will put the client at a disadvantage. We will return to this issue in the latter part of the chapter.

PROFESSIONAL SELF-REGULATION

The three leading professional bodies (RICS, ISVA, NAEA) all had procedures for dealing with complaints about their members. We were able to look in some detail at those of the NAEA and less fully at those of the other two bodies, which did, nonetheless, seem to be substantially similar in the way they operated. The outstanding characteristics of the complaints system in each case are the length of the proceedings necessary to reach a full disciplinary hearing and the deflective and conciliatory nature of the stages leading up to the hearing. In this the professional bodies reflect the ambiguity of their role as, on the one hand, professional bodies concerned to protect the public when the conduct of their members falls below acceptable standards, and on the other, their character as trade associations designed to protect the interests of members. The solution to these conflicting interests is to protract the proceedings for the complainant so as to deter all but the serious, determined and articulate from reaching the full disciplinary tribunal stage. For the minority of complaints which do reach that stage, the professional body is then under pressure to demonstrate good faith and so tends to find for the complainant and impose a penalty upon the errant member.

In the case of the NAEA this penalty could range from a reprimand to expulsion, and could include a fine and an order for the compensation of the complainant where appropriate, and the award of costs. Complaints to the NAEA are dealt with initially by the compliance officer, whose first task it is to establish the nature of the complaint and to verify that it is something that the NAEA can take on, i.e., that it appears to involve allegations of misconduct that break the NAEA's rules, and that it clearly involves one of their members. The complaint is then referred to the respondent, who is allowed four weeks to reply in writing to the allegation. This response is then passed back to the complainant who is asked to provide written comments within a further four weeks. The stated purpose of this toing and froing, which may take three months to complete, is to establish the common ground between the parties and the precise basis of the dispute. In practice it was used also to deflect and foreclose complaints. Compliance officers' comments to the complainants were found to include such phrases as 'I trust that this reply has managed to clarify the situation'; 'although I cannot at this stage see that there has been a contravention of the Association's Rules of Conduct'; 'I sincerely hope you will accept this letter of regret in the spirit in which it was given'; 'I regret that the NAEA cannot become further involved in this matter'.

Such remarks clearly riled some complainants, who replied, *inter alia*, 'This effectively turns the NAEA into a cosmetic organisation with power neither to investigate or to discipline'; 'I do not intend to let this matter rest and I intend to expose the folly of your association as widely as possible through the media' (all comments from NAEA closed disciplinary files). When it was clear that the complainant would persist, the compliance officer referred the case to the business practices officer (BPO) for formal consideration. As the chairman of the disciplinary subcommittee put it: 'Fortunately for the committee the initial investigations dispose of the majority of complaints without involving a full hearing' (*Estate Agent*, Summer 1986, p. 25).

If the BPO is satisfied that there is prima facie evidence of a breach of the Association's rules, the case may be referred to the Disciplinary Tribunal for an oral hearing. The BPO is charged with preparing a statement of the case and the case papers, as well as notifying the parties of their right to attend and give evidence, or to rely on written submissions. After hearing the evidence, the tribunal reaches its verdict in camera and then delivers judgment. There is a right of appeal by members (but not for complainants) to an appeals committee. Beyond that cases may be appealed to the County Court. This sometimes happens, though in the experience of one senior officer no disciplinary decision by the Association has been reversed by a court in the past 15 years. The outcome of cases is normally published and although the Association may require confidentiality, again this has never been imposed in the past 15 years.

Besides reviewing a number of closed files we observed the proceedings of the Tribunal in three cases, all of which resulted in a finding for the complainant. The first was all but a foregone conclusion since it involved allegations of racial discrimination against clients and the case had been investigated and supported by the Commission for Racial Equality. The second involved allegations of sexual harassment by a client which stopped short of serious assault but was clearly improper and unethical. Once again, the tribunal found for the complainant and issued a severe reprimand and required a letter of apology. The final case involved allegations of dishonesty on the part of a member and the most detailed interrogation of the complainant, who had alleged essentially that the agent had a personal interest in the sale of the property. In finding for the complainant the tribunal imposed a £750 fine, compensation of over £600 and £150 costs, though the fine was suspended provided no further complaints of dishonesty were substantiated.

In these cases the NAEA was clearly concerned to show that it could act on behalf of a complainant in serious cases and discipline its members, but cases such as these had a substantial symbolic element. Rather than the complaints process acting as a means of redressing grievances by the public, it acted to test the determination of complainants, both to pursue a complaint through to a hearing, and resist having it abandoned, conciliated or diverted, and the complainant's capacity to mount an effective and coherent case — the NAEA offered no assistance in this latter respect and regularly sought to test the quality of the case against its member. Resort to complaint against the professional body is hence likely to prove frustrating and ineffective for the majority of complainants who lack the necessary capacity. For the minority who can stay the course there is the prospect of some satisfaction.

In respect of the ISVA and RICS, less access was allowed, but it seems that procedures were similar to those of the NAEA. Complaints at ISVA are dealt with by the professional services officer (PSO), who refers them to the member concerned and in turn passes on the member's comments to the complainant. If this does not resolve matters, and if the PSO accepts that there was a case to answer, it is referred to the Professional Practices Committee, which can reprimand members or reject a case. If the case is considered serious it is referred to the Disciplinary Committee, which can suspend and expel (but not fine) members. At this stage the parties can attend in person and give evidence. There is a right of appeal against the decision of the disciplinary committee, and the results of serious cases are published. It was estimated by ISVA that three or four complaints a week were received, in the past about gazumping, now more usually mismanagement or failure to recognise a defect in a property. Half were filtered out, leaving the Professional Practices Committee to deal with about 10 complaints a quarter, of which perhaps seven or eight would be taken on. The more extensive tiering of the committees and the lack of powers to impose fines suggests that ISVA is weaker in its treatment of complaints than the NAEA. Certainly it shares the same evident tendency to divert and deflect complaints.

The situation is similar at the RICS. It was suggested by the head of professional conduct that most complaints arose because complainants did not understand the system of buying and selling houses, and hence were outside RICS rules. Complaints were initially dealt with by the secretariat, with advice as appropriate from the Professional Conduct Committee. The latter has powers only to reprimand or require an undertaking not to repeat the conduct. More serious cases are referred to the Disciplinary Board, which can expel members, who can appear to give evidence in person. There is a right of appeal to a further Board. The secretariat attempts to be helpful to a naïve complainant such as a first-time buyer, though a professional complainant such as a solicitor will be expected to mount a complaint unassisted. Table 11.1 details complaints over a year in 1989–90. No figures were available on the numbers which were transmitted for hearing at the Disciplinary Board, and the outcome of such hearings, but it was evident from discussions with the officers involved that this was a small proportion of complaints received. As a percentage of the RICS membership of some 63,000 corporate, and 21,000 unattached (students etc.) the rate of complaint

Table 11.1 RICS — Complaints received against members 1989 to 90

	1989		1990											Total
	Nov	Dec	Jan	Feb	Mar	Apr	May	Jun	Jul	Aug	Sep	Oct	
Advertising	3	2	2	2	3	3	3	3	6	3	6	4	40
Auction sales	1	1	2	2	1	1	–	–	1	1	2	3	15
Bankruptcy	–	–	1	–	–	–	–	1	–	1	–	–	3
Conflict of interest	4	3	5	4	5	4	5	4	5	5	4	4	52
Criminal convictions	1	–	–	–	1	1	1	–	–	–	1	2	6
Designations	2	1	3	2	5	5	4	3	6	4	3	3	41
Estate agency	15	13	17	14	20	19	22	19	17	15	20	16	207
Failure to account	3	3	2	2	4	4	2	2	3	4	4	5	38
Failure to reply	7	4	8	5	11	12	5	8	7	8	9	10	94
Fees	19	14	20	15	17	21	19	20	22	19	20	26	232
Managing agents	11	8	8	6	7	9	11	6	12	11	12	12	113
Negligence/incompetence	50	39	49	39	48	41	51	43	57	47	52	43	559
Solicitation	4	5	3	4	2	2	3	4	5	4	8	11	55
Others	3	3	1	1	1	2	1	2	2	3	4	4	27
Total	123	96	121	96	124	124	127	115	143	125	145	143	1,482

Source: RICS

is clearly quite low. It should also be recognised that these figures cover all RICS members, the majority of whom do not practise as residential estate agents — only 13,000 are estimated to derive some or all their income from this. In the case of RICS members especially, where commercial relationships are involved, litigation is likely to be a more frequent recourse, justified by the sums of money at issue.

Like the ISVA and the NAEA, the complaints system at the RICS does not appear to be a much used, consumer friendly or very effective course of redress for the public. So much was more or less explicitly recognised by the RICS itself recently.[1] The general practice director, Adrian Britton, wrote:

The Institution does not have the power to investigate allegations of negligence, which account for more than a third of the complaints received by the professional conduct department. The absence of such a power mystifies such complainants, who fail to understand why the Institution appears to them to be uninterested in the competence of its members.

The RICS arbitration scheme can deal with such matters but use of it is not compulsory for members, some of whom evidently insist on leaving complainants no recourse other than expensive civil legal action. Britton's advice to members was blunt: 'professional self-regulation is under attack, which may only be withstood if the profession provides adequate consumer protection and redress'.

In each case the complainant has to be confident, articulate, determined, and have a clear grievance to pursue in order to stand much chance of success. Complaints and disciplinary procedures provide an outlet for this minority of complainants but for the most part they must be regarded as ineffective. Further, these systems rely entirely upon the initiative of the public to complain, rather than upon the professional body to ensure that its rules are complied with. None of the professional bodies had compliance officers who made random visits to members' practices to ensure that the rules were observed, still less engaged in dummy enquiries where professional inspectors impersonated the public to verify that the responses and level of service offered were of a professional standard.

CORPORATE OMBUDSMAN: OCEA

The Ombudsman for Corporate Estate Agents (OCEA) was introduced in September 1990, and hence had completed one full year and produced a report by the time of the conclusion of our research. By the end of its first year the scheme included 28 corporate estate agents, large and small, with a total of 4,300 branches. The essence of the scheme is simple. It offers redress against the actions of any of its members for the public where the agent has:

- infringed your legal rights
- treated you unfairly

[1] General Practice Members Information Service, April 1992, p. 3, *Settling Disputes on Competence*.

— been guilty of maladministration (including inefficiency or undue delay) in a way that results in you losing money or suffering inconvenience.[2]

The ombudsman's terms are hence drawn broadly and the OCEA code of conduct is available to the public (or should be) at all branches of member agencies. The code covers all the legal obligations of estate agents and emphasises the prohibition upon conditional selling of properties — forced tie-in sales of financial services products. It also outlaws such matters as overvaluation to obtain instructions and the erection of 'for sale' boards against clients' wishes. Complainants are offered the prospect of an independent inquiry into their complaint with compensation of up to £100,000 in each case.

The scheme was designed to be attractive to the public as an earnest expression of the good faith of the corporates and as a means of impressing upon their staff the importance of good service and practice — the converse of a successful complainant bringing disciplinary proceedings against the estate agent responsible. The publicity given to the scheme, its broad terms of reference and the high maximum for compensation evoked widespread scepticism among independent estate agents, professional bodies and others. We record here, without adopting it as our own judgment, that the OCEA scheme was all but universally regarded as 'window-dressing' by the corporates. There is an element of sour grapes on the part of some of those rushing to this judgment. As we have seen, independent estate agents do not have much to boast about on this score. In our view, the scheme has been operating for too short a time to reach a secure judgment about its qualities as a means of redress. We were not able to investigate the administration of the scheme in detail.

The ombudsman's first report records that 1,236 enquiries indicating evidence of a complaint were received but 586 concerned non-member agencies. The 517 enquiries including member agencies involved 738 complaints. The source was vendors in 281 cases, purchasers in 208 cases, both (because the agent was the same) in eight cases, and unknown in 20 cases. Of the 62 cases closed after formal review by the end of the first year, three were found to be outside the terms of reference, five were settled by negotiation, 25 were decided against the complainant, and 29 against the member agency. The highest award of compensation was £2,750, with the median in the £100–500 range. The breakdown of cases is shown in table 11.2 on page 259.

Towards the end of his second year's work, the ombudsman told us that complaints had increased by about 60 per cent but that those coming within his terms of reference only by about 30 per cent. He put the increase down to greater public awareness of the scheme. The vast majority of complaints continued to be of maladministration, and where the ombudsman found for the complainant this was, in the second year, in all cases but two, because of maladministration or professional misjudgment rather than deliberate mal-

---

[2]Consumer Guide, First Annual Report, p. 18.

practice. In his first annual report the ombudsman offered the following
leading remarks:

Table 11.2   OCEA complaints 1990 to 91

Complaint	Total received	Total to formal review
Maladministration	276	59
Commission, fees, expenses	132	19
Sales particulars	76	12
Communication of offers (purchasers)	65	7
Gazumping	37	4
Communication of offers (vendors)	35	7
Discrimination	24	2
Viewing and keys	18	4
Valuation for sale	14	5
Conflict of interest	13	1
Purchaser's finances	13	2
Sale boards	8	2
Category not disclosed	27	–
Totals	738	124

Source: OCEA

> Consumer ignorance of the legal requirements placed upon estate agents in
> the practice of their profession is widespread and matched by a lack of
> awareness and appreciation of the sensitive area in which an agent operates
> between two or more parties with directly conflicting aims. While his primary
> responsibility rests with his vendor client, whose understandable preoccupa-
> tion is to achieve the best price possible in the existing market for his property,
> the estate agent has a duty of care and fair treatment to all prospective
> purchasers, who are both competing with each other and endeavouring to
> purchase the property of their choice as cheaply as possible. (2.2.)

> I would particularly single out the problems faced not only by first-time
> buyers but also those of first-time sellers who find themselves grappling
> both with the practical problems of coordinating the sale of one property
> and the purchase of another and of understanding the nature of their
> different relationship with their estate agent(s) in the two transactions.

> If I am asked for one bit of advice to give any member of the general public
> engaged in the buying and/or selling of residential property, it is that they

should ask questions of their estate agent until such time as they are absolutely satisfied that they fully understand both to what they are committing themselves and what the next stage of the process should entail. (5.3, 5.4.)

It is interesting that the ombudsman, who is not an estate agent by background, should have been impressed by precisely the same issues of consumer ignorance and the two-way obligations of estate agents that we have emphasised. Like the other redress and complaints schemes reviewed above, the ombudsman filters most of the complaints out, either as beyond his terms of reference or by conciliation through the member's agency, perhaps with an offer of compensation. In only a small minority is he therefore asked to adjudicate. It is not clear how much support he is able to offer less articulate complainants in preparing a case, and it may be that this will prove to be a difficulty in respect of the staff resources required in the future if complaints continue to increase. It is also of interest that the great majority of complaints involve what is in the end incompetence and negligence rather than deliberate malpractice, since this bespeaks the need for improved standards of competence widely accepted in the industry, and which seemed to be particularly lacking, on the evidence of our consumer survey, among the corporates. It does not sit well with the claim by the government (see below) that the problems with estate agency are predominantly those of ethics not competence.

ESTATE AGENTS ACT 1979

This Act, it will be recalled from chapter 3, was salvaged from the collapsing Callaghan administration by all-party agreement, and is widely regarded as unsatisfactory because of poor drafting and limited provisions. We shall come below to the difficulties that trading standards officers (TSOs) have in discharging their responsibilities to enforce the Act. Its other weakness until 1991 was that many sections of the Act were not brought into force by statutory codes and it has only been as a result of sustained pressure on the Office of Fair Trading and thence on the Department of Trade and Industry, that a series of orders were made specifying 'undesirable practices', which entitle the Director General of Fair Trading to issue a warning notice or barring order. Between May 1982 when the Act came into force, and March 1993, actions taken by the OFT were as shown in table 11.3.

It is evident that the Act has not been a very savage weapon in the hands of the OFT particularly in the light of the fact that, whilst warning orders can only be triggered by breaches of the Act, prohibition orders may be the result of criminal convictions as well as of breaches of the Act. It was not possible for the OFT to distinguish among the 182 cases between those which were an automatic response to a conviction for dishonesty or other specified offences, and those which were the outcome of regulatory inquiry.

This does not necessarily imply that the Act has been ineffective in raising standards of conduct. We found widespread concern to conform to the provisions of the Act, notably the 1991 orders, and there seems little doubt that the gradual implementation of the Act has been beneficial to some degree in establishing the limits of acceptable conduct. It is therefore worth reviewing briefly the provisions of the Act in its present form.

Table 11.3 OFT action under the Estate Agents Act

	Total 1982–93	1991	1992
Total prohibition orders served	182	33	24
Partial prohibition orders served	9	1	0
Warning orders served	9	1	0
Undertakings accepted	59	13	13
Warning letters sent	59	–	–
Advisory letters sent	87	–	–

Source: OFT.

At the outset of a relationship with a client, the agent is required to specify fees and charges (such as advertising) in writing, together with the circumstances in which fees become payable, and any additional payment. Where sole agency or sole selling rights or the provision of a ready, willing and able purchaser, are part of the contract, the meaning and implications of these phrases must be set out in terms specified under the Act. Clients must be told if any services such as mortgage arrangement are proposed to be offered to prospective purchasers, though the amount of commission at issue need not be specified. Further, all involvement in the transaction by any connected person must be disclosed, whether this involves introducing an associated property developer as the purchaser, or the referral of purchasers to a financial services business in which the agent has an interest. The definition of a connected person is drawn very widely indeed to include any business associate, and any relative or family member (including stepchildren). There is a prohibition upon seeking a deposit for the sale of a property in which the agent has a personal interest. The effect of the provisions is to try to ensure that the agent acts clearly in the client's interest and that the terms of the contract with the client are unequivocal.

During negotiations the agent is required to ensure that all parties are treated equally, fairly and promptly, thus introducing a specific duty to the purchaser. Offers must be transmitted to clients promptly and a written record of them kept, and the client must be kept up to date as to the provision of services to the purchaser. Discrimination of any kind against a purchaser who does not wish to take up ancillary services is illegal — for example, failing to provide information to them, failing to forward property particulars in due time, and requiring them to have a mortgage survey before passing on an offer. Clients must not be solicited on the basis of misleading information such as claims of the availability of cash purchasers for their properties, or that potential buyers are known to the agent, unless there is good evidence of these claims.

Clients' monies, whether by way of initial deposit, or the deposit at exchange of contracts, is required to be meticulously accounted for in client accounts that are regularly audited, with records kept for 10 years. Trading standards officers are required to be allowed access to these records. Interest is payable to the client on any deposit over £500 if it amounts to £10 or more.

Warning orders can be issued by the OFT if the provisions of the Act are breached in relation to: information on charges, definition of terms, personal interest, information on clients' offers, information to clients on services provided to buyers, misleading statements, avoiding bias against buyers, and payment of interest on clients' money. The OFT in issuing warning and prohibition orders is required to allow 21 days for the agent to explain why the order should not be made. Prohibition orders barring the agent from some or all kinds of work may be made if the agent: has breached any of the provisions under warning orders, been convicted of fraud, dishonesty or violence, committed racial or sexual discrimination, or been convicted of any of a considerable variety of offences under other Acts such as the Financial Services Act 1986, the Company Directors Disqualification Act 1986, the Consumer Credit Act 1974 and the Data Protection Act 1974. Thirty-eight offences under 13 Acts are specified.

In 1991, out of 752,779 complaints received by the OFT, 2,477 were about estate agents, quite a low proportion of the total but nonetheless an increase of 57 per cent on the previous year.

Because local TSOs are responsible for enforcing the 1979 Act and aspects of other legislation involving estate agents, and we heard that they experience some difficulty in doing so, we canvassed their views and received a significant and often vehement response. One office which takes a proactive view of its responsibilities under the Act, pointed out that estate agents legislation is 1/180th of the office's total workload. Complaints about estate agents to trading standards officers were generally reported to be low, and given the difficulties of enforcement and the competing demands of more serious matters — counterfeit goods, verification of new equipment, public compaints about quality and pricing of goods etc. — many offices give estate agency a very low priority. The strategy of this office was, however, to attempt to achieve compliance by estate agents by regular informal visits in which the requirements of the Act are discussed, and as in other areas with a similar pattern of regulation,[3] there is some prospect of modest success, including the identification of those businesses likely to be the source of trouble. It is evident, however, that most TSOs are so frustrated by the inadequacies of the legislation that they have more or less forgone enforcement, save in response to specific complaints.

It was pointed out that the 1979 Act creates only one criminal offence, that of failing to keep proper accounts; all other matters have to be referred to the OFT for action by way of warning or banning orders. In the case of accounts

[3] Cf. B. Hutter, *Environment and Enforcement* (Oxford University Press, 1988).

offences, however, there are various difficulties. The Act only gives TSOs powers of entry if there is reasonable cause to suspect an offence, in contrast to most other legislation under which they act, which gives powers of entry to ascertain whether an offence has been committed. In addition it was said that the accounts regulations are written in such a way that an offence could expire before the date of its discovery and that there are no standards specified to which accounts are required to be produced. The impossibility of even investigating other offences under the Act was generally excoriated: TSOs generally see themselves as the supporters of consumers, but in this case have no powers to investigate an offence either to judge its gravity or to identify other complaints, but can only refer the matter to the OFT. This was particularly complained of in respect of failure to declare an interest in the sale of the property (self-dealing and related abuses) which, it was pointed out, is neither a criminal offence under the Act nor the ground of a civil action.

In addition to the 1979 Act, TSOs are, or will be, also responsible for enforcing the Property Misdescriptions Act 1991 (see below) and the Courts and Legal Services Act 1990 in respect of its ban on tie-in sales of financial and other services. The Property Misdescriptions Act 1991 was brought into effect by a ministerial order specifying what aspects of property were to be subject to its provisions, until April 1993. In debate 25 items were identified as recommended by the OFT, covering almost all aspects of a property.[4] On the assumption that the provisions would be wide-ranging, the Act was given a broad welcome by TSOs as likely to be reasonably effective. The same could not be said of the Courts and Legal Services Act 1990 which was denounced by one officer as absurdly complex, 'a lawyer's paradise', 'quite one of the most dreadful pieces of legislation I have ever seen'. Prospects for enforcement were hence not very rosy.

Overall it is evident that the 1979 Act and related legislation are of symbolic rather than instrumental significance. Standards of conduct appropriate to a number of important areas of estate agency are established, but the means of enforcement are exceedingly weak, and its accessibility to the public generally poor. Whilst, like similar legislation such as race relations and sexual discrimination law, it may have and have had a long-term beneficial effect in raising the standards of the majority of practitioners, it falls a long way short of effective regulation. In particular, it says very little about the most sensitive area of estate agency, relations between vendor, agent and purchaser during negotiations.

PROPERTY MISDESCRIPTIONS ACT 1991

The enactment of this private member's Bill is significant less for its content and force as a regulatory measure than for the manner of its passage. Essentially the Act brought estate agency in line with the Trade Descriptions Act 1968, the penalties being £2,000 in a magistrates' court or an unlimited fine in the Crown Court. This resolved such obvious anomalies as the

---

[4]Parliamentary Debates, Commons, vol. 186, col. 1255 (1 March 1991) (2nd reading).

illegality of a hotelier claiming his premises are next to the railway station but the legality of an estate agent doing so.

The interesting question is why it took so long for this protection to be offered to the public, particularly given the notoriety of estate agents' descriptions of properties, with their bloated language and puffery so grotesque that it gave rise to the success of a celebrated independent London estate agent, Roy Brooks, who sent up the pretensions of his profession by deliberately describing his clients' properties in bathetically negative terms and achieving good sales.[5] As far back as 1984 the Director General of Fair Trading, in a review of the 1968 Act, recommended that it should be extended to property, given that this is the most important purchase made by most citizens. He was unimpressed by the objections to its extension, although he commented that 'there is no reason to doubt that the omission from the Act of any provisions to deal with misstatements about houses for sale or rent or by lease was deliberate'.[6] He did accept, however, that there were difficulties with property, notably the necessity of estate agents taking on trust claims by vendors about their properties, for example, about the date and exact nature of repairs, improvements, guarantees, or fixtures such as central heating. He therefore accepted that the absolute liability imposed under the 1968 Act should be modified in respect of property to require *mens rea*. This was specified as requiring (a) that the statement be made about a property not owned by the person making it (i.e., by an agent), (b) that it was made recklessly or knowing it to be false, and (c) that it was made with the object of inducing a sale.[7]

We have been unable to ascertain why it should have taken a further 15 years to implement these recommendations. Part of the reason would seem to lie in the diversion of legislative energies to other ends, but in this case it is odd that one of the arguably leading sources of the notoriety of estate agents should be neglected. It seems likely that the difficulties that the strict liabilities of the 1968 Act would impose on estate agents were seen as a stumbling-block. This problem was probably made the greater by the shift in the view of the OFT, at the time of a further review to the extension of the 1968 Act as part of the office's consultation process on estate agency in 1990. The OFT's conclusion then was that dealing with property misdescription by

---

[5] Roy Brooks's estate agency flourished in the late 1950s and 1960s in Chelsea and Pimlico, then far less grand than they now are. Brooks achieved both success and notoriety by inverting the puffery of conventional estate agents' language and in doing so appealing to a characteristic element of the British sense of humour. So much were his advertisements appreciated that they gained a readership among those who were not even seriously looking for property. Comments such as 'So-called garden with possibilities — best solved by saturation bombing'; 'Back bedroom suitable only for dwarf or placid child'; 'Derelict dosshouse fashionable Pimlico (will now only sell to gentle people for single family)' and 'Desperate English man and French girl would consider anything sordid' are characteristic of his style which, for all that it became something of a cult (and sold properties), was not widely imitated. Brooks himself died in 1971 and the business failed in January 1992.

[6] *Review of the Trade Descriptions Act*, a report by the Director General of Fair Trading Cmnd 6628 (October 1976), para. 71.

[7] Ibid., paras 116–17.

orders under the 1979 Act would involve inadequate penalties and that strict liability should be maintained for property. The 1991 Act does not do this, but its provisions for a defence of due diligence nonetheless aroused the indignation of Hugo Summerson MP, a member of the RICS, who pointed out that the job of estate agents is to market properties not survey them, and that the requirements in the Bill for agents to verify information supplied to them by the vendors were excessive. He provoked some excitement by asking whether the fact that he was asked by the environmental health officer to lay two feet of concrete in the basement of his house in Marylebone, because it had been built on the site of a plague burial pit would be required to be declared under the Bill. Significantly the reply came from the government minister:

> If an estate agent said that the house was in an historic spot well noted over the centuries for its healthy nature, he might be liable if he failed to reveal that, many centuries ago it had been the site of a plague burial pit. He would not be liable if he did not make any admission as to the healthy nature of the site over the centuries.[8]

By 1991 matters had clearly moved on in estate agency regulation to the point at which consumer protection was taken for granted as a legitimate regulatory aspiration and all parties were against sin. The government gladly expressed its support for the Bill, having undertaken the previous year to extend the Trade Descriptions Act 1968 to property. The Bill also enjoyed official Labour Party support, its spokesman's main complaint being the delay in achieving this modest and necessary reform and in failing to legislate more widely. The Bill also had the explicit support of a number of the professional bodies, including the RICS, ISVA and the NAEA, as well as the Consumers' Association and the Institute of Trading Standards Administration.

QUALIFICATIONS AND STANDARDS OF COMPETENCE

One section of the Estate Agents Act 1979 notable for the lack of its implementation is s. 22 concerning the establishment of minimum standards of competence. Although there were those who remarked that the Act was so drafted as never to make it likely that s. 22 would be implemented, since there was no indication as to who was to be responsible for this, it has been a bone of contention almost ever since the passing of the Act. It will be recalled that the impetus of the profession was to establish a code of conduct which was enforceable, and minimum standards of conduct alongside this. The standard argument in respect of the need for standards of competence has been, first, that no profession can be credible without specified professional expertise, and, secondly, that a code of conduct has to be made intelligible to practitioners by adequate training and education in what the

---

[8]Parliamentary Debates (Hansard), Commons, 6th ser., vol. 186, col. 1249 (1 March 1991).

job entails: in short that whilst some kinds of misconduct are self-evident or easily specifiable, a proper appreciation of how to conduct oneself in the complex relationship with client, purchaser and other parties (brokers, lawyers, mortgage lenders etc.) can only be reached by professional socialisation, a combination of on-the-job experience and specialist education. For this reason there has for long been widespread support for the principle of general standards of competence as a requirement for estate agency practice, though a certain practical diffidence has remained.

For the senior professional bodies (RICS and ISVA) who have their own training schemes and qualifications and conceive of their members as qualified beyond the minimum level in any case, support for tests of competence has long been unequivocal. For the NAEA, with a more market and sales-oriented view of estate agency, the arguments have been accepted in principle since 1962[9] but there has been a concern that any tests of competence should make adequate provision for the benefits of experience and that agents should not be debarred from what is essentially a selling business by the imposition of unduly high or complex educational standards. Nonetheless, the link between standards of competence and the capacity to live up to standards of conduct has been accepted.

This position has been explicitly rejected since 1979 by the Department of Trade and Industry, and successive Ministers of Consumer Affairs, and by the OFT. Thus:

> The main subject of consumer complaint in this area is about unethical conduct rather than about incompetence. The introduction of a licensing or minimum qualification system would not therefore remedy the problem and might prove a deterrent to those who would otherwise be well suited to estate agency work.[10]

The view of the OFT can be seen in the following quotations from the Director General:[11]

> I am not convinced that a case has yet been made out for introducing *compulsory* standards of competence. The introduction of mandatory requirements must have some restrictive effect on market entry and lead to disadvantages to the public from the resulting reduction in choice and in competition. These factors need to be weighed in the balance against the anticipated benefits of statutory competence qualifications, and it is not at all obvious what are the minimum standards necessary or desirable for an estate agent to have when handling a typical private house sale or purchase. In any case, it needs to be emphasised that qualifications are no guarantee of integrity. By way of illustration my officials can and do take

---

[9] Why all Estate Agents Should Be Licensed by Law (NAEA, 1962).
[10] DTI, Consumer Affairs Division, personal communication, 17 June 1992.
[11] Sir Gordon Borrie, who retired in 1992.

preemptive action prohibiting solicitors who have been struck off by the Law Societies for wrongdoing from entering estate agency.[12]

Legally binding rules of univeral application must be the principal — and the most satisfactory — way of dealing with malpractice, developing more transparency in the vendor/estate agent relationship and building on the basic rules of the common law and the requirements of the Estate Agents Act. I always have a certain wariness about self-regulation, which can often be in the interests of the regulated rather than the public.[13]

There appear to be a number of *non sequiturs* in these remarks from a regulator of great experience and very widespread respect. Would he prefer lawyers not to be subject to tests of competence, since passing such tests is no guarantee of integrity? That the standards of competence appropriate to estate agents are not self-evident is no basis for failing to explore what they should be. It borders on contempt towards an occupation, the demands upon which our research have shown to be complex and substantial, to refuse to recognise that property transactions require expertise and that clients and the public will benefit from those who have that expertise and suffer from those who do not. It may be that most of the complaints reaching the OFT concern 'ethics not competence', though, as indicated above, we would question whether the two are always or even frequently neatly divisible — one needs competence to recognise ethical issues and how best to handle them. Complaints reaching the OCEA ombudsman and our own consumer survey both indicate that incompetence, poor judgment and maladministration are greater problems by far than outright exploitation. To refuse to contemplate the development of standards of competence is, as we have seen, out of line with practice in a number of other countries and to relegate estate agency to the status of second-hand car sales. Anxiety about excluding competition is, we believe, ill founded and we question what faith the public is likely to place in the totally unqualified and inexperienced salesman who launches upon a venture into estate agency. We suspect that if the public knew of such lack of experience and competence they would give such an agent a wide berth. We are in no doubt that if our research demonstrates anything it is that standards of competence among estate agents need to be identified, fostered and increased over time, alongside specific prohibitions on undesirable conduct. Whilst this may not be immediately possible given the state of the industry, we believe that the insistence on minimum standards of competence should be an urgent objective both of the industry and of government and, more to the point, we believe that much abuse and misery would have been avoided if it had been such an objective at least since 1979.

---

[12]Speech to NAEA, April 1992, para. 16. Emphasis in original.
[13]Sir Gordon Borrie, 'Estate agents and bankers — regulation or self-regulation?', *Current Legal Problems*, 1990, pp. 15–34.

Happily the situation is not quite as dismal as this. Despite its official position, the OFT has been having discussions in 1992 with the RICS, ISVA and NAEA with a view to establishing a code of practice for estate agents. The OFT has wanted to add to this some form of redress scheme in the event of complaints, and the societies were reluctant to accept this unless in anticipation of future legislation to make it mandatory. The revised code was at the time of writing being discussed with the European Property Agents Group, which represents estate agents in all EC countries. Consultations were also taking place with OCEA to try to agree a common code.[14] The aspiration towards a code of conduct appears hence to have revived after a decade or more but to be subject to the same difficulties as before, that the professional bodies do not want their members tied to, and required to fund, a code and compensation scheme which would leave non-members free to ignore its provisions. In most other countries that we have considered, this problem is resolved by compulsory registration of estate agents and the requirement that they adhere to legislation, including a code of conduct, and that they pass tests of competence of increasing stringency.

National Vocational Qualifications in estate agency

Nor has the practical pursuit of standards of competence been entirely abandoned even by the government. Through the Department of Trade and Industry and the long-term initiative to establish national vocational qualifications for a range of occupations, the government created a lead body to set up NVQs for estate agency. Although led by an able civil servant, the body, working in cooperation with private training consultants to develop the standards and curricula, drifted. The corporates, the most heavily represented group on the body, became frustrated and threatened to develop their own standards unless there was action, and the body was duly converted into a company with a board of 24 and an industry chairman, the Real Estate Agency Training and Education Association (REATEA). Most of the corporates are now represented, the notable exception being one whom we have come across as subject to adverse comment in respect of its estate agency practices. Independents have also joined and the professional bodies and educational institutions such as the College of Estate Management are also members. By 1992 when the first qualification (level 3 senior negotiatior/junior manager) was launched, it had taken three years to achieve this, together with some development of other (area managers and lower clerical) standards.

Although the application of the standards was formally voluntary, the consensus of opinion at REATEA was that they should become compulsory. The prime difficulty was achieving reconciliation with courses offered by the professional bodies and establishing assessors, an assessment centre and awarding organisation, especially for the independents. The corporates have the resources to undertake such tasks internally and to integrate NVQs into their existing training programmes.

---

[14]ISVA personal communications, 10 June 1992, 23 July 1992.

For the corporates, establishing common accepted standards was important in several respects. It is part of the process of establishing careers for estate agents; it is a means of dealing with malpractice, and it is a means of establishing uniform standards of estate agency practice — corporates on REATEA were reportedly appalled at the range of competence and practice evident in the estate agencies they bought up. This confirms our view that there is considerable variation in effectiveness and competence, but that the public are only poorly aware of this.

The development of NVQs is very much to be welcomed as a first step in the introduction of uniform standards of competence. We have not been able to observe the teaching of the new qualifications, nor were we privy to the meetings which led to the development of the syllabus, but our interest was welcomed by REATEA, who provided us with a copy of the outline syllabus (*Standards of Competence: Selling Residential Property* (REATEA, May 1991)) from which we quote two elements from unit 1.

There is not the space here to review this in detail, and in any case the success or failure of the qualifications will depend to a significant degree, first, upon the effectiveness of their teaching, and, secondly, upon the extent to which material transmitted is either built upon in subsequent working experience or rejected and abandoned as irrelevant. One trusts, for example, that the desirable respect for clients' and customers' interests evident in the NVQs does not suffer the same fate as the respect Hendon police cadets are taught to develop for ethnic minorities, where subsequent socialisation 'on the job' restores racial stereotyping. It is no doubt inevitable in the development of qualifications in which the corporates have had a leading role that there should be an overall sense of proceduralisation to the programme, and that reference to financial services products should arise before obtaining instructions to sell a property. Nonetheless, the sample elements quoted do provide some reassurance that a measured approach to the client is required, in which identifying needs and aspirations takes a leading place, rather than the overeager promotion of the estate agent's services. Certainly some of the agents we observed could have benefited from such a training programme, both in terms of understanding how to go about their job, and in terms of reversing the simple priorities of 'getting the property on', and 'selling additional services', as against identifying customer needs.

Unit 1   Promote property selling and associated products and services
Element 1.3   Promote associated products and services to customers
Range
Associated products and services — valuations, surveys, financial services, specialist services, local sources of legal representation
Services promoted — by telephone, in person, in writing

Performance criteria
a)   appropriate questions are used to establish customer interest in associated products and services
b)   benefits and features of associated products and services offered are relevant to customer needs and are described clearly and accurately
c)   where appropriate, acting to progress the provision of associated products and services is agreed
d)   where relevant, accurate additional information is supplied
e)   requests for associated products and services are passed on to the appropriate person promptly and accurately
f)   records are complete, accurate and legible

Assessment guidance
a)   *Specialist services* include property management, property maintenance, overseas property purchase, lettings, rent appeals, chattels disposal
b)   *Types of survey available* include financial institution report, housebuyer's valuation, structural survey

Unit 1   Promote property selling and associated products and services
Element 1.4   Secure instructions from sellers
Range
Property price — low, medium, high
Sellers — estate of deceased owners, corporate sellers, private individuals
Methods of sale: private treaty, auction, tender

Performance criteria
a)   information is obtained from customers to establish reliability and propensity to sell
b)   benefits, features and costs of agency services, relevant to customers' needs are presented clearly and accurately
c)   customer objections are recognised, addressed and overcome wherever possible
d)   actions taken are appropriate to secure instructions
e)   complete details of instruction are agreed with customers and recorded accurately and legibly
f)   marketing methods to promote property and dates and methods to review progress are agreed with customers
g)   written confirmations of agreement and cost are complete, accurate and legible and supplied to customers within the timescale required by law
h)   reasons not to accept a particular customer's instructions are recorded clearly and accurately

Assessment guidance
'details of instruction' includes services required, asking price (or price guide), authority of agency, timing of promotion and viewing arrangements

In addition to these two elements we thought it appropriate to look at two sensitive points in the sales process: valuation and negotiating the sale. In the former case (element 2.1) some, but only some reassurance against over-valuation to obtain instructions is evident:

Unit 2   Prepare individual properties for sale
Element 2.1   Prepare and present market appraisals of commonly available residential property
Range
Property condition — excellent, average, poor
Property price — low, medium, high
Property age — pre 1919, pre 1950, 1950 and after
Property type — terraced, semi-detached, detached, multi-dwelling building
Market appraisals — written, oral

Performance criteria
a)   appraisal reflects benefits, features, characteristics and location of property
b)   market appraisal price is based on relevant market data
c)   price band suggested optimises the chances of sale on the best terms available having regard to the sellers' objectives
d)   sellers are encouraged to make clear their reasons for obtaining a market appraisal and to disclose any factors which would have a bearing on the availability of the property for sale
e)   sellers' objectives are accurately summarised
f)   details of the market appraisal are confirmed to sellers clearly and accurately

Assessment guidance
Relevant market data — state of local property market, information on recent sales, current local employment conditions, availability of finance
Characteristics — judgments on the construction and condition of property plus the ways to remedy major defects

---

The strategy is plainly a market appraisal, which includes the vendor as a feature of the market, rather than a valuation, and this leaves room for the agent to exercise a degree of latitude when it comes to actual pricing. It is not made explicit, still less emphasised, as it should be, to the vendor that there are a variety of values to a property and that, dependent on the state of the market, it may be more or less possible for the agent, even if experienced and well-informed, to reach an accurate judgment of value. Further, especially in a weak market, there may be a considerable discrepancy between an agent's reasonable judgment of the market value and the selling price the agent may be able to achieve in the normal selling period. In short, the situation is, as we detailed earlier in the book, much more complicated that element 2.1 allows, though, of course, a good teacher would remedy this.

Our final illustration is the negotiation of a sale, where the danger is that the interests of vendor and/or purchaser are subordinated to those of the agent, both in achieving a sale and in directing a sale to a purchaser likely to take additional services such as a mortgage and insurance:

Unit 4a   Negotiate the sale of properties
Element 4.4   Negotiate on behalf of sellers to obtain acceptable price and conditions
Range
Sellers — from choice; reluctant; inexperienced; experienced
Buyers — experienced, inexperienced requiring finance, not requiring finance; part of a chain
Market conditions — 'buyer's'; 'seller's'; 'balanced'

Performance criteria
a)   realistic price band and other boundaries of negotiation for acceptability of offers are agreed with sellers
b)   negotiations are consistent with sellers' instructions and within legal constraints
c)   buyers' likely maximum offer is established accurately
d)   offers are assessed accurately in terms of ability to pay and other conditions
e)   opportunities to overcome difficulties are identified and appropriate suggestions are offered promptly
f)   offers, with any conditions, accepted by sellers subject to contract are recorded accurately
g)   agreement to proceed with sale subject to contract is confirmed with buyer and seller
h)   where a second or subsequent offer is received negotiations are conducted with buyer and seller according to law
i)   in cases where a chain of sales is involved sufficient accurate information is obtained to advise sellers

Once again the general approach which implies due care and attention to the situation and the interests of both selling and buying parties is reassuring, but the position of the agent and the agent's interests is not explicitly recognised. Perhaps this is because the emphasis is upon bringing the two parties together, and the notion that the estate agent's interest might compromise rather than promote this is unthinkable. We believe that good training should require trainees to think the unthinkable and to be aware of, confront and manage potential conflicts of interest.

The qualification as it stands is, of course, only a start, and its impact will much depend upon the relationship between it and professional socialisation. We suggest that a good deal could be done to bridge the gap between the qualification and ongoing professional experience by the use of modern teaching techniques involving groups and the use of interactive computer learning. In the latter case, trainees would be subjected to scenarios by a computer which would require them to respond and which could teach them the consequences of failing to ask the right questions at the right time by showing that reaching decisions about the delivery of an appropriate service subsequently became more and more problematic. What such techniques are less effective in achieving is identifying not only the right questions to ask, but the right way to ask them, especially having regard to such factors as the demeanour of the client (confident, hesitant, knowledgeable etc.) and factors such as age and gender on both sides. Here role playing of a variety of situations in groups under the guidance of a tutor could, we believe, contribute significantly to the development of appropriate styles and of sensitivity. These techniques would go some way to meeting the overall problem, expressed by a senior source at REATEA that 'NVQs describe outcomes not processes ... provided the agent secured the instruction, which style he used was not important'. We believe to the contrary that such matters of 'style' are vitally important in determining whether the overall character of the relationship between agent and client is that of a satisfactory professional service or one of manipulation and even exploitation.

CONSUMER ORGANISATIONS AND CONSUMER AWARENESS OF ESTATE AGENCY

Although there has been an increase in the interest of the two leading consumer bodies, the government-sponsored National Consumer Council (NCC), and the independent Consumers' Association (publishers of *Which?*), concern by them about estate agency has remained at a relatively low level. The NCC gave evidence to the OFT during its review of estate agency regulations and the Consumers' Association published some articles critical of estate agents as a result of sending its representatives to agents incognito, and pretending to be interested in buying or selling properties. These forays involved very limited numbers, although the results were critical of estate agents' quality of service and attempts to push financial services products, and were responded to by estate agents as unrepresentative and rather underhand.

On the whole we do not believe that consumers have been well served by the consumer lobby in respect of estate agency, though we would not wish to hold the two leading organisations responsible for a failure which, whilst regrettable, is a reflection of their very wide remit and limited resources, and of the public's unduly passive view of estate agents. The public may be ready to deride agents in opinion polls and laugh at them when portrayed in comedy shows, but it shows little interest in informing itself about estate agency, either in respect of what it involves and therefore what it is reasonable to expect from an estate agent, or in respect of the quality of service available from different agents. Both these are areas that cry out for remedy and we believe that both agents and the consumer organisations should address them.

As far as the first issue, the basic education of the public about what estate agency involves, is concerned, we believe that present circumstances offer an unprecedented opportunity for estate agents to take the initiative. On the one hand, the past decade has seen the entry into the property market of large numbers of people with no previous experience of it, and very limited knowledge, many of them young. The comfortable assumptions of the past that property owners were middle aged, middle class, family men, is now absurdly out of date and it is time the estate agency profession addressed the issue seriously of the considerable variation in the levels and sophistication of knowledge about how the property market works and estate agents' role in it.

The recent unheavals in estate agency itself, consequent upon the arrival of the corporates, should serve to reinforce this impetus. Just as the effort to establish minimum standards of competence through NVQs constitutes an attempt to fix uniform standards of service on the part of estate agents, so the establishment of a basic level of knowledge on the part of the relevant public about the property market and the role of estate agents constitutes a necessary counterpart to the establishment of satisfactory long-term relationships between estate agents and the public. True, some agents have made limited efforts in this direction through the preparation of brochures about their services, but this has been designed principally to inform and promote public awareness of 'Jones and Co. estate agents', not estate agents in general.

Estate agents often lamented to us that the public are prejudiced against them because they do not understand what they do or the services they provide. Whilst we think it doubtful that even the most energetic propaganda will result in a surge of public affection for estate agents, we do believe that a well-directed campaign by estate agents as a profession could raise public awareness of what estate agents do. If this can be achieved, the basis will have been laid for a dialogue with the public about what they want from estate agents, a dialogue that can only take place meaningfully in the light of what they can reasonably expect. As an example of this, we have noted in our analysis of the consumer survey that there is a minority who would probably be interested in a fee-based service. Agents are generally sceptical of such an idea and claim that it reflects public ignorance of the way estate agency works. That may be so, but we draw agents' attention again to the fact that some clients resent the levels of payment which result from the commission system, and believe that agents 'do not really earn their money'. If the agents' general view is correct, a properly informed public would accept the necessity and benefits of the commission system, and the resentment presently harboured by some would be dispelled.

Such an effort to better inform the public about estate agency could not be mounted effectively except by the profession as a whole. It represents, therefore, an opportunity for a now severely fragmented occupation to come together to promote its own image. We foresee not inconsiderable benefits to all parties from such an effort, which would necessarily involve the cooperation of independent and corporate agents and the professional bodies in a common campaign to identify plainly what estate agents do and what the public can reasonably expect from them — and hence what it is not reasonable to expect from them.

Information on the basics of estate agency and the property market is, of course, very different from information on the comparative quality of service offered by different agencies. This is a consumer issue. To provide a comparative reference point, we believe that consumer awareness of the comparative merits of estate agencies is now at roughly the stage that consumer awareness of the comparative merits of restaurants was in the 1950s. Since that time, Christopher Driver's *Good Food Guide* has worked, if not miracles, at least a remarkable transformation, and the guide now has a number of counterparts both for restaurants and for hotels, pubs and cafés.

Both the government and estate agency bodies have emphasised in recent years the vital importance of competition among estate agents as a means of ensuring quality. The market, it is said, will produce quality. It appears to be true that the market does tend to drive out marginal operators who are prepared to be systematically unscrupulous. It does not, however, act very effectively at present in respect of the vast majority of agencies, simply because the market is very substantially under-informed. Although agents widely expressed the view that the best source of business was word-of-mouth recommendation of clients, and clients returning because of previous satisfaction, the actual proportion of such business is very small, partly as a result of the recent expansion in home ownership, and partly as a result of the rapid personnel changes and reassigned identities of agencies in the course of the corporate takeovers, but also because the public do not use estate agents very often and, in any case, have very little awareness not only of their relative merits, but of how to go about determining them.

There is a crying need for an assertive consumer campaign to remedy this. What member of the public, for example, would contemplate asking an estate agent for a list of his most recent 30 clients with a view to telephoning a random sample of six or 10 to check levels of satisfaction with service? Agents would almost certainly refuse to divulge the information though, of course, the prospective client could do an approximate job personally, as we have done in our consumer survey, by working with property details available from agents. We would like to see local efforts along these lines, perhaps with the support of the national consumer bodies, with the results regularly published. There are considerable differences between the quality of service offered by different estate agents, and the public are entitled to discover that. We do not wish to offer here a blueprint by which the detailed consumer awareness which we believe is required should be achieved, but we are clear that it is necessary to have some regular appraisal by the consumer lobby of the levels of satisfaction of clients of (and purchasers from) specific agents (that is, at branch or office level, not just the agency as a whole because there can be enormous variations between branches, as branches can vary over time). The results should be published regularly.

Such consumer services could be supplemented both by agents and by consumer organisation's incognito inspectors who arrive, in the manner of the *Which?* initiatives, purporting to be interested in buying or selling a property. The merit of this approach is that the consumer reporting is sophisticated and not naïve or easily flattered, and, second, that a pitch can deliberately be made to identify a client or purchaser with characteristics likely to elicit bad practice, if that is a tendency in the agency. Once agents have overcome their sense of outrage at being subjected to systematic critical consumer review they will, we hope, take the lesson to heart and appoint their own compliance staff, who will arrive not only for regular inspections to see that all systems are working and everything is professionally shipshape, but will also arrive anonymously in the guise of prospective client or purchaser to verify that staff regularly do conduct themselves as they should when dealing with the public.

The effect of greatly increased consumer pressure on quality of service will be, we hope, to put real pressure upon agencies to improve staff training and to drive out of business agencies that fail to compete in terms of quality of service. This need not, in agencies with several branches, involve the demise of the agency as a whole, of course, but it may involve the wholesale restaffing of a branch. Such systematic and regular consumer pressure should constitute a significant counterweight to the pressures of sales and profit targets. We are under no illusions that it can be achieved quickly. It will require a great deal of effort in a large number of localities, and it will require that effort to be sustained. Here the national consumer bodies could perform a useful service by providing support for local efforts. The impact of such critical consumer investigation and appraisal, however, will, we believe, have a considerable impact on estate agents' attitudes to the public.

VALUATION

We have devoted some space earlier in this book, notably in chapter 5, to the complex character of valuation, particularly as undertaken by estate agents in the course of taking instructions to sell a property. The professional valuation of property is, however, a separate matter, as we have noted at several points, and for that reason we have declined to comment on it at length. The most frequent form of professional valuation in connection with residential sales is in connection with a mortgage application or as part of a structural survey. Many surveyors now offer an intermediate form of buyer's survey which is more detailed than the mortgage valuation and less detailed than a structural survey. Although we have noted that valuation for different purposes can lead to a different figure being put on a property — mortgage valuations tend to be slightly conservative, for example — we have also pointed out that the essential elements of valuation are the same in most cases. Residential valuation rests on a foundation of comparability between properties, adjusted for special features such as locality, aspect, improvements and general condition, and the state of the local market. We have not observed structural surveys taking place with any frequency but we have observed mortgage valuations, from which it is evident that the same techniques are used to reach a judgment as are used by estate agents in valuation in the course of taking instructions for sale. In many cases a mere drive past the property getting a glimpse of its basic features, and of course the location, is enough to suggest a figure which is subsequently confirmed by a cursory inspection. There is no difference then, in many instances between a 'professional' valuation and a 'market appraisal' or 'listing advice' as regards the techniques used and the time taken, albeit that a professional valuer is likely to be more experienced, and would defend his or her capacity to reach a rapid judgment by reference to this experience.[15]

[15]It should be noted that although the RICS has compiled an extensive series of Statements of Asset Valuation and Practice (the Red Book) these mainly concern commercial property valuations. No specific guidance is given to members on domestic property valuation, see A. Cherry, 'The Statements of Asset Valuation Practice and Guidance Notes (the Red Book)', *Journal of Property Valuation and Investment*, vol. 9 (1991), pp. 247–51.

The problems of professional valuation do not stop here, however. Valuers may derive a significant part of their income from mortgage lenders and there is plenty of evidence of lenders exercising pressure on valuations. A number that we spoke to said that during the property boom of the 1980s there was regular verbal and implicit (though rarely written) pressure from lenders to put in valuations in line with the sale price so that the mortgage could go through, and the lender obtain business, despite the valuer's opinion that the sale price was above real value. Lenders normally took the view that discrepancies would be eliminated in a few months anyway because of rising prices, and securing market share was the name of the game. Such practices are confirmed in detail by a surveyor and valuer in a recently published article.[16] Not content with thereby adding to house price inflation and overborrowing by purchasers, mortgage lenders have recently turned on valuers in the wake of the wave of repossessions. Lenders have recently taken to suing valuers in repossession cases where it appears that the valuation during the boom was overoptimistic. This often takes place as part of the lender's claim on indemnity insurance, when it seeks to recoup the difference between the repossession sale price and the mortgage, with many cases being settled out of court. As a result, valuers have reacted by becoming exceedingly cautious in their judgments so again contributing to an accentuation of the market trend, this time further into slump.[17]

Lenders have further contributed to lower prices by refusing to allow householders with negative equity to sell their properties if the sale price does not allow full repayment of the mortgage, preferring to repossess, even though that results in an even lower resale figure, because the difference can then be recouped through mortgage indemnity cover.[18] Mortgage lenders, through tactics nakedly designed to further their own interests, have hence arguably had a malign effect upon property market values on several occasions. In doing so they have been able effectively to subordinate valuers to their purposes.

The situation worsened in 1992 with complaints that mortgage lenders, notably those who have substantial estate agency chains, have taken further steps to protect their interests, regardless of those of the public, in the face of the recession. First, there has been a move to take valuation in-house on the part of some lenders. Whilst this is a considerable safeguard against the collusion of valuers with mortgage fraudsters, from which lenders have suffered in the past,[19] it reduces the independence of the valuation and increases the likelihood of a valuation which reflects the interests of the lender at the time. In a well publicised example the Household Mortgage Corporation reduced its valuation panel to 13 for the whole of England and Wales, thereby making it inevitable that many valuations would have to be undertaken 'out of area', where valuers lacked local knowledge. Overall, the

---

[16]M. Bar-Hillel, 'The use and abuse of valuation practices', *Chartered Surveyor Weekly*, 30 April 1992.
[17]'Low values stall house prices', *Times Business News*, 21 March 1992.
[18]'Estate agents attack societies for holding back the market', *Guardian*, 24 August 1991.
[19]See M.J. Clarke, *Mortgage Fraud* (Chapman and Hall, 1991).

effect of restricting valuers' access to mortgage valuation is to reduce competition, and it is claimed that valuation fees — charged to applicants — have been increased dramatically. In addition the implication is, as has been confirmed in practice, that a mortgage applicant who has a structural survey may be asked to pay for a valuation survey in addition because the structural surveyor is not on the mortgage lender's panel.[20]

Further, the practice of reciprocal business generation has increasingly come to dominate mortgage valuation. Surveyors are told that if they wish to remain on a lender's panel and continue to receive valuation business, they must reciprocate with, say, one mortgage referral for every four valuations. The increasingly incestuous relationship between valuers and mortgage lenders was referred to the OFT in 1991 by the RICS and the cause was taken up by the Consumers Association. The OFT expressed its disquiet and took the matter up with the Council of Mortgage Lenders[21] and in 1993 the issue was referred to the Monopolies and Mergers Commission whose report is expected in 1994. Meantime the Cheltenham and Gloucester Building Society took the plunge and in February 1994 abolished application and valuation fees for house purchasers taking new mortgages or further advances.

Valuation reports are now the only professional advice undertaken by 85 per cent of purchasers, according to the RICS. Given that it is the purchasers who pay for the valuation, and the effects which we have noted above that compromised relations between lenders and valuers can have on valuers and the housing market, it is important that mortgage valuation is protected and independent and not the creation of lenders. Abuse of mortgage valuation was, we saw, a significant element in the savings and loan débâcle in the USA. In Britain until the 1980s there was a substantial element of professional independence in such valuations. To put valuers in the pockets of lenders, as has happened in the past decade, is a retrograde step incompatible with the public interest and one upon which it is regrettable that the OFT has not acted more vocally and decisively.

REGULATORY REFORM

The reader will by now be informed in a number of respects as to our views on the regulation of estate agents and we shall not repeat our arguments at length. The brief review of the practicalities of current regulation in this chapter demonstrates the utter confusion which exists. Regulation is conducted by the State, by professional bodies and by the corporate estate agents with different powers and aspirations. It is in each case weak and ineffective, though not without benefits. In the case of State regulation the situation is ludicrous: a badly drafted Act, implemented piecemeal over time is enforced by trading standards officers locally who find their powers entirely insuffi-

---

[20] Bar-Hillel, op. cit. (note 16). See also 'Lenders defend stance on valuers', *Money Marketing*, 25 June 1992.
[21] Bar-Hillel, op. cit. (note 16). 'OFT investigates lenders links with valuation panels', *Money Marketing*, 28 October 1991.

cient; nationally it is enforced by the OFT, which is committed to an almost paranoid policy of concern not to deprive wholly unqualified and almost entirely unverified members of the public of the right to decide that they will practise as estate agents on the absurd grounds of maximising competition, absurd because the public is too ill-informed about estate agents to require them to compete properly, and is at risk from the incompetence and corner-cutting of fly-by-night entrants to estate agency. The OFT and the DTI take comfort in the fact that complaints about estate agents are limited in number without recognising the fact that public knowledge about estate agents is poor and expectations of them low. This regulatory mess constitutes, if it constitutes anything, a vicious circle wherein regulatory efforts are limited, regulatory standards low, public expectations are limited, public views of estate agents are negative, estate agents feel themselves slighted and treated by some of the public with contempt, and even exploited. It is a recipe for cynicism, low expectations and low performance all round.

We have recounted the efforts of estate agents through their professional bodies to break out of this towards higher enforceable standards. We have recently seen the recognition by the corporate estate agents that a broad effort to improve standards is necessary. Just as the professional bodies have failed to achieve this by themselves, so we believe the corporate estate agents will fail if they act by themselves — and in their case there are additional grounds for concern, to which we will come below. Only if the State, the corporates and the professional bodies act in concert on a broad front can this vicious circle be broken, and a virtuous one be installed in its place. It is to the achievement of this objective that the suggestions that follow are directed.

The professional aspiration

In making those suggestions, and in our analysis so far, we should not wish to be seen as unsympathetic to the professional aspirations of estate agents. We believe that history demonstrates, first, that professional self-regulation as the clear principal basis of regulation is unachievable and politically unacceptable, and second that the ambiguity of estate agency as between its selling and service aspects make the achievement of full professional status impossible (even if, for example, radical changes such as a shift from commission to fees took place). On the other hand, the aspiration of workers in any occupation to do the job well and give honest value for money is, of course, to be supported. It is particularly to be supported where the job is subject to ambiguities and conflicts of interests, as we have documented, and where the transaction involved is lengthy and of great financial (and other) significance. We believe therefore that a successful regulatory system should be structured to support the professional model espoused by the bodies that have emerged to represent estate agency since the 19th century. This cannot be achieved, in our view, without a measure of State intervention: we propose below the establishment of a register. It also cannot be achieved without an explicit provision for the protection of consumers, not only because of the tendency of professions to put their own interests before those of clients in certain circumstances, even if, in general, established to provide dispassionate, competent service, but particularly in the case of estate agency because of the explicit market-oriented element of the work, which accentuates that risk. We see only limited benefits from the formal proceduralisation of services espoused by the corporates (on which more below), because properties, their buyers and their sellers, and their circumstances, are unique and require individual, case-by-case, flexible and sensitive responses. The very nature of estate agency requires that its aspiration to professionalism be given firm external support if it is to have any chance of succeeding. In essence our proposals amount therefore to a hybrid of professional and State regulation.

Estate agents, vendors and purchasers

It cannot be stated too often that at the heart of estate agency lies a profoundly ambivalent relationship between the estate agent, the vendor client, and potential and actual purchasers. This relationship is and will remain a slippery one requiring constant attention and sensitivity at each stage of every property transaction, unless — and we see no obvious model for this — estate agency undergoes a structural transformation which eliminates the ambiguities in the competing interests of the three parties. To put it at its very simplest, it is vital that all parties are aware that (a) the vendor is the estate agent's client and is paid on commission by the vendor; (b) the agent's interest is in completing the deal, otherwise the agent does not earn the commission; (c) the purchaser is the vital means to this end and besides may (but only may) be a source of commission income from financial and other services. Conflicts of interest are hence persistent and endemic to property transactions. We doubt that they can be resolved, but at least three things can be done which would have a direct effect on mitigating them — more effective regulation overall would, of course, also be beneficial.

Purchaser representation and the Scottish system

Our analysis of property transactions in Scotland led us to the conclusion that the often-touted merits of the sealed bidding system in eliminating gazumping and chains are counterbalanced by a variety of other problems, that the system is by no means immune from abuse, and that in any case it appears to be moving in practice towards the English system of negotiated bids. The one single advantage that it has is the bringing in of the lawyer on the purchaser's side at a much earlier stage, a lawyer who in Scotland is much more likely to act as a practical adviser on the details of property purchase than his or her English counterpart, whose role is normally confined to the technicalities of conveyancing. We doubt whether the Scottish system is transferable elsewhere, because it is dependent upon lawyers also being estate agents, but we do believe that the issue of purchaser representation needs further careful consideration by all relevant parties. Given the trend to specialisation now among English solicitors, it may be that some could offer an enhanced service offering advice to purchasers at an earlier stage. The corporates have recognised the problem, or at least the Leeds Building Society has in creating and advertising a property arranger whose job it is to assist and guide purchasers. Estate agents too might consider whether they could provide paid and contractual help to purchasers in certain circumstances.

The commission system

Enhanced services to purchasers might be more feasible if there were alterations in the commission system. It will be recalled that our consumer survey identified a minority that is resentful of the amount paid in commission and concerned to explore a fee-based system. Whether that would be acceptable once clients realised that fees would be payable regardless of whether a sale was achieved is, of course, open to question, but we believe that the question should be put and the answer not assumed. Further, there is no reason why purchasers should not pay a fee or commission for the assistance of an agent. Indeed, given the amount of time agents spend on purchasers and their essential role in completing the deal, it might be said to be a truer reflection of the situation. It is also one which is accepted in other countries, notably France, where the ambiguities of estate agency would seem to be reflected in variations in commission practice. We do not wish to make firm recommendations here, only to suggest that the commission system should be reviewed in the light of what the public might want. At present it seems to us to operate with an artificial clarity in a situation which is complex and thereby to contribute in practice to confusion.

The public's knowledge of estate agency

Changes in the commission system would, of course, create more confusion if canvassed in the present context of widely varying levels of sophistication by the public about estate agency and property transactions, and, we believe, very large areas of ignorance. We have argued above for a campaign to remedy this to be conducted by estate agents which, we believe, could have the benefits of reducing public reliance on stereotypes, most of them unflattering to estate agents, making the establishment of relations between the estate agent, clients and purchasers easier, and less subject to suspicion, antagonism and confusion, and lay the ground for at least some sections of the public to consider whether they would benefit from contracts with estate agents other than the standard one based on the vendor paying commission on completion of a sale. We do not wish to specify how such a public education and information campaign should be carried out, but we do caution against a simple media-reliant public relations operation, which is likely to be counter-productive. A successful campaign will, we believe, need to be long-term, low-key and multifaceted. It will also need to be agreed by corporate and independent estate agents, and such agreement will itself be both an achievement and a long-term benefit.

Consumer awareness

Besides public information about estate agency in general, we have also made a case above for much greater consumer awareness of the quality of estate agencies branch by branch. We are under no illusions about the scale of largely voluntary effort required to make this a real success, but equally we believe that enhanced consumer awareness and regular quality and comparability reports could have a powerful impact upon the quality of service offered by estate agents, and produce, for the first time, real competition, that is, competition to produce better service and results, not merely to grab more clients and properties. The national press could be helpful here in sponsoring surveys and in publishing the results of enquiries in regular columns. There is no reason why the critical evaluation of estate agencies should not become an element of the regular residential property features pages of the press.

Registration

None of this addresses the regulatory mess. We believe that the example of other countries should be heeded, that regulation of an occupation so subject to conflicts of interest as estate agency, and so profoundly ambiguous as between its service-oriented and professional and its market-oriented salesmanship cannot be left either to the market or to the professional bodies to achieve regulation. The market simply does not regulate, it has to be hedged with rules and institutions to do so in this as in any other case. The professional bodies are too weak and disorganised and too self-interested to be relied upon to regulate. The State must intervene and take decisive control.

This requires a national registrar with a secretariat empowered to identify, accredit and license estate agents, and to discipline them by fines, suspension and bans. Identification needs to be unequivocal both for individuals and firms to prevent identity switching in cases of abuse. Accreditation should involve at least a fit and proper person test and compulsory adherence to a compensation scheme to protect the public against abuse and insolvency, and a test of competence. The latter need not be onerous, at least in the case of those aspiring only to be employed as estate agents rather than to be principals, but we do not believe that the public interest is served by allowing the wholly ignorant to set up as principals. The introduction of such a system need not be precipitate or oppressive, and should seek, as most regulatory regimes do, to achieve a continuous gradual increase in standards over time.

Such a regime would require primary legislation, but we are satisfied that the current situation justifies it. The Estate Agents Act 1979 will need to be replaced, though much that has been learned in administering it can be incorporated in the new legislation. The staff of the registrar will need to have experience of estate agency, but the office of the registrar should be unequivocally a State one, not a collective representation of estate agents. Of course, agents and their professional bodies will be free to make representations to the registrar, and there may even be an advisory representative body for that purpose, but we are clear that what is called for is State regulation not self-regulation. Only State regulation will command public confidence and avoid the taint of self-interest. In addition, we do not believe that estate agents have demonstrated the capacity to reach professional status and the self-regulatory discretion that goes with it. Given their ambivalence as between their selling and professional service aspects, they are never likely to.

Enforcement will also need radical revision. A centralised system for public complaints and financial redress against estate agents should be established that will become well-known to the public, with procedures that render it reasonably accessible. Such a scheme would render the recent efforts of the corporates with OCEA superfluous, but we would not wish to outlaw such additional schemes if parts of the industry wished to continue to run them. Enforcement of standards locally would seem to be most appropriately undertaken by trading standards officers, but their remit will need to be considerably clarified and strengthened. If consumer awareness of estate agency grows in the way we aspire to, local trading standards officers are likely to acquire an increased workload in respect of estate agency. They will need additional resources, particularly staff, to discharge this, as well as an unequivocal clarification of their powers when the law is revised. We do not wish to specify here what officers should or should not be able to do. What is essential is that their powers and resources should be adequate to investigate and enforce the law where they are responsible. We also see a significant role for them in acting as the initial recourse for the dissatisfied member of the public who may use them to seek informal redress against an agent, and clarification as to whether a wrong has been done. If it has, the trading standards officer might advise on making a formal complaint to the registrar, with a view to redress or disciplinary action. Trading standards officers would hence have a significant educational role both for the public and for estate agents, besides investigative powers, and powers to refer specific breaches to the magistrates' court and/or to the registrar for disciplinary action.

Competence and training

We have referred above to tests of competence as one of the criteria for admission to estate agency through a registrar. We do not believe that the registrar should have sole authority over such tests, but rather that this should be predominantly the province of estate agents themselves. NVQs are a first step in the right direction, and should be built on, with the support of all branches of estate agency. Eventually overlapping sets of tests should become available which, on the one hand, satisfy the requirements for registration at different levels — notably employed estate agents and principals — and, on the other hand, reflect the developing profession of estate agency, its managerial skills and requirements, and its developing specialist expertise, which in turn will mesh with the qualifications of the professional bodies, notably the RICS. The requirement to pass tests of competence before admission to estate agency will, as it is phased in, naturally enhance their status and contribute to the process of developing a structured career for estate agents, enhancing the occupation's profile, as well as skill levels, and contributing to job satisfaction, as well as capacity to serve the public. Although we accept that selling is a significant part of estate agency, it follows from the position adopted here that we do not regard estate agency as 'just selling', nor do we regard the selling of residential property as 'just selling', but rather as a specialised and complex kind of selling with special responsibilities on the part of the salesperson.

The registrar will need to have a right of representation on the body representing standards of competence and training of estate agents, and we suspect that this body should be a quango, that is, have State backing even though dominated by the industry, as REATEA is at present. Its responsibilities will be to satisfy the registrar that the courses and standards are, where appropriate, up to his or her requirements, and to ensure the effective administration of the training and education regime by establishing teaching and examining staff, assessment and training centres and examination procedures in liaison with estate agencies, large and small. Besides an educational function, this body will have an important role in pulling the various branches of estate agency together, since it will have the powers to determine standards and to apply them practically across the board. Although the body may hence have difficulties in recruiting staff and gaining representation from the various branches of estate agency initially, it should in time acquire self-confidence and independence of mind and seek to act as the leader of the industry, not merely to represent and reflect its constituencies.

The corporates

Corporate estate agency may currently be likened to a loose cannon in a man-of-war: in itself a powerful potential contributor to the common good and the common purpose, but unless lashed down securely, liable, because of its weight, to roll about in an uncoordinated way and wreak havoc. The corporates have made a number of serious mistakes since they surged into estate agency with the blithe intention of making a lot of easy money and of putting estate agency to rights. They have recognised some of their mistakes, but they are in many ways benighted by an arrogance born of their size, wealth and long historical establishment. For a variety of reasons we think it unlikely that the large quantities of humble pie that the corporates ought to be consuming at present will even be considered in many quarters. Some, it is true, will probably back off from estate agency, but corporate estate agency will probably remain and it will consciously attempt to constitute a new form of estate agency. Whether it will be successful is very much open to question. In the meantime, the considerable contradictions and conflicts of interest to which the corporates are subject will require vigilant attention on the part of the regulatory authority (whether that is the registrar we envisage or some other authority).

These contradictions are, in the first place, between the individualism characteristic of working estate agents and the bureaucracy characteristic of the corporates, and their need to control and constantly evaluate their estate agency staff and branches. This has translated recently into a proceduralised view of estate agency service and quality appraisal which is at odds with the professional client orientation characteristic of the better independents. Further, the career aspiration of the independent agent to setting up as a principal or becoming a partner has no counterpart in the corporates, and career paths remain to be properly developed. Rising upwards means a move into management and the corporate's bureaucracy and away from practising estate agency, a problem that also needs to be tackled. These problems, as we have seen, have been recognised in various ways by some of the corporates, but none have yet resolved them. Where the outcome has been a formalised and proceduralised service and a strong emphasis upon targets, we believe that the public have cause for concern at standards of competence and at the consequences of target pressures for conflicts of interest.

Conflicts of interest are for the corporates greater than for independents. Besides the basic conflict referred to above, of the agent's interest in doing a deal to earn commission as against the vendor's in best price and the purchaser's in fair treatment and the right property, besides lowest price, corporate estate agents are subject to the additional conflicts deriving from the sales of financial services products. Even though their stance has become much more sophisticated here in recent years, and they now expect, for example, to use their financial services high street presence to sell products independently of their estate agency presence, and although all accept that tied sales are unacceptable, the plain fact is that the corporates are there for the additional business potential offered by estate agency and the targeting of financial services referrals; the integration of financial services advisers into overall branch profitability reflect this. The following is a particularly brazen example of the thinking involved, albeit from an independent consultant rather than a corporate estate agency:

> When the purchaser opens the door to his new house, he finds on the mat a personal letter from the consultant welcoming him to his new home. Three months later another letter or phone call from the consultant to check that everything is in order and whether another meeting is required. Thereafter service-led sales calls or letters can be issued at six monthly intervals.
>
> Opportunities will be apparent from the initial 'fact find', e.g., the renewal date of an existing buildings insurance policy etc., and these could generate specific sales approaches. With an average life span of only a handful of years the ideal situation would be the purchaser recontacting the consultant to arrange his mortgage when he moves again. The situation has then become one of 'relationship marketing' rather than a continual series of one-off sales.
>
> An estate agent will possess at any time a number of lists of names, all with varying degrees of information on the customer. These may comprise prospective purchasers, vendors, past vendors, purchasers and previous purchasers who have also been sold other products. These lists may be contained on files or even on a computer and can be used to cross-sell other products, to generate leads for consultants or simply to enhance the relationship as an investment for financial sales activity....

The next step in the exploitation of the 'affinity group' formed by these lists of names is the development of the estate agency as a separate sales force comprised of financial consultants trained to advise on wider financial services than just those related to a mortgage. The lists will then be used to provide the lifeblood of leads for these direct salesmen.[22]

Some at least of the corporates now have such a 'separate sales force' in place and it is to prevent the brazen assault on anyone who has ever unwittingly left his or her name and address with an estate agent and answered a few personal questions that regulatory attention needs to be devoted. Bringing mortgages within the regulatory ambit of the Financial Services Act 1986 would be a modest step in the right direction, but would plainly not deal adequately with the risks of abuse evident in the above quotation. The right of the corporates to use information on estate agency clients to stuff every new financial services package they introduce down their throats over an indefinite period requires, to put it mildly, careful regulatory attention. Detailed comment is beyond the scope of this book, which is concerned with estate agency proper, but the point should be clear that the issue of 'forced tie-in sales' cannot be resolved by a simple ruling which bans the straight selling of a property to a purchaser on condition of taking out a mortgage through the estate agency.

The difficulty with the corporates, then, is that, first, they are a different kind of estate agent and will probably have long-term problems, as well as what are perceived as short-term problems of adjustment, because of their distinctive features. Further, however, because of their financial services parents they spill over from estate agency into the financial services sector, and so pose additional regulatory problems. The estate agency regulator will hence need to be in regular liaison with the financial services regulator (which looks at the time of writing as though it will be the Personal Investment Authority to replace FIMBRA and LAUTRO) in order to identify undesirable practice. Powers to make regulatory orders in this respect will need to be coordinated as between the two authorities. At present our impression is that the corporates believe they are close to 'getting estate agency right', that is, producing an acceptable model, based on staff training, network restructuring, investment and heeding the negative publicity they generated in their brash initial days. It is important that powerful regulators disabuse them of any complacency on this score. The corporates, because of their additional conflicts of interest, are likely to need regular interventions, both advisory and regulatory, over the indefinite future. If either the estate agency regulator or the financial services regulator is or becomes compliant and lacking independence and resolve, the future for the consumer in these sectors is bleak. The capacity of the financial services corporations through their size and marketing strength and their expertise to persuade the public that all is for the best in the best of all possible worlds is considerable.

---

[22]D. Livesey, 'House marketing and all that!' *Building Societies Gazette*, December 1989, pp. 38–9.

CONCLUSION

Are we being absurdly optimistic in our proposals for regulatory reform, both in their prospects for implementation and in what they may achieve if implemented? Naturally, we believe we are not. Our proposals are mostly capable of implementation separately, and each will have benefits both for estate agency and for the public. If implemented collectively we believe that our proposals could initiate substantial change in estate agency. Whilst we doubt if there will come a time when the public will love estate agents, we believe that there can come a time when users of estate agents regard them as more than a 'necessary evil' (to use a phrase from a respondent in our consumer survey), and when users become discriminating customers, and relations between them and estate agents become constantly respectful and no longer subject to the suspicion and lack of esteem which we have documented in this book.

We began our research with the prejudices, as individuals, common to the public about estate agents, and with substantial ignorance of their work. Our research has left us better informed and more sympathetic to estate agents, but also sadder at their predicament. Their floundering attempts at self-improvement over almost a century seem to have become no more effective in recent times, even when assisted by the corporates. It is our hope that this book will go some way to informing the interested public about what estate agents do and their constraints in doing it, and that it will stimulate estate agents, regulators and other interested parties to make a concerted attempt at regulatory reform. Only if that attempt is concerted is it likely to see results substantial enough to more than tinker. And perhaps the time for this is now coming. After a decade and more of blind faith in the unfettered market as the solution to this and most other problems, sentiment in Britain and America seems finally to be turning to a recognition that markets and their actors serve the public — rather than the most powerful market participants — better if they are properly monitored and carefully regulated. There are probably a good many estate agents who view this prospect with disquiet if not outright horror. We ask them in reading this book to reflect upon what they have achieved by their own efforts and how well it sits with their aspirations to provide a service to the public and a profession for themselves. We suggest that they have little to fear from further regulation. To those who believe that estate agency is no more than 'flogging houses' — and these days mortgages and insurance too — we reply that what they are flogging is a dead horse. Estate agency will always be selling, but it should not be permitted to be mere selling.

Index